D1667011

2090 -15

91

Sustainable Development and Urban Form

European research in regional science

Infrastructure and regional development
edited by R W Vickerman

2 **Sustainable development and urban form**
edited by M J Breheny

p Pion Limited, 207 Brondesbury Park, London NW2 5JN

European research in regional science   2

Sustainable Development and Urban Form

Editor M J Breheny

Series editor   P W J Batey

European research in regional science

Series editor
P W J Batey   University of Liverpool

Editorial board
M J Breheny   University of Reading
R Cappellin   Luigi Bocconi Università Commerciale, Milan
R Maggi   University of Zurich
J B Parr   University of Glasgow
R Vickerman   University of Kent

ISBN 085086 160 8
ISSN 0960-6130

© 1992 Pion Limited

British Library Cataloguing in Publication Data
A CIP catalogue record British Library.

published by Pion Limited, 207 Brondesbury Park, London NW2 5JN

Printed in Great Britain by Page Bros (Norwich) Limited

Contributors

D Banister
Bartlett School, University College London,
Wates House, 22 Gordon Street,
London WC1H 0QB, England

M Barrett
Earth Resources Research Ltd,
258 Pentonville Road, London N1 9JY, England

H Barton
Severnside Research and Consultancy Unit,
Department of Town and Country Planning,
University of the West of England at Bristol,
St Matthias, Oldbury Court Road, Fishponds,
Bristol BS16 2JP, England

A Blowers
School of Social Sciences, Open University,
Walton Hall, Milton Keynes MK7 6AA, England

M J Breheny
Department of Geography, University of Reading,
PO Box 227, Reading RG6 2AB, England

V Despotakis
Department of Geodesy, National Technical
University of Athens, PO Box 14069,
Athens 11510, Greece

A Faludi
Institute of Planning and Demography,
University of Amsterdam, Jodenbreestraat 23,
1011 NH Amsterdam, The Netherlands

M Giaoutzi
Department of Geodesy, National Technical
University of Athens, PO Box 14069,
Athens 11510, Greece

A Gillespie
Centre for Urban and Regional Development
Studies, The University,
Newcastle upon Tyne NE1 7RU, England

D Hutchinson
London Research Centre, Parliament House,
81 Black Prince Road, London SE1 7SZ,
England

P Lasschuit

Faculty of Economics and Econometrics,
Free University, De Boelelaan 1105, Amsterdam,
The Netherlands

P Nijkamp

Faculty of Economics and Econometrics,
Free University, De Boelelaan 1105, Amsterdam,
The Netherlands

L Orrskog

Department of Regional Planning,
School of Architecture, Royal Institute
of Technology, S-100 44 Stockholm, Sweden

S Owens

Department of Geography,
University of Cambridge, Cambridge CB2 3EN,
England

P A Rickaby

Rickaby Thompson Associates, Regency Court,
220 Upper Fifth Street, Milton Keynes MK9 2HR,
England

Y Rydin

Department of Geography,
London School of Economics, Houghton Street,
London WC2A 2AE, England

F Snickars

Department of Regional Planning,
School of Architecture, Royal Institute
of Technology, S-100 44 Stockholm, Sweden

F Soeteman

Faculty of Economics and Econometrics,
Free University, De Boelelaan 1105, Amsterdam,
The Netherlands

P J Steadman

Centre for Configurational Studies,
Design Discipline, Open University, Walton Hall,
Milton Keynes MK7 6AA, England

A van der Valk

Institute of Planning and Demography,
University of Amsterdam, Jodenbreestraat 23,
1011 NH Amsterdam, The Netherlands

Contents

Sustainable Development and Urban Form: An Introduction

M J Breheny
University of Reading

1 Introduction

The environmental debate runs and runs. There have been occasions in the past when an apparent political and popular commitment to environmental issues has proved to be mere fashion. This time the commitment appears to be genuine and sustained; at least to the extent that political commitments are ever genuine and sustained. At the time of writing, the Rio 'Earth Summit' has just finished, and, although there are the predicted disappointments at the refusal of national governments to put aside economic self-interest in favour of global environmental benefits, the issue remains high on the political agenda.

Much of the environmental debate has focused on the notion of 'sustainable development'. Although there is some frustration at the way that this phrase has come to dominate the debate, and at the loose way that it is used, there is little doubt that many researchers and policymakers do find it useful, albeit in very idiosyncratic ways. The commonly adopted definition is that from the Brundtland Report (WCED, 1987): "Sustainable development is development that meets the needs of the present without compromising the ability of future generations to meet their own needs" (page 8). A further elaboration that is popular amongst researchers is that of Pearce and colleagues (Pearce and Makandya, 1989; Pearce et al, 1989). This defines development as the economic, social, and environmental aspirations of groups, which may or may not have economic growth as a priority. The achievement of these aspirations, however, is subject to a set of conditions. These include intergenerational equity, which requires that the stock of environmental resources passed on to the next generation should not inhibit their aspirations, and intragenerational equity, which seeks to increase the likelihood that the current aspirations of different groups will be met. A basic underlying principle is that the stock of natural resources should not be depleted beyond its regenerative capacity.

This set of ground rules for sustainability is generally accepted by the contributors here. However, in a number of instances they add the dimension of space. Whereas time is a explicit dimension in most notions of sustainability, space is generally ignored. If, however, we wish to talk of regional sustainability or urban sustainability, then it is necessary to be explicit about the spatial dimension. Although it may be possible to talk about achieving sustainable development—the meeting of development aspirations while not breaching the environmental conditions—at the global level, this cannot be possible at any other geographical levels.

Even at the continental or national levels, there will be cross-boundary flows of resources, and even of pollution and waste. Therefore a conception of sustainability is required that both accounts for (1) the openness of regional or urban areas, and (2) the need for institutional arrangements that recognise this openness. A number of the authors of the papers presented here try to develop this additional dimension of sustainability.

There is now a growing realisation that much of the sustainability debate has an urban focus. The world's cities are the major consumers of natural resources and the major producers of pollution and waste. Thus, if cities can be designed and managed in such a way that resource use and pollution are reduced, then a major contribution to the solution of the global problem can be achieved. The role of cities in the debate is seen to be greater still if we appreciate that they are also the focus of most other human activities. Thus, if the relationship—and possibly trade-off— between environmental and social, economic and cultural aspirations is part of the debate, then the role of cities looms large. This collection of papers is intended to cast some light on the urban and regional dimensions of sustainability, and in particular on what environmental gains might be achieved by planned changes. This review of planning possibilities ranges from strategic perspectives, which focus on urban form and transport, to local perspectives concerned with a wide range of finer grained initiatives.

The large majority of the papers presented here were commissioned by the editor for a session on "Sustainable Development and Urban Form" held at the 22nd Annual Conference of the British Section of the Regional Science Association at Mansfield College, Oxford, in September 1991. The papers by Rydin and by Orrskog and Snickars were added afterwards to give further breadth to the coverage.

2 Summaries of the papers

The papers here are loosely presented in an order that moves from the general to the particular. Thus, for example, Blowers at one extreme considers general questions of the political context of sustainability, whereas at the other Hutchinson assesses the role of combined heat and power (CHP) systems in reducing energy consumption. Within this general structure, the papers can also be considered in groups. The Blowers; Nijkamp, Lasschuit, and Soeteman; and Gillespie papers are all context setting to varying degrees. They discuss political, definitional and technological issues. The Owens; Orrskog and Snickars; Breheny; and van der Valk and Faludi papers are all concerned with questions of the sustainability of different urban forms, and with the reconciliation of sustainability and other objectives. Banister; and Rickaby, Steadman, and Barrett seek to find evidence on the energy-efficiency of different urban forms; the former focusing on empirical sources and the latter on modelling approaches. Barton; Rydin; Despotakis, Giaoutzi, and Nijkamp; and Hutchinson are concerned with specific aspects of the sustainability debate: with the role of light rail transit, with the role of geographic information systems (GIS), with the behaviour of the property market, and with the prospects for CHP, respectively.

The first paper, by Andrew Blowers, sets a profound, and ultimately pessimistic, context for the remaining papers. The focus is on the political prospects for achieving sustainable development. The political realities of the sustainability debate are investigated in detail. Blowers begins by reviewing this debate and by welcoming many of the local, national and international initiatives of recent years. However, many of these initiatives are only acceptable to politicians and public alike because they "tend to provide reassurance that present patterns of growth can be sustained provided there are marginal shifts in behaviour" (page 25). This, he argues, is nonsense because the achievement of sustainability would require revolutionary changes: in the nature of production and consumption; in the balance of relations between developed and developing countries; and in the self-interested attitudes of nation-states.

The political constraints on the prospects for such revolutionary change are then reviewed. Self-interest, Blowers argues, will always be the determinant of change. Politicians will be motivated by: the net benefits of resource use, international competitive advantage, and short-term political survival. While self-interest is served by environmental degradation, it is likely to continue. Only when the disbenefits arising from environmental damage outweigh the benefits, is self-interest likely to be compatible with sustainability. By the time such conditions arise for the developed countries, it may be too late. By then, access to resources may have become the basis of a new round of social decay and global conflict.

Blowers argues that four groups of initiatives are necessary (but probably not sufficient) for sustainability to become anything like reality: (1) "for the nation-state to surrender power upwards to supranational authorities and to devolve powers to regional and local authorities" (page 35); (2) "for the environmentally damaging operations of multi-national corporations to be prevented by effective national and international controls" (page 35); (3) "planning within a participative democratic political system must be introduced at all levels to coordinate and enforce the conservation of resources and the control of pollution" (page 36); (4) "Resources must be redistributed to give priority to environmental conservation" (page 36). Without these kinds of initiatives, he concludes that "for some time to come the limits to change are more likely to be determined by political, not environmental, constraints" (page 37).

Peter Nijkamp, Petra Lasschuit, and Frits Soeteman address the question as to what *regional* sustainable development (RSD) can mean. They begin by asking the question: "can a meaningful and operational concept of RSD—and rules for policies to obtain RSD—be postulated on the basis of the global concept of SD?" (page 39). As a basis for the further elaboration of the concept, RSD is defined as having to fulfil two goals: "(1) it should ensure for the regional population an acceptable level of welfare, which can be sustained in the future; and (2) it should not be in conflict with SD at a supraregional level" (page 41).

The characteristics of regions are discussed in relation to these goals. The authors acknowledge that a major problem must be the openness of a spatial system of regions. Regions will inevitably import and export goods and services, natural resources, and pollution and waste. Closed regional systems do not exist, but the degrees of openness will differ considerably. Also, it may be possible that regional specialisation may be appropriate to sustainability. For example, some regions may make 'sacrifices', such as accepting higher levels of resource loss, in order to satisfy sustainability aspirations at a supraregional level. In general, there is scope for trade-offs of varying kinds at interregional, global–regional, and intertemporal levels.

The authors continue by considering various aspects of RSD within a framework which cross-references key factors—intergenerational and inter-regional trade-offs, multiple use of environmental resources, sustainable use of renewable resources, risk and uncertainty—against socioeconomic issues in regional development—population patterns, production structure, regional income, and regional investment. Each of these cross-linkages is discussed in turn. For example, the relationship between the prospects for intergenerational sustainability is linked to the question of intragenera-tional income differences and the likelihood of greater income equality reaping environmental benefits. Another instance is the discussion of environmentally optimal regional population levels. It may be appropriate in some circumstances to discourage population growth; in others, envi-ronmental improvements may lead to in-migration that undermines those very improvements. A crucial issue is the relationship between production structures and interregional trade-offs. Various possibilities emerge. Environmentally damaging production may be best focused in a few regions, or spread more equitably between them. Production costs may be significantly raised in areas of stringent environmental policy. This may induce economically backward regions to attract industry and forego environmental benefits.

Having reviewed a range of conceptual and technical issues that arise as RSD is considered, Nijkamp et al turn to the question of the institutional arrangements necessary to deliver genuine RSD. They see the problem as one of determining who does what: a question of 'institutional assignment'. They identify a problem that has only recently emerged: that is, the traditionally separate functions of local and regional government—for example, health, employment, physical and social planning—now militate against the integrated policymaking required to tackle environmental problems. The circumstances in which certain environmental policies might be assigned to levels in the policy hierarchy are then discussed. It is demonstrated that assignments that are appropriate for economic, social, or environmental policies, or indeed for different environmental policies, will often not coincide. The institutional assignment question is then pursued further by discussing appropriate assignments in relation to each of the key factors—intergenerational and interregional trade-offs, multiple use of environmental resources, sustainable use of renewable resources, risk and uncertainty—discussed earlier in the paper. The conclusion is that, in relation to most of these key issues, assignment to a central, regional authority seems appropriate.

Andrew Gillespie contributes to the debate on sustainability and urban form by asking whether advances in telecommunications will tend to produce greater urban dispersion; and to what extent "might the *energy-consuming* effects which are associated with a more spatially dispersed metropolitan form be mitigated or even reversed by the *energy-conserving* substitution of physical movements (of people, of goods and services, and of information) by their telecommunications-mediated equivalents (such as telecommuting, teleshopping, electronic data interchange, video-conferencing, and so on)?" (page 68).

Popular conventional wisdom has it that, as telecommunications facilities become more sophisticated, so there is less need for people and activities to congregate in cities. Gillespie quotes Brian Berry's idea that such telecommunications act as a 'solvent' on the city, allowing the dispersal of the city's activities in space and time. The postwar phenomenon of urban decentralisation is often assumed to have been hastened by this 'solvent' effect of telecommunications. Gillespie challenges this view.

As a background to a review of the likely solvent effect of telecommunications on cities, Gillespie assesses the 'limits to technological forecasting'. He argues that, just as it is difficult to conceptualise the relationship between technology and society generally, so it is difficult to conceptualise that between communications technology and urban form. There is a tendency for commentators to assume the 'technological sublime'; that is, that advances in communications technology will change dramatically the nature and the geography of our lives. The uncritical acceptance of the dispersal scenario is part of this assumption.

Gillespie goes on to review the evidence for his counterview: that "advances in telecommunications are revalorising the city, and enabling it to reap considerable benefits from nodality within increasingly global networks" (page 68). This review is based both on historic and contemporary evidence. It is not denied that the city exists historically because of the need for communication. What is challenged is the view that, as the need for physical proximity diminishes, so the city will inevitably disperse. Gillespie argues that, to understand the centralising rather than decentralising effects of communications technology, it is necessary to consider the economic, social, political, and cultural contexts within which advances in telecommunications are made and used. In particular, he stresses that cities have always been centres for the control of communication and access to information. Many cities have prospered because they have managed to control channels of communication. Gillespie cites New York. There, the effect of an earlier introduction of new communications technology—the telegraph—was to place New York at the core of a new network.

Thus, 'hub and spoke' communication technologies confer advantages on nodes (as is also the case with the expanding high-speed rail system in Europe). Inevitably, the major nodes will be the major business centres: the cities. And, because communication systems remain inherently nodal, the cities will maintain this advantage. The corollary of this, of course, is that many rural areas are likely to be 'bypassed', particularly by advanced networks. The electronic cottage is feasible, but it will not be a very sophisticated cottage.

Gillespie's assertion, then, is that, far from telecommunications acting as an urban solvent, they are more likely to act "as a very powerful magnet, an 'electronic superglue', which is enhancing and extending the influence of the city within nodal communications networks" (page 72). He demonstrates this by reference to examples—in cities in the United States, Japan, and Europe—of urban teleports, which are business complexes built around superior global communications technologies. These teleports have now become major foci of more general economic promotion initiatives, as global and regional cities become increasingly conscious of their competitiveness.

In his conclusion, Gillespie returns directly to the question of sustainable urban forms. Although cities are likely to exert even stronger controls over national and international communications, he acknowledges that at a more local level new communication technologies can have a dispersing effect; through, for example, back office activities and—in principle, but as yet barely evident in practice—telecommuting. Thus, metropolitan areas are likely to get larger, and involve longer (but possibly fewer) journeys. On the central question—will telecommunications encourage or discourage physical movements and hence energy consumption— Gillespie is ultimately agnostic. It is unlikely to be the technologies themselves that determine which outcome prevails, but the context in which they are used.

Susan Owens addresses the question of the potential role of land-use planning in contributing to greater sustainability. She begins by pointing out that the notion of urban sustainability—now a much used phrase—is a contradiction. Urban areas will always be net consumers of resources, drawing them in from the world around them. They are also likely to be major degraders of the environment, simply because of the relative intensity of economic and social activity in such places. However, although it will not be possible to achieve absolute urban sustainability, the term is a useful label for those who seek to move towards a greater degree of sustainability in urban areas. Thus, the issue is how to reduce resource inputs to urban areas and how to reduce degrading outputs from such areas.

Owens is at pains to point out the limited role that urban planning can have on environmental issues, but is equally anxious to emphasise the degree to which environmental issues are urban in origin and, hence, are susceptible to planning. She estimates that as much as 70% of delivered energy may be subject to the influence of land-use planning.

The focus of the paper is on the relationship between energy consumption, urban form, and planning. She builds up the argument carefully, arguing that policy measures can range from those that are cost effective to all concerned—a 'no regrets' policy—to those that require increasing public intervention as cost-effectiveness becomes more difficult to establish.

The range of possible energy-efficiency measures in urban areas is then reviewed. The review starts at the most local intraurban scales and builds up to a consideration of strategic land-use and transport planning. At the building scale, the insulation benefits of terraces of houses or flats relative to other forms of dwellings are considered; and the merits of layouts and orientation in making optimum use of solar gain and microclimate conditions are reviewed. Considerable progress could be made on these issues, Owens argues, but at present responsibility tends to fall between planning and building regulation procedures, and little is achieved. Moving up the urban scale, the possible role of CHP schemes is considered. Here, Owens argues, much could be achieved. She reviews the circumstances in which the contribution of such schemes is likely to be optimised. In some circumstances, existing urban areas provide the appropriate conditions; in others, greenfield sites provide the best prospects.

Potentially the biggest contribution that planning could make to the reduction of energy consumption and pollution is to design urban forms to minimise the need for travel. Owens stresses the difference between the need for travel and actual travel behaviour. Planning may be able to influence the former, but possibly not the latter. The available evidence on the relationship between urban densities and travel behaviour does suggest that high urban densities—by reducing necessary travel distances and facilitating public transport—do correlate with lower fuel consumption. Owens acknowledges that, at particularly high densities, the energy-consumption benefits may begin to be outweighed by the disbenefits arising from congestion. It is suggested that a form of 'decentralised concentration', with a number of centres functioning within an urban area with overall high densities, might be particularly efficient. This conclusion, however, also depends on assumptions about the prevailing propensity to travel. If the propensity is high, as is likely with low fuel costs, then the local availability of facilities may make little difference to travel behaviour. Where the propensity to travel is low, then local facilities are likely to be used and fuel consumption relatively low. Consideration of land-use patterns that reduce travel demand must include public transport. Owens suggests that high-density urban areas are likely to facilitate public transport patronage, but also that urban forms can be designed that provide for higher densities adjacent to public transport routes.

Owens turns from theoretical considerations to a review of practice in the implementation of environmental policies. She begins by commending the Dutch government's National Environmental Policy Plan, and then turns to the results of her own survey of English local authorities. Her findings are that environmental issues now receive much more attention than in the past, but that these concerns have not yet been converted into policy or action in any meaningful way. The paper concludes with a summary of planning policy options for the future. Owens opts for future urban form based on policies of containment, higher densities in appropriate locations (such as along transport routes), avoidance of dormitory developments, mixed land uses, avoidance of employment and service locations that are car dependent, and the encouragement of walking and cycling.

Lars Orrskog and Folke Snickars begin their contribution by exploring what they call the "two repellant poles" in the sustainability debate: the instrumental standpoint which is progrowth and which relies on technological solutions and the ecological standpoint which emphasises the need for integration between human activities and nature. They speculate as to how this argument will develop in the future. One of the concerns of the paper is "whether the ecologically sustainable city has a different spatial form from the economically, socially, or politically viable city" (page 110).

They try to develop a view of the prospects for building more sustainable cities by assessing the relative prospects of changing different parts of cities. They argue that city cores can be changed very little because of the sheer scale of investment already made and the slowly changing nature of infrastructure. They see greater prospects in outer parts of cities, in suburbs, and at the urban fringe. They regard urban fringes as being of particular interest in relation to sustainability, suggesting that they "resemble the ecologically important shorelines where land meets water" (page 109).

Much of the focus of the Orrskog and Snickars paper is on the question of the increased greening of urban areas, which may be in conflict with the popular policy option of increasing urban densities. One of the observations made is that additional green space provided at the edge of the city is less vulnerable in the long run than such space provided nearer to the core. The latter will always be subject to pressures for development.

The authors focus from general observations on urban sustainability to a discussion of the practical application of sustainability criteria in the planning of Greater Stockholm. The question facing policymakers is "how to allocate new built-up areas so that contacts between different areas of economic and social interest are supported, as well as to guarantee the functioning of ecological systems to support life in the city" (page 111).

Stockholm has been planned around radial rail and road lines, with green fingers in between. The three major options being considered at present are: to build in the green-finger areas, thus creating a more compact city but losing green space; to expand further into existing suburban areas along the radial routes; or to focus more on the towns within Stockholm's hinterland, with better access between them. The environmental considerations have to be made consistent with the economic aspiration of ensuring that Stockholm remains an 'internationally competitive region'.

Orrskog and Snickars argue for both regional strategic planning that incorporates sustainability criteria—in this case covering the Greater Stockholm area—and the needs for an environmental focus in local planning. At the local level, they envisage a different agenda; one that covers issues of building scale, densities, mixing of uses, ambient sources of energy, balances of green and exploited spaces, and public participation. The paper finishes with a discussion of principles for building sustainable urban structures. The overall emphasis is on the question of appropriate balance. Urban densities can be increased to reduce travel, but this must be weighed up against the need to respect the ecological 'carrying capacity' of cities. An important issue concerns the scale at which this balance has to be struck. Is it within cities, or is it within a city region?

The overall preference seems to be for: a moderately dense urban system, composed of major cities and with satellites that accommodate most of the growth; with intervening open areas of sufficient size to be agriculturally productive; with high levels of accessibility; with facilities for urban recycling; with CHP systems and ambient energy sources; and sufficient greenery in all areas to remind everyone of their reliance on nature. The whole approximates, as the authors acknowledge, to a modern version of Ebenezer Howard's Social City.

There is an assumption amongst European planners and environmentalists that the best practice on environmental issues is to be found in the Netherlands. It is there that the government appears to be brave enough, unlike other national governments, to introduce radical measures in full knowledge that these might have unpopular repercussions. Arnold van der Valk and Andreas Faludi explain the general moves being made to expand environmental policies. They discuss the National Environmental Policy Plan, the designation and objectives of 'ROM' areas (ROM being the acronym for physical planning and environment), the linking of physical and environmental planning, and thoughts on the development of the 'nature-city'. Their main purpose, however, is to reflect on one aspect of these policies: the promotion of more 'compact' cities. They explain briefly the postwar history of national physical planning in the Netherlands. The latest phase in this history, in the Fourth Report, has a new 'doctrine' of urban compactness, which replaces the earlier focus on controlled decentralisation. There are three main motives for the new focus. One is the desire to rejuvenate the big cities which have seen their

population and income bases fall with decentralisation. A second is
economic regeneration, which has inevitably to focus on the 'engine'
economies of the Randstad cities. A third and more recent motive, which
arises from the Fourth Report 'Extra' of 1991, is that of sustainable
development.

Van der Valk and Faludi find these changes laudable, but have doubts
about the merits of the new single-minded focus on the compact city.
They argue that the policy fails to take account of uncertainty in population growth and dispersal, and is out of step with the major determining
forces of modern urbanisation. They are also worried that: the urban
focus of the policy neglects both rural communities and the earlier growth
centres; open space in cities is being taken up; environmental quality
suffers; real estate prices rise as does social segregation.

They review the nature of recent growth pressures in the Netherlands in
order to demonstrate that the 'compact-city' policy runs counter to very
powerful and well-established forces. Despite wild fluctuations in forecasts
of housing need, they show that there will be large-scale growth—between
a half and one million new homes up to the year 2015—that cannot
reasonably be accommodated within existing cities and towns. They argue
that the Dutch government has taken a great risk in committing itself to a
policy that is inflexible and has been based on remarkably little research.
They propose in place of the compact-city policy the concept of 'growth
regions'. The logic behind this proposal is a simple extension of the
'concentrated deconcentration' idea, but a logic that also builds upon the
experience of 'growth-centres' policy that prevailed before the Fourth
Report. This experience is reviewed briefly by van der Valk and Faludi.
They explain how efforts in the 1950s and 1960s to adopt growth-centre
policies failed because of problems of implementation. By 1970 these
problems had been overcome, and the policy began to have a substantial
effect. The growth-centre initiative has now petered out because of a
combination of factors including reduced housing subsidies, which had
been the backbone of growth-centre policies, general reduction in funding,
and the new compact-city policy.

Van der Valk and Faludi call for growth regions of 50000 plus houses,
possibly in a series of linked settlements, administered by new-style
authorities with planning, transport, economic, and environmental powers.
Growth regions would be as self-contained as possible, with localised
compactness and green surrounds. The *villes nouvelles* of Cergy-Pontoise,
Melun-Sénart, and St Quentin-en-Yvelines, in the Paris region, offer
models, and within the Netherlands the area of Het Gooi, near Amsterdam,
and Almere come close to the ideal. However, the example which has
inspired them most is the proposal for a polynucleated 'Park City' in
the area between the Hague, Zortermeer, and Rotterdam. The feature that
most distinguishes the earlier growth centre policy and the authors'
proposed growth regions is the question of administrative arrangements.

They propose a public–private partnership arrangement for their growth regions. The paper finishes with a radical suggestion that the growth-region concept could be put into practice by building a Park Metropolis in the Green Heart of the Randstad; the equivalent in the United Kingdom of suggesting that the green belt around London should be built on.

Michael Breheny's contribution focuses on a critique of one particular solution to the urban sustainability problem that has gained some currency recently: that of the 'compact city'. Before beginning this critique, he argues that the recent debate on sustainability has served to integrate discussions on urban and regional issues that were previously compartmentalised. For example, issues such as quality of life, counterurbanisation, environmental protection, strategic planning, scales and locations of growth, urban intensification, and others, now have to be related together very closely. The effect is to give a boost to academic debate and to draw academics and practitioners together.

Although it is not the only source of the compact city proposal, Breheny focuses on the European Commissions's *Green Paper on the Urban Environment* (CEC, 1990) because it comes from an important organisation that usually puts into practice what it proposes. He argues that there is a danger that the Commission's proposal—which is largely assertion—will be taken up as policy before it has been properly examined. The proposal is to promote throughout Europe high-density compact cities on the grounds that such a solution is both environmentally desirable, in that it reduces travel distances, and delivers a higher quality of life. The report advocates an end to urban sprawl—to the degree that all future development should take place within existing urban boundaries—and promotes a return to mixed land uses in cities. The high-density city, the report argues, will recreate intensive, innovative, culturally rich, urban milieux.

Breheny welcomes the report as an important stimulus to debate, but suggests that much of what it says is merely assertion and is highly contentious. He provides a critique of the idea of the compact city by way of what he calls 'contradictions' of the compact city; a mixture of internal contradictions and potential conflicts with other desirable policy stances. The contradictions that are explored are those between the compact city idea and: energy efficiency; suburban qualities of life; the green city; telecommunications–rich dispersal; renewable energy sources; and rural economic development. Before investigating these in turn, the paper suggest that there is one even more fundamental problem with the compact city proposal: that of the prospects for reversing deep-seated decentralisation trends. These are now so strong that a policy advocating the containment of all future growth within existing urban boundaries seems very naive.

Breheny reviews the available literature on the relationship between energy consumption, urban form, and transport. This consists of a mixture of empirical evidence, hypothetical modelling, and policy proposals.

The arguments are contentious and the evidence often contradictory. The issue of suburban quality of life revolves around the questions as to whether total urban containment is possible and, if possible, desirable. Breheny demonstrates that in the United Kingdom it is impossible, without unimaginable draconian measures. In the UK case, where there is a profound fondness for suburban and semirural living, it is unlikely to be regarded as desirable. At the moment there seems to be a general consensus that our cities should be made greener. Indeed, the European Commission itself urges this. What it does not do is explain how this is consistent with the idea of increased urban densities.

The compact city proposal is totally at odds with another proposed approach to the sustainability problem: that of decentralised living, enhanced with telecommunications. A number of authors see this approach, based on urban decentralisation, a return to rural values, and greater degrees of self-containment, plus the benefits of telecommunications, as a viable future. The proposal may also be at odds with two other desirable policies. One is the promotion of the use of wind and solar power, which cannot be used efficiently in high-density urban environments, but which may need to be near to the point of consumption. The other is the protection of vulnerable rural economies, which may be threatened by a focus of activity within existing cities and towns. Breheny concludes by arguing that the contradictions of the compact city proposal demonstrate that the sustainable city issue is complex, and needs much more thought and debate before major, and possibly counterproductive, initiatives are taken.

David Banister also addresses the question of the relationship between transport, urban form and energy consumption. He begins with a review of the contribution of transport, and particularly road transport, to the energy and pollution problem. The brief review of likely future trends in transport makes gloomy reading: "The background is one of increasing demand for travel, greater levels of car ownership, and longer trip distances" (page 164). The focus of the paper is on the identification of evidence which relates energy consumption from transport and urban form. This is attempted by a review of four approaches: one based on the relationship between energy consumption, modal shares, journey lengths, and vehicle occupancy; one which looks at modal shares, trip distances, and settlement types; one which relates urban density, the intensity of land use, and energy consumption; and one which relates energy consumption to journey-to-work self-containment.

The first of these two approaches report on Banister's own attempts to use empirical information to cast some light on the energy and urban form issue. His analysis of the UK National Travel Survey data suggests that per capita fuel consumption from travel is highest in more rural areas, but that the largest cities (in this case London) are likely to be less efficient that medium-sized and smaller towns, presumably because of the effect of congestion offsetting gains from shorter travel lengths in the largest cities. His second approach, based on survey data in a rural area of England, supports the first in that it provides consistent evidence that the smallest of rural settlements are the least energy-efficient.

Banister's third approach reviews evidence both from attempts to correlate urban energy consumption rates with densities, and from hypothetical modelling of urban form and energy consumption. The first of these areas of work—also reviewed in Breheny's paper—suggests that higher density cities around the world tend to exhibit lower fuel-consumption rates. This, it is suggested, is a function of shorter travel distances and the availability of public transport in high-density cities. This leads to policy prescriptions in favour of urban containment and public transport provision. The modelling work reviewed by Banister tends to suggest that 'decentralised concentration'—that is the promotion of urban and suburban cores—might be a fuel-efficient urban form. The paper here by Rickaby, Steadman, and Barrett gives a more up-to-date report on this line of work, suggesting that more recent modelling runs are less conclusive about appropriate urban forms. The final approach concerns the degree to which certain sizes and types of towns exhibit greater journey-to-work self-containment, and hence lower energy consumption. The cases of British new towns and villages, and Dutch medium-sized towns are considered.

Banister concludes his paper by trying to identify common threads from the approaches he reviews. He suggests that: single objectives in the pursuit of greater energy-efficiency will be misguided; that a balance should be struck between transport and other social, economic, and environmental objectives; that some degree of urban containment is required; that new residential developments should be related to jobs and services; that satellite development close to, and integrated with, existing urban areas are likely to be energy-efficient; as are towns of about 25 000 population.

Although the question of the relationship between urban form and energy consumption has become a fashionable area of study only in the last few years, Peter Rickaby and colleagues have been developing models to investigate this link since the 1970s. The paper by Rickaby, Phil Steadman, and Mark Barrett reports on progress in this work. The paper begins with a simple explanation of the responsibility for CO_2 emissions: 24% from transport and 45% from space heating and lighting, both of which can be affected by planning and building design. Thus, the search for efficient planning solutions at strategic and local scales is important.

The use of two models in simulating energy consumption and travel behaviour is explained. The first model, PASS, is an accounting framework, operating at the national level, which calculates likely changes in fuel consumption and emissions, as assumptions about switches in travel mode, journey lengths, and vehicle-load factors are introduced.

Some indications about likely responses to changes are available, but as yet no specific results are forthcoming.

The second model, TRANUS, is being used to experiment with changes to an archetypal English town of about 100 000 people. This hypothetical town has been modelled on data for some twenty actual towns. Five modified versions of the town are then modelled in order to assess their relative changes in energy consumption: three versions with development within the original urban area, and two with peripheral expansion. In each case, change is modelled over a twenty-year period, in five-year intervals. The results were disappointing in that there were no significant differences in fuel use, in either transport or domestic heating, between the five options. This contrasted sharply with earlier work, in which the archetypal town was placed in a regional context, thus allowing greater variability in the possible locations for development. The result then was that two options—a concentration in the town core, and a village dispersal strategy—showed significant fuel savings. However, in no option was there any noticeable switch from car to public transport.

Rickaby et al draw a number of conclusions from their modelling work. The comparison of the earlier, regional, version of the model and the later, strictly urban, version suggest that it is urban density which accounts for different levels of fuel consumption. Higher densities result in shorter journeys and fuel savings. They also conclude that significant switches from private to public transport are unlikely to result just from the planned location of new development. Measures to discourage travel, such as higher taxation of fuel, would also be necessary; a point made by other contributors, such as Owens and Banister.

There is little dispute, in these papers or in the wider debate about sustainability, that improved public transport in urban areas is desirable. Hugh Barton, in his contribution, takes one specific form of transport, light rail transit (LRT), in one specific place, the city of Bristol in southwest England, in assessing this claim. In many cities in the world LRT systems are being introduced or contemplated, in part because of the supposed environmental benefits. Thus, an assessment of the validity of this claim is timely.

Barton begins with an explanation of the transport problem in Bristol, which has car ownership levels well above the UK average, a high rate of traffic growth, increasingly severe congestion, a high level of car dependence, and consequent pollution levels. Decentralisation of people and jobs from the city has exacerbated car dependency. The response from the local authorities has been to emphasise environmental policies, including greater energy efficiency. Despite this, the proposal for an LRT system has come from the private sector—Advanced Transport for Avon (ATA)—who hope to finance the scheme from enhanced land values along the route.

Before looking at the role of the LRT proposal in reducing energy consumption in Bristol, Barton reviews the depressing evidence on 'business as usual' traffic growth, energy consumption and pollution. He explains that in the "Bristol Energy and Environment Plan" (BEEP) targets for lowering CO_2 emissions have been set. This is followed by a review of the evidence available on increased patronage resulting from the introduction of LRT schemes in European cities. He considers the likely effects of increased use of public transport, including: the direct primary energy use of public transport, relative to car use; the responses of motorists to newly available road space; and the effects on urban congestion. The greatest gains, Barton argues, have occurred where public transport provision is part of a major investment in green strategies of transport integration, car restraint, enhanced pedestrian facilities, etc.

Barton reviews the prospects for the introduction of improved public transport systems in a situation in which "Current land-use trends are progressively undermining the function of public transport" (page 207). Dispersal of cities, and the resulting lower densities, result he argues in "increased car dependence, profligate energy use, and global pollution". He then reviews the Dutch work which has recognised this problem, and which has proposed policies based on three key concepts: higher urban densities; concentration of jobs and facilities at public transport nodes; and compact urban development linked into public transport and cycling networks. Each of these three concepts is then assessed against the British context of: the power of the market, worries over 'town cramming' and urban greening, relatively low prevailing densities, and existing development control regulations.

Barton ends with a discussion of the principles by which land-use and transport planning might be better integrated to produce more efficient urban development. Forms of 'decentralised concentration' are preferred, with the least flexible elements—rail systems, commercial development, etc—providing a starting point for designs. The keys to more sustainable urban forms, he concludes, are integrated land-use and transport planning and firm commitment on the part of both local and central government.

The contribution by Yvonne Rydin starts with the observation that much of the debate about urban sustainability is concerned with land-use issues, and tends to ignore the socioeconomic processes by which sustainability is to be achieved. This concern is particularly heightened now because of the increased reliance on market-based instruments to achieve public policy, including environmental policy. Thus, an understanding is required of the "ways in which market-based decisions frustrate environmental policy, and the most effective points at which to direct instruments for change" (page 217). The focus of the paper is on the property market; a sector which obviously has a direct bearing on the urban sustainability debate, but one that has rarely been included in that debate.

The paper begins with a review of the relationship between the property market and the environment. Land and buildings have an impact on the environment as they are produced, consumed, and continue to exist. The production of the built environment entails the use of natural materials, the consumption of energy, and localised impacts on habitats, for example. During their lifetimes buildings can create problems, irrespective of their use: they leak CFCs and store up problems with asbestos, for instance. Clearly, buildings are the focus of considerable environmental problems.

Rydin suggests that an understanding of these issues does point to more sustainable ways of managing built form, but that in addition an understanding of the ways in which property-market decisions react to environmental impacts is crucial. Only with this understanding will it be possible to anticipate ways in which the property market will undermine environmental policy aspirations. Three specific features of the property market – environmental impact relationship are identified as important: timescales and the temporal distribution of impacts; the spatial scale of impacts; and their riskiness or unpredictability.

The temporal issue is important because there may be a conflict between the long-term, intergenerational concerns of sustainability and the relatively short time horizons used by the property market. Environmental impacts beyond a certain date are likely to be ignored by developers. Environmental impacts from a building that are exported beyond the locality—even if collectively such effects are severe—will also be of less concern to a developer. The property market will also have to take into account environmental risks in making decisions. For example, the probability of sea-level rises, or future outfalls of pollution or, indeed, restrictive government environmental policy are all risks that have to be considered.

Rydin then takes her consideration of the relation of the property market to the environment through an analysis of the different interests in property: occupational interests, development interests, and investment interests. The environmental issues that arise from the point of view of each of these interests are considered under the timescale, spatial scale and predictability dimensions introduced earlier. This section of the paper explores the circumstances under which pressures for environmental improvements are likely to come from the three interests. For example, in a depressed market developers will conform with occupiers' 'green' demands.

The occupiers – developers – investors framework discussed in principle by Rydin is then used to investigate the housebuilding industry in some detail. The attitudes of the three groups to environmental issues are explored via surveys of estate agents, housebuilders, and mortgage lenders, plus extensive literature searches. Occupiers of houses, as evidenced by the views of estate agents, put environmental issues very low on their agenda of desirable features of houses. Although housebuilders appear to be more concerned about environmental issues, Rydin found a disappointing lack of any serious attempts to put sustainability ideas into practice in housebuilding. Likewise, mortgage lenders showed no particular interest in promoting or favouring dwellings with higher environmental standards.

The contribution by Vassilios Despotakis, Maria Giaoutzi, and Peter Nijkamp considers the role that GIS might play in arriving at planning policies that enhance environmental sustainability. The possibilities are explored by using a hybrid GIS-sustainable development (GIS – SD) system developed in the GIS Laboratory of the Free University, Amsterdam, as applied to an area of the Greek Sporades islands. To evaluate the results of different policy scenarios, the GIS – SD system is also linked to a decision support system (DSS).

The paper begins with a formal definition of sustainable development as used in the paper. Development is defined as a nonnegative change of socioeconomic and ecological welfare over time. The nature of the goals of sustainable development are then introduced. These goals can only be discussed when the dimensions of sustainability are made clear. These relate to time and to space. There then follows a brief discussion of how sustainability can be regarded at different spatial scales. Regional scale sustainability, which is the focus of the paper, is defined as: "... a development which ensures that the regional population can attain an acceptable level of welfare—both at present and in the future—and that this regional development is compatible with ecological circumstances in the long run while at the same time it tries to accomplish a globally sustainable development" (page 245). The authors go on to discuss substitutability of different economic and ecological stocks, and the carrying capacity of regions.

They then explain, stage by stage, the construction of the GIS – SD system. The system is built up around 'stocks', 'flows' (into and out of stocks, and determined over time), 'converters' (any functions of time entering the model), and 'connectors' (possible relations between stocks, flows or converters). The final GIS – SD model is made up of eight submodules: spatial modelling; nonspatial modelling; stock – layer linking; dynamic simulation; suitability analysis; sustainability check; allocation; and presentation. Each of these modules is explained in detail. The 'engine' of the model is the dynamic simulation element. Within this, interactions between four submodels—ecological, terrestrial, economic, and marine—are simulated for the islands. The sustainability module checks that sustainable development constraints on stocks are being satisfied. If they are not, the model stops and asks the user for instructions. At this stage, constraints may be changed, scenarios respecified, or simulation submodels revised. Once sustainability constraints have been satisfied, the system finally allocates land uses and presents these.

After the detailed system specification, the authors discuss its application to the Greek Sporades islands. The islands exhibit classic conflicts between the desire for economic development (tourism and fishing) and environmental protection. The system was used to evaluate the effects of change in two ways: first, transport – no transport scenarios were simulated, which lead to very different spatial patterns of development; second, a series of scenarios were developed which adopt different foci for development. The results are presented in map and tabular form. The effects table shows scores for each of four criteria against five scenarios. It is imported into a DSS, which uses a multicriteria method to produce an overall ranking of scenarios. The preferred option is the most sustainable because it meets economic and ecological aspirations most fully.

A large proportion of fossil fuel energy consumption is accounted for by domestic and industrial heating and cooling. In turn, this consumption accounts for a high proportion of pollution, and in particular CO_2 emissions. David Hutchinson addresses this problem in his paper by reviewing the role that CHP systems can play in increasing the efficiency with which energy is used. The problem is that the production of electricity is inefficient, with an average of 37% of energy input actually being used; with the remainder lost as heat waste and flue gases. CHP systems, by making use of the heat produced in energy production, can raise efficiency levels to between 70% and 90%.

Hutchinson reviews the four systems that can produce both heat and electric power: steam turbines, internal combustion engines, gas turbines, and combined cycle gas turbines. The development and use of combined heat and power and district heating schemes (CHP/DH) is most advanced in Scandinavia. In Finland, for example, approximately 25% of building space is heated by district heating schemes and 25% of all electricity is produced by CHP. In Helsinki these figures approach 80%. In the Danish city of Odense 95% of homes are heated by CHP. In Sweden it is a statutory requirement that local authorities have up to date plans for energy supply, distribution, and use.

The rapidly increasing interest around the world in the possible adoption of CHP systems is reviewed by Hutchinson. He reports on initiatives in China, Australia, and the United Kingdom. The UK government has only recently taken a positive interest in CHP, but has done so in a forceful manner, asking local authorities to include energy questions in development plans and encouraging the adoption of CHP. Although this general encouragement is new, the government has sponsored a number of pilot schemes in British towns. The criteria that the government has adopted in assessing the validity of schemes is that they must be sufficiently attractive commercially to be run by the private sector.

Hutchinson reviews in some detail CHP schemes carried out in Leicester, southeast London, and the City of London. The Leicester experience was encouraging and the consortia involved in the study recommended the establishment of a joint public – private company to run the scheme. To date this has not happened, in part because of complications arising from the privatisation of the electricity industry. The southeast London scheme, again investigated by a public–private consortium, will start in 1994. This is to be a scheme based around incineration of waste, and will sell electricity to London Electricity and supply heating to 7500 homes and to local schools. The City of London scheme, which will burn natural gas to supply electricity and heat, will also proceed as a public–private venture. It will supply mainly buildings owned by the City of London Corporation.

Although historically CHP systems have been developed on a large scale, the technology now exists for small-scale schemes, or 'micro-CHP systems', which could supply individual buildings or groups of buildings such as hospitals, universities, and sports centres. Legislative changes in the United Kingdom have also given a boost to such small-scale CHP.

Hutchinson reviews UK experience with heat-only district schemes. Generally, the experience has not been very satisfactory. Such schemes, usually providing public-sector housing developments, have often been unable to provide heat at a lower cost than conventional systems and have a poor reputation amongst users. An exception to this poor record has been the city of Sheffield, where the local authority has made a considerable investment in its incinerator-driven system since the 1960s. The now extended scheme provides heating to a large number of dwellings and to business premises in the city centre. The scheme is now to be expanded and run in conjunction with a Finnish private investor.

The paper concludes on a positive note, suggesting that with positive practical experience of such schemes now available, with CHP schemes seen as making a positive contribution to the reduction of CO_2 emissions, with microscale systems becoming available, and with encouragement from governments, CHP systems seem set to make a significant contribution to sustainability at the local level.

3 Emerging themes

What, then, do we learn from reading these papers? We should not expect a nice, neat set of agreements to emerge. As explained earlier, the sustainability debate is not yet at the stage, and may never be, where such consensus can emerge. However, some concluding thoughts can be offered, covering: questions of definition; the role of local solutions; institutional arrangements; the wisdom of 'going against the grain'; the achievement of balance; consensus on urban form solutions; and on marginal change versus existing urban structures.

3.1 The definitional question

There is a general unhappiness in the sustainability debate that the term is bandied about much too loosely; that it has become an umbrella term that somehow encompasses any altruistic thoughts about the environment. A number of the contributors here have tried to be more specific, particularly in adding a spatial dimension to the notion of sustainability.

Thus, Nijkamp et al have tried to define regional sustainable development, as well as identifying issues that arise as this scale and this definition are adopted. Owens has discussed the impossibility of urban sustainable development, given the flows of resources and pollution and waste across boundaries. Rydin's discussion of the behaviour of actors in the property market shows interesting parallels with these notions of sustainability at the regional or urban levels. Their behaviour is also dependent on the degree to which environmental effects are internalised or exported.

3.2 The limited role of localised solutions

The papers here are useful in putting local solutions to environmental problems in their place. There is at the moment an enormous groundswell of support in favour of, and willingness to engage in, environmental initiatives. There is a dilemma here. On the one hand, for the sake of realism, these enthusiastic activists need to be made aware of the limited contribution of their efforts in the face of broader national and international forces. Blowers paints a pessimistic picture of the political constraints on governmental action (and the subsequent Rio 'Earth Summit' seems to bear him out); Owens explains that, without governmental efforts, as say with fuel taxes, local changes to urban form or transport policy will come to very little. Indeed, as this introduction is being written, the UK Secretary of State for Transport has announced that the government will continue, despite all of its supposed commitment to the environment, to rely on the private market to determine the nature of the transport system. At the same time he announced that a stretch of the M25 motorway around London is to be widened from six to fourteen lanes. On the other hand, nothing must be done which reduces local enthusiasm. Local initiatives do make a small contribution, and, as a number of the contributors here stress, land-use changes do have a potential bearing on a large proportion of environmental issues. In the absence of clear governmental initiatives, the exhortation to 'hope global, act local' does seem appropriate. Also, it may be the force of local commitment that will in the long run persuade national politicians to put environmental issues on a par with economic ones.

3.3 Appropriate institutional arrangements

It is clear from a number of papers—notwithstanding the point above about the place of local initiatives—that a major barrier to progress on environmental initiatives may be the legacy of institutional arrangements. Nijkamp et al have attempted a systematic consideration of what they call 'institutional assignments'; that is, given a knowledge of what regional sustainability means, what tasks should be assigned to what institutions. They discuss vertical assignment, to levels of government, and horizontal assignment, to networks of agencies and actors. In practice, constraints on appropriate arrangements will be largely a result of present compartmentalisation of functions. In the United Kingdom, for example, the system of land-use development plans is regarded by central government as the major focus of environmental policy, but is regarded by many as an inappropriate vehicle for broad-ranging environmental policy.

There is a general consensus here that at the subgovernmental level, environmental issues must be addressed in an integrated way at the regional or city-regional level. This is stressed forcefully by Nijkamp et al; van der Valk and Faludi; Owens; and Orrskog and Snickars. Orrskog and Snickars stress the importance of linking this with local level initiatives, based on a specific localised agenda. There are interesting differences of opinion over the structure of institutions. The majority of papers imply a heavy reliance on public-sector intervention, seeing recent experiments with deregulation and privatisation as a barrier to environmental planning. Van der Valk and Faludi, in contrast, argue strongly in favour of pubic – private partnerships.

The question of institutional arrangements also raises the question of institutional competence. This is an issue not raised directly here, but it is one that Despotakis et al raise indirectly. Many of the issues discussed in this volume are complex and contentious. How likely is it that regional or local authorities can carry out thorough analyses and derive appropriate environmental policies if supposed experts are so uncertain? How many can carry out the kind of sophisticated analysis presented here by Despotakis and colleagues? These questions cannot be answered here, but must be given consideration if ideas in theory are to be carried into practice.

3.4 The problem of 'going against the grain'

A theme running through a number of papers concerns the wisdom of adopting environmental policies that 'go against the grain' of well-established and powerful trends. These trends are established in the market, in politics, in domestic life, and in geographical changes that reflect these trends. For example, suggestions that people should give up cherished suburban life-styles, as in the compact city proposal, may be very unrealistic. Likewise, the assumption that counterurbanisation, which has been the dominant urban force since 1945 in most Western countries, can suddenly be halted and even reversed, is naive. Thus, proposals that promote the compact city in its extreme form, such as that by the European Commission, are unrealistic in the extreme. There is something of a consensus in the papers presented here that policymakers would be wise to redirect trends or practices, where they are well established, rather than try to beat them back, Canute-like. One obvious example of this is the adoption of some form of decentralised concentration as a basis for settlement planning. This has been proposed here in different forms by Owens; Orrskog and Snickars; Breheny; and van der Valk and Faludi. Another example is given by Rydin, when she explains the conditions under which the property market is more likely to be sympathetic to environmental policies.

3.5 The achievement of balance

Another point that emerges from the papers here, and one that is closely related to the question of 'going against the grain', concerns the balance of environmental and other policies. Radical environmentalists are likely to argue for the absolute superiority of environmental initiatives. The problem with this authoritarian approach is that it is likely to be self-defeating. Given the popular support for environmental causes, initiatives that generate a backlash are to be avoided. Thus, draconian policies that reduce the quality of social and economic life in order to achieve environmental objectives are likely to be very unpopular and in consequence undermined. A better approach is one that achieves a balance between environmental and other objectives. This question of balance has been addressed here by Banister; Breheny; and Orrskog and Snickars.

3.6 Policies on sustainable development and urban form

The papers here have demonstrated that the question as to whether certain urban forms are more sustainable than others is a complex one. The simple answer probably still remains: 'it depends'. Nevertheless, there may be a glimmer of consensus of certain points. These might be:

(a) Urban containment policies should continue to be adopted, and the decentralisation process slowed down.

(b) Extreme compact city proposals are unrealistic and undesirable.

(c) Various forms of 'decentralised concentration', based around single cities or groups of towns, may be appropriate.

(d) Inner cities must be rejuvenated, thus reducing further losses of people and jobs.

(e) Urban (or regional) greening must be promoted.

(f) Public transport must be improved both between and within all towns.

(g) People-intensive activities must be developed around public transport nodes, along the Dutch 'right business in the right place' principle.

(h) Mixed uses must be encouraged in cities, and zoning discouraged.

(i) CHP systems must be promoted in new and existing developments.

3.7 Marginal change versus existing structures

An issue that emerges, if only weakly, from the papers concerns the role of new increments of growth in achieving environmental gains, relative to existing urban structures. Much of the discussion of urban sustainability focuses on the marginal change. But, even in areas where this change is relatively high, as van der Valk and Faludi explain is the case in The Netherlands, it is still in any year a tiny fraction of what exists. The vast majority of energy consumption and pollution of a city will be accounted for by this existing stock. The real challenge, then, is to redesign existing urban form. Some important elements can be changed quickly, such as bus routes which might be redirected to serve suburb-to-suburb movements. Other elements, such as railways or commercial buildings, can only be changed infrequently. Planners need to devise and adopt a set of specifically intraurban sustainability principles, covering issues such as public transport, private car restraint, density targets, urban greening, development of transport nodes, mixed uses, etc.

3.8 Finally: 'do no harm'

Although some of the issues discussed here have received sporadic attention over many years, the current intensity of academic research and political debate is very recent; dating generally from the Brundtland Report of 1987 (WCED, 1987). Thus, the debate is relatively immature. This is reflected in the variety of, sometimes conflicting, views presented here. A few points of consensus do emerge, but the hard-pressed practitioners in cities and regions may be frustrated at the lack of clear guidance. It is incumbent upon researchers to help produce such guidance on this eminently practical issue. However, the 'precautionary principle' advocated by environmentalists implies that we would be unwise to advocate profound policy switches without being sure of their consequences. Florence Nightingale's first principle of care was: 'do no harm'. We would be wise to bear this in mind.

References

CEC, 1990 *Green Paper on the Urban Environment* EUR 12902 (Commission of the European Communities, Brussels)

Pearce D, Makandya A, 1989 *The Benefits of Environmental Policies* (OECD, Paris)

Pearce D, Makandya A, Barbier E, 1989 *Blueprint for a Green Economy* (Earthscan, London)

WCED, 1987 *Our Common Future* (The Brundtland Report) World Commission on Economic Development (Oxford University Press, Oxford)

Sustainable Urban Development: The Political Prospects

A Blowers
Open University, Milton Keynes

1 Environmental security—a key issue

As the final decade of the twentieth century opened, the environment appeared to be fully established as a key political issue at every level. Environmental problems had long been a matter of local political concern in the richer countries. The environment has now become a prominent issue of national politics, taking its place alongside more traditional issues such as health, education, or defence as a subject of electoral significance. At international level, as the Cold War subsided, the fear of nuclear Armageddon was replaced by the possibility of environmental catastrophe. The environment emerged as "an issue, at once, both genuinely global, and politically divisive" (Imber, 1991, page 201).

Political concern for the state of the environment reflected and responded to the evidence of public opinion. A UK poll in 1989 revealed that 30% of a sample population (unprompted) regarded the environment and pollution as an important issue to deal with (up from only 8% three years earlier) (ENDS, 1989). In the EC a survey found that over half the population (55%) regarded protecting the environment and preserving natural resources as necessary conditions to assure economic development and only 7% felt that economic development should take priority over the environment (OECD, 1991, page 254).

This political concern about the environment was given some coherence by the concept of sustainability. The idea that we should at least ensure the earth's natural resources are conserved or replenished and bequeathed to succeeding generations has attracted extraordinary support as the unifying theme of environmental policy. Sustainable development is a principle subscribed to by scientists, environmentalists, politicians, and the business community alike. Almost, it seems, effortlessly a powerful coalition has been mobilised to deal effectively with some of the most intractable problems facing the world today.

This enthusiasm for sustainable development is likely to fade as the full implications are grasped. In this paper, I shall argue that the concept is sufficiently vague to enable quite disparate interests to subscribe to it (section 2). Consequently, its impact on policymaking is likely to be marginal rather than fundamental (section 3). Scientific uncertainty and political realities dictate that governments should pursue their short-term interests rather than any long-term common purpose (section 4). In the final part of the paper (section 5) I conclude that fundamental social change to ensure sustainable development is likely to be uneven and to be achieved in conditions of conflict. My intention is to take a broad approach examining the global political context within which national and local policies for sustainable development must be evaluated. Sustainable urban development will be subsumed within this broader picture and will only be referred to where its specific features need to be identified.

2 The implications of sustainable development
Sustainable development is a concept whose "strength is its vagueness" (Redclift, 1991, page 36), but therein lies also its weakness. Sustainable development draws its political sustenance from its unifying, consensual, and essentially conservative connotations. It serves a variety of sociological purposes. It provides status and support to the scientific community; it endows environmentalists with much-desired credibility; it creates a platform for politicians; and it transforms the image of business (Buttel et al, 1990). But maintaining the consensus will ensure that effective action in the pursuit of sustainable development is likely to be strictly limited.

The vagueness surrounding the concept of sustainable development derives largely from the much-quoted key phrase in the Brundtland Report, "Sustainable development is development that meets the needs of the present without compromising the ability of future generations to meet their own needs" (WCED, 1987, page 8). This begs questions concerning the meaning of development, needs, and future generations.

First, it must be clear that development is not synonymous with growth. Growth involves a physical expansion of the economy. Sustainable growth is ultimately contradictory as expansion will run up against the physical limits imposed by the capacity of the earth's natural resources. By contrast, sustainable development is the "qualitative change of a physically nongrowing economic system in dynamic equilibrium with the environment" (Daly and Cobb, 1990, page 71).

A precondition of sustainable development is the conservation or regeneration of the natural capital stock. During the period of modernisation the stock of natural resources has tended to be regarded by some economists as 'free goods', substitutable by humanly created resources. It is now widely recognised that the regenerative capacity of the earth's physical systems can only be assured if its natural assets are properly valued. If a procedure of assigning values to natural resources is adopted, the result is likely to be considerable changes in the patterns of production, settlement, and transportation. Therefore, policies that exhort industry and households "to conserve valuable raw materials, reduce damage to the environment and save money, by minimising or preventing wastes, especially at source" (DoE, 1989, page 19) are useful but, in terms of sustainability, inadequate. They tend to provide reassurance that present patterns of growth can be sustained provided there are marginal shifts in behaviour.

The inadequacy of present policies is further underlined when we examine the meaning of needs. Brundtland emphasises that sustainable development means "meeting the basic needs of all and extending to all the opportunity for a better life" (WCED, 1987, page 44). At present there is a profligate consumption of resources to support the standards of living expected by the rich nations. The poor lack the resources to meet basic necessities. Meeting the demands of the rich and the needs of the poor is likely to place intolerable burdens on the natural resources of the environment. A redistribution of resources with an emphasis on conservation will be necessary.

The need to make some present sacrifices is also inherent in the meaning of future generations. Stewardship implies that the present generation should avoid irreversible damage to the environment. Unfortunately, this requirement has almost certainly been broken. The loss of species cannot be remedied; the risks from toxic or radioactive waste cannot be entirely eliminated no matter how carefully they are managed. If this criterion of sustainability is to be met, we must desist forthwith from those activities which may rob or imperil future generations.

The implications of sustainable development are nothing short of revolutionary. Achieving sustainable development involves a change in the nature of production and consumption, replacing resource exploitation with resource conservation. It requires a redistribution of resources to ensure that gross disparities in living standards and environmental conditions are eliminated. And it envisages a withdrawal from those activities likely to inflict harm on future generations. Such revolutionary changes are exceedingly unlikely, certainly in the short run, for reasons set out in the next section.

3 Limited scope for progress
The political prospects for sustainable development will be determined by the relative power of interests, as they always have been. Political concern for the environment is nothing new. Preoccupation with the relationship between society and nature can be traced back to ancient times (Glacken, 1967) with a continuing oscillation between pessimistic ecocentric and optimistic technocentric views on the relationship. The pessimistic perspective with its neo-Malthusian emphasis on the ultimate limits of the earth's capacity to sustain human demands upon its resources is now accepted in principle by a majority of scientists and politicians. This does not necessarily presage anticipatory action to avoid the checks of famine, disease, war, and pollution that are forecast to overwhelm us. Action is only likely when it is clear that inaction will prove more costly. "If there is a single historical lesson to be drawn from the early history of conservation ... it is that states can be persuaded to act to prevent environmental degradation only when their economic interests are shown to be directly threatened" (Grove, 1990, page 13).

Despite the support for sustainable development and the predictions that serious harm will be the consequence of a failure to act, we have probably not yet reached the point where national interests appear to be sufficiently threatened for fundamental changes in the economic base to be seriously contemplated. But in the affluent countries the environmental concern has stimulated an emphasis on sustainability.

It would be foolish to disregard the progress being achieved towards sustainable development in the short term. There is broad agreement on some important basic principles. There is a general awareness of the need for adopting the precautionary principle, that is acting "where there are good grounds for judging either that action taken promptly at comparatively low cost may avoid more costly damage later, or that irreversible effects may follow if action is delayed" (DoE, 1990, page 11). There is, too, a recognition that environmental action requires an integrated approach. This has three aspects. One is the need for integrated pollution control (IPC) to take into account the fact that pollution can pass through different environmental pathways. Second, there is a need for horizontal policy integration to take into account the environmental consequences of sectoral policies. And, third, policies must be vertically integrated between the different levels of government.

There have been some notable achievements. At the local level in the United Kingdom many councils have developed environmental charters, initiatives, audits, programmes, and action plans. These have resulted in more emphasis on recycling, conservation of habitats and improvement of landscapes, planting of woodland, etc. There has been greater cooperation with conservation bodies and with business in creating environmental improvements. At national level there has been a major white paper, *This Common Inheritance* (DoE, 1990), a substantial Environmental Protection Act, and commitment from all parties to the idea of sustainable development. Within the EC there have been over a hundred environmental directives and the fifth environmental action programme is now being drawn up. Although there have been long delays, action has been taken to reduce acid rain, to clean up beaches, to reduce pollution in the North Sea and the Rhine, and to regulate international trade in toxic and hazardous wastes. Finally, at global level there has been the agreement to phase out CFCs under the Montreal Protocol initiated in 1987. The problem of global warming has been the subject of a major report by the Intergovernmental Panel on Climate Change (Houghton et al, 1990) and was a major subject of the UN Conference on Environment and Development (UNCED) held in Rio de Janeiro in 1992. Outside government, the business community has proclaimed its commitment to sustainability through environmentally friendly products, environmental audits, and through declarations such as that made at the Second World Industry Conference on Environmental Management (WICEM II, 1991) at Rotterdam in March 1991.

It would be unwise to magnify the progress so far made. It has been confined to what is feasible within political limits that do not fundamentally threaten powerful interests. Self-interest has been the prime motivation. At local level there has been a response to public opinion for a cleaner environment. But this is often voiced by relatively privileged groups, anxious to protect or improve the environmental benefits they enjoy. They are quick to protest against locally unwanted land uses (LULU) (Lake, 1987) such as a nuclear waste repository which brings risk and blight to the community. They are able to mobilise sufficient political power to ensure that hazardous activities end up in 'pollution havens' or 'nuclear oases' (Blowers et al, 1991) where the power to resist is weakened by economic dependence on the activity.

A similar process of imposing negative externalities on less powerful communities operates at international level. Polluting industries often seek locations in developing countries where investment is needed and pollution controls are weak. The rich countries have used some of the poorest as dumping grounds for toxic waste materials. There are two circumstances in which it may be possible to prevent the international transfer of negative externalities. One is where agreement is reached between developed countries, as in Europe in the case of acid rain, trade in toxic wastes, clean up of the Rhine, or pollution of the North Sea. The other is where there is an immediate threat to the global commons as in the case of depletion of the ozone layer. This stage has not been reached in the case of global warming, for reasons I shall come to in a moment.

So far progress towards sustainable development has been dictated by self-interest with occasional rhetorical gestures towards a higher moral purpose. Undoubtedly there will be environmental improvements in some areas, though a basic pattern of environmental inequality will persist. Sustainable development in its fullest sense implies concessions, costs, and sacrifices on the part of powerful interests which they show no inclination at present to make. Under present circumstances of scientific uncertainty it is possible both to support sustainable development in principle and to take little action in practice.

4 Consensus in principle, conflict in practice
4.1 Scientific uncertainty—the case for delay
Agreement to take precautionary action presumes there is sufficient knowledge on which to base a judgment of the effects of that action. Scientists have played a central role in identifying a range of environmental problems. For example, there has been the discovery of the depletion of the ozone layer; the evidence of the widespread loss of species and habitats; the monitoring of acid rain; the identification of relationships between radioactivity and certain cancers; and latterly the predictions of global warming. Perhaps for the first time there has developed a scientific consensus on a number of environmental issues

which challenges the exploitative basis of modern technologies and production systems. Unsurprisingly environmentalists have gratefully grasped the evidence that endorses their claims.

In the case of many environmental processes, "Logical deduction appears much more certain than empirical induction" (Yearley, 1991, page 39). In cases where empirical data are incomplete or contestable and under conditions of theoretical uncertainty, scientific predictions rely on judgments that are provisional and, therefore, revocable. They are also, ultimately, subject to political interpretation. Just as scientific evidence can be used to urge the necessity of precautionary action, the uncertainty of the evidence can endorse a strategy of delay.

For example, the controversy over the precise cause and effect of acid rain enabled the British electricity industry to disclaim responsibility for damage to Nordic countries for many years.

Although fossil fuel power stations are a major source of SO_2 which, emitted from tall stacks, can form into acid rain, they are not the only source because pollutants from motor vehicles also contribute to the problem. Moreover, it is very difficult to pinpoint the exact source and precise effects of acid rain damage. The incidence and impact of acid rain vary according to a complex combination of meteorological, biological and geological conditions and the effects are cumulative. It was only after considerable political pressure from within the EC that the United Kingdom eventually acceded to the desulphurisation programme and even then it managed to negotiate lower targets and a longer time-scale than some of its EC partners.

Similarly, it is extremely difficult to prove the link between nuclear facilities and cancer. The statistical correlation between childhood cancers and proximity to the Sellafield nuclear plant is well attested (for example, see Craft and Openshaw, 1987), but the authoritative Black Report made the obvious point that an observed relationship does not prove a causal relationship. Consequently, the hypothesis that there is a causal relationship is "not one which can be categorically dismissed, nor, on the other hand, is it easy to prove" (Black, 1984).

The most spectacular of the recent scientific environmental pronouncements has been the prediction of global warming by the Intergovernmental Panel on Climate Change (Houghton et al, 1990). But there is considerable uncertainty about the degree of warming (a range of between 1.5 and 4.5 °C within the next half century), its timing and the geographical extent of the consequences of drought, flooding, and other climatic hazards (Mohnen et al, 1991). It can readily be seen that "current consensus on the greenhouse effect has raced ahead of the quality and quantity of scientific data on the issue" (Buttel et al, 1990, page 58).

Politically, the question of responsibility for global warming is of extreme interest. The data on the sources of greenhouse gases are incomplete and contain many assumptions leaving them open to widely differing interpretations. Interpretations which seek to pin the responsibility on the developed countries emphasise the fact that around half of energy use comes from the OECD countries and that average consumption per head of fossil fuels in the North is eleven times that of the South (or seven times if biomass is included) (Holmberg et al, 1991, page 26). Conversely, the World Resources Institute (WRI) has compiled a composite greenhouse index combining the heat-trapping potential of the major greenhouse gases (CO_2, methane, and two CFCs). These figures show that three of the top six emitters for 1987 are developing countries (Brazil, China, and India) and that, by including the EC as one country, there are five developing countries in the top ten. Moreover, the United States on this estimate produces only 17.6% of the total, though it produces over a fifth of the CO_2 from fossil-fuel burning. The WRI index has been criticised on several counts: for basing its assessment on just one year's figures (a year in which deforestation in Brazil was very high); for underestimating the impacts of past emissions and the lingering impact of CFCs; for overestimating the effects of deforestation; and for the widely varying accuracy of the different data fed into the index (data for methane are very unreliable compared with data for the other gases).

The political implications of the data are immense: "WRI has succeeded in constructing an opaque methodology which can only lead to confusion and disagreement among those who wish to negotiate and monitor a climate convention" (McCully, 1991, page 164). The WRI index purports to demonstrate a shared responsibility for the problem of global warming between North and South. It neglects the problem of equity, the needs of the South as against the luxuries of the North; it discounts the feasibility of reducing greenhouse gases in the North (eliminating CFCs and reducing CO_2 levels) as against controlling the smaller scale and dispersed sources in developing countries; and it fails to recognise that curbing fossil-fuel power production will conserve nonrenewable resources and prevent other forms of pollution at the same time. By treating gases together rather than separately, the United States will be able to claim that it will stabilise its greenhouse gas emissions by the year 2000, masking a 15% increase in CO_2 by equivalent reductions in other gases.

The question of responsibility for greenhouse gases is deeply political and divisive. On this issue, as on others of vital importance to sustainability, the scientific basis for identifying cause and effect and forecasting future trends is incomplete and contestable, a situation described as "pragmatic uncertainty" (Yearley, 1991, page 39). But it provides a platform for dissension between North and South whose fundamental interests are in conflict. The prospects for progress towards sustainable development are further diminished by the political constraints on action.

4.2 Political reality—the case for procrastination

Political agreement at international level on the reduction of greenhouse gases is the absolute key to sustainable development. Agreement will exert pressure on individual countries and on individual localities to conserve energy and resources and reduce waste and pollution. Without it, progress towards sustainable urban development will be uneven. In the short term, at least, there are several political constraints that must be satisfied and which are likely to hinder the chances of effective progress towards sustainable development.

4.2.1 Costs and benefits

A primary political constraint is the need to balance the costs of environmental protection against the presumed benefits. At the national level this means avoiding burdens on business which may prejudice their competitive position or profitability. At the same time politicians must respond to public demands for environmental enhancement. Politicians must avoid offending the business community on whom they depend for economic growth while, at the same time, appeasing the public to whom they must appeal for votes (Lindblom, 1977). Although business has, in many countries, burnished its green image, there are strict limits to this. The more far-reaching changes in industrial location, production, and structure implied by sustainable development are simply not practical in the short term.

At the international level there has been some success in ensuring that polluters pay the costs of transboundary pollution. The measures to clean up SO_2 emissions in Europe and to cut CFCs at a global level are examples. But the costs of reducing greenhouse gases have yet to be faced. Any effective reduction will require the rich North both to cut back on its energy production and to provide finance and technology to developing countries to assist them in reducing their growing contribution to global warming. Given the problems of apportioning responsibility already referred to, the rich will be able to support their reluctance to pay with excuses for delay. Whatever progress is made in principle, the pace of implementation is likely to be slow and hesitant.

4.2.2 Competitive advantage

Avoiding responsibility can also be justified by a second political constraint: that of ensuring that competitive advantage is not surrendered. This point is linked to costs. It is argued that unilateral action which places burdens on one country that are not imposed on others can result in investment withdrawal, increased prices, and loss of markets. It is a matter of interests. The tragedy of the commons provides a key to national behaviour (Hardin, 1968). Individual countries are likely to continue to pollute so long as they gain an advantage from doing so (that is, the costs of pollution are less than the gains from increased growth). If, as is likely, all countries behave in this way the degradation of the global commons is likely to occur well before the impact of a deteriorating environment is sufficient to cause individual countries to curb their pollution. By this time it may be too late to avoid the consequences of an overloaded environmental system. This is the case at the present time. The onset of global warming is subtle and almost invisible, and there is no urgency to make sacrifices now to avoid a possible future peril.

Nation-states are also liable to behave towards each other in the same way as the prisoners in the prisoner's dilemma who have to guess each other's likely action. States are unlikely to impose environmental controls if they feel that others, particularly rivals, will not follow suit. The tragedy of the commons and the prisoner's dilemma suggest that states will not adopt pollution control measures "either because they do not see it as in their interests to do so, whatever the others may do, or because they do not believe that an agreement can be effectively monitored, that some might break it" (Johnston, 1989, page 138). International agreement to desist from pollution will only be secured if it is in the mutual interest of the parties. In the case of the EC, acceptance of supranational authority on environmental control, however reluctant, has been secured on the basis of the wider economic benefits that issue from a common market. At the global level we have not reached the point where the widely perceived common interest encourages international cooperation in a serious attempt to halt pollution and encourage resource conservation.

4.2.3 Political survival

Political horizons are, inevitably, short, whereas environmental policies are long term. Political survival, whether in democracies or dictatorships, depends on providing security, meeting material needs and responding to aspirations for consumption. Political survival depends on avoiding the unpalatable consequences of action. A shift towards sustainable development sounds attractive in prospect and is sometimes portrayed as merely a shift in the emphasis of policies. Even the Brundtland Report rather underplays the significance of the changes in patterns of development: "Changing these patterns for the better will call for new policies in urban development, industrial location, housing design, transportation systems, and the choice of agricultural and industrial technologies" (WCED, 1987, page 59). Under present technological regimes such changes would mean a severe reduction in the use of personal transport, a change in agricultural practices, restrictions on the consumption of nonrenewable resources in consumer goods, a reduction in energy supply, an emphasis on reuse and recycling, and heavy restraint on polluting activities. Such changes cut right across the grain of modern capitalist industrial economies which are designed to maintain economic growth by the exploitation of resources, the encouragement of consumer demand, and the development of individual opportunity and mobility.

Governments in the developed countries are hardly likely to sacrifice the very things that make them popular. They will only undertake changes when the alternative is unmistakably better and likely to improve their standing. The shift towards free market capitalism undertaken in Britain and elsewhere in the 1980s was in good part a response to the perceived failures of the social democratic state (Gamble, 1988). Despite the growing environmental consciousness in the West, there is little sign that it is inducing more than marginal changes in behaviour among a small minority of people. Porritt claims that "Hard evidence that the world is falling apart around us...is multiplying on every side" (1991, page 16). One can only say that, for the majority of people, such evidence is easy to ignore so long as it does not affect their daily lives. In such circumstances it would be a foolish government that risked opprobrium by imposing unpalatable costs and restrictions which the public felt to be unjustified.

5 The political conditions for sustainable development
For the present, then, there is little real incentive for the rich countries to bear the economic and political costs of a fundamental shift towards sustainable development. They have an interest in environmental improvements which are part of the quality of life in affluent societies. Hence, the rich countries have undertaken environmental protection policies, land-use planning, and pollution controls to improve amenity, conserve heritage, and encourage environmental management. They have also reduced the transboundary pollution they impose on their rich neighbours. We may expect further progress in policies for sustainable urban development within the rich countries.

In the poor countries day-to-day survival is the preoccupation of the majority of the population. They "are forced to forego the needs of the future to meet the needs of today" (Holmberg et al, 1991, page 32). As Brundtland puts it, "Poverty reduces people's capacity to use resources in a sustainable manner; it intensifies pressure on the environment" (WCED, 1987, page 49). For the poor the issue is not environment, but development.

Here we come to the crux of the problem. For the rich, sustainable development is a means to achieve a better environment; for the poor, it is the way forward for development. In urban terms, "the basic problem with Northern cities is that they are unsustainable, and that of Southern cities that they are underdeveloped" (Holmberg et al, 1991, page 31). The concept of sustainable development has come to endorse particular interests rather than reconcile them. Sustainable policies have been embraced while production and consumption have carried on largely as before. There is a danger that sustainability will exhaust its popularity as conflicts of interest between economy and environment, between rich and poor, between short and long term require difficult choices to be made.

It is unclear what those choices will be and when and how they will be made. There is an assumption, rapidly becoming a belief, that we must move from our present economic system to one based on sustainable development. The process of this transformation has been undertheorised. An optimistic or utopian view, somewhat parodied, is that changes in the environment and changes in technology and values will precipitate a fundamental change in attitudes and behaviour that will transform political relationships. In the rich countries people will be happy to consume less, confine their travel, and organise their social and cultural life in self-sustaining communities. The transformation will be achieved both because it is necessary and because it is preferable. The problem with the utopian prescription is that it neglects to explain how or even why it will be achieved.

An alternative, pessimistic neo-Malthusian perspective suggests it is more likely that fundamental changes, if they do occur, will be undertaken in circumstances of rapid environmental deterioration and be accompanied by considerable conflict and upheaval (Gorz, 1980). The rich will cling onto their privileges and there will be wars over resources with the looming prospect of environmental catastrophe through gross pollution or nuclear proliferation. The problem with this perspective is that there is no vision of the future beyond a gradual and inevitable deterioration of living conditions.

In both cases action is required either to achieve utopia or avoid the abyss. The attainment of a sustainable urban development presupposes some fundamental changes in social, political, and economic organisation. The political conditions for sustainable development will involve a challenge to the power of the nation-state and the multinational corporations and an emphasis on planning and redistribution of resources.

5.1 The nation-state
Political power has become increasingly centralised in the nation-state. The modern industrial state has focused primarily on promoting economic growth. Environmental protection policies to clean up pollution and to conserve resources have been introduced by the state to ameliorate the problems of industrialisation. But the nation-state is not competent to deal with the problem of externalities imposed on other countries. There is a need for supranational authority to deal with the problems of global warming, pollution of the oceans, deforestation, transboundary pollution, or loss of species. Conventions, protocols, and other negotiations may achieve substantial results as we have seen. "One of the functions of international organisations is to act as a forum, in which states can overcome the temptation of the prisoner's dilemma, and negotiate public, simultaneous and binding commitments to improved standards of conduct" (Imber, 1991, page 210). But, in any conflict between international and national need, vital national interests will always take priority so that compliance is always likely to be unreliable and fragmented. This problem can only be overcome by a surrender of state power to a higher body.

At the same time there is a need for authority to be devolved downwards to regional and local governments. It is at this level that the detailed policies of sustainable urban development will have to be delivered. In terms of scale, commitment, planning and implementation it makes sense to encourage localised control over the production of energy, the management of water and other resources, the development of land, waste management and pollution control, and transportation strategy. Thus a first condition for the achievement of sustainable urban development is for *the nation-state to surrender power upwards to supranational authorities and to devolve powers to regional and local authorities*.

5.2 Multinational corporations

Multinational corporations (MNCs) have a major impact on the exploitation of oil resources, minerals, timber, and other raw materials, and the production of a range of primary agricultural products and manufactured consumer goods. Their investment, production plants, and markets are widespread and mobile. They may seek out pollution havens, usually where environmental controls are weak and labour plentiful. Their size and economic significance place them substantially outside the control of individual states or international organisations. Although many MNCs are environmentally conscious, their conversion to 'green' consumerism or to environmentally friendly production processes is likely to be tactical. The drive to increase market share through greater profitability, investment, and sales is bound to take precedence over environmental needs. For this reason it is vital that the MNCs are brought under effective political control. Therefore a second condition for sustainable urban development is for *the environmentally damaging operations of multinational corporations to be prevented by effective national and international controls*. But, for reasons previously stated, the chances of this happening before global deterioration becomes unavoidable are slim.

5.3 Planning

Although certain market mechanisms might be used to implement sustainable policies, the achievement of sustainable development will require comprehensive coordination, monitoring, and implementation. This will mean intervention by supranational, national, and local authorities to control production and consumption. For example, at the international level the targets, time-scale, and distribution of CO_2 reductions must be planned. National strategies for controlling the environmental impacts of sectoral policies will be required. There will need to be a hierarchy of plans to ensure strategic coordination of land development, resource management, waste management, and pollution control. Participation in the development of plans can, no doubt, be encouraged, but inevitably planning for sustainable development will involve some restriction on individual freedom in the common interest. It is difficult to visualise a democratic system delivering policies of self-restraint, but direction by a coercive state is likely to prove unacceptable. Therefore, a third condition is that *planning within a participative democratic political system must be intro-duced at all levels to coordinate and enforce the conservation of resources and the control of pollution*.

5.4 Redistribution

The preceding conditions if applied would reduce the power of the nation-state and the multinationals and increase the role of participative planning at different levels of government. The fourth condition envisages a transfer of resources from rich to poor. Redistribution is advocated both as a moral principle to enable more equitable development but also as a necessary mechanism to prevent further environmental deterioration. Thus environmental quality will be a consequence of social equality. For all the reasons set out earlier the rich countries will resist providing aid to the poor if at the same time they have to cut back on their own pollution. The reduction in living standards this could involve would be difficult to justify on the basis of a putative but hardly imminent environmental calamity. Nevertheless, the following condition is essential for the achieve-ment of sustainable development on a global basis. *Resources must be redistributed to give priority to environmental conservation*.

6 Conclusion

The four conditions outlined are necessary but not sufficient for the achievement of sustainable development. Institutional changes must be preceded by changes in values and behaviour. The signs of change are, at present, superficial. People in the advanced countries have, no doubt, become more environmentally conscious. Some of them have modified their buying habits, but very few have basically changed their life-style. Nor is there a broad movement of environmental activists waiting in the wings to spearhead the revolution when the political moment is ripe. Those groups most likely to be mobilised have been seduced by the pleasures of conspicuous consumption. On the whole their conservationist instincts have been devoted to preserving their own environments, often at the expense of someone else's.

It is likely that people will be prepared to put up with a great deal more congestion, pollution and general environmental deterioration so long as they continue to enjoy the freedom and comforts of modern consumerist society. Moreover, it is likely that individuals and nation-states will fight to retain their privileges. After all, the projected environmental catas-trophe is likely to be a gradual process, not a sudden event. It has even been suggested that global warming may benefit some areas. Conflicts of interest may well be expressed in military conflicts to secure resources. Within forty or so years it is possible that "environmental deterioration and economic decline will be feeding on each other, pulling us into a downward spiral of social decay and political upheaval" (Brown, 1991, page 9).

It may be that the world is on the threshold of a major social transformation. There has been much discussion of the characteristics of late capitalism (postmodernism and post-Fordism). As the scale of technology has grown so the fundamental characteristics of capitalism, growth, competition, and resource exploitation have begun to destroy the natural resources on which survival ultimately depends. Moreover, capitalism is a mode of production in which it is impossible to limit or suppress growth while simultaneously distributing goods more equitably. If capitalism is in its terminal phase its successor may be what has been described as ecologism, a social condition in which care for the environment "presupposes radical changes in our relationship with it, and thus in our mode of social and political life" (Dobson, 1990, page 13).

If that is the case we should not expect the transition to be accomplished peaceably. Capitalism's development was accompanied by conflict, gross exploitation and degradation of the environment. Its benefits will not be lightly surrendered. The contemporary concern for the environment and development will make some impression on policies for sustainable development. There will important changes and improvements especially at the local level. But, for some time to come the limits to change are more likely to be determined by political, not environmental, constraints.

References

Black D, 1984 *Investigation of the Possible Increased Incidence of Cancer in West Cumbria* report of Independent Advisory Group, chairman Sir Douglas Black, Department of Health and Social Security (HMSO, London)

Blowers A, Lowry D, Solomon B, 1991 *The International Politics of Nuclear Waste* (Macmillan, London)

Brown L R, 1991, "A sustainable future" *Resurgence* number 147, 8–13

Buttel F H, Hawkins A P, Power A G, 1990, "From limits to growth to global change: constraints and contradictions in the evolution of environmental science and ideology" *Global Environmental Change, Human and Policy Dimensions* **1** 57–66

Craft A, Openshaw S, 1987, "Children, radiation, cancer and the Sellafield nuclear reprocessing plant", in *Nuclear Power in Crisis* Eds A Blowers, D Pepper (Croom Helm, Beckenham, Kent) pp 244–271

Daly H E, Cobb J B, 1990 *For the Common Good* (Green Print, London)

Dobson A, 1990 *Green Political Thought* (Unwin Hyman, London)

DoE, 1989 *Sustaining Our Common Future, A Progress Report by the United Kingdom on Implementing Sustainable Development* Department of the Environment, 2 Marsham Street, London SW1P 3EB

DoE, 1990 *This Common Inheritance: Britain's Environmental Strategies* Cm 1200 Department of the Environment (HMSO, London)

ENDS, 1989 *Report 173* 11 June, Environmental Data Services Ltd, Unit 24, 40 Bowling Green Lane, London EC1R 0NE

Gamble A, 1988 *The Free Economy and the Strong State* (Macmillan, London)

Glacken C J, 1967 *Traces on the Rhodian Shore* (University of California Press, London)

Gorz A, 1980 *Ecology as Politics* (South End Press, Boston, MA)

Grove R, 1990, "The origins of environmentalism" *Nature* **345** 11 – 14

Hardin G, 1968, "The tragedy of the commons" *Science* **162** 1243 – 1248

Holmberg J, Bass S, Timberlake L, 1991 *Defending the Future: A Guide to Sustainable Development* , (Earthscan, London)

Houghton J T, Jenkins C J, Ephraum J J (Eds), 1990 *Climate Change: The IPCC Scientific Assessment* Report of the United Nations Environment Programme, Intergovernmental Panel on Climate Change (IPCC) (Cambridge University Press, Cambridge)

Imber M F, 1991, "Environmental security: a task for the UN system" *Review of International Studies* **17** 201 – 212

Johnston R J, 1989 *Environmental Problems: Nature, Economy and State* Belhaven Press, London)

Lake R W(Ed.), 1987 *Resolving Locational Conflict* (Center for Urban Policy Research, Rutgers University)

Lindblom C E, 1977 *Politics and Markets: The World's Political – Economic Systems* (Basic Books, New York)

McCully P, 1991 "Discord in the greenhouse: how WRI is attempting to shift the blame for global warming" *The Ecologist* **21** 157 – 165

Mohnen V A, Goldstein W, Wei-Chyung Wang, 1991, "The conflict over global warming: the application of scientific research to policy choices" *Global Environmental Change, Human and Policy Dimensions* **1** 109 – 123

OECD, 1991 *The State of the Environment* (OECD, Paris)

Porritt J, 1991, "Global warming" *New Statesman and Society* **10** 15 – 16

Redclift M, 1991, "The multiple dimensions of sustainable development" *Geography* **76** 36 – 42

WCED, 1987 *Our Common Future* The Brundtland Report, World Commission on Environment and Development (Oxford University Press, Oxford)

WICEM II, 1991, "Official report, Second World Industry Conference on Environment and Management", in *Environment Strategy Europe* (Campden Publishing, London) pp 71 – 107

Yearley S, 1991, "Greens and science: a doomed affair?" *New Scientist* 13 July, pages 37 – 40

Sustainable Development in a Regional System

P Nijkamp, P Lasschuit, F Soeteman
Free University, Amsterdam

1 Regional ecologically sustainable economic development

The notion of 'sustainable development' (SD) has been discussed extensively in recent years (see Archibugi and Nijkamp, 1989; WCED 1987). However these discussions have often taken place on a global scale, and to a large extent they focused on conceptual issues. Consequently, it is not surprising that the lack of empirical applicability has been a major source of criticism. A more operational treatment of this—appealing but highly abstract—concept of SD seems the only way for it to survive in the current debate on our common future. Thus the practical applicability of this concept has to be emphasised, as SD analysis should offer operational guidelines for the contents and the steps to be taken in order to meet the objective of SD.

The inherent logic of a regional sustainable development (RSD) analysis stems from the belief that this analysis may make functional interdependencies at the regional level more manageable in view of a given development. Clearly, from a management and policy point of view, a regional scale is more suitable for control and transformation than the global scale. And hence it is evident that the objective of SD may be achieved more easily, if the process of socioeconomic development and environmental change at a regional scale are clearly understood and properly managed (see Kairiukstis, 1989). The interdependencies may be either one-dimensional (or single faceted) (for example, in the case of transport, commuting, industrial, infrastructural, communication, or recreation activities) or multidimensional (broader social, economic, or economic–ecological phenomena). Clearly, regional development objectives may vary from analytical–theoretical to descriptive–empirical or prescriptive. The goal of concrete regional management issues may be a rationalisation of policy behaviour (ex-ante or ex-post) with respect to one or more facets. A unidimensional objective may be operationalised by means of conventional optimisation strategies, whereas with a multidimensional policy analysis a 'satisficing' strategy may be more appropriate (see Simon, 1967).

In this paper, we will first discuss *sustainable development at a regional level* (RSD). In this context a methodological question which is relevant to real-world problems and policy questions is: can a meaningful and operational concept of RSD—and rules for policies to obtain RSD—be postulated on the basis of the global concept of SD?

Another question concerns the openness of a spatial system of regions. Given an internal (that is, intraregional) policy of sustainable development, an important question is: what are the restrictions in economically and ecologically 'open regions' to render an internal RSD policy effective in a broader spatial system? Therefore, in section 3 we will briefly discuss the notion of a 'region' in this context. The main question is: in the context of sustainable development, which are the specific dimensions of this RSD notion? It will be argued that the *relative openness* of a region, the *specific regional circumstances* (precluding a regional levelling out of global developments, and leading to global impacts of regional problems), and the *level of authority on the common environmental goods or resources* of a region are of importance.

Usually the interdependencies in RSD are clearly multidimensional; this will be discussed further in section 4, where the emphasis will be on some descriptive–theoretical thoughts about the objective of SD at a regional level. In our approach, we will link the notion of RSD to a welfare–theoretical approach, in which RSD will be related to intergenerational trade-off, multiple use of environmental resources, and sustainable use of resources (Nijkamp and Soeteman, 1989).

We will particularly emphasise one of the key factors for successful implementation of regional sustainable policies: the *institutional structure of RSD management and policy*. Therefore in section 5 we develop some prescriptive–analytical guidelines for an institutional structure.

It is evident that—in contrast to the notion of 'regional economic growth'—the multidimensionality of RSD calls for a satisficing policy analysis, based on compromise optimisation strategies. Consequently, in section 6 we discuss a set of possible feasible policy strategies.

2 Towards a definition of regional sustainable development
In the framework of RSD an integrated economic and environmental approach to policymaking is needed to minimise conflicts between resource–using activities, to enhance socioeconomic opportunities (like optimising productivity), and to bequeath an environmental estate for the benefit of future generations (Cloke and Park, 1985). Quite often an RSD-orientated strategy is carried out by evaluating the implications of environmental standards or by putting constraints on industrial, agricultural, or transport developments. A particular project (proposed or implemented) may increase or decrease welfare levels of society at different (intergenerational) points in time and (interregional) points in space, while the aggregated welfare measured over all these points may still be positive in all cases (depending inter alia on the social rate of discount used). Thus there are distributive implications for income, employment, and environmental amenities over space and time.

If no acceptable environmental solution can be found for some (new) regional activities, a way out may be to search for compensating measures. These can be applied both to spatial and to time scales. The idea of compensation is appealing in as far as it provides for alternative policy choices. However, in various practical situations many questions still have to be answered to make this option really operational. For instance: how should compensation be used (what are the environmental and socioeconomic consequences of the compensating project); are there time lags between destruction of environmental amenities and their reconstruction; what are the costs to be borne by various groups? Recently, various interesting proposals have been made. One example is to replant forests in Central America as a compensation for the carbon dioxide produced by a new power station in New England. The idea of compensation is of course easier to apply to large individual projects with a single or few decision-makers. For numerous small daily decisions by individuals (painting a house, driving a car, smoking a cigarette) direct compensating measures are hard to carry out because of the so-called large number case.

An alternative way of looking at RSD in an open spatial system is to conceive of it as a long-term balance of flows of regional imports and exports, both ecological–physical flows, and trade–monetary flows. The physical flows are determined not only by cross-boundary flows of groundwater, surface water, or air (the physical means of transport), but also by socioeconomic activities such as trade, capital flows, and migration.

This view of RSD is appealing, but is still too much region orientated. RSD refers essentially to more than just balanced flows for a given area. From a welfare viewpoint, it makes more sense to define RSD as *a development which ensures that the regional population can attain an acceptable level of welfare—both at present and in the future*—and that this regional development is compatible with ecological circumstances in the long run while at the same time it tries to accomplish a globally sustainable development (Nijkamp and Soeteman, 1989). Consequently RSD has to fulfil two goals: (1) it should ensure for the regional population an acceptable level of welfare, which can be sustained in the future; and (2) it should not be in conflict with SD at a supraregional level.

The second goal implies that RSD for a single region is compatible with global SD. Consequently, if all regions of a global system have an RSD, then development in the global system will also be sustainable. Clearly, the RSD paths of specific regions may have different characteristics because of specific regional circumstances (availability and use of natural resources and socioeconomic capital, environmental vulnerability and resilience, and socioeconomic distribution of income and employment), so that it is not easy to typify a general RSD.

Given the existence of trade, transport, dispersion of species, and other socioeconomic and ecological linkages between regions, it may be possible to attain SD at a global level without having an RSD path at the regional level. In extreme cases it might be possible that global SD demands regional '*sacrifices*' to the detriment of regional development (or environ-mental sustainability). Such a development may be acceptable from a supraregional or global human need perspective. By 'sacrifice' we mean here a reduction in welfare for the regional population, which will be in contrast to the first goal of RSD. This may happen when certain regions are used for specific environmental or economic purposes (such as conservation of natural areas, concentration of industrial activity, or dumping of waste). According to the Brundtland Report (WCED, 1987, page 45) it is unrealistic to suppose that every ecosystem (which may encompass more than one region) can be preserved intact everywhere. In these cases we have to look for regional implications of SD, which may require solutions to the difficult problems of regional compensation.

3 Aspects of a regional analysis of sustainable development

RSD runs the danger of transferring the 'global rhetoric' (Pezzy, 1989) of sustainability towards a micro or meso level of application. Clearly, a regional treatment of sustainable development falls in between a macro (or global) systems level and a micro (or project) level approach, as analysis of RSD is spatially a meso level analysis. However, practical, efficiency, or analytical reasons may necessitate flexible use of different spatial scales. Also, management reasons may necessitate a differentiated level of treatment of RSD, both for legislative tasks and for control (or executive) tasks. Thus, RSD presupposes a meso level of analysis, but not on an a priori fixed spatial scale of a region.

Regions are not uniquely defined spatial entities. Demarcation of a region may depend on the purposes of analysis but may also be the result of an analysis. The following rather abstract and analytical definition of a region, which is often used in the regional economic literature, may be applied: "a set of spatial points that are either homogeneous with respect to some characterization (criterion of homogeneity) or more intensively interrelated among each other than with other spatial points (criterion of functional dependence)" (Siebert, 1985, p 126). A region is seen as a subset of a global system. Consequently, it would be straightforward to define RSD as a translation of the global concept of sustainable development to the regional level. For instance, if for a given region RSD is possible and independent of the rest of the world, then it is self-sufficient. However, it follows from the above definition that regions are open systems with respect to many characteristics, so that they are to a large extent dependent on other regions for their development. Interactions and trade-offs between regions are especially relevant.

It is noteworthy that for RSD a closed system seems a rather unrealistic abstraction of the real world. First, for a global system all processes are in principle internally determined, but for a region many factors are externally determined (scarcity and prices of resources, imported pollution, and even climatic conditions). Second, global developments do not uniformly and smoothly impact on all regions. Global warming of the atmosphere may have positive effects on the total of organic production in the world, but will certainly result in socioeconomic and ecological disasters in parts (regions) of the world. Also the consequences of the finity of natural resources on a global scale may have important different consequences at a regional scale. The depletion of resources primarily originating from one region may be compensated by surpluses of other regions. However, such compensations will only be possible if there exists a wide diversity among regions and if the resources are mobile. In the case of land (an immobile resource), the interrelation of regions may also ease the mobility of human activities when the pressure on this resource becomes too high. Thus, on a regional level of analysis and policy there is much scope for various trade-offs: interregional, global–regional, and intertemporal. It is *necessary* to consider RSD in relation to *interactions with other regions* and their respective development. The resulting kind of RSD depends on the type and amount of goods and services the region can sustainably offer and on the sustainable importation of goods and services from the rest of the world.

If the purpose of demarcation is taken as a central aim, a less abstract definition may be used. The demarcation is a starting point instead of a result of the analysis. If institutional considerations are taken as a focal point, a region may be defined as: "an area within which there is enough community to support an authority that represents and serves the common good" (Daly, 1989, page 74). A government that wishes to serve the regional common good needs a programme consisting of goals, objectives, and finally measures or projects. As with the global concept of SD, it is not easy to arrive at a sustainable development path by coordination of individual projects impacting on these common goods. Among complicating issues are multiple uses of natural resources, multiple and often conflicting objectives of social groups, dynamic interdependence within and between social actions and environmental evolution. In this definition interregionally complicating factors are not yet taken into consideration. If there are any relevant interregional connections, the region would simply have to be enlarged to encompass them. Clearly, this may not always be possible in a policy context.

Consequently, RSD differs from SD in three essential aspects: the openness (or interrelatedness) of a region; the aspects which are—in contrast to global treatment—not levelled out on a regional scale; and the regionalised authority of common goods. These aspects should be considered explicitly to make SD operational on the basis of (supra-) local, regional, or supraregional—but regionally differentiated—decisions. These three dimensions justify separate attention for RSD.

4 Welfare considerations of RSD
4.1 Introduction
A recent publication (van den Bergh et al, 1989) has given the key factors that are relevant in an RSD approach: intergenerational and interregional trade-offs, multiple use of environmental resources, sustainable use of renewable resources, risk and uncertainty. These key factors will be discussed in relation to the following socioeconomic issues which are

of crucial importance for regional development: population pattern, production structure, regional income, and regional investment. Not all potential issues of RSD planning will be discussed fully here. We will concentrate only on those socioeconomic issues which are regarded as most important in a regional setting.

4.2 Intergenerational trade-offs

4.2.1 *Regional population structure and intergenerational trade-offs*
There exists a mutual relationship between population and the environment. The rate of population growth influences the speed of extraction of environmental resources, and the environment provides necessary resources for existence, survival, and growth (UNEP, 1987).

The rate of population growth is, amongst other things, a function of the structure of population. A fast rate of population growth has often been regarded as one of the most important factors accelerating environmental degradation (for example, see Ehrlich and Holdren, 1971; Hardin, 1972). There are others who disagree that there is such a causal relation. A representative of a more synthetic view is Wilkinson (1974), who considers both population and technology to be causes of environmental degradation. In his view ecological imbalance will force people to look for new resources and new exploitation methods that require increasingly complicated technologies. These new technologies may induce new problems, and so a spiral effect may come into operation of ever changing technologies that result in an increasing interference with the environment.

Clearly, the rate of population growth is closely related to the structure of the population, while the use of environmental resources is also related to the rate of per capita consumption. The relation between population structure and the welfare of future generations may be manifest in different consumption patterns and engagements in the production process by different age groups. For example, the activity level of older people may decrease with age. This may mean relatively fewer environmental externalities and less use of environmental resources. The need for infrastructure is also a function of population structure (for example, commuting). For an RSD the fulfilment of present needs may preclude the realisation of new needs in the future. The aging of the rural population may cause a lack of successors in the agricultural sector, leading to a more concentrated form of cultivation of farmland by fewer farmers. The resulting agricultural production processes will show more mechanisation and an increase in monocultures (that is, 'industrial farming'). The final result may be a loss of environmental amenity for future generations.

Although population structure evidently plays a clear role in questions of intergenerational trade-offs, hard facts are difficult to obtain. Macrofigures about issues such as population growth, consumption, and production are relatively more easily available. For example, in the Netherlands, between 1960 and 1985, the amount of waste per capita increased by 83%, whereas population grew by only 26%. Thus, less than a third of the increase can be attributed to population growth (CBS, 1987).

Whatever the main cause of regional environmental degradation, the population structure also plays an important part. Therefore, to ensure RSD, there has to be a balance between population structure and the use of environmental potentials (like natural resources), not only today, but in the future. Intergenerational trade-offs have to be made; society has to choose (implicitly or explicitly) between the use of natural resources for economic development by the present generation and their conservation for later use by future generations.

Such a sustainable development is unlikely to come about automatically (Kirsch, 1986; Krutilla and Fisher, 1975; Kula, 1988; Nijkamp and Rouwendal, 1988). Individuals make decisions on the basis of the value they attach to the environment. To obtain this value at any moment in time, the net benefits derived from the environment are weighted by a discount factor. The discounted value is a decreasing function of time, which implies that the benefits of the environment that accrue to the individuals in the near future are valued higher than the benefits in the distant future. The value of the discount rate partly depends on the time preference (or the consumption rate of interest) which may differ with age. Older people will probably have a relatively high time preference rate (they value present consumption relatively highly), as they know their remaining lifetime is likely to be short. Consequently, an allocation of resources meant to support the next generations is probably not very highly appreciated by them. Young people, on the other hand, may value the future benefits much more highly, because the probability that they will also enjoy (a part of) these benefits is higher. Thus age (or population structure) is one of the factors that explains the difference in time preferences—and thus discount rates—of different generations. Another factor which explains differences in discount rates is the welfare level of the population: people living near subsistence level tend to have a very high time preference.

It is not always true that the time horizon of people is limited to their lifespan. They may also be concerned about the future of their children and grandchildren. But there is a general consensus among economists that concern about the future consequences of our decisions quickly decreases with time; empirical evidence shows that people seldom look further than one or two generations (Hilhorst, 1987). This feature may lead to discrimination against future generations, as they are the ones who will to a large extent bear the consequences of decisions taken by the present generation, although they do not have any say in this decision-making process.

To overcome this dilemma it will be necessary to influence current decisions of individuals and institutions by means of a proper environmental policy. Sustainability requires—at least implicitly—that the discount rate be a derivative of future welfare positions and not the other way round [compare Rawls's ideas of social justice (see Kula, 1988)]. Such a policy would have to decide how much environmental capital should be preserved and what its composition should be (James et al, 1989; Opschoor, 1987). Clearly, this proposition is fraught with many uncertainties, because various assumptions have to be made about: future population, both in terms of size and structure (for example, interregional migration may change the pressure on regional environmental resources); future demands (for example, regional changes in preferences); technological developments through which the natural potential limits may be shifted (new substitution possibilities or recycling methods, new extraction methods; although the regional dimension is less evident in the second case); and the future assimilative capacity of the environment (various environmental effects of activities in the past or present may only come about in the future and it is hard to determine beforehand the temporal and spatial impacts as well as the intensity of these delayed effects; here the regional aspects appear more clearly).

It will be clear from the above observations that the relationship between intergenerational trade-offs and population structure is multi-dimensional. No easy and straightforward answers can be generated for a particular region. In a system of interrelated regions, robust answers about the time perspective are even harder to provide.

4.2.2 Regional income and intergenerational trade-offs
An equal distribution of income within and between regions is often regarded as essential in a policy for sustainable development (WCED, 1987; World Bank, 1987). Although the link between income and environmental degradation is somewhat obscure, it is generally accepted that severe poverty has a negative impact on the environment. An unequal income distribution—which implies the concentration of means and power in the hands of a few people, whereas what is left has to be distributed among the large majority—is a characteristic phenomenon in many less developed countries. The same imbalance appears between countries in the world. The fast growth rate of population, the growing need for food and other basic requirements, and the limited access to resources drive the mass of poor people to an unsustainable use of environmental resources. Although they are often aware of the potential dangers of their decisions, in many areas they have no alternatives in their struggles to survive (their time preference is necessarily very high).

From an opposite point of view, one may claim that high levels of income may lead to an unsustainable use of the environment. A high material standard of living implies more needs and wants and therefore a greater stress on environmental resources. The per capita consumption of cereals in the United States is 4.5 times as high as in India and the energy consumption 60 times as high (Opschoor, 1989).

These two issues show that there is a close relation between the intergenerational distribution of income-generating capacity of the environment (and consequently of welfare) and the intragenerational distribution of income. A more equal distribution within one country may lead to an alleviation of poverty and therefore enable people to take more consideration of the limited capacity of the environment. But a decrease in income of the very wealthy people may reduce their 'overconsumption' which also may have positive effects on the environment, not only now, but also in the long run.

In an international setting there is some evidence that the higher developed countries have the ability to take care of their environmental resource base. From an environmental viewpoint it is not clear whether international redistribution of welfare will have positive environmental effects. Clearly, there is a severe lack of research.

One possible contribution to a more sustainable use of environmental resources is an increase in resource prices to a level where the true costs of depletion and pollution are reflected (Daly, 1986). For nonrenewable resources the increasing relative scarcity instead of absolute scarcity in the market at a certain time should be reflected in their price. For renewable resources, the market price should at least reflect all the costs of sustainable production. Such price rises may bring about more environmentally sound production processes. The income effects of such changes may work out in different ways depending, amongst other factors, on the time period under consideration. For example, higher resource prices for industries in a certain region may have a negative effect on employment and income when these price increases cannot be passed on to consumers. Some regions may be worse affected than others. The same can be said for environmental regulations by the government. The result may be that the more heavily affected regions lag behind in their development, thereby decreasing the production and income opportunities for future generations.

It should be added that an environmental investment will either imply a reduction in consumption or a decrease in nonenvironmental investments. When the environmental investment is unproductive and squeeezes profits, it may induce a negative impact on new investments and thus on the income-generating capacity of future generations (Meissner, 1986).

4.2.3 Investment and intergenerational trade-offs

Industrial investment in specialised plant and equipment often represents an irreversible commitment of capital. If the investment has been misjudged, there will be a loss of capital value. When information necessary to meet future demands for capital goods has been lost (for example, because of a misjudged investment), the options available for future generations will be reduced, which will imply a welfare loss for society as a whole (Krutilla and Fisher, 1975). The option value of an investment in land degradation implies gains from being able to learn about the future benefits—benefits otherwise foregone by a development of this land—if one does not develop it immediately (Fisher and Hanemann, 1985).

Not all investment implies a technological irreversibility. Some restriction or compensaton is possible, but here again there are difficulties, because: restriction and/or compensation may take time and there might be considerable time lags before the desired effects are manifested; and perfect restriction is very hard to realise, and leaves us with the problem of the absence of authenticity in a reproduction or a restoration.

Another issue related to investment and intergenerational trade-offs concerns the discount rate. Individuals try to maximise the present value of their investment. In their decision they will consider both the time preference regarding consumption and the productivity of the investment (Kula, 1988). Regional differences in the discount rate may therefore lead to regional differences in investment and therefore influence the production capacity of future generations.

4.3 Interregional trade-offs

4.3.1 *Population structure and interregional trade-offs*

Interregional trade-offs between population structure and the environment are an important issue in the light of an integrated environmental economic policy. In the case of land (an immobile resource) the interrelation of regions may ease the mobility of people. If the pressure on land increases through fast population growth, migration to less populated regions may alleviate the pressure. There are also examples of pressure increasing on land because of outward migration of farmers, leaving the land fallow and prone to erosion (see Manning, 1988). On a regional level there is much scope for trade-offs between economic and environmental decisions (see also Siebert, 1985).

In order to achieve RSD, the regional population, given its activity level, would have to be balanced with respect to the environmental potential. The population size may be larger, if more resources are allocated to technologies that serve to minimise environmental degradation or if interregional sustainable resource exchange is possible. One problem is that no one can exactly determine an optimal size of regional population from this perspective, ignoring historical circumstances or public preferences (in contrast to a more isolated issue like the determination of an optimal fish population in fishery management).

It will be clear that free fluctuations in population may have severe ecological consequences in ecosystems under stress. Therefore a policy may be needed to control the regional population structure. Meissner

(1986) has suggested two policies:

(1) *Control the number of jobs* The region may become more or less attractive for workers and this may result in an increase or decrease in the supply of labour. Then, the wage level will be affected (for example, through labour shortage) and the region will become more or less attractive for firms.

(2) *Control the number of dwellings* Furthermore, the price of houses will be affected, which will even further increase or decrease the attractiveness of the region.

Regional environmental policy itself may influence the growth of regional population. Stringent environmental measures and high environmental taxes may induce people to move to regions where a less stringent environmental policy is implemented.

A common feature of all these policy measures is that their effects are socially and spatially discriminating. Only affluent people can afford to stay in the region and to pay the higher costs (for transportation, housing, taxes) that are associated with these policies. Interregional welfare effects come to the fore. We may conclude that institutional regulations or incentives may influence the way these interregional trade-offs will work out. The level of institutional assignment of responsibilities is of primary importance.

4.3.2 *Production structure and interregional trade-offs*

Economic growth—or increase in GNP—and environmental quality are both components of human welfare. Evidence from the past has shown us an antagonistic relation between these two components. Particularly in regions with a high concentration of human activities (agriculture, industry), the environmental burden has been heavy.

A policy to alleviate the problem may try to spread these activities over a larger area. This will surely result in a reduction of environmental pollution in the most heavily concentrated regions. But the other side of the coin is an extension of the number of regions that will endure environmental damage, although to a less intensive degree (Bresso, 1989).

Another policy option may be based on the spatial separation of polluting activities in (parts of) regions that will be given up ('blackspots') in order to safeguard other (parts of) regions against environmental damages resulting from these activities (Siebert, 1987). An example of this spatial functionalisation is the concentration of industrial activities in specially designated industrial zones in order to maintain the recreational or natural function of other regions.

Such policies oriented to alleviate environmental degradation may lead to a rise in production costs; the additional efforts and increased costs that have to be borne will often not be compensated by extra output. In the case of free trade and mobility of production factors (including capital), regional differences in environmental policies may induce the relocation of certain polluting activities from regions where a stringent policy is implemented to regions with a more flexible environmental policy (for example, the industrial free zones in developing countries have replaced the most polluting hotspots of the OECD countries). In the case of free mobility of production factors, activities will relocate according to the principles of absolute advantages. Only in the case of immobility of production factors will relocation take place on the basis of comparative cost advantages (Daly, 1989). The environment (including environmental policy) may become (or already is?) the most important immobile production factor, and consequently this factor will to a large extent determine the future production structure. One more aspect of the mobility of production processes has to be mentioned. If, because of stringent environmental legislation production moves to more easily accessible spots in the world, it becomes increasingly important that the consumption process is controlled (for example, no imports of cars from countries where the pollution in production already exceeds environmental standards, and no imports of tropical wood from countries with insufficient reforestation programmes).

Although practical evidence about the relationship between structural change and environmental effects is as yet rare, the study by Jänicke et al (1988) of thirty-one countries has shown that a clear relationship exists between the level of production (GNP), the growth rate of GNP, and the change in resource use. The four input factors used in this study (steel, cement, energy, and freight transport) show a delinking from GNP in the highly developed countries: the rate of growth in use of these inputs has been smaller than (or is sometimes even negatively related to) the growth rate of GNP.

4.3.3 Income and interregional trade-offs
When regional environmental investments are less productive than non-environmental investments, an opportunity cost will arise which implies a decrease in potential regional revenues. Less revenue may imply less investment and fewer regional employment opportunities. So the effect on regional income should be considered from a spatial, as well as a temporal, perspective. The closure of polluting industries because of stringent environmental policy regulations may bring about their relocation to other regions, thereby also relocating income and employment opportunities (see also Siebert, 1985).

It is possible that the increased production cost will be passed on to the consumers, so that revenues may ultimately remain the same. Employment in such an environmentally controlled sector may increase (see below). Pollution control may lead to a decrease in other costs (through energy saving or recycling). Therefore, it is very hard to predict what the final result of environmental policy will be with respect to income.

In an interregional setting one would expect that comparative disadvantages will lead to some redirection of regional income and consequently of regional employment.

However, empirical studies show that in most cases the net effect (the positive effect of investment on the short run and the negative price and income effect on the long run) of regional environmental policies on employment is positive. Between 1970 and 1975 the net employment effect in the United States was an increase of 524 000 jobs (man–years). For Germany, the increase was about 300 000 jobs (man–years) (Meissner, 1986). This may be in accordance with the viewpoint of Potier (1986, see section 4.3.4) that the interregional trade-offs of environmental policies are of less importance.

These studies have, however, been carried out for developed economies. For less developed countries, it is likely that price and income effects offset the investment effects because of less value added in the production structure (capital investments caused by environmental legislation may necessitate imports of new technologies or capital goods).

4.3.4 *Investment and interregional trade-offs*
Besides the temporal implications of investments, as discussed in section 4.2.3, investments also have a spatial dimension. Investments may differ among regions because of:

Economic factors: differences in (the speed of) development (and consequently in means, knowledge, and power) may enable some regions to invest more, and more successfully than others. Regional differences in income imply that people in poor regions—who are close to subsistence—will have a high time preference. Present consumption, in relation to future consumption, is valued very highly and therefore the rate of investment will be relatively low. Regional differences in property rights may also influence investments; when environmental property rights are weak, marginal user costs and marginal external costs may both be ignored. This will result in a private rate of return that will exceed the social rate of return and may lead to an unsustainable use of environmental resources (Pezzy, 1989).

Political factors: regional differences in investment may also result from the goal of maximising national welfare. Some regions may be selected where pollution-intensive investments will be concentrated ('blackspots') in order to save other regions from being polluted (Siebert, 1985). Industrial activities may be concentrated in a certain region to maintain the recreational function of other ones. The location of a certain new activity may be influenced by the bargaining power of the region. R&D and investments in pollution control and prevention may be stimulated by the government by way of subsidies, tax exemptions, etc. A study carried out by the OECD among its member states in 1977 indicated that the financial assistance for pollution control and prevention—measured as a percentage of total environmental investment—varied between 0.004% and 26.9% for different countries (Potier, 1986). Not only financial differences, but also more stringent environmental regulations may induce industries to search for and implement new technologies. In the United States the investments in favour of the environment are much higher than in Italy, where the environmental regulations are much less intensive.

Infrastructural factors: lack of infrastructure (because of low population density) may hinder research and development, but the pressure on the natural resource base may be less, simply because the means and knowledge are not available to exploit and transport natural resources (Boserup, 1981).

Natural factors: the production potentials of regions differ with respect to natural production factors (Munn, 1989), because of differences in soil composition, vegetation, climate, geographical location, etc. The confrontation of natural threats may induce the search for and implementation of new technologies that will increase the resilience of the region. Lack of potentials may induce investments (for example, greenhouses in regions with a shortage of sun-hours and, hence, low temperatures).

4.4 Multiple use of environmental resources

4.4.1 *Multiple use of environmental resources and investments*

From an economic viewpoint, resources are to be allocated in their most productive direction. Often, this may imply regionally a single use of a specific resource. However, sustainable resource use (for example, with respect to risk management) gives some scope for the idea of diversifying uses as much as possible. In cases where one use would exclude the use of a resource in other directions, less profitable uses would be stimulated either by subsidies or by regulations. When more uses of one resource would not conflict, it would be reasonable from a welfare viewpoint to promote all these uses in such combinations that total welfare (including environmental amenities) is maximised.

Thus, for a specific region, from an SD perspective the investments (which make up part of regional resources) should not be directed to just one profitable use, and one use should certainly not preclude other uses in the future.

4.5 Sustainable use of renewable resources

4.5.1 *Production structure and sustainable use of renewable resources*

In many regions all over the world the sustainable use of renewable resources has become problematic. The increasing population and intensification of economic activities have resulted in great stress on the natural resource base, whereas cross-boundary environmental effects (for example, acid rain, ozonisation) have made control over the natural resource base much more difficult (Archibugi, 1989).

To find a balance between economic development and ecological sustainability, conventional economic policy—based on maximisation of income, production, profits, etc—would have to be oriented towards an ecologically sound policy, based on increasing efficiency [that is, increasing throughput, not output (Daly, 1973)], while maintaining an acceptable standard of living (Simonis, 1989).

Regional differences in efforts to change the production structure to the benefit of the environment may be caused by differences in physical circumstances (for example, regional assimilative capacities) and regional preferences (for example, with regard to environmental stress). Hot and dry climates may reduce the impact of certain effluents from production processes, or high rainfall levels may reduce the impact on air quality of some types of emissions (Walter, 1975).

Of all sectors, agriculture uses renewable resources most intensively. The idea that this sector benefits from sustainable use is certainly not reflected in its production structure. At least in the well developed countries this structure may be identified as highly diversified and specialised. External effects of one level influence the production results of other levels. Specialisation may exhaust specific organic growth potentials, while the environment becomes polluted with chemicals and pesticides. An integrated long-term viewpoint on renewable production has still to be developed. In a regional perspective a material balance in the production structure seems a reasonable condition to enhance sustainability. Consequently, the stratification of production—which has resulted in very high yields in past decades—should now be carefully reconsidered in view of the stratification of material uses. The interrelation between production sectors is also increasingly important in a regional context. A coherence between, for instance, waste treatment and agriculture seems (economically) almost impossible. In this respect a source-oriented policy may imply a change in production process and products, so that they become less polluting (Bresso, 1989). Technological innovations in pollution-control equipment, recycling processes, conservation, and recovery techniques may all contribute to the reduction of environmental pollution.

To ensure such changes in production, a strict planning system would be necessary, as one would not expect such changes to be implemented voluntarily. One way is to stimulate the implementation of pollution-control technology, but this policy has its shortcomings. Stimulating effective pollution-control technology for one environmental pollutant may lead to a neglect of pollution control of other environmental pollutants, thereby shifting the problem and not solving it (Voelzkow, 1986). A spatially orientated policy is a second option to change the production structure in order to find an optimal sustainable combination of different uses. Key issues in this policy are regulation of activities, land-use zoning, and assimilation of plans. Thus from an SD viewpoint we need a coherent spatial–economic, sectoral–economic, and source-oriented policy.

4.6 Risk and uncertainty

4.6.1 *Investment, risk, and uncertainty*

Since World War 2, technological innovations have led to an enormous increase in investment and economic growth. However, these innovations have also often coincided with the exploitation of natural resources, the decrease (or elimination) of ecological habitats, and environmental pollution. One reason for the one-sided economic approach toward technological innovations may be that the economic benefits of an investment up to a certain point often increase as a proportion of the scale of its application, while many of its social and environmental effects evolve in a highly nonlinear way. The result might be that "technological activities become strongly established with influential vested interest long before the disbenefits begin to manifest themselves" (Brooks, 1986, page 263).

Investments in new technology are surrounded by much environmental risk and uncertainty. For a specific region, this risk and uncertainty is related to the following (Siebert, 1987):

Accumulation, interaction, and spatial transportation of pollutants. An investment in one region may cause environmental effects in others through interregional diffusion of pollutants (externalities). Also, environmental effects may only appear after considerable time has passed. Thus, the investment decision will necessarily be based on incomplete information, in which no full account may be taken of externalities. This will result in a nonoptimal investment decision.

Damage caused by a given quantity of pollutants. Besides uncertainty about the environmental decay caused by an investment in a certain region, the damage caused by a given quantity of pollutants, both in time and magnitude, is also surrounded by uncertainty.

The irreversibility of the environmental use. A new investment may imply such a modification of the regional environment that the changes become irreversible. Then the possiblity of learning about future benefits by retaining the option to preserve or invest in the future is excluded.

The costs of abatement. It is not always easy to identify which investment has caused the environmental damage in a certain region. Therefore it is difficult to identify the responsible actor for the abatement, or the compensation for the damages incurred by society.

From the viewpoint of a regional environmental policy, risk and uncertainty relate to the impact of the new investment on regional environmental quality. The more uncertain the environmental impact, the higher the environmental quality targets may be set. Higher environmental quality can be interpreted as an insurance against environmental degradation or, in other words, as a risk premium. Investment in technological diversity implies a greater survival potential in an environment subject to surprises from causes that accumulate over long periods of time: "The existence of and the considerable depth of technological options is a potential source of systematic self-renewal and adjustment to new circumstances"

(Brooks, 1986, page 263). There is a striking similarity with genetic diversity: a variety of genetic processes maintains the values of parameters that define the ecosystem. If natural variability is constrained, it will lead to self-simplification and to fragility of the ecosystem (Holling, 1986).

Which risk level is acceptable for certain investments is often a matter of political choice, based on estimates about the tolerance of society. Although such a numerical approach to risk levels may encounter several societal, ethical, and scientific problems, it may be a useful means to help to prevent an unsustainable use of environmental resources. Risk levels should be incorporated in a broader system that also considers source-related elements. Such an integrated system may encompass the following criteria (Wams, 1989):

(1) *Justification*. The risk level of a development, an activity or a product should be weighted against that of all its alternatives. In the case of serious (potential) environmental dangers, the zero option also should be considered.

(2) *ALARA principle*. When the development, acitivity, or product is justified, one should try to prevent risks as far as is technologically feasible. The ALARA principle, which stands for 'as low as reasonably achievable', implies the prevention of avoidable environmental degradation and the application of the most suitable means available.

(3) *Environmental standards*. When criteria (1) and (2) are met, environmental standards can be enforced in order to resist the pressure for socioeconomic aims at the cost of the environment. In other words, environmental standards should be used as a kind of control function.

5 Institutional assignment

5.1 Introduction

In section 2 RSD was defined as a regional development of economic and environmental conditions to accomplish a globally sustainable development, while at the same time ensuring that the regional population can attain an acceptable level of welfare, both at present and in the future and that this regional development is compatible with ecological circumstances in the long run. It was also argued that in the framework of RSD an integrated economic and environmental approach to policymaking is a necessity. However, its implementation will face a variety of difficulties. One of these is related to the institutional structure of regional planning (Zimmerman, 1982). In this context, the institutional structure refers to the whole system of rules and regulations by which competencies, tasks, and responsibilities are divided among actors.

When production factors are relatively immobile or no free trade is allowed between regions, a regionally differentiated RSD is always considered desirable (Ewringmann and Hansmeyer, 1980; Frey, 1980). Clearly, these issues are time-related (as in the very long run everything is mobile).

With a limited mobility and free trade, however, there is still sufficient environmental evidence to warrant policy. But does this also give satisfactory scope for regional authority? An integrated regional policy can be centrally planned or delegated to lower levels (regional, local) or can be organised from the viewpoint of functionalisation. This assignment problem of competencies and operational tasks is a matter of concern in this section. Our aim is not to give a clear-cut answer (if ever possible) to this question, but to make a first step in designing a framework for integrated regional policy organisation orientated towards the achievement of sustainable development.

5.2 Facet planning

Present planning structures have evolved over a long period. Problems show up in due course. In general, new governmental tasks and responsibilities may evolve as a result of a perceived imperfect working of the market economy (external economies, economies of scale, equity considerations, imperfect supply of social utilities). Consequently, rooted in specific historical backgrounds, separate planning cultures have evolved (housing programmes resulted from bad hygienic circumstances at the end of the last century, and employment planning in the period before World War 2). Physical planning became popular in the 1920s as a result of imbalanced development between industrialisation, housing, and transport. Environmental and social planning are the most recent developments.

A historical characteristic of many of these planning efforts is that in early phases of planning the emphasis was mainly on prohibitions and regulations, whereas in later phases more emphasis has been on development. This is certainly true for environmental planning. It started with measures coping with the negative environmental externalities of production and consumption processes (for example, end-of-pipe technologies). Nowadays there is a tendency towards more source-orientated policies. An inevitable development in the near future will be an integrated development policy in which environmental policy will be an integrated development policy in which environmental policy will be a key factor for welfare development (for example, integrated spatially oriented policy).

It will be clear that such a development is impossible without a simultaneous design of coordination channels between the several functional areas. The main coordination problems may be the result of the historical roots of separate planning fields. Consequently, significant differences in planning culture can be identified: in more recent planning fields the firefighting approach of problem-solving is practised, whereas established fields may be characterised as development orientated. The coordination problems may also be the result of the different educational backgrounds of specialists, separate planning languages, separate planning horizons, use of different databases, lack of integrated formal and evaluation models, and use of different performance indicators.

5.3 Hierarchical design

Hierarchical structuring is a second issue in the context of coordinated and integrated planning. It can be regarded as a hierarchy of responsibilities and tasks delegated to various levels or as a hierarchical division of goals. The first viewpoint is related to a problem-orientated policy; a specific issue is emphasised from several functional viewpoints (economic, social, spatial, environmental) and these viewpoints determine the level of assigned responsibilities and tasks.

An advocate of a more economic approach is Zimmermann (1982), who formulated some guidelines about the level at which an environmental policy should be carrried out.

(a) *Regional preferences* about certain environmental and socioeconomic goods and services (especially their equity aspects). When interregional preferences are rather homogeneous, a national policy may be most appropriate; for example, minimum health standards. However, the more the impacts of certain acitivites on specific environmental goods differ among regions, the more heterogeneous interregional preferences may be (for example, noise nuisance), and a more decentralised policy may be recommended.

(b) *Economies of scale* in the supply and provision of environmental goods (especially their efficiency aspects). The marginal cost of supplying the region with specific environmental goods or services may decrease with growing quantity (for example, waste treatment). Therefore, efficiency—in the sense of economies of scale—might serve as a criterion for the implementation of regional environmental policy, in cases of changes in the marginal cost of supply.

(c) *Spillover effects* (equity and efficiency aspects are both relevant here). If the costs and benefits of an environmental good or service are internalised within a region, its provision may become more efficient and equitable, because in this case those who benefit from the provision of the environmental good or service will also pay for it. This criterion for the assignment of a regional environmental policy can only be used in a limited way, because striving for an internalisation of all costs and benefits of environmental goods and services would make the region equal in size to the whole system. Therefore the cost of not internalising all environmental effects should be balanced with the positive welfare effect of regionalised planning organisation.

Thus economics provides some meaningful guidelines for a demarcation of planning responsibilities. But ecological considerations should also be taken into account.

Administrative and legal boundaries seldom coincide with those of the environmental problem region. As a result solutions to environmental problems are often carried out on the basis of assigned responsibilities, without special emphasis on the spatial dimensions of the environmental problem. In order to carry out a proper policy—orientated towards sustainability—the assignment should also take into account the spatial ecological characteristics of the problem (Klijn, 1988).

Figure 1 is an illustration of some environmental problems and the spatial range of their impact. For example, climatic change is a process that takes place in the atmosphere and works through the whole ecosystem. Therefore, an efficient policy to influence this process necessitates a global planning approach. Thus, a plausible conclusion is that from an ecological point of view, the institutional assignment should be derived from the spatial impact of the environmental problem (see also Clark and Munn, 1986).

Both considerations for institutional assignment offer clues to the design of an appropriate framework for an institutional structure of balanced planning for RSD. However, when these two approaches are combined the problem arises that the economic efficiency and equity aspects do not often

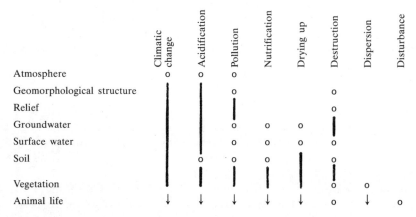

o is an intervention point and ↓ is the impact of environmental problems on the ecosystem.

Figure 1. Environmental problems and the spatial range of their impact (source: Klijn, 1988).

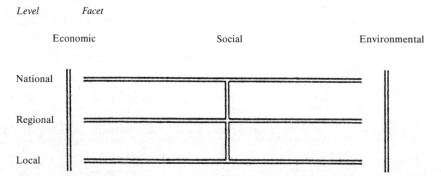

Figure 2. Facet planning and institutional level.

coincide with the intervention points of the ecological problem. Moreover, an optimal response assignment may vary wildly for all the above reasons.

In figure 2 the approaches are visualised by means of vertical lines. The approach starts from one discipline; side conditions are derived from this, for the treatment of the next discipline, and so on. This is how actual planning is often carried out. For RSD such an approach does not suffice; a more integrated approach is necessary.

5.4 Integrated RSD policy: a goal-oriented approach

There are many economic and ecological exchange relations between regions (Ewringmann and Hansmeyer, 1980). These relations may exist because (Siebert, 1987): emissions in one region may affect other regions by way of interregional diffusion; regional differences in environmental policy induce migration of production factors, people, and goods; or environmental policy in one region may be pursued which take into account the environmental quality of other regions, thereby raising the question of the compensation problem of functional specialisation and differentiation between regions.

A proper environmental policy should take account of these inter-dependencies between regions. According to Odum (1971) the main goal of environmental policymakers should be to minimise the impact of human activities on the environment from the perspective of the eco-system. In our opinion such an ecocentric viewpoint has no direct policy meaning, because it implicitly abandons the trade-offs between socioeconomic development and a sustainable environment. The National Physical Planning Agency in the Netherlands defines environmental policy as:

"The stimulation of certain spatial and ecological conditions in such a way that:

—the real aspirations of individuals and groups in society can be realized to full advantage

—the diversity, coherence and sustainability of the physical environment can be guaranteed as much as possible"

Clearly, because environmental and socioeconomic variables influence each other in an interrelated system, an integrated policy is needed to balance these variables. Moreover, integration may be desirable from the perspective of compensation. From this viewpoint, the level of regional welfare is determined by the total sum of separate welfare components. Equalisation of regional welfare may thus be achieved, without the necessity for a strict interregional equality of the separate welfare components.

An integrated policy does not mean that it should automatically be implemented on one centralised level. This would result in a top level carrying too heavy a burden and being charged with issues that could be more efficiently dealt with at a lower level. When decentralising national policy, however, other difficulties may also arise: regional or local agencies may try to maximise the welfare of their own regions, thereby neglecting the interregional effects of some of their activities or measures (spillover problems) (Siebert, 1985); and environmental media may differ in their spatial extent. This implies that the planning regions will overlap, which will create coordination problems (Ewringmann and Hansmeyer, 1980).

Decentralisation of environmental policy may be justified because regional authorities are best suited to identify regional preferences and to implement regional targets, and they will be better informed than national authorities about the implementation of environmental policy instruments (Siebert, 1985).

In this context it might be useful to distinguish between institutional policy and executive policy aspects. Institutional policy aspects related to the distribution of responsibilities over various policy levels (constitutional power). Executive policy aspects relate to decisions taken during the policy period to ensure that the policy goals are achieved (executive power).

An integrated policy means:

(1) *An integrated institutional policy* or vertical coordination between policy levels. Here the following guideline seems relevant: lower level authorities should be well informed about decisions to be taken by higher level authorities, since higher level authorities should be informed about the decisions to be taken by lower level authorities (the latter are micro-constraints to the former).

(2) *Integrated executive policy* or horizontal coordination between authorities at the same level of different policy departments and of the same policy department, but of different regions. This will be expecially important in the case of externalities.

In the second case horizontal coordination between economic authorities and environmental policy may also lead to more efficiency. Economic authorities could provide the environmental authorities with essential information. However, economic policy often has a short-term planning horizon. Economists are concerned with the income and employment effects of an investment but environmentalists may be concerned with the long-term effects of such a new investment, for its effect may become manifest over long periods of time or the investment might imply an irreversibility, in the sense that it precludes other developments in the future.

6 Attributes of sustainability: a guideline for institutional assignment

A goal-oriented approach—as discussed in the previous section—is another way of arriving at an integrated planning system. This approach is in line with the sustainability framework developed in the first sections of this paper. To make this welfare-theoretic approach operational, in the following subsections the attributes of welfare as discussed in section 4 will serve as guidelines for the hierarchical policy assignment.

6.1 Intergenerational trade-offs and institutional assignment

As we have seen in section 4.2 the relation between population structure and intergenerational trade-offs cannot be neglected when discussing institutional assignment in the context of sustainable development.

When considering this relation we have to deal mainly with equity aspects. Because regions differ in terms of environmental resource base, production structure, and regional preferences, the future effects of current institutional decisions will not be homogeneous among regions. Policies affecting population structures (for example, densities of population) with the aim of RSD may be hard to implement. Because of the open character of this kind of socioeconomic and environmental instrument, such policies should necessarily be carried out on an interregional or national level. Moreover, interregional and intertemporal equity issues necessitate an environmental policy at a more comprehensive level, as regional agencies may only be concerned with the welfare of the people in their own region.

As far as income is concerned, environmental policies are mainly directed to equity issues. It is hard to assess the general relationship between the institutional assignment of environmental policy and income effects. The abatement of pollution may lead to increasing production costs or consumption prices, which will have a negative effect on real income and future income. Pollution-control techniques may also lead to a more efficient use of environmental resources and production costs may decrease, instead of increase, while at the same time environmental resources will be saved. The kind of environmental pollution and the range of its impact may be decisive for the institutional assignment.

6.2 Interregional trade-offs and institutional assignment

When considering interregional trade-offs and population with regard to institutional assignment, both equity and efficiency aspects have to be considered. As far as equity is concerned, the institutional level should comply with the spatial range of environmental effects and measures on population. So, if there are any spillover effects, a policy that exceeds the regional level will be necessary. From an efficiency point of view, a national policy may be appropriate when this implies economies of scale. This will mainly depend on the way measures affecting population levels can be handled and on their foreseeable impacts. In general, the planning and legislative tasks should whenever possible be in the hands of a central government within the boundaries of this planning framework. Thus, it will be clear that it is not possible in general to identify the most suitable institutional assignment.

In order to let changes in either production processes or products have a significant effect, these changes have to materialise on a national (or even international) level. If a polluting production process is forbidden in one region only, while the demand for its output remains, profit-seeking entrepreneurs will simply relocate their production to other regions. The same applies to products. If the sale of a polluting product is prohibited in a certain region, people may import it from other regions. Therefore, a national policy will be necessary, both in the conext of interregional trade-off and use of renewable resources.

Regional specialisation may lead to more efficient production. Consequently, this may result in a more economic use of resources and therefore—in the context of sustainability—have a positive impact on the environment. However, specialisation of production may also imply concentration of pollution and environmental degradation in certain regions, to such an extent that the limits to ensure an RSD will be exceeded. Therefore, a national policy may be required to take decisions about such interregional trade-offs.

It will be clear from the openness of the spatial system and the benefits of physical or economic specialisation that the institutional assignment of environmental policy will necessarily be on an supraregional level (multiregional or international). At this level thoughtful decisions may be taken that encompass the whole regional system.

According to an empirical study by Zimmerman and Ullman (1981), it seems that intraregional changes have been more important than interregional changes in production structure. Other studies, although not directed to the spatial dimension of changes in the production structure, also point in this direction. In the Netherlands 66% of the equipment industries are located in the western part of the country. Environmental policy may come into play in the sense that subsidies given to control environmental damage may stimulate industries to develop and implement less detrimental production processes (Potier, 1986). This evidence may weaken the need for the regional institutional structure of environmental planning.

Closure or no new investments in polluting industries would decrease income and employment. Because these effects are mainly regional, a policy focusing exclusively on a regional level has the danger that a self-interested policymaker is only concerned with his or her own region. Therefore it is not likely that such stringent measure will easily be implemented, especially when other regions do not follow them. Thus, a supraregional assignment of regional environmental policy would be a proper strategy. This will certainly be true for the legislative tasks of authorities, but possibly also for the executive tasks of local or regional officials.

6.3 Multiple use of environmental resources and institutional assignment

Environmental resources can often be used for different purposes (water can be used for drinking or waste disposal). Multiple use of resources also exists (water for fishing and transportation). Quite often different uses are in conflict.

It is clear from table 1 that not all different land uses are compatible. The task of the regional planner is to find an optimal sustainable combination of different uses. There are several management approaches, key elements of which are (Cloke and Park, 1985; Leeflang, 1989):

(1) *Regulation of activities*. The degree of compatibility of land use determines the scope for manoeuvre in allocating land to compatible uses in the planning process. When different land uses are incompatible, they can be regulated by a system of permits.

(2) *Land-use zoning* (physical separation of land uses within a given tract) is an option when different land uses are incompatible. In particular, it is used to allocate available land-use resources as equitably as possible and among competing resource users and for different purposes. Land-use zoning policies tend to be more effective when applied to the planning of new developments, particularly for public land.

(3) *Assimilation of plans*. The spatial impacts of environmental problems of different land uses are often regional. Therefore, policymakers should incorporate physical planning in their environmental policy, which would contribute to priority setting in the case of multiple use of land.

Table 1. Compatibility and multiple land use.

Primary land use	Compatibility with secondary land use[a]								
	U	R	A	F	G	T	WR	W	M
Urban (U)		0	0	0	0	1	0	1	1
Recreation (R)	0		1	2 – 4	0 – 1	1	2	5	1
Agriculture (A)	0	1		0	0	0	1	2 – 4	2
Forestry (F)	0	6	0		0.5	0	0	6	2 – 4
Grazing (G)	0	6	0	1		0	2 – 6	6	2 – 6
Transport (T)	0	0	0	0	0		0	0	0
Water resources (WR)	0	2 – 6	1	1	2 – 4	0		2 – 6	1
Wildlife (W)	0	6	1	4	4	0	2		1
Mineral production (M)	0	2	2	3	3 – 4	3	2	2 – 3	

[a] 0 none, 1 very poor, 2 poor, 3 fair, 4 moderate, 5 fairly high, 6 high.

6.4 Sustainable use of environmental resources and institutional assignment

The answer to the question about the most appropriate institutional level of environmental policy in respect of the use of renewable resources and production structure, may point to a more centralised level. This is because there may be a danger that the closer the relation between the decisionmaker and the polluter, the more sensitive the decisionmaker may be to social and economic arguments (for example, employment) and the less inclined he or she will be to take measures which benefit the environment (de Rijk, 1989).

6.5 Risk and institutional assignment

The institutional setting in which such an integrated risk approach—as discussed in section 4.6.1—should be carried out depends on the related elements at hand. The ALARA principle should be pursued by the central authority and implemented by the organisation responsible for the activity or development. Environmental standards suggest central legislation, although they may be specified regionally. Implementation and control may be regionally or locally specified. The justification for policy will depend on the activity or development under consideration. For developments with extraregional consequences, the level of authority should be supraregional.

6.6 Concluding remarks

By way of illustration of a welfare approach to RSD we have discussed the question of institutional assignment. From this discussion we may conclude that the hierarchical assignment of responsibilities often points to a central authority. When intertemporal and interregional aspects have to be considered, lower level authority may bring about suboptimal results. The same arguments hold when we consider risk and and the use of renewable resources. However, as soon as the executive character of a policy gains importance—as we discussed with respect to multiple use—lower levels of authority come to the fore as a reasonable option. We have only briefly mentioned some aspects of executive responsibilities. In the context of RSD, horizontal and vertical assignment, and the coordination and integration of executive responsibilities still need further consideration.

References

Archibugi F, 1989, "Comprehensive social assessment: an essential instrument for environmental policy-making", in *Economy and Ecology: Towards Sustainable Development* Eds F Archibugi, P Nijkamp (Kluwer, Dordrecht) pp 169–188

Archibugi F, Nijkamp P (Eds), 1989 *Economy and Ecology: Towards Sustainable Development* (Kluwer, Dordrecht)

Boserup E, 1981 *Population and Technological Change* (Basil Blackwell, Oxford)

Bresso M, 1989, "Environmental policy in relation to territorial distribution and productive activities", in *Economy and Ecology: Towards Sustainable Development* Eds F Archibugi, P Nijkamp (Kluwer, Dordrecht) pp 261–278

Brooks H, 1986, "The typology of surprises in technology, institutions and development", in *Sustainable Development of the Biosphere* Eds W C Clark, R E Munn (Cambridge University Press, Cambridge) pp 123–136

CBS, 1987 *Statistisch Jaarboek* (Central Bureau voor de Statistiek, Amsterdam)

Clark W, Munn R E (Eds), 1986 *Sustainable Development of the Biosphere* (Cambridge University Press, Cambridge)

Cloke P J, Park C C, 1985, "Integrated management strategies", in *Rural Resource Management* (Croom Helm, Andover, Hants) pp 408–448

Daly H E, 1973 *Towards a Steady-state Economy* (W H Freeman, San Francisico, CA)

Daly H E, 1986, "Equity and efficiency—problems of implicit redistribution", in *Distributional Conflicts in Environmental-resource Policy* Eds A Schnaiberg, N Watts, K Zimmerman (Blackmore Press, Shaftesbury) pp 85–94

Daly H E, 1989, "Environmental–economic policy and sustainable regional development", in *Economy and Ecology: Towards Sustainable Development* Eds F Archibugi, P Nijkamp, (Kluwer, Dordrecht) pp 73 – 88

de Rijk M, 1989, "Een onverdiende reputatie" *Intermediar* **24** 4 August, page 31

Ehrlich P R, Holdren J R, 1971, "The impact of population growth" *Science* **171** 1212 – 1217

Ewringmann D, Hansmeyer K, 1980, "The institutional setting of regional environmental policy", in *Regional Environmental Policy* Eds H Siebert, I Walter, K Zimmerman (Macmillan, London) pp 152 – 166

Fisher A C, Hanemann W M, 1985, "Endangered species; the economics of irreversible damage", in *Economics of Ecosystem Management* Eds D O Hall, N Myers, N S Margaris (Kluwer, Dordrecht) pp 129 – 138

Frey R L, 1980, "Interregional welfare comparisons and environmental policy", in *Regional Environmental Policy* Eds H Siebert, I Walter, K Zimmerman (Macmillan, London) pp 97 – 108

Hardin G, 1972 *Exploring New Ethics for Survival: The Voyage of the Spaceship* (Beagle, New York)

Hilhorst M T, 1987 *Verantwoordelijkheid voor Toekomstige Generaties? Een Sociaal-economische Bezinning op Bevolkinsaantal, Kernenergie, Grondstoffen en Genetica* (Kok Agora, Kampen)

Holling C S, 1986, "The resilience of terrestrial ecosystems: local surprise and global change", in *Sustainable Development of the Biosphere* Eds W Clark, R E Munn (Cambridge University Press, Cambridge) pp 292 – 317

James D E, Nijkamp P, Opshoor J B, 1989, "Ecological sustainability and economic development", in *Economy and Ecology: Towards Sustainable Development* Eds F Archibugi, P Nijkamp (Kluwer, Dordrecht) pp 27 – 48

Jänicke M, Mönch M, Rannenberg T, Simonis U E, 1988, *Structural Change and Environmental Impact: Empirical Evidence on Thirty-one Countries in East and West* (WZB, Berlin)

Kairiukstis L, 1989, "Ecological sustainability of regional development: background to the problem", in *Ecological Sustainability of Regional Development* (International Institute for Applied Systems Analysis, Laxenburg, Austria) pp 1 – 5

Kirsch G, 1986, "Solidarity between generations: intergenerational distributional problems in environmental and resource policy", in *Distributional Conflicts in Environmental-resource Policy* Eds A Schnaiberg, N Watts, K Zimmermann (Blackmore Press, Shaftesbury) pp 381 – 404

Klijn F, 1988, "Milieubeheergebieden: CML-mededelingen 37", Centrum voor Milieukunde, Rijksuniversiteit, Leiden

Krutilla J V, Fisher A C, 1975 *The Economics of Natural Environment* (Johns Hopkins University Press, Baltimore, MD)

Kula E, 1988 *The Economics of Forestry: Modern Theory and Practice* (Croom Helm, Andover, Hants)

Leeflang H, 1989, "Physical planning and environmental protection in the long term", in *Economy and Ecology: Towards Sustainable Development* Eds F Archibugi, P Nijkamp (Kluwer, Dordrecht) pp 279 – 294

Manning E W, 1988, "The analysis of land-use determinants in support of sustainable development", collaborative paper, International Institute of Applied System Analysis, Laxenburg, Austria

Meissner W, 1986, "Employment, income and welfare implications of environmental policy", in *Distributional Conflicts in Environmental-resource Policy* Eds A Schnaiberg, N Watts, K Zimmermann (Blackmore Press, Shaftesbury) pp 38 – 48

Munn R E, 1989, "Towards sustainable development: an environmental perspective", in *Economy and Ecology: Towards Sustainable Development* Eds F Archibugi, P Nijkamp (Kluwer, Dordrecht) pp 49–72

Nijkamp P, Rouwendal J, 1988, "Intergenerational discount rates in long-term planning plan evaluation" *Public Finance* **43** 271–288

Nijkamp P, Soeteman F, 1989, "Economic development and ecological sustainability: coevolution with special reference to agricultural land use", research paper, Department of Economics, Free University, Amsterdam

Odum E P, 1971 *Fundamentals of Ecology* (W B Saunders, Philadelphia, PA)

Opschoor J B, 1987, "Duurzaamheid en verandering, over ecologische inpasbaarheid van economische ontwikkeling", inaugural address, Department of Economics, Free University, Amsterdam

Opschoor J B, 1989 *Na Ons Geen Zondvloed: Voorwaarden voor een Duurzaam Milieugebruik* (Kok Agora, Kampen)

Pezzy J, 1989, "Economic analysis of sustainable growth and sustainable development", WP 15, Environment Department, The World Bank, Washington, DC

Potier M, 1986, "Capital and labour reallocation in the face of environmental policy", in *Distributional Conflicts in Environmental-resource Policy* Eds A Schnaiberg, N Watts, K Zimmermann (Blackmore Press, Shaftesbury) pp 253–271

Siebert H, 1985, "Spatial aspects of environmental economics", in *Handbook of Natural Resource and Energy* Eds A V Kneese, J L Sweenley (Stanford University, Cambridge, HA) pp 125–164

Siebert H, 1987 *Economics of the Environment: Theory and Policy* (Springer, Berlin)

Simon H A, 1967 *Models of Man: Mathematical Essays on Rational Human Behaviour in a Social Setting* (John Wiley, New York)

Simonis U E, 1989, "Ecological modernization of industrial society—three strategic elements", in *Economy and Ecology: Towards Sustainable Development* Eds F Archibugi, P Nijkamp (Kluwer, Dordrecht) pp 211–228

UNEP, 1987 *The State of the World Environment 1987* (United Nations Environmental Programme, Nairobi)

van den Bergh J, Soeteman F, Gilbert A, 1989, "SPIDER", working paper, Department of Economics, Free University, Amsterdam

Voelzkow H, 1986, "The organization of interests in the pollution control industry", in *Distributional Conflicts in Environmental-resource Policy* Eds A Schnaiberg, N Watts, K Zimmermann (Blackmore Press, Shaftesbury) pp 272–286

Walter I, 1975 *International Economics of Pollution* (Macmillan, New York)

Wams T, 1989, "Risciobenadering VROM verbrokkeld en aanvaardbaar" *Nieuwe Beta* **3** (September) 10

WCED, 1987 *Our Common Future* (Bruntland Report) World Commission on Environment and Development (Oxford University Press, Oxford)

Wilkinson R G, 1974 *Armoede en Vooruitgang* (Prisma, Utrecht)

World Bank, 1987, "Environment growth and development", Committee Pamphlet 14, World Bank, Washington, DC

Zimmermann K, 1982, "Institutional aspects of integrated planning process", in *Integrated Physical, Socio-economic and Environmental Planning* Eds Y J Ahmed, F G Muller (Tycooly International, Dublin) pp 35–62

Zimmermann A, Ullmann, 1981, "Umweltpolitik and Umweltschutzindustrie in der Bundersrepublik Deutschland" *Berichte 6* (Erich Smidt, Berlin)

Communications Technologies and the Future of the City

A Gillespie
CURDS, University of Newcastle

> "Our understanding of the impact of information
> technology on cities is still woefully inadequate"
>
> Batty, 1990

1 Introduction

In the debate over sustainable urban futures, an important area for examination concerns the potential impact of new information and communications technologies. Like all significant communications improvements, the advances in telecommunications which are now occurring in the wake of the 'digital revolution'—such as greatly increased bandwidth, making possible the high-speed transmission of data and images—are leading to considerable time–space convergence. By collapsing the relative distance between locations, albeit unequally and differentially, communications technologies are necessarily implicated in the establishment of new spatial interrelationships and new forms of spatial organisation.

Telecommunications, and its convergence with computing to form a hybrid field of 'telematics', is of particular importance in this respect, because of structural changes in the nature of advanced capitalism. As Hepworth (1987; 1989) has demonstrated, multilocational computer networks are becoming more and more centrally embedded in the internal management and operation of organisations, and in the transactional structures which connect them to other organisations.

Whether these developments reflect the growth of an 'informational mode of development' (Castells, 1989), or rather the transition from a 'Fordist' to a 'post-Fordist' form of economic organisation [see Gillespie (1991) and Robins and Gillespie (1992) for discussions of the role of advanced communications in this hypothesised transition], there can be little doubting the contemporary significance of telecommunications within new forms of spatial organisation. Questions concerning the future of the city, and the form of internal spatial organisation it will embody, cannot therefore afford to ignore the implications of the rapid growth in telecommunications use.

Current developments in communications technologies can be expected to affect the sustainability of the city in a number of different though interrelated ways. First there is the question of the very sustainability of the city itself as a spatial entity. As Berry (1973) argued nearly twenty years ago:

> "It was the demand for ease of communication that first brought men into
> cities. The time-eliminating properties of long-distance communication

and the time-spanning capacities of the new communications technologies are combining *to concoct a solvent that has dissolved the core-
oriented city* in both time and space, creating what some refer to as an
'urban civilisation without cities' " (page 54, emphasis added).

Even if the city does not dissolve entirely into the ether, Berry's
contention raises a number of related questions concerning the spatial
form of the future metropolitan region; if the impact of advanced communications is to loosen substantially the metropolitan fabric, what will the
implications be in terms of environmental sustainability, particularly in
energy consumption terms? Clearly, if communications improvements
simply facilitate a spreading of the city beyond its existing functional
boundaries, then the energy-consumption effects are likely to be deleterious.

However, the possiblity of substituting telecommunications for physical
movement, in certain circumstances at least, could lead to countering
effects. To what extent, therefore, might the *energy-consuming* effects
which are associated with a more spatially dispersed metropolitan form be
mitigated or even reversed by the *energy-conserving* substitution of physical
movements (of people, of goods and services, and of information) by their
telecommunications-mediated equivalents (such as telecommuting, teleshopping, electronic data interchange, video-conferencing, and so on)?

The main concern of this paper will be to examine critically the
proposition advanced by Berry that communications improvements will
dissolve the core-oriented city, leading to "an urban civilisation without
cities". On the basis of an interpretation of historical and contemporary
evidence, a very different conclusion is reached, namely that advances in
telecommunications are revalorising the city, and enabling it to reap
considerable benefits from nodality within increasingly global networks.
At the same time, it will be argued that the spatial extent of such 'revalo-
rised' metropolitan regions is likely to continue growing under the impact
of communications improvements, but that the hypothesised substitution
effects are likely to be less than anticipated.

2 The limits to technological forecasting
In an attempt to grapple with the complex questions raised by developments in communications technologies for the future of the city, for its
spatial form and for its sustainability, a crucial starting point is to accept
that the technologies themselves cannot provide the answers. As Gold
(1985) has argued, "A more sophisticated view is necessary of the relationship between technology and urban society ... a large proportion of
future city schemes have been essentially exercises in technological
forecasting. Their authors were deeply impressed with the potential of
technology and adopted a facile, implicitly deterministic view of its powers
to transform ... without a more balanced view of the complexities involved,
forecasting becomes superficial and flatulent" (page 99).

Conceptualising the relationship between communications technology and future urban form has long proved problematic and intractable, for many of the same reasons that have bedevilled attempts to understand the nature of the relationships between technology and society more generally. In what Carey (1981) has termed "the rhetoric of the technological sublime", in which "it is the machines that possess teleological insight", the potential embodied in new technology is often deterministically assumed to be responsible for a forthcoming transformation in the way we live and in the geography of human organisation.

Within the familiar discourse of postindustrialism, for example, developments in communications technologies are seen to herald an era in which information, "the raw material of truth, beauty, creativity, innovation, productivity, competitiveness and freedom" (Maisonrouge, 1984, page 31), become equally and plentifully available to all, thereby dissolving forever the sources of social and spatial inequality (Gillespie and Robins, 1989). Nowhere is this rhetoric of the technological sublime more in evidence than in the discourse concerning the future of the city in the postindustrial era, particularly in the contention that convergent developments in information and communications technologies would undermine the very rationale for the existence of the city.

There have been many expressions of this vision, including Dizard's (1982) evocation of an 'electronic Eden', Martin's (1978) 'wired society', and Toffler's (1981) 'third wave' society, comprised of decentralised communities and equal interdependent subeconomies, with the fundamental social unit being the electronic cottage. In all such utopian visions, the decentralising impacts of communications technology are regarded as unproblematic and self-evident. In the remainder of the paper, the inadequacies of this assumption are exposed both through a historical treatment of the role of communications in urban development and through a consideration of contemporary developments in the provision of urban communications infrastructure.

3 Communications technology and the 'monopoly of knowledge' by the city

That there is an important relationship between communications technology and urban development is undeniable, as much historical evidence testifies. As Berry suggests above, it can indeed be argued that the city first developed as a device for maximising the ease of communication; or, as Schaeffer and Sclar (1975, page 8) put it, "to avoid transportation ... mankind invented the city".

The scale of the city too has historically been conditioned by what Mumford (1966) termed "the range of collective communications systems":

"Early cities did not grow beyond walking distance or hearing distance. In the Middle Ages to be within the sound of Bow Bells defined the limits of the City of London; and until other systems of mass communication were invented in the nineteenth century, these were among the effective limits to urban growth. For the city, as it develops, becomes the centre of a network of communications ... the permissive size of the city partly varies with the velocity and the effective range of communication" (page 80).

What then does the future hold for the city in an era of electronic communication, in which both the velocity of communications and its effective range have been so drastically increased? Is it not inevitable, as Berry and Toffler and others would have had us believe, that the city will cease to reap the benefits of communications nodality, that its centripetal and centralising power will simply dissolve; or is it more likely, as Gottman (1977) contends, that the increased velocity and expanded range of modern communications will serve rather to promote agglomeration and facilitate the development of 'megalopolitan formations'?

In attempting to resolve the contradictory positions adopted by these protagonists, particular attention needs to be paid to the economic, social, political, and cultural contexts in which technology is applied and used. As Robins and Webster (1988) remind us, technologies and their implications are integral to particular social formations, and necessarily embody the dominant social relations and values of those formations.

When the history of communications advances is looked at from this perspective, and related to developments in the pattern or form of urbanisation, we can begin to comprehend the role of the city not simply as a centre of communication but rather as a centre for the *control* of communication and access to information. The earliest forms of urban power, the citadel and the priesthood, owed their power precisely to the effective exercise of such control:

"If anything proves that the city was primarily a control centre, long before it became a centre of communication, the persistent restrictions exercised over the extension and communication of knowledge would support this interpretation" (Mumford, 1966, page 120)

As recognised first by Innis (1951), the significance of advances in the technologies of communication has been both to extend geographically existing 'monopolies of information' and, on occasions, to pose challenges to these monopolies [see Gillespie and Robins (1989) for a discussion of Innis's contribution to the geography of communication].

The changing historical fortunes of individual cities have frequently been closely associated with how effectively they have managed to control channels of communication. A particularly well-documented example of this is provided by Pred's (1973) study of the historical growth of New York's hegemony within the US urban system (for a summary of this work see Salter, 1981). New York and more particularly the merchants, firms and elites based within it, came by 1840 to control an increasingly centralised system of information which extended north into Canada and south as far as New Orleans; interconnections between southern cities, for example, were poor, and they dealt with one another and with the North only by channelling communication through New York.

The coming of the telegraph in the middle of the 19th century did not seriously challenge the effective hegemony of New York over channels of communication; rather it was used to extend such control, with New York the hub of the national telegraph network and the gateway into international networks. As DuBoff (1983) has described, not only did the telegraph first link New York with other major cities, but potential users at intermediate points on the telegraph network were often denied access through circuit congestion, with priority given to traffic between and within the major cities.

As this example demonstrates, the assumption that communications advances, with their space-transcending capabilities, will necessarily lead to a weakening of the 'monopoly of information' of the city is to ignore some rather important lessons from the history of communications geography. These demonstrate that communications technologies have the parallel capability to 'bind space together' more effectively, and, in so doing, to facilitate further expansion of the monopolies of information enjoyed by certain nodal points in communications networks. With such lessons in mind, let us return to contemporary developments and to the myth of the dissolving city.

4 Communications nodality and the remaking of the centrality of the city
From their rather different starting points, both Castells (1989), in his explorations of 'the informational city', and Gottman (1983), in his analysis of 'the transactional city', are well aware of the complex nature of the relationship between communications technologies, economic change, and urban spatial outcomes. Castells, for example, contends that "the newly emerging forms of the informational mode of development, including its spatial form, will not be determined by the structural requirements of new technologies seeking to fulfil their developmental potential, but will emerge from the interaction between its technological components and the historically determined process of the restructuring of capitalism" (page 21).

Both authors conclude, however, on the basis of the evidence that they marshal, that modern communications technologies are serving to enhance rather than undermine the functional authority of the major city. Castells (1989), drawing on the empirical work of Moss (1986; 1988), contends that "telecommunications is reinforcing the commanding role of major business concentrations around the world" (page 1), whereas Gottman (1983) argues that "Urban settlements will not dissolve under the impact of this technology, although they may evolve and, indeed, are evolving. For transactional activities, the new technology is rather helping concentration in urban places; first, in large urban centres, already well established transactional cross-roads; and second, in a greater number of smaller centers of regional scale or highly specialised character" (page 28).

Why is this so? Quite simply because there is mutually reinforcing interaction between the existence of information-intensive and communications-intensive activities and investment in the advanced infrastructure needed to support advanced telecommunications services. As Hall has recently argued, echoing the findings of Gottman, Moss, and Castells, "technical advance will be most rapid in the existing centres of informational exchange, above all the world cities, where demand produces a response in the form of rapid innovation and high-level service competition" (1991, page 19).

One of the more commonly advanced myths is that the 'new electronic grids' are ubiquitously available. Although they are certainly capable of going anywhere, and although they undoubtedly span the globe, they remain inherently nodal. Indeed, the combination of increasingly specialised networks and more market-driven systems of regulation are serving to exacerbate rather than diminish this nodality.

We are, in effect, moving into an era of 'nonuniversal service' (Gillespie and Robins, 1991), in which cities are very well placed to capture a disproportionate share of the benefits associated with the use of advanced communications networks (Goddard, 1990). For rural areas, there are very real fears that they will become 'bypassed' by advanced networks, unable to demonstrate sufficient levels of spatially concentrated demand to justify the investment needed to provided specialised services (Gillespie et al, 1991; Hudson and Parker, 1990; Price Waterhouse, 1990).

The 'electronic highway' analogy has previously been criticised on the grounds of its failing to recognise the essentially private and proprietary nature of many of the advanced telecommunications networks (Gillespie and Hepworth, 1988). Even for those networks that provide switched services, and which can be regarded as publicly available, 'electronic railways' would be a more appropriate analogy than electronic highways, for it draws attention not only to network infrastructure but also to the need for place-specific access to the network through stations or other terminal facilities. For many rural areas, the new electronic communications networks can 'pass through' en route to somewhere else, without providing access points, as the Mercury Communication network in Britain well illustrates (Economic and Transport Planning Group, 1989; Gillespie and Williams, 1990).

Far from acting, then, as Berry (1973) foresaw, as a "solvent which would dissolve the core-oriented city", advanced communications technologies are rather acting as a very powerful magnet, an 'electronic superglue' which is enhancing and extending the influence of the city within nodal communications networks. As Gottman (1983) has astutely observed, "the centrality of the city is constantly being re-born" (page 15). A particularly good example of the process of rebirth through the spatial selectivity of access to advanced communications facilities is provided by the development of teleports.

5 Teleports as metropolitan communications hubs

The world's first 'teleport' was opened in New York in 1985. The concept was pioneered by the Port Authority of New York and New Jersey, and contained three elements: (1) a large parcel of land to accommodate satellite dishes operated by different communication companies; (2) an office park for telecommunications-intensive businesses: (3) a fibre-optic loop around New York to provide direct access to the satellite facility. A private firm, Teleport Communications Inc., was established as a joint venture between the Port Authority and Merrill Lynch to develop and operate the telecommunications facilities and fibre-optic network (Merrill Lynch are now sole owners). There are currently twenty satellite earth stations at the facility, which is on Staten Island, more than one million square feet of office space in the associated office park, and 250 customers connected to the 174 mile fibre loop (Moss, 1991).

The undoubted success of the New York Teleport has spawned a wave of imitators, initially in North America but increasingly in Japan and Europe. Many North American teleports are little more than 'facilities bypassers', finding market niches in a fully liberalised telecommunications environment characterised by chronic congestion in metropolitan local loops. In Japan and Europe, however, the application of the teleport concept has accentuated its potential with respect to urban redevelopment, enhancing the competitive advantage of those cities with such high-grade— and highly marketable and image-laden—communications facilities.

In Japan, the teleport approach is being pursued with remarkable vigour, with major schemes having being completed or initiated in Osaka, Tokyo, Yokohoma, Nagoya, Kobe, Sendai, and Fukuoka. In each of these cases, the teleport is seen not only as a local real estate or urban development project, but also as a very conscious attempt to strengthen the role of the city within Japanese and Pacific Region communication networks. As the brochure announcing the opening of the Osaka Teleport in 1989 put it, "the Kansai District extends its global presence".

Within Europe, teleports have been developed or projects initiated in nearly twenty locations (figure 1). The European teleport projects are characterised by marked diversity in the sectoral focus of the end-users at which they are targeted. Some, of which Rotterdam is the best and most fully developed example, are targeted specifically at port-related logistical functions; others (such as Amsterdam and Edinburgh) are oriented towards financial services; others (notably Cologne) are aimed primarily at the media and audiovisual sectors; and the Île de France teleport is intended to have four interlinked nodes (at La Défense, Roissy, Marne-la-Vallée, and Saclay) targeted at financial services, air transport, media industries, and research and innovation, respectively.

Notwithstanding this sectoral diversity, however, each of the European teleport projects are seen as actively promoting the development of the city in which the infrastructure investment is planned and to which it is intended that downstream users will be drawn. To take one example, the Amsterdam Teleport has been developed as part of an integrated strategy to promote Amsterdam within Europe and beyond as an 'information city', with the teleport as one element within a so-called 'telematics belt' along the southern banks of the Y-estuary, and linked into the rest of the conurbation by a recently completed fibre-optic network.

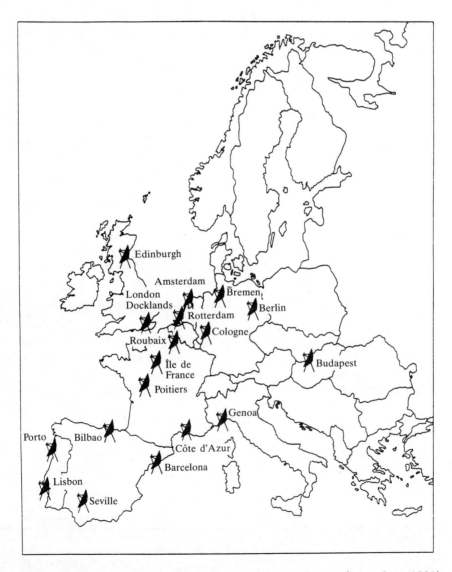

Figure 1. Teleport projects completed or initiated in Europe (as at June 1991) (source: World Teleport Association, Europe).

Initiatives such as these provide firm indication of the 'rebirth of the centrality of the city' through advanced communications technology. Cities are competing amongst themselves to become regional or even global information hubs, with the teleport as one of the more potent symbols of this competitive process. There will of course be winners and losers in this process, just as there have always been winners and losers in the competition between cities, and their commercial, cultural, and political elites, for control of communications networks and the information channelled through those networks. It is surely clear, however, that 'the city' will be the main beneficiary of the highly specialised and demand-driven communications networks that are being developed through the convergence of telecommunications and computing technologies.

6 Communications technology and urban spatial form
This is not of course to deny that there are strong co-existing possibilities inherent in these technologies to facilitate decentralisation. Such decentralisation is, however, most likely to occur within the context of extended metropolitan regions, as the evidence relating to the relocation of back-office activities confirms (Moss and Dunau, 1987; Nelson, 1986). The same is true for the much heralded, but slow to develop, phenomenon of 'teleworking' [so slow to develop in fact that Steinle (1988, page 8) has commented that "there are more people doing research on telework than there are actual teleworkers"].

The eventual development of teleworking is likely to contribute to expanding the commuting fields around the major metropolitan centres, allowing a partial substitution for some journeys to work and business trips. Contrary to the romance of the rural telecottage scenario, sustained by advertising campaigns such as the one recently run by the Highlands and Islands Development Board in Scotland, it is not the remote rural areas that are likely to benefit most from the growth of teleworking, but rather the fringes of the largest cities (Price Waterhouse, 1990). In this sense, teleworking will have a positive impact on the sustainability of major cities such as London, improving the quality of life of the 'competence-based' professionals that are likely to constitute the main category of teleworkers (Quortrup, 1992).

If telecommunications is likely to improve the quality of metropolitan life in this way, this is not necessarily to argue that the city will become more sustainable in energy-conservation terms. The large metropolitan region is likely to get larger, and to incorporate increasingly distant territory into its commuting field. Journeys to work are likely to be fewer in number, because of the partial substitution effect of teleworking, but quite possibly to be longer than previously. Certainly the implications of incorporating modern communications capabilities into flexible working arrangements is likely to militate against any development of the type of 'compact city' which has been proposed on energy-saving grounds. All the evidence suggests rather that telecommunications will facilitate the linking of activities over increasingly long distances.

Further, the partial substitution potential of teleworking should not be allowed to obscure the fact that for most human activities, telecommunications is not a substitute for the physical movement of people or goods or services, but rather a facilitator or even a *generator* of such movements. A good example of this is provided by advanced logistics in goods distribution, in which electronic communication is able to support and coordinate considerably more frequent 'just-in-time' delivery.

Depending on the circumstances in which it is used, therefore, telecommunications could contribute to the sustainability of the city in energy-consumption terms by substituting electronic for physical movements; or to the squandering of energy through facilitating more dispersed urban forms and more movement-intensive forms of economic activity. As always, it will not be the technology itself which will determine which of these outcomes prevails, but rather the economic, social, political, and regulatory context in which the technologies are developed and used.

A further issue concerning the 'sustainability' of the city associated with the proliferation of communications technology applications is their possible contribution to a process of 'internal fragmentation', which a number of commentators have argued characterises the post-Fordist or postmodern city [for a recent postmodernist perspective on the city see Sennett (1991)].

Sharpe and Wallock (1987), for example, suggest that the city is becoming 'distorted and decentred', with the time-eliminating and time-spanning properties of the new communications technologies producing a new kind of 'decentred urban field'. In similar vein, Virilio (1987) sees the city as becoming 'overexposed' and becoming increasingly 'disorganised' by the electronic technologies that are penetrating its fabric. Dematteis (1988) suggests that network interconnections between sectors in different cities are prevailing over interdependencies based on territory, and that in the process the city is losing its cohesion, becoming what he terms a 'weak metropolis': "the city loses its territorial identity and breaks up into as many fragments as the number of networks it is traversed by" (page 38).

In conclusion, there remain considerable uncertainties about the implications of advances in communications technologies for the future of cities. Although it is my contention that 'the city' will benefit considerably from the enhanced global reach of communications networks and from a 'remaking' of its centrality within such networks, at the same time there are aspects of these same technologies that may be contributing to the loss of internal coherence and cohesion within metropolitan regions.

The city, but what sort of city? Beyond the technologically deterministic futurology that has so dominated thinking about urban futures, there remains, as Batty (1990) reminds us, a 'woeful inadequacy' in our understanding of the implications of new information and communications technologies for cities and for their sustainability as places to live and work.

References

Batty M, 1990, "Intelligent cities: using information networks to gain competitive advantage" *Environment and Planning B: Planning and Design* **17** 247-256

Berry B J L, 1973 *The Human Consequences of Urbanisation* (St Martin's Press, New York)

Carey J W, 1981, "Culture, geography and communications: the work of Harold Innis in an American context", in *Culture, Communication, and Dependency: The Tradition of Harold Innis* Eds W H Melody, L Salter, P Heyer (Ablex, Norwood, NJ) pp 73-91

Castells M, 1989 *The Informational City* (Basil Blackwell, Oxford)

Dematteis G, 1988, "The weak metropolis", in *World Cities and the Future of the Metropolis* Ed. L Mazza (Electa, Milan) pp 33-42

Dizard W P, 1982 *The Coming Information Age* (Longman, Harlow, Essex)

DuBoff R B, 1983, "The telegraph and the structure of markets in the United States, 1845-1890" *Research in Economic History* **8** 253-277

Economic and Transport Planning Group, 1989, "Telecommunications in rural England", report to the Rural Development Commission and OFTEL, Rural Research Series number 2, Rural Development Commission, 141 Castle Street, Salisbury, Wilts SP1 4TP

Gillespie A E, 1991, "Advanced communications networks, territorial integration and local development", in *Innovation Networks: Spatial Perspectives* Ed. R Camagni (Belhaven Press, London) pp 214-229

Gillespie A E, Hepworth M E, 1988, "Telecommunications and regional development in the information economy: a policy perspective", PICT Policy Research Papers number 1, Programme on Information and Communications Technologies, Economic and Social Research Council, Polaris House, North Star Avenue, Swindon SN2 1US

Gillespie A E, Robins K, 1989, "Geographical inequalities: the spatial bias of the new communications technologies" *Journal of Communications* **39**(3) 7-18

Gillespie A E, Robins K, 1991, "Non-universal service: political economy and communications geography", in *Cities of the 21st Century: New Technologies and Spatial Systems* Eds J Brotchie, M Batty, P Hall, P Newton (Longman, Harlow, Essex) pp 159-170

Gillespie A E, Williams H P, 1990, "Telecommunications liberalisation and the future development of Scotland", a report to the Scottish Development Agency, Newcastle PICT Centre, Centre for Urban and Regional Development Studies, University of Newcastle upon Tyne, Newcastle upon Tyne

Gillespie A E, Coombes M G, Raybould S, Bradley D, 1991, "Telecommunications and the development of rural Scotland", a report to Scottish Enterprise, Newcastle PICT Centre, Centre for Urban and Regional Development Studies, University of Newcastle upon Tyne, Newcastle upon Tyne

Goddard J B, 1990, "The geography of the information economy", PICT Policy Research Papers number 11, Programme on Information and Communications Technologies, Economic and Social Research Council, Polaris House, North Star Avenue, Swindon SN2 1US

Gold J R, 1985, "The city of the future and the future of the city", in *Geographical Futures* Ed. R King (The Geographical Association, Sheffield) pp 92-101

Gottman J, 1977, "Megalopolis and antipolis: the telephone and the structure of the city", in *The Social Impact of the Telephone* Ed. I de Sola Poole (MIT Press, Cambridge, MA) pp 303-317

Gottman J, 1983 *The Coming of the Transactional City* (Institute for Urban Studies, University of Maryland, College Park, MD)

Hall P, 1991, "Three systems, three separate paths", special feature on 'The coming global metropolis: the longer view' *Journal of the American Planning Association* **57** 16 – 20

Hepworth M E, 1987, "Information technology as spatial systems" *Progress in Human Geography* **11** 157 – 180

Hepworth M E, 1989 *Geography of the Information Economy* (Belhaven Press, London)

Hudson H E, Parker E B, 1990, "Information gaps in rural America: telecommunications policies for rural development" *Telecommunications Policy* **14** 193 – 205

Innis H, 1951 *The Bias of Communication* (University of Toronto Press, Toronto)

Maisonrouge J, 1984, "Putting information to work for people" *Intermedia* **12**(2) 31 – 33

Martin J, 1978 *The Wired Society* (Prentice-Hall, Englewood Cliffs, NJ)

Moss M L, 1986, "Telecommunications and the future of cities" *Land Development Studies* **3** 33 – 44

Moss M L, 1988, "Telecommunications: shaping the future", in *America's New Market Geography: Nation, Region and Metropolis* Eds G Sternlieb, J W Hughes (Rutgers University Press, New Brunswick, NJ) pp 255 – 275

Moss M L, 1991, "The new fibers of urban economic development" *Portfolio* **4**(1) 11 – 18

Moss M L, Dunau A, 1987, "Will the cities lose their back offices?" *Real Estate Review* **17**(1) 62 – 68

Mumford L, 1966 *The City in History* (Pelican Books, Harmondsworth, Middx)

Nelson K, 1986, "Labour demand, labour supply and the suburbanisation of low-wage office work", in *Production, Work, Territory* Eds A J Scott, M Storper (Allen and Unwin, London) pp 149 – 171

Pred A, 1973 *Urban Growth and the Circulation of Information* (Harvard University Press, Cambridge, MA)

Price Waterhouse, 1990, "The economic impacts of information technology and telecommunications in rural areas", final report to DGXIII.F, Commission of the European Communities, Brussels; Price Waterhouse, 31 London Bridge, London SE1

Quortrup L, 1992, "Telework: visions, realities, barriers", in *Cities and New Technologies* (OECD, Paris) pp 77 – 108

Robins K, Gillespie A E, 1992, "Communications, organisation and territory", in *Understanding Information: Business, Technology and Geography* Ed. K Robins (Belhaven Press, London) pp 147 – 164

Robins K, Webster F, 1988, "Athens without slaves ... or slaves without Athens? The neurosis of technology" *Science as Culture* **3** 7 – 53

Salter L, 1981, " 'Public' and mass media in Canada: dialectics in Innis' communication analysis", in *Culture, Communication and Dependency: The Tradition of Harold Innis* Eds W H Melody, L Salter, P Heyer (Ablex, Norwood, NJ) pp 193 – 207

Schaeffer K H, Sclar E, 1975 *Access for All: Transportation and Urban Growth* (Pelican Books, Harmondsworth, Middx)

Sennett R, 1991 *The Conscience of the Eye: The Design and Social Life of Cities* (Faber and Faber, London)

Sharpe W, Wallock L, 1987, "From 'great town' to 'non-place urban realm': reading the modern city", in *Visions of the Modern City* Eds W Sharpe, L Wallock (Johns Hopkins Press, Baltimore, MD) pp 1 – 50

Steinle W J, 1988, "Telework: opening remarks on an open debate", in *Telework: Present Situation and Future Development of a New Form of Work Organisation* Eds W B Korte, S Robinson, W J Steinle (North-Holland, Amsterdam)

Toffler A, 1981 *The Third Wave* (Pan Books, London)

Virilio P, 1987, "The overexposed city" *Zone* **1**(2) 15 – 31

Energy, Environmental Sustainability and Land-use Planning

S Owens
University of Cambridge

1 Introduction: energy, sustainability, and urban development

Sustainable urban development is arguably a contradiction in terms. By definition, urban areas require the resources of a wider environment for their survival. Partly for this reason, a strong thread of antiurbanism has always run through environmentalist thought. It can be traced from its roots in the 19th-century reaction against economic liberalism (Lowe and Goyder, 1983) through publications of the early 1970s, such as "Blueprint for survival" (Goldsmith et al, 1972) and the writings of Paul Ehrlich (for example, Ehrlich and Holdern, 1971) to the present-day decentralist philosophy of the 'deep green' movement. Schumacher (1976) argued that urban expansion had only been made possible by the removal, predominantly through the use of nonrenewable fossil fuels, of tight constraints on agricultural productivity and mobility, implying that urban sustainability was in question unless alternative sources of energy could be found.

Given current development patterns throughout the world, however, the likelihood of a return to a decentralised pattern of quasi-self-sufficient small communities is remote, and indeed it is highly questionable whether such a pattern would be sustainable at present and projected levels of population. Urban areas are here to stay. In considering the question of sustainable urban development, therefore, we must think not only in terms of urban areas themselves, but in the sense of their wider impact on regional and global ecosystems. Urban sustainability has both internal and external dimensions.

It is widely accepted that sustainable development at all scales must involve the more efficient use of energy. Energy is a crucial resource, and the currently dominant forms are not renewable. They are associated with many serious environmental impacts, including urban air pollution, regional transfrontier problems like acidification, and global-scale impacts, the most important of which, as far as we are currently aware, is the enhanced greenhouse effect. Concern about the environmental impacts of energy cycles is reinforced by security of supply considerations, complacency having been rudely dispelled by the Gulf War of 1991.

In this paper I am concerned with the contribution that land-use planning might make to sustainable urban development through its influence on patterns of energy demand. Towns and cities are major energy consumers (OECD, 1990). At the same time it is clear that energy systems are related in complex but fundamental ways to patterns of land use and the structure of the urban environment. Throughout history, the nature and availability of energy resources have influenced the distribution of human activities and urban form. During the 20th century the absence of energy constraints has had the most marked impact: in much of the developed world, falling real energy prices have permitted increasing physical separation of activities and the outward spread of urban areas at decreasing densities. Urban structure is itself an important determinant of energy demand, especially for transport and for space heating (or cooling) in buildings. This influence is substantial: in the United Kingdom, for example, transport and space heating account for well over half of delivered energy needs and it is estimated that as much as 70% of delivered energy may be subject in some way, and at some time, to the influence of land-use planning (Barton, 1990).

Given the relative permanence of urban infrastructure and the major uncertainties surrounding both the global environmental impacts of energy cycles, and future energy supplies, it may seem self-evident that land-use planning should be concerned with energy supply, demand, and conservation. As this argument is rapidly becoming part of the conventional wisdom (in rhetoric if not in practice), it merits scrutiny before we consider how urban areas might in fact be made more energy efficient.

In simple terms the case is clear. Energy and land use are related; greater energy efficiency is desirable; planners influence land-use patterns and therefore some aspects of energy demand in the longer term. What tends to be left out of this equation is cost. We need to consider not only the benefits of improving energy efficiency, but the costs of doing so, and there is a logic to adopting first those measures which are most cost-effective. In fact, energy conservation is often economically attractive in its own right, but because markets for energy and energy efficiency are imperfect for reasons which are now well understood (for example, see HCEC, 1991a), intervention is needed to ensure that the 'optimal' investment in energy efficiency takes place. This is an argument that can be applied to land-use planning, a long-standing regulatory instrument. It does not imply, however, that all measures which might make the built environment more energy efficient can be justified in these terms.

Where energy-efficiency measures cannot be justified on (narrowly defined) economic grounds alone, we can resort to another, increasingly compelling, argument. Given the widely accepted need to control the environmental effects of energy cycles, improvements in energy efficiency, even if they incur real costs, can often be shown to be the most cost-effective way of controlling pollution and other forms of environmental degradation. Again, this is not invariably the case—some efficiency measures may be more costly than, for example, pollution controls or fuel switching, but true internalisation of environmental costs would almost invariably lead to greater emphasis on energy efficiency. This is another argument which might favour energy-conscious land-use planning—but it applies only to those measures whose costs do not clearly outweigh the benefits when environmental (and other) externalities are taken into account.

Land-use planning policies to promote energy efficiency could therefore be justified as a means of removing barriers to efficiency improvements which are cost-effective in their own right (essentially a 'no regrets' policy) or as an instrument of environmental policy in a wider sense (in both cases, we should be careful not to define costs too narrowly). The problem, of course, is that planning, forecasting, and internalising environmental costs are all very inexact sciences. Given that land-use planning also tends to operate over long timescales, we simply will not know, in many cases, whether planning policies aimed at promoting energy efficiency will be 'cost-effective' or not.

Though we are dealing with much uncertainty, we can nevertheless retain some notion of balance. It seems reasonably likely that neglect of energy considerations will mean continued development of energy-intensive urban areas which may not be sustainable in the longer term. Application of the precautionary principle would therefore suggest that land-use planners should at least be aware of the energy implications of alternative policies, and should include energy efficiency among their objectives. It does not suggest that they should pursue energy-efficient patterns of development at all costs, but in any case it is extremely unlikely that they would be permitted to do so. A related point, which introduces a recurring theme in this paper, is that land-use planning in isolation is unlikely to be an effective means of promoting energy efficiency and environmental sustainability. Unless other social and economic forces are working in the same direction, it may even be counterproductive. With the potential contribution of land-use planning in perspective, in the rest of this paper I consider the mechanisms through which energy and land use are related, planning policies which might improve energy efficiency in theory, and some of the problems of implementation in practice, with particular reference to a recent survey of English planning authorities.

2 Energy demand and urban form: defining the connections
The form of the built environment exerts its major influence on energy demand in the transport and space heating or cooling sectors. In both cases, land-use patterns and built form affect intrinsic energy needs as well as the efficiency with which energy needs can be met. Low-density urban sprawl, for example, generates a greater need to travel than more compact structures of mixed land uses in which the physical separation of activities is small, and the technical and economic viability of certain energy technologies and transport systems are affected by factors such as urban density and the location and mixing of different land-uses. Such considerations need not be unduly restrictive, but they do need to be taken into account at an early stage in the land-use planning process.

Interaction between energy systems and urban structure takes place at all scales from that of the individual building to the region. At all these levels it could be influenced by forward planning and development control. It is argued later, however, that energy-conscious land-use planning at any one level alone is unlikely to make a major contribution to sustainability. Here we begin by exploring the relationship at the fine grain of urban development, then move upwards to consider such issues as urban-scale combined heat and power (CHP), and transport systems operating at the urban and regional levels.

2.1 Energy and planning at the microscale
At the neighbourhood scale, measures to conserve energy in the urban environment should be the concern of both land-use planning and building regulations: the important requirement—not currently achieved—is that both work together towards a common objective. In this paper I am not concerned with measures such as thermal insulation, which do not have major implications for the form of urban development, though high standards of thermal insulation are crucial to any comprehensive urban energy policy. The discussion here focuses on the influence of built form on intrinsic energy needs and on the potential for passive solar and micro-climatic design. Both have land-use planning as well as architectural implications.

2.1.1 *Built form*
Built form exerts a systematic influence on energy requirements for space heating. Theoretical calculations show that detached houses can require as much as three times the energy input of equivalent intermediate flats (Barnes and Rankin, 1975; BRE, 1975), though in the real world the relationship tends to be obscured by the large number of variables involved in determining heating requirements (Grot and Socolow, 1973; Loudon and Cornish, 1975).

There can be little doubt that any systematic trend towards built forms like terraced housing or low-rise flats could result in significant reductions in energy demand. As such a trend would imply generally higher net densities, there are implications for planning at the urban scale. Energy-efficient built forms might also incur costs in terms of loss of amenity. But this can be weighed against the fact that smaller housing units, often in the form of terraces or flats, are particularly suited to meeting projected household needs, which in many countries are no longer dominated by the requirements of the nuclear family. In the United Kingdom, 85% of new households will be accounted for by single people by the year 2001 (DoE, 1988). The opportunity to take advantage of energy-efficient built forms should therefore be considerable.

2.1.2 *Passive solar design*

Over the past decade an excellent understanding has developed of the ways in which siting, design, orientation, layout, and landscaping can make the optimum use of solar gain and microclimatic conditions to minimise the need for space heating (or cooling) of buildings from conventional sources. Guidelines for different climatic and microclimatic conditions are now available [for example, see the guidelines produced for the United Kingdom by the Building Research Establishment, (BRE, 1990)]. It is essential, however, that these principles are taken into account at an early stage of the urban development process when important key factors like road layout are decided; the potential for later intervention or adaptation is limited.

The use of passive solar energy can lead to significant savings in conventional fuel at little or no economic or environmental cost: demonstration projects in Milton Keynes in the United Kingdom suggest that in the 'ideal' situation (passive solar houses on an ideal site) energy demand for space heating might be reduced by 11–12% (NBA Tectonics, 1988). But there are some important implications for urban design arising from the advantages of a north–south building orientation and the need to avoid overshadowing, which in turn affect layout and development density.

Although it entails some departure from conventional practice, passive solar design does not require unattractive repetitive layouts and/or very low-density housing, as has sometimes been implied. Advantage can be taken of solar gain with up to a 30° variation from a north–south axis, and, with attention to layout and orientation, 80% of the maximum possible savings can be achieved in passive solar houses on real sites with densities of up to 40 dwellings per hectare (NBA Tectonics, 1988). Densities of new private-sector development in the United Kingdom are typically around 25 dwellings per hectare.

The most significant constraints are likely to be the size and shape of some urban infill sites, which are often developed to higher densities and where overshadowing by existing buildings may limit the scope to choose appropriate orientation and layout for exploitation of passive solar energy. The less restrictive the site, the more opportunity there will be to take advantage of the principles of energy-conscious development at the micro-scale.

One recent study for the Department of Energy suggests that at densities at which they are normally built, 100% of detached and semi-detached houses and bungalows, 50% of terraced houses and 25% of flats could achieve the full energy-saving potential from passive solar design (NBA Tectonics, 1988). Many UK planning authorities however, do not currently feel able to provide any more than mild (and ineffectual) encouragement to developers to take such considerations into account. The reasons for this are discussed in more detail later.

2.1.3 *Other microclimatic considerations*

Attention to microclimate can reduce heat loss from buildings in a number of ways, for example by controlling wind speed and by raising external ambient temperatures. Appropriate measures include the use of particular materials, attention to building layout, landscaping, and planting shelter belts of trees. The influence of these factors on energy demand is less well researched than passive solar design, but preliminary results suggest that savings might be of the order of at least 5% and perhaps considerably more on exposed sites (BRE, 1990). Ideally, microclimatic considerations would also influence the location of new development (avoiding very exposed sites, for example), but in most urban areas where land is scarce, the important requirement will be to make the best use of microclimate on sites selected for other reasons.

There is little reason why the principles of passive solar and micro-climatic design should not be applied in a substantial proportion of new developments. In general they are not, however, because they often fall into a policy vacuum between planning and building regulations. There is scope here for a significant policy initiative to ensure that these simple cost-effective measures are considered at an early enough stage in the urban development process. This applies not only to new development, but to redevelopment and renewal projects where there may be opportunities to improve energy efficiency through urban structure at the 'micro-scale' as well as through more conventional means such as better standards of thermal insulation.

2.2 Urban design and combined heat and power systems

Conventional power stations convert primary fuel into electricity with a maximum efficiency of about 38%. Combined heat and power (CHP), in which heat produced during the process of electricity generation is used for space and water heating, increases the efficiency of conversion of primary fuel (for example, coal or natural gas) to around 80% and there-fore leads to reductions in environmental impact per unit of delivered energy. It is widely acknowledged that CHP could make a substantial contribution to environmental sustainability. It also has implications for urban structure.

During the 1970s the Combined Heat and Power (CHP) Group (estab-lished by the Secretary of State for Energy in 1974) conducted theoretical analyses of the factors affecting the economic viability of large-scale CHP, including certain urban structural factors such as density and land-use mix (CHP Group, 1977; 1979). More detailed analyses of real cities were subsequently conducted in the 'lead-city' studies (Atkins and Partners, 1982).

The CHP Group estimated costs for three hypothetical situations—a small 'green field' development (10 000 people), an existing small city (100 000 people), and an existing large city (one million people)—

and compared them with the costs of individual gas-fired central heating for the new development and with the existing fuel mix in the other cases.

The economics of urban-scale CHP were sensitive to density, but this sensitivity was mediated by other factors. For example, in the case of the existing small city, with a 10% discount rate (over a sixty year period) and with the assumption of constant real fuel prices, the breakeven density was more than 250 dwellings per hectare. Reducing the discount rate to 5%, or assuming that real fuel prices will double every 18 years, reduced the breakeven density to about 50 dwellings per hectare in each case. These results were obtained assuming a modified existing power station 15 km from the edge of the scheme (costs are sensitive to this assumption).

In the green field case, on the assumption of CHP from two small back-pressure sets, the breakeven density was about 75 dwellings per hectare with a 10% discount rate and constant real fuel prices, coming down to less than 25 dwellings per hectare or 37 dwellings per hectare by modifying the discount rate or fuel price assumptions as above. The economics are more favourable for green field development because heat mains and connections can be installed at the point of construction. However, it should be noted that the group was comparing new development ('green field') with installation in built-up areas ('existing city') and not the merits of different locations and forms of urban development per se.

Feasibility studies for the lead-city schemes which followed this work concentrated on 'high-density heat load' areas, defined as those having a net density of at least 20 MW km^{-2}, which would be typical of areas with dwelling densities of 44 or more dwellings per hectare. However, circumstances have changed in the intervening period (for example, fossil fuel costs have fallen, but there is more concern to internalise environmental costs). It is therefore difficult to draw conclusions about threshold densities, and there seem to be no current operational figures (D Green, Director of CHP Association, personal communication, 1991).

The other significant structural factor is a mix of different land uses—residential, industrial, and commercial—which spreads the demand for heat and electricity and improves the viability of CHP schemes. A large and stable heat load is now the key requirement, because electricity can be sold to the grid (though negotiation of contracts, after electricity privatisation, has presented an obstacle in at least one case in the United Kingdom).

For urban-scale CHP schemes, development should ideally be dense, mixed, on a reasonably large scale, and capable of being reached by heat mains without significant disruption elsewhere in the urban system. Because of the costs involved in routing the heat mains, much would depend on the location of the power station in relation to the areas being served.

Though in theory CHP is more viable in new development, because heat mains can be installed more cheaply, most of the above conditions are more likely to be met in existing urban areas (where a large and stable core heat load could be negotiated in advance, for example); additional development within the urban area might then further improve the economics of the scheme. In a new settlement, development could in theory be planned to be compatible with a CHP scheme from the outset, but the fact that there are no powers to compel firms or households to connect to the network would seem to present a major obstacle in areas where there is no existing development. In Denmark, under the 1979 Heat Supply Act, town councils have the right to stipulate that all potential consumers of district heating must be connected: in Kalundborg, for example, this right was exercised in 1984, requiring connection by 1993 (Danish Ministry of Energy, 1987). Any proposal to extend such powers to local planning authorities in the United Kingdom would be certain to excite considerable controversy.

Refuse-based schemes (which currently benefit from the Non-Fossil Fuel Obligation) probably need to be big enough to support two (or even three) furnaces, so that one can be out of action if necessary. In Newcastle, a three-furnace plant takes around 200 000 tonnes of refuse per annum from an area of about half a million people. Smaller schemes might be possible, but a number of limitations have to be borne in mind. First, siting of any new incinerator is likely to be difficult and contentious; second, industrial as well as domestic refuse is burnt, implying mixed development; third, a 'sustainable' community would arguably be one in which much less waste was generated than at present, tending to push up the size of population which could support such a scheme; and, fourth, the concept of a relatively small community importing refuse does not seem immediately practicable.

CHP systems which operate at the scale of the individual building or group of buildings (providing both electricity and heat) are considerably more flexible in relation to different forms of urban development because they avoid the need to lay expensive heat-distribution mains. Plentiful supplies of natural gas (and the new structure of the electricity supply industry) make units with output as low as 10 kWe viable and prospects for such systems seem more positive than those for widespread application of urban-scale CHP. Constraints are related mainly to the cost of backup electricity and the price offered for any local electricity exports (CHP Association, 1991). Again, however, no one can be compelled to participate, and the greatest potential for such schemes is seen to be in buildings such as hotels, hospitals, and sheltered housing. The obstacles to using small-scale CHP in ordinary residential or mixed development seem to be institutional rather than technical.

The availability of small-scale CHP schemes means that (if fiscal and institutional problems could be overcome) CHP could be tailored to any size of community. In Denmark, CHP schemes using a range of fuels operate or are planned to serve communities on many different scales, including areas of relatively low-density development (Danish Ministry of Energy, 1987). Investment in modular units is to some extent 'lumpy' because they tend to come in specific sizes (for example, 10, 20, 40, 100 kWe), and there are probably some economies of scale (D Green, personal communication, 1991). It is difficult to judge how sensitive urban-scale schemes are to size, but in the CHP Group's theoretical analysis costs were of the order of 10% higher in the small-city scheme than in the large-city scheme.

Because experience of CHP outside the industrial sector is very limited in the United Kingdom, and much recent analysis has been scheme specific, it is difficult to generalise about the viability of CHP in different forms of urban development. Costs are probably more sensitive to site-specific variables and financing arrangements than to the type of development per se. Key factors are the fiscal environment, the availability or proximity of a suitable power station (for urban-scale schemes) and the willingness of potential customers to connect. There are nevertheless a number of significant land-use planning implications relating to the need to understand where CHP would be most viable, site requirements, and institutional arrangements.

2.3 Integrating land-use and energy-supply planning

Different energy-supply systems can clearly have different requirements in terms of urban structure. Ideally, urban development and redevelopment should be planned from the outset to be structurally compatible with a desired energy-supply and conservation strategy. With full cooperation between urban planning authorities, developers and energy utilities (especially if the utilities have adopted 'least cost planning', which effectively treats conservation opportunities on an equal financial footing with supply), urban areas could be planned to accommodate the most efficient combination of energy-supply systems and conservation measures, making an important contribution to sustainable development. This does not necessarily imply a single efficient form: in different geographical areas different supply systems (natural gas grid, district heating network, or passive solar energy, for example) may be feasible or nonviable for a variety of reasons—the point is that the planning of new development should permit the best possible combination. Where constraints prevent the most efficient supply-systems being installed, particular emphasis could be given to built form and to standards of thermal insulation.

Considerable progress with energy-integrated planning has been made in Scandinavian countries. In Denmark land-use planning and the planning of heat supply take place simultaneously (Danish Ministry of Energy, 1987), and in Sweden work is continuing on models designed to optimise heat supply and energy conservation within a given settlement structure, existing or planned (Bergman, 1976; Lundqvist, 1989; Wene and Ryden, 1987). But in the United Kingdom, land-use planning and planning for energy supply are still conducted as largely separate processes, apart from essential consultation between local planning authorities and energy utilities. This is another area where there may be considerable scope for policy initiatives in the interests of sustainability.

2.4 Energy, transport, and urban form

The postwar period has been one in which trends in both land-use and travel patterns have reinforced each other to produce an increasingly mobile society. Higher levels of mobility have benefits for the individual and for the economy, but also impose costs, many of which are external- ised. Rapid growth in car ownership has permitted more dispersed patterns of urban development; these land-use patterns in turn require longer journeys for most daily activities and have become increasingly difficult to serve by energy-efficient modes of transport.

The energy and environmental implications of these trends are alarming because predicted traffic growth is likely to outstrip measures to improve the energy efficiency and environmental performance of vehicles unless other policy measures are introduced. In the United Kingdom, for exam- ple, whereas the energy efficiency of vehicles is projected to improve by a maximum of 28% by 2010 (ETSU, 1989), a 'low' forecast for vehicle kilometres projects an increase of 41% (Department of Transport, 1989). EC legislation requiring all cars to be fitted with catalytic converters will help reduce emissions of nitrogen oxides, hydrocarbons, and carbon monoxide in the short term, but these are likely to start to rise again early in the next century if traffic increases in line with government forecasts (ERRL, 1989).

Policies for sustainable urban development should therefore include measures to reduce the need for movement and to provide favourable conditions for energy-efficient and environmentally friendly forms of transport. Land-use planning has a key role to play in the attainment of these objectives.

2.4.1 *Reducing the need for movement*

Some land-use patterns are potentially efficient in the sense that they reduce the need for travel, though not always without cost in other terms. At the urban scale the most important factor is the physical separation of activities. This affects travel needs, and therefore energy requirements for transport. Modifying land-use patterns will not guarantee transport-energy savings, for reasons discussed below, but the smaller the physical separa- tion, the lower travel needs are likely to be, and the more feasible it is to meet them by the most environmentally friendly transport modes, walking and cycling.

The key variables in this relationship at the urban scale are density and the degree of mixing of different land uses. Theoretical work, much of which was conducted in the aftermath of the oil crisis of 1973–74, shows fairly unambiguously that, as urban density increases, energy use for transport falls (for example, see Clark, 1974; Edwards and Schofer, 1975; Keyes, 1982; Roberts, 1975). These findings are broadly confirmed by empirical studies. One of the best known, a cross-sectional analysis by Newman and Kenworthy (1989) of thirty-two cities throughout the world, showed a strong inverse relationship between urban density and energy consumption for transport. Similar results have been obtained from data collected within urban areas: in Toronto, for example, people living in low-density outer suburbs travel more than twice as far by car and emit more than twice as much carbon dioxide as their counterparts in the higher density urban core (Canadian Urban Institute, 1991). (Public transport networks as well as reduced travel distances are important factors in these empirical studies; the role of more efficient transport is considered in more detail below.)

One way to reduce travel needs would be to bring homes, jobs, and services together in a relatively compact urban centre to achieve a high level of accessibility with little need for movement. Many studies suggest that concentration of development is an energy-efficient form (Clark, 1974; Edwards and Schofer, 1975; Fels and Munson, 1975; Rickaby, 1987; Roberts, 1975; for a summary and assessment, see Owens, 1986a; 1990). It is a development pattern strongly endorsed by the European Commission in its recent "*Green Paper on the Urban Environment*" (CEC 1990). Higher densities also have other energy advantages, as I have shown in the previous section: they tend to be associated with energy-efficient built forms, and they increase the viability of district heating or CHP systems which could make a major contribution to energy savings. But there are drawbacks too: above a certain size of centre, there are problems of congestion, leading to inefficient energy use and loss of accessibility, and high densities limit the scope to use some forms of ambient energy, such as passive solar power (though not to the extent that has sometimes been implied).

Concentration of development in existing urban centres may also contribute to their rehabilitation and revitalisation, which in turn helps to make development within the cities a more attractive proposition. But there is also concern about the potential loss of urban green spaces, and 'town cramming', and these reservations need to be addressed if urban development and redevelopment are to be sustainable in the widest sense of the word. One important factor here, however, which it is easy to overlook, is the large amount of land currently demanded by the private car in urban areas. A Norwegian study (in progress) suggests that if dependence on the car could be reduced, considerable amounts of land might be released, minimising potential conflicts between the need for urban green space and a more compact pattern of urban development (Naess, 1991).

An alternative way to reduce the physical separation of activities is to decentralise some jobs and services and relate them to residential areas, either within a single large urban area, or to form freestanding settlements which may or may not retain links with the original centre. In theory 'decentralised concentration' often emerges as relatively efficient in terms of travel and energy requirements (for example, see Albert and Banton, 1988; Clark, 1974; Hemmens, 1967; Owens, 1981; Romanos, 1978; Stone, 1973).

However, there are major uncertainties about the potential energy advantages of decentralised mixed development. Reducing travel require-ments may incur costs in terms of amenity or access to a range of jobs and services: what matters is how individuals trade off these different costs against each other. When alternative development patterns are modelled and ranked according to energy efficiency, the results tend to be sensitive to assumptions about future life-styles and the way in which people value mobility and choice. They suggest that, if rising energy costs or policy restraints restrict mobility, a pattern of 'decentralised concentration' will be energy efficient because people will tend to use the jobs and services which are close to them. If travel costs pose only a minimum deterrent, such a pattern is likely to be more energy intensive than centralisation, because of the potentially large amount of cross-commuting and other travel.

In practice, it is the latter situation that seems recently to have prevailed in many countries. In the United Kingdom, decentralisation over the past few decades has produced suburbs and freestanding settlements with the potential to be self-contained, but the level of autonomy typically attained is small, even where self-containment was an explicit objective, as in the new towns. Although the autonomy of settlements tends to increase with size, it is also a function of relative isolation (Breheny, 1990).

All of this implies that an energy-efficient form of urban development cannot be defined without qualification, though it is reasonable to con-clude from the available evidence that peripheral or ex-urban residential development unrelated to jobs and services is an energy-intensive pattern. In this sense dormitory suburbs and settlements do not perform well on the criterion of sustainability. Rickaby (1987) suggests that both central-isation and 'decentralised concentration' are likely to be more energy efficient, but involve different sets of costs. A relatively robust form involves development in centres large enough to provide access to a good range of jobs and services without the need for long journeys, and with good public transport links to employment and other facilities to offer a viable alternative to the private car.

In another sense, too, reducing the distances which people need to travel may be a necessary but not a sufficient condition to reduce energy demand. Dangerous and unpleasant conditions inhibit walking and cycling in many urban areas. Although 43% of journeys in the United Kingdom are between one and three miles, only about 13% are undertaken on foot or by bicycle. As well as reducing the physical separation of activities, therefore, planning for sustainability would mean positive discrimination in favour of walking and cycling, making them feasible not only in terms of distance but also by providing a safe and clean environment.

2.5 Promoting public transport through land-use planning

The above discussion has been concerned mainly with the way in which land-use patterns can influence the need for travel. But the location and form of urban development also affect choice of transport mode, and therefore the energy and environmental implications of meeting particular travel needs. The interactions between land use, travel needs, and transport mode need to be recognised and incorporated into an integrated system of land-use and transport planning for urban areas within their regional context.

This means that land-use planning must be sensitive to the requirements of public transport. Rail and bus systems are generally more energy efficient than cars, and less environmentally damaging. On the basis of average passenger loads, a bus travelling in uncongested road conditions uses least energy per passenger-kilometre, and a car used for commuting in an urban area the most; rail systems occupy a position somewhere in between (Hughes, 1991; Maltby et al, 1978). The higher the load factor for public transport, the more significant its energy advantages become. A shift from private to public transport could therefore help to achieve wider energy and environmental objectives, and land-use planning has a role in encouraging this shift to take place in the medium to long term. This means relating development to new or existing public transport routes, and giving consideration to the types of development pattern that will maximise their use.

It is important to consider transport implications at the planning stage of urban development, because certain land-use patterns are better suited to the efficient and economic operation of public transport than others. Conventional bus and rail, for example, are poorly adapted to dispersed low-density areas typical of residential suburbs (Keyes and Peterson, 1977), whereas relative concentration of homes and facilities maximises accessibility to transport routes and encourages people to use them (Jamieson et al, 1967; Roberts, 1975). In the Netherlands, it has been found that proximity of employment to public transport nodes is effective in discouraging car use for the journey to work (Netherlands Ministry of Physical Planning, 1990). Linear urban forms are particularly conducive to public transport. This need not mean 'ribbon development', but could involve, for example, broad bands of urban development combining high densities along a bus or light rail route with moderate overall densities. A number of investigators have suggested that such forms could be entirely compatible with a high-quality urban environment (for example, see Barton, 1987; Steadman, 1980).

Appropriate planning policies would therefore include discouragement of dispersed low-density residential areas or any significant development heavily dependent on car use; some degree of concentration, though not necessarily centralisation, of activities; integration of development with public transport facilities and the maintenance of moderately high densities along transport routes. Where transport networks do not already exist, they should be planned in an integrated way with the development of land. Such policies could be applied, with the necessary adaptation to local circumstances, to green field sites and to redevelopment, growth, and infilling in existing urban areas.

There are important qualifications to these conclusions. Both with the reduction of travel needs and the promotion of energy-efficient modes, appropriate development patterns provide a necessary but not a sufficient condition for success. Land-use planning needs to be combined with investment in transport facilities as well as fiscal and regulatory constraints on private vehicles. Policies imposed in isolation are likely to have unintended effects. Encouraging decentralised concentration, for example, may increase the amount of travel unless accompanied by fiscal restraints; and making city centres unfriendly to cars, unless combined with appropriate planning policies, may lead not to the intended modal shift but to energy-intensive development in out-of-centre locations. Land-use planning is a long-term strategy, likely to be most effective as an integral part of the wide range of policy measures which will be essential if we are to move towards an environmentally sustainable urban land-use and transport system. Transport represents an immense challenge in this respect, for it

Table 1. Influence of urban form on energy demand (source: adapted from Owens, 1986a).

Land-use variable	Mechanism	Effect on energy demand
Combination of factors (shape, size, interspersion, etc)	travel requirement (especially trip length and frequency)	variation of up to 150%
Interspersion of activities	travel requirements (especially trip length)	variation of up to 130%
Shape of urban area	travel requirements	variation of up to 20%
Density or clustering of trip ends	facilitates economic public transport	energy savings of up to 20%
Density or mixing of land use and built form	facilitates combined heat and power	efficiency of primary energy use improved by about 100%
Layout, orientation, design	passive solar gain	approximately 12% energy saving in cool temperate conditions
Siting, layout, landscaping, materials	optimise microclimate	energy savings of at least 5%, more on exposed sites

would be dangerous to underestimate political opposition to significant restraints on mobility or, as Mishan (1990) reminds us, to assume that because something must be done, it will be done.

2.6 Potential energy savings

It is clear from the above discussion that policies influencing urban development from the building to the city scale have important implications for energy demand and therefore for environmental sustainability. Energy-efficient urban structure could in theory result in substantial energy savings in the longer term (table 1). Theoretical savings will never be fully achieved in practice, but they may not be realised at all unless appropriate land-use planning policies are adopted. As long timescales are involved, it is important to begin to make the necessary adjustments now.

3 Planning for sustainability: experience in practice

Elements of energy-integrated planning can be found in many countries, ranging from energy-conscious development at the microscale to integrated land-use and transport planning imposed at national level (as in the Netherlands). There are also some cases of comprehensive urban energy management, incorporating land-use planning, one of the best known of which has been implemented in Davis, California, since the 1970s. These examples of energy-integrated land-use planning have been extensively described, and to some extent their success analysed, elsewhere (Craig, 1982; Lee, 1980, pages 26-27; MKDC, 1982; Netherlands Second Chamber of the States General, 1989). One of the lessons that emerges is the need for energy-integrated land-use planning to be coordinated at all scales, as well as integrated with other kinds of policy measures.

The Milton Keynes initiatives, for example, have provided an important demonstration of potential energy savings at the microlevel (arising from building and site design combined with nonstructural measures) and have shown that many of these savings can be cost-effective. They have played a major role in information dissemination. To some extent, however, the energy projects have been made possible by the special status of the Milton Keynes Development Corporation, whose powers are not enjoyed by all planning authorities in the United Kingdom. Although individual projects have a key role in showing what can be achieved, higher level policy commitment is essential if energy-saving initiatives in the built environment are to become the rule rather than the interesting exception. Sustainability is not very meaningful in isolated pockets.

Similarly, although urban-scale initiatives such as that in Davis have been widely commended, and may stimulate more general interest in energy efficiency, they raise the issue of how much can be achieved in the absence of a comprehensive national policy framework. When individual cities pursue energy-management policies in isolation, there is a danger that energy-intensive and environmentally damaging activities (for example, dispersed growth) will simply be displaced. This is illustrated to some extent by the growing attraction of Davis for Sacramento commuters (Barton, 1990). Ultimately, there must be a commitment to energy management at all scales if achievements in specific locations are not to be undermined by developments elsewhere.

An excellent illustration of such a commitment is provided by The Netherlands "National Environmental Policy Plan", which establishes emission ceilings for nitrogen oxides, hydrocarbons, carbon dioxide, and noise for the transport sector for the years 2000 and 2010. It begins by attempting to define what is sustainable, then works through to the necessary policies. A wide range of measures, including land-use planning, is proposed in order to achieve these objectives and it is expected that the anticipated growth in car use to 2010 (from 1986) will be reduced by 48% as a result (Netherlands Second Chamber of the States General, 1989). Policies include location criteria for housing, employment, and recreation facilities, measures (including traffic restraint) to encourage the use of bicycles for journeys of 5 to 10 km and a specific new policy of matching the accessibility profiles of locations to the mobility profiles of firms and services. Although it is too early to tell how successfully the measures in the plan will be implemented, they do provide a good example of a national policy commitment to reducing the energy needs and environmental impacts of travel. This provides a framework within which individual cities can formulate and implement their own policies.

The absence of such a framework seems to be a major inhibiting factor in the progress of energy-integrated land-use planning in the United Kingdom. This finding emerged clearly from a recent survey of English planning authorities, the results of which are worth considering in some detail.

3.1 The experience of English planning authorities
During 1990, a postal survey of all strategic planning authorities in England, and a sample of districts, London boroughs, and metropolitan authorities was conducted (for full details, see Owens, 1991). Authorities were asked about the extent to which they took energy considerations into account in land-use planning, whether they thought energy efficiency should receive more attention, and if so what might help them to achieve this. The analysis which follows is based on the replies of thirty-four strategic planning authorities (about 90% of the total), forty-three district planning authorities (about 90% of the sample), the two national park planning boards, and six London boroughs and metropolitan authorities (86% of the sample).

The survey reveals an increased awareness of energy issues compared with the early 1980s (Owens, 1986b) and an increasing commitment to take them into account. However, there is great variation in planning authorities' attitudes, ranging from strong commitment to almost total neglect, and considerable confusion about the legitimacy of treating energy efficiency as a land-use planning issue.

County planning authorities demonstrate a fairly high level of awareness of energy-conservation issues. More than a third (35%) make some explicit reference to energy efficiency in the structure plan, predominantly in policies or in the explanations for them and occasionally as an overall goal or criterion for evaluation. Almost as many again (a further 29%) mentioned policies in which the more efficient use of energy is implicit. Most frequently the policies cited are concerned with transport, either directly as an element of transport strategy or indirectly in relation to settlement or other location policies. A handful of county planning authorities have given very detailed consideration to energy issues (for example, see Cornwall County Council, 1989; Nottinghamshire County Planning Department, 1989).

Concern about the environment, especially global warming and the environmental impacts of traffic, has been an important stimulus for current or planned emphasis on energy efficiency. In contrast to the early 1980s, when resource depletion dominated the rationale for conservation, a wider concept of environmental sustainability now seems to be the focus of concern. Several authorities mentioned greater awareness of these issues among officers, members, and the public, and the need therefore to incorporate them into strategic planning. Bedfordshire, for example, said that energy issues were now included "in recognition of concern for the environment, which would otherwise be incomplete"; Devon noted "more public/member awareness", and Humberside felt that energy efficiency is "a more important issue now than a few years ago, especially as far as officers are concerned". Warwickshire was conscious of "the growing awareness politically of the need to conserve energy".[1]

Perhaps even more significant is the apparently strong commitment to develop energy efficiency as a strategic planning issue in future, even among authorities which currently give it no explicit consideration. More than two thirds of the latter group expected energy issues to become more prominent within the next five years. Hertfordshire, for example, said that:

"Despite the perceived problems the County Council will be considering energy consumption and conservation along with other 'environmental' issues very seriously in the next five years. It intends to produce a 'State of the Environment Report' for the County which will try to assess energy consumption along with other environmental indicators."

Similarly, both Oxfordshire and Suffolk expected energy efficiency to be an element of environmental audits and action plans which were being prepared for their respective counties, and Northumberland was typical of

[1] Quotes from the various planning authorities are all from correspondence with the author during the 1990 survey.

a number of county planning authorities in anticipating that:

> "Energy efficiency will assume increased importance in the formulation of strategic planning policies.... The present escalation in energy costs together with growing concern for the environment will provide a focus for strategic thinking on energy issues."

In spite of existing policies and good intentions, however, there is little evidence that energy considerations are yet integrated into the strategic planning process in any meaningful sense. In many cases, this is only to be expected because the policies are very new (sometimes still only in draft form), but the situation seems little better for those planning authorities with a fairly long-standing policy commitment to energy efficiency. In fact, hardly any planning authorities could claim that energy-related policies had yet been effective, or even that energy issues had ever been raised or discussed in appeals or in consultation with district planning authorities.

Where energy considerations formed part of the justification for settlement policies, a handful of authorities felt that they had had some effect. Cambridgeshire, for example, said that "the continued thrust in the Settlement Policies, for concentrating new development in main centres and towns, is influenced by energy conservation considerations". Dorset and Warwickshire made similar points. But the effectiveness of these policies, largely adopted for nonenergy reasons, is almost certainly independent of any reference to energy efficiency. Energy is rarely raised as an issue in development control: it was mentioned only by Derbyshire, in relation to a proposed out-of-town shopping centre.

The inclusion of energy-related policies in a significant number of structure plans is encouraging because it demonstrates quite clearly that such policies can find a place within the strategic planning framework. As yet, however, most references to energy are brief and fairly rhetorical. Typically, energy efficiency is employed as an additional justification for land-use or transport policies which would be pursued in any case. This point is emphasised by the fact that essentially similar policies, for example relating new housing to employment opportunities, are justified with reference to energy efficiency in some structure plans, but entirely on nonenergy grounds in others. All of this suggests that energy efficiency, and the related environmental implications, are increasingly recognised as important, but have not yet acquired the practical significance associated with more traditional planning considerations.

3.2 Constraints as perceived by the counties

Strategic planning authorities offer a variety of reasons for their relative neglect of energy issues. Similar factors were cited by authorities that give energy some explicit attention (but presumably feel it merits more) and by the substantial minority that have not yet taken it on board. The reasons given fall into two main groups: the relative priority of energy considerations, and their legitimacy as a strategic planning issue.

One fifth of the planning authorities suggested that other matters were more important than energy, though many of the issues cited (such as housing, settlement patterns, 'conservation', and congestion) clearly have an energy dimension.

Nearly half of the authorities (44%) expressed reservations about the legitimacy of energy efficiency as a strategic planning issue. Many cited the 'land-use format' of structure plans and the difficulties of justifying energy-related policies in the absence of relevant legislation or guidance; as a result, such policies were perceived to be difficult to formulate and to implement. Cornwall, for example (a planning authority which has devoted an unusual amount of attention to energy supply and demand), found "difficulty in justifying energy efficiency as a land-use planning consideration"; Essex said that it was "not a major factor in broad strategic planning"; Hertfordshire outlined the perceived difficulties of implementation as follows:

"Energy conservation within the home, related to the design layout and construction of houses, is not a proper matter for a land-use based Structure Plan while the location of new development is the subject of many and varied parameters of which energy conservation would be just one";

and North Yorkshire commented that:

"The Structure Plan has been prepared in the context of advice ... on policy content issued by the Central Government. In the sphere of energy consciousness it is singularly lacking in guidance."

Other reasons, mentioned by a small number of authorities in each case, included limited resources and the relatively low political significance of energy and environmental issues at the time of structure plan preparation.

Two things are particularly striking about these responses. One is the prevailing sense that energy conservation is not a 'land-use' issue. The other is that it is often perceived as a separate issue, which merits treatment in its own right if at all. Yet the main argument for energy-integrated land-use planning is that land-use patterns are important determinants of energy demand and this relationship has significant environmental implications. It is in making this connection, and therefore in confirming that energy is indeed a legitimate issue for consideration within a strategic planning framework, that planning authorities most urgently need explicit direction from central government.

This policy gap is confirmed by planning authorities' own assessment of what would help them integrate energy considerations into the land-use planning process. Overwhelmingly they express a need for statutory support and policy guidance from the Department of the Environment on this issue.

3.3 District planning authorities

Authorities responsible for development control and the preparation of local plans (or unitary development plans) have made less progress towards the integration of energy considerations than the counties. About 18% of respondents make explicit, though typically very brief, reference to energy efficiency in their plans (or existing informal policies, if plans are not yet complete); relevant policies are typically to encourage, or look favourably upon, developments incorporating energy-conscious design features, or the use of renewable energy in various forms. A further 8% said their policies took energy into account implicitly.

Energy efficiency has rarely been an issue in development control. About 16% of respondents said that it had been raised at some point, either by the planning authority or by environmental groups. The circumstances varied. Peterborough City Council, which is among the planning authorities giving the most detailed attention to energy efficiency, had met 'significant resistance' when it tried to encourage developers to incorporate energy considerations into larger scale proposals. The impact of solar panels was reported as a development control issue by three planning authorities. The Peak Park Joint Planning Board, for example, had refused an application for installation of solar panels because these would 'spoil the appearance' of a building in the centre of a village, and Brighton has produced guidelines relating to the use of solar panels in Conservation Areas. Both Great Yarmouth and Westminster were involved in negotiations about possible CHP schemes.

3.4 Constraints as perceived by the districts

Nearly half of the nonstrategic planning authorities (47% of respondents) felt that energy efficiency was not a land-use planning issue, or at least that it was not traditionally perceived as such: 16% cited the lack of government advice or any statutory requirement to take energy into account. Other problems, mentioned by several authorities in each case, included a low level of political awareness, constraints on time and resources, and lack of information and expertise. One authority (Blackpool) felt that the opportunity to plan for energy efficiency was limited in a tightly constrained urban area; Derbyshire Dales and West Dorset both suggested that in a rural district it was difficult to take energy considerations into account.

A number of authorities (some 14%) felt that refusal of an application on the grounds of energy efficiency would not be upheld on appeal, and several added that costs might be awarded against the local planning authority. Redditch, for example, considered that:

"Any conditions imposed may at present be outside the scope of planning legislation and ultimately therefore unenforceable, unlikely to be upheld on appeal and likely to give rise to a claim for costs against the local planning authority for imposing them."

Once again, the need for a statutory and policy framework emerges very clearly. More than a third of the respondents felt that legislation or government guidance were prerequisites for giving greater attention to energy efficiency in local (or unitary development) plans and development control. Interestingly, it is guidance from the centre that is demanded, rather than simply an appropriate framework in the structure plan. Only a handful of the nonstrategic planning authorities referred to the existence or lack of structure plan policies on energy efficiency. In Cambridgeshire, where the structure plan contains well-established explicit energy-related policies, Peterborough and South Cambridgeshire have developed the issue in local plans, but Fenland felt that the local plan was "not ... a vehicle suitable for advancing policies in respect of energy efficiency" and in Huntingdonshire energy efficiency "has not featured in any way in the preparation of the Local Plan". Hampshire's structure plan has virtually no explicit energy-related policies, but Portsmouth's Draft City Plan contains one and Rushmoor intends to produce an environment strategy "which will deal with these issues".

As with the strategic planning authorities, there are good intentions for the future. Of the districts and boroughs which do not currently give energy any explicit attention, 45% thought that it would become a more important consideration. Nearly half of them mentioned the environment as a stimulus for concern, often in the context of a 'Green Charter' being adopted by the local authority.

Results of the survey show growing awareness among local planning authorities of the significance of energy efficiency. There is also a fairly strong willingness to act on this issue, especially among the county planning authorities, but a variety of constraints mean that practical and effective energy-integrated policies in forward planning and development control are rare. One of the most important inhibiting factors is clearly the lack of a statutory framework and policy guidance to require and legitimise consideration of energy efficiency as a land-use planning issue.

4 Options for the future

In many cases, the principles of energy-conscious urban design are well established. The requirements for implementation are information dissemination, political will, and policy coordination. This is particularly true for action at the building or neighbourhood scale, involving: measures affecting individual buildings (which have not been discussed here, but are clearly essential, such as insulation); siting and other microstructural factors in relation to microclimate; design to optimise use or efficiency of particular energy sources (for example, district heating network or passive solar energy).

Mechanisms to put these principles into practice are not always established. In the United Kingdom considerations relating to building orientation are covered by neither the planning nor the building regulations.

In response to a recommendation from the House of Commons Energy Committee (HCEC, 1991a, paragraph 106) that "applicants for planning permission be required to state what account they have taken of the energy efficiency aspects of layout and design", the government replied that energy efficiency "is primarily a building control issue", and that "the energy implications of microclimate or orientation will seldom be sufficiently weighty ... to justify refusing planning permission" (HCEC, 1991b, paragraph 21). It was conceded that the Department of the Environment would consider guidance on these issues to local planning authorities. Establishing urban-scale CHP has also been difficult, but the Energy Committee's calls for the government to remove certain fiscal barriers to its development also met with a lukewarm response.

There is a need to consider the extent to which elements of best practice may successfully be transferred from one national and urban context to another; not all measures are universally applicable because of institutional, cultural, and political differences. We need to understand these constraints if we are to disseminate information and learn from others' experience of urban energy management.

At the wider urban scale it must be accepted that there will never be total certainty about the effects of particular policies on energy consumption because much depends on variables (such as the propensity to travel) which are inherently difficult to predict. Nevertheless, there are certain principles which can be applied in most circumstances. The available evidence suggests that authorities responsible for land-use planning in urban areas should:

(1) Make the efficient use of energy resources an explicit goal of land-use development plans.

(2) Consider the energy implications of alternative policy options in plan preparation.

(3) Make energy efficiency an explicit consideration in urban planning policies. The most appropriate policies will vary with the local context, but the key principles are to minimise the physical separation of activities and to relate development to transport facilities. This is likely to mean: mixing of land uses at a scale which provides a reasonable choice of jobs and services; a positive attitude to higher densities in appropriate locations (for example, along public transport routes), subject to high standards of design; avoidance of dispersed development; avoidance of dormitory development in suburbs or new settlements, especially where these are unrelated to public transport facilities; location of employment areas and service facilities where these are not dependent upon access by car, or likely to generate significant numbers of additional car-based trips; provision of every facility to encourage walking and cycling, discriminating against cars wherever there is conflict.

(4) Adopt a positive attitude towards environmentally benign energy sources, subject to full assessment of the environmental impact of any specific proposals.

(5) Engage in early discussion with energy suppliers with a view to achieving the optimum combination of supply facilities and efficiency measures in new development.

(6) Seek a better understanding of patterns of energy consumption within the urban area, and monitor the influence of energy-related policies in the urban plan.

(7) Coordinate transport investment priorities to achieve strategic objectives for increased energy efficiency.

5 Conclusions

It has been argued in this paper that the development of environmentally sustainable patterns of urban development must entail, amongst other things, improvements in energy efficiency, and that land-use planning has a role in achieving this objective in the longer term. Many of the arguments are now well rehearsed, and there are some encouraging signs that the issue is being taken on board by local planning authorities. At this point, therefore, it is worth reiterating certain key conclusions and qualifications where these are likely significantly to affect the success with which theory can be translated into practice.

First, although it is not difficult to justify land-use planning for energy efficiency in broad terms, this does not mean that all possible measures will be effective or desirable. Although many costs (and benefits) are likely to remain stubbornly unquantifiable, we should not lose sight of the need to consider them, however broadly they may be defined.

Second, it should be stressed again that energy-conscious planning is not an exact science, especially at the urban and regional scales. Because of many intrinsic uncertainties in urban and energy systems, we are unlikely to be able to identify development patterns which would be the most energy efficient under all possible future circumstances. But research suggests that it is possible to identify land-use patterns and built forms which are robust and flexible. To achieve this, it may be necessary to conduct some form of environmental or energy assessment of land-use planning policies.

Third, greater integration emerges as an important ingredient of planning for sustainability—integration of land-use and transport planning, and integration of the planning of the built environment with that for energy supply and conservation. Institutional change is likely to be necessary in many urban areas to achieve genuine integration of energy considerations into the urban development process. There is also a need for 'vertical' integration of appropriate planning policies at different scales. The very concept of sustainability implies commitment from national to local level.

Spatially isolated examples of good practice are interesting, but they are not 'sustainable'.

Fourth, we should not expect to be able to measure the 'success' of all energy-integrated land-use planning policies quickly or directly. It may be possible to assess the impact of certain measures with some accuracy. For example, it is estimated that gradual implementation of passive solar design in new development in the United Kingdom over a twenty-year period could lead to energy savings of 0.2 million tonnes of coal equivalent per annum (NBA Tectonics, 1988). But for broader land-use planning policies, such as those designed to reduce the physical separation of activities and encourage more compact urban development, it will be difficult—perhaps impossible—to measure 'success' directly in terms of energy or money savings; the long time scales involved will make it problematic to isolate the influence of urban structure from that of many other variables determining urban energy demand.

Fifth, and perhaps most significantly, energy-conscious land-use planning will be necessary but not sufficient for the improvement of urban energy efficiency. Land-use planning must be set within the context of local, national, and international policy frameworks employing the full range of policy instruments—public investment, information, fiscal measures, and regulation. Some policies can be implemented at local level by municipal authorities, but other measures can only be taken comprehensively by central government. What is important, if sustainable urban development is to be achieved, is for policies at different levels to be coordinated and for all policy instruments to work in the same direction. Regulations which seek to change travel patterns or improve energy efficiency in buildings, for example, will cause conflict and encounter resistance unless energy price signals give essentially the same message.

It is within this wider framework that land-use planning has a significant role in improving energy efficiency and contributing to sustainable development. In isolation, it is unlikely to have much impact on urban energy consumption, and, as shown above, may even be counterproductive. But a policy package designed to achieve environmentally sustainable urban development in the longer term would be incomplete if land-use planning proceeded to ignore the opportunities to reduce energy consumption for travel and within buildings. When a range of policies is employed to achieve the same objective, the whole is likely to be greater than the sum of the parts.

Acknowledgements. The survey of local planning authorities discussed in this paper was commissioned by the Council for the Protection of Rural England (see Owens, 1991). My ideas on energy and land-use planning were further developed in conducting a study for the Department of the Environment (DoE) on the land-use planning implications of climate change, in contributing to the DoE-sponsored 'New Settlements' Project run by Professor Michael Breheny, and in preparing a paper for the Urban Affairs Division of OECD.

References

Albert J D, Banton H S, 1978, "Urban spatial adjustments resulting from rising energy costs" *Annals of Regional Science* **12** 64–71

Atkins and Partners, 1982 "CHP/DH Feasibility Programme: stage 1, summary report and recommendations for the Department of Energy" W S Atkins and Partners, Woodcote Grove, Ashley Road, Epsom, Surrey KT12 5BW

Barnes D, Rankin L, 1975, "The energy economics of building construction" *Building International* **8** 31–42

Barton H, 1987, "The potential for increasing the energy efficiency of existing urban areas through local planning policy", M Phil thesis, Department of Town and Country Planning, Bristol Polytechnic, Bristol

Barton H, 1990, "Local global planning" *The Planner* 26 October, pages 12–15

Bergman L, 1976, "An energy demand model for the Swedish residential sector", Document D4 1976, Swedish Council for Building Research, Stockholm

BRE, 1975, "Energy conservation: a study of energy consumption in buildings and means of saving energy in housing", CP 56, Building Research Establishment, Garston, Watford, Herts WD2 7JR

BRE, 1990 *Climate and Site Development* Digest 350, Parts 1–3, Building Research Establishment, Garston, Watford, Herts WD2 7JR

Breheny M, 1990, "Strategic planning and urban sustainability", paper presented to Town and Country Planning Association Conference on Planning for Sustainable Development, London, 27–28 November; copy available from the author, Department of Geography, University of Reading, Reading, Berks

Canadian Urban Institute, 1991, "Cities and global warming", prepared for meeting of the Climate Institute, 12–14 June, Canadian Urban Institute, Toronto

CEC, 1990 *Green Paper on the Urban Environment* (Commission of the European Communities, Brussels)

CHP Association, 1991, Evidence, in *Third report [session 1990–91]* "Energy efficiency third report", House of Commons Energy Committee, (HMSO, London) volume 2, pp 56–61

CHP Group, 1977, "District heating combined with electricity generation in the United Kingdom" *Energy Paper 20* discussion document prepared by the District Heating Working Party of the Combined Heat and Power Group (HMSO, London)

CHP Group, 1979, "Combined heat and electrical power generation in the United Kingdom" *Energy Paper 35* report by the Combined Heat and Power Group to the Secretary of State for Energy (HMSO, London)

Clark J W, 1974, "Defining an urban growth strategy which will achieve maximum travel demand reduction and access opportunity enhancement", RR 73, Department of Civil Engineering, Washington University, Seattle, MA

Cornwall County Council, 1989 *Energy and Planning in Cornwall, Report for Cornwall Energy Project* Ref: HQ/8X/3/HR, Cornwall County Council, Truro

Craig P P, 1982, "Energy, land use and values; the Davis experience", in *Energy and Land Use* Eds R W Burchell, D Listoken (Center for Urban Policy Research, Rutgers University, New Brunswick, NJ) pp 510–525

Danish Ministry of Energy, 1987 *District Heating in Denmark* Danish Ministry of Energy, Copenhagen

DoE, 1988 *1985 Based Estimates of Numbers of Households 1985–2001* Department of the Environment, 2 Marsham Street, London SW1P 3EB

Edwards J L, Schofer J L, 1975, "Relationships between transportation energy consumption and urban structure: results of simulation studies", Department of Civil and Mineral Engineering, Minneapolis, MN

Ehrlich P, Holdern J R, 1971, "The impact of population growth" *Science* **171** 1212–1217

ERRL, 1989, "Atmospheric emissions from the use of transport in the UK: Volume 1, the estimation of current and future emissions" report for Worldwide Fund for Nature (WWF) UK Ltd, Earth Resources Research Ltd, 258 Pentonville Road, London N1 9JY

ETSU, 1989, "Energy use and energy efficiency in the transport sector to 2010", Energy Technology Support Unit, Harwell, Oxon

Fels M F, Munson M J, 1975, "Energy thrift in urban transportation: options for the future", in *The Energy Conservation Papers: A Report to the Energy Project of the Ford Foundation* Ed. R H Williams (Ballinger, Cambridge, MA) pp 7–104

Goldsmith E, et al, 1972, "Blueprint for survival" *The Ecologist* **2** (1) (whole issue)

Grot R A, Socolow R H, 1973, "Energy utilization in a residential community" WP W-7, Center for Environmental Studies, Princeton University, Princeton, NJ

HCEC, 1991a *Third report [session 1990–91]* "Energy efficiency third report", House of Commons Energy Committee (HMSO, London)

HCEC, 1991b *Fifth special report [session 1990–91]* "Government observations on the 3rd report from the Committee (Session 1990–91) on energy efficiency, House of Commons Energy Committee (HMSO, London)

Hemmens G, 1967, "Experiments in urban form and structure" *Highway Research Record* number 207, 32–41

Hughes P, 1991, "The role of passenger transport in CO_2 reduction strategies" *Energy Policy* **19** 149–160

Jamieson G, Mackay W, Latchford J, 1967, "Transportation and land use structures" *Urban Studies* **4** 201–217

Keyes D L, 1982, "Reducing travel and fuel use through urban planning", in *Energy and Land Use* Eds R W Burchell, D Listoken (Center for Urban Policy Research, Rutgers University, New Brunswick, NJ) pp 214–232

Keyes D L, Peterson G, 1977, "Urban development and energy consumption", WP 5049, Urban Land Institute, Washington, DC

Lee H, 1980, "The role of local governments in promoting energy efficiency", DP-E-80-12, Energy and Environmental Policy Centre, J F Kennedy School of Government, Harvard University, Cambridge, MA

Loudon A, Cornish P, 1975, "Thermal insulation studies" *Building Research Establishment News* **4** 4

Lowe P, Goyder J, 1983 *Environmental Groups in Politics* (George Allen and Unwin, London)

Lundqvist L, 1989, "A model system for strategic metropolitan energy studies", in *Spatial Energy Analysis: Models for Strategic Decisions in an Urban and Regional Context* Eds L Lundqvist, L-G Mattson, E A Erikson (Gower, Aldershot, Hants) pp245–269

Maltby D, Monteath I G, Lawler K A, 1978, "The UK surface passenger transport sector: energy consumption and policy options for conservation" *Energy Policy* **6** 294–313

Mishan E J, 1990, "Economic and political obstacles to environmental sanity" *National Westminster Bank Quarterly Review* May, pp 25–42

MKDC, 1982 *Energy Projects in Milton Keynes* Milton Keynes Development Corporation, Milton Keynes

Naess P, 1991, "Environment protection by urban concentration", paper presented at Conference on Housing Policy as a Strategy for Change, Oslo, copy available from Norwegian Institute for Urban and Regional Research, Oslo

NBA Tectonics, 1988 *A Study of Passive Solar Energy Estate Layout* Department of Energy, Thames House South, Palace Street, London SW1E 5HE

Netherlands Second Chamber of the States General, 1989, "National Environmental Policy Plan, Session 1988 – 89" **21** 137, numbers 1 – 2, Ministry of Housing, Physical Planning and Environment, The Hague

Newman P W G, Kenworthy J R, 1989, "Gasoline consumption and cities: A comparison of US cities with a global survey" *American Planning Association Journal* **55** 24 – 37

Nottinghamshire County Planning Department, 1989 *Nottinghamshire County Structure Plan* Nottinghamshire County Council, Nottingham

OECD, 1990 *Environmental Policies for Cities in the 1990s* (OECD, Paris)

Owens S E, 1981 *The Energy Implications of Alternative Rural Development Patterns* PhD Thesis, School of Environmental Sciences, University of East Anglia, Norwich

Owens S E, 1986a *Energy, Planning and Urban Form* (Pion, London)

Owens S E, 1986b, "Strategic planning and energy conservation" *Town Planning Review* **57** 69 – 86

Owens S E, 1990, "Land-use planning for energy efficiency", in *Energy, Land and Public Policy* Ed J B Cullingworth (Transactions Publishers, Center for Energy and Urban Policy Research, University of Delaware, Newark) pp 53 – 98

Owens S E, 1991 *Energy– conscious Planning* Council for the Protection of Rural England, Warwick House, 25 Buckingham Palace Road, London SW1W 0PP

Rickaby P, 1987, "Six settlement patterns compared" *Environment and Planning B: Planning and Design* **14** 193 – 223

Roberts J S, 1975, "Energy and land use: analysis of alternative development patterns" *Environmental Comment* September issue, pages 2 – 11

Romanos M C, 1978, "Energy price effects on metropolitan structure and form" *Environment and Planning A* **10** 93 – 104

Schumacher E F, 1976, "Patterns of human settlement" *Ambio* **5** 91 – 97

Steadman P, 1980, "Configurations of land uses, transport networks and their relation to energy use", Centre for Configurational Studies, Open University, Milton Keynes

Stone P A, 1973 *The Structure, Size and Costs of Urban Settlements* (Cambridge University Press, Cambridge)

Wene C – O, Ryden B, 1987, "A comprehensive energy model in the municipal energy planning process" *European Journal of Operational Research* **33** 212

On the Sustainability of Urban and Regional Structures

L Orrskog, F Snickars
Royal Institute of Technology, Stockholm

1 Introduction

The seriousness of current threats to the environment is in marked contrast to prevailing urban policies. Given that the threats are real, ecological catastrophies will occur more frequently unless priorities and policies change radically. From this perspective, it is difficult to decide what can be regarded as realistic urban and regional futures as opposed to utopian ones. In this paper, we outline some of the range of possible future visions that involve increased ambitions of sustainability. The dimensions of this range are technical change, production conditions, and life-styles. The sustainable urban region or city, and its transportation and communication functions, are described for some of the defined futures.

The city houses firms engaged in trade and industry, working under different productivity conditions, and households practising different modes of living. The perspective of sustainability deals with exchange between the human society and nature. The sustainable city cannot become a reality unless production and living conditions are adapted to the requisites that nature provides.

Transportation is a sign of evolving trends in the economy, impinging on the environment in at least two ways. One is the effect of energy conversion in transport. The other impact comes from materials and people being moved in society in a dispersed way, which makes re-collection and recycling more difficult. The first problem applies to transportation both of people and of goods. The second phenomenon applies primarily to transportation of goods.

We deal with strategic urban planning on the assumption of only modestly increased political ambitions in the environmental area. The strategic task is to organise the city spatially and functionally so it provides for a better adaptation in the future between urban society and nature.

2 Scientific views on sustainability

Today's arguments for a new thinking in urban and regional planning are often triggered by environmental problems. Solutions are increasingly based on environmental considerations. A short description follows of the current knowledge of the threats to the environment, of their origin, of what should and could be done in planning, and of hindrances to a breakthrough for environmental arguments. The list of arguments is typical of the current knowledge base for green urban planning.

The environment is threatened through the greenhouse effect. The layer of ozone that protects life on earth from ultraviolet radiation seems to be damaged. Lakes and seas are overfertilised and polluted, and fresh water is becoming a scarce resource. The productivity of agricultural land is not increasing as rapidly as during earlier decades. Species are being extinguished and the regenerative ability of different kinds of biotopes is damaged. The capacity of the life-supporting systems is being undermined.

Environmental problems emanate from the burning of fossil fuels such as coal and petroleum and from the ruthless exploitation of nature in many extraction regions. They also follow from the way we handle organic substances. Some areas are being impoverished while others are enriched with nutrients. The handling of inorganic substances, including toxic ones, in production processes is another contributory factor. Components are mixed so that recycling becomes difficult following the concentration of materials in consumer areas.

Unanimity prevails among scientists and many citizen groups on policies relating to renewable sources of energy and recycling of waste products. Part of the reason why adjustment of production and consumption is slow is that pollution comes mainly from diffuse sources associated with our overall life-style. Environmental problems can arise far away from their regional source. Phenomena such as the warming up of the atmosphere are not felt to be significant in everyday life. To a large degree these are matters of tendencies and threats rather than of manifest problems, accurately measured in scientific scales. Scientists now understand that the functions of nature are dynamic and often exhibit discontinuity, whereas everyday life tells most people that nature is well-balanced and predictable (for example, see Wiman, 1988).

The current debate has existed since the regional and global consequences of the industrial society became publicly known. The standpoints concerning the linkages between nature and humankind have their roots far back in Western history.

One of the standpoints is instrumental. Among its characteristics are that humans are masters over nature, and that spontaneous technical development will make us even more skillful when it comes to controlling nature as well as controlling small-scale environmental problems. Implicitly, nature is assumed to be very tolerant. The hope is for boundless economic growth in the well-organised human society. The boundless society can be described in terms of work distribution and specialisation to make production ever more effective. The unboundedness comes from the fact that economic man has created a value system which purports to be fundamentally applicable to processes in both society and nature.

The opposite is the ecological standpoint. Here humankind and human society are regarded as an integral part of nature. Everything that we do must be subordinated to the normal functions of sensitive nature, in delicate balance with itself.

Technologies operating from the ecological standpoint do not always follow the trends in the local community. On the other hand, spokespeople for the local community pay special attention to simplicity and participation. They talk about self-sufficiency in the sense that every local society should have control over its supply of goods and services to fulfill basic needs. During the second half of the 1980s, some ecological villages were built in Scandinavia which may be said to attempt to materialise this ideal.

Between these standpoints a struggle is going on concerning the privilege of problem formulation, which can be compared with the struggle that existed between the industrial–capitalistic and the cooperative or anarchistic ideas during the late 19th century (for instance, see Hettne, 1983).

Today the economic paradigm seems to have superiority, but what will public opinion be in a decade or two? Will trade, commerce, and environmental policy build on a new dominant consensus? Where on the scale between the two repellant poles will the social and economic system be found? Will there be large shifts in public opinion? Why would such changes in preferences be exhibited at this particular moment in time?

In a recent white paper on metropolitan problems in Sweden by Metropolitan Investigation (1990a; 1990b), arguments have been put forward for denser urban regions to shorten travel times and distances, thereby reducing the burden on the regional as well as the global environment. Investigations within the European Community seem to have arrived at the same conclusion. Spokespeople for the ecological villages and representatives of the so-called permaculture school, on the other hand, have put forward alternative settlement structures which are very similar to the rural village.

Those advocating denser regions do not take into account what can be called the city's metabolism, and how that process can cooperate with nature's functions. Against dense structures stands the fact that these structures will depend increasingly on the external world. The vision of the sustainable city, which involves socially and economically novel ways of thinking, is utopian in the sense that the proposed settlement structures are basically free from today's urban reality.

Against the arguments for self-sufficient local communities it is contended that the economy in a municipality is today hooked into regional, national, and global economic processes. The environmental problems one is confronted with may emanate from sources far away, and activities in municipalities may have consequences in other communities, regions, and nations. Decisionmakers and opinion creators in the local community belong to complex structures of global loyalty, and operate in information and communication networks on higher levels of regional arenas.

3 The urban planning question in Sweden
Traditionally there are two forces involved in building the city of the industrial society and the metropolitan region. They are economic and social ambitions, and technical abilities to construct buildings and infrastructure.

Distance from the city centre is a determining factor for land values and density of land use. The overriding momentum is an economic force that springs from the marketplace function of the city. This economic truth is present in planned and market economies alike, and was a force at work in cities long before the industrial revolution. Von Thünen's economic model of land use in the isolated city was constructed in the early 1800s. Its applicability to contemporary urban problems has been convincingly shown by Alonso (1964) and a whole range of researchers working in the same model tradition.

Tension has developed between rural and urban areas. The borderline between urban and rural is given by the equity in land value from using the land for urban and rural purposes. The classical rural purpose was agricultural production. In most modern societies, the agricultural sector is not fully exposed to market competition, thus blurring the strict border-line which would arise from economic forces. Another reason for the borderline not being sharp is the dynamic character of the city, with a continuing game between landowners and real estate developers over land-value increases from urban economic activity.

The structure of the city will be difficult to change radically in the vicinity of the core, because the building capital of a city consists of a slowly changing infrastructure. With increased distance from the city centre the freedom of action increases fast. Access to open space will increase with the radius of the city. In an expanding region, economic modelling will point to the high likelihood that the city will be sprawling, containing patches or belts of rural land within the ultimate city limits. These green belts, and the limits between them and urban land, are areas of special interest for sustainability. They resemble the ecologically impor-tant shorelines where land meets water.

Figure 1 illustrates some theoretical structures for land use in an urban area surrounded by rural land. The starting point is a completely differen-tiated pattern of land-use with workplaces centrally located. The question is what pattern of development will occur if more activity is to be housed and what environmental effects will result from these patterns. The example in the figure deals with expanding workplace activity.

The urban region in figure 1 has come to the situation where no nonurban land remains within the city borders. The existing strategy to build a com-pletely separate city can no longer be used. It will not be viable to demolish building stock. There are three principal alternatives for workplace expansion. One is to increase the density in formerly residential districts by locating the workplace expansion there, either uniformly or as close as possible to the workplace district, as illustrated in figure 1(b). The second is to increase the density in the earlier workplace district [figure 1(c)]. The third is to build on nonurban land at the urban periphery [figure 1(d)]. The three alternatives will have different proximities between land uses. In the first case, the links between dwellings and workplaces will become stronger.

The density of exploitation will increase in part or all of the residential district. The second alternative will promote better contacts among workplaces at the expense of space standards. The third will promote contacts between dwellings and workplaces but will increase the distance from existing residential and workplace districts to rural land.

A real-world city does not exhibit the simple properties of figure 1. Pecularities of the landscape, local natural and man-made amenities, ownership structure, and activity pattern will influence the land use and its potential change over time. The changes will be determined by a complex web of decisions by individuals and organisations. The city needs to be sustainable in social, economic, and political terms as well as in ecological terms. One of the principal issues discussed in this paper is whether the ecologically sustainable city has a different spatial form from the economically, socially, or politically viable city. If there is a conflict in spatial terms there will also be one in the nonspatial arenas. To discern potential conflicts it is necessary to formulate objectives by which to assess goal fulfilment. It is also necessary to employ a split perspective as regards the regional resolution of the analysis.

Sustainability means that costs and benefits should be distributed over time and between individuals in such a way that everybody gets a fair share. A spatial structure of a city is not sustainable if it changes radically

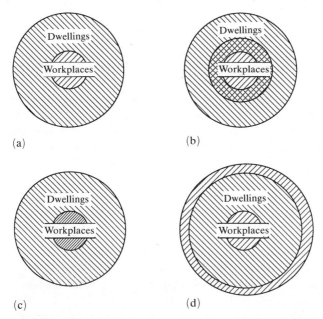

Figure 1. Four patterns of land use in a dynamic circular city: (a) completely differentiated starting point, (b) new workplaces among dwellings, (c) new workplaces among workplaces, (d) new workplaces on nonurban land.

over the long term. It is stated in environmental literature that connectness among green areas in a city is one of the intermediary goals for ecological sustainability. There are at least two reasons for this. One is that the functioning of the ecosystems is improved if there are connected areas of nonurban land. Another reason is that the chance that nonurban land becomes urban increases quickly if it is interspersed with settlements or cut off from the rural hinterland surrounding the city. Thus, in figure 1 there would be a possibility of keeping land vacant within the city limits during the dynamic development phase. Such land would run a higher risk of being brought into urban use in the long run than land at the urban fringe.

We here provide an example of ecological-planning considerations of the type outlined above by referring to the expanding region of Stockholm. The reasoning is taken from thoughts that have emerged out of today's debate on Greater Stockholm and its extension to the west into the northern and southern shores of Sweden's third largest lake, Mälaren. We focus on rules of new development outside or close to the Stockholm region within the larger geographical and ecological region called Mälardalen. The planning issues differ with the spatial level. The relevant levels are defined by labour and housing market conditions in commuting regions and by administrative boundaries. We distinguish here mainly between the local and the regional level.

A primary planning problem at the metropolitan or regional level in a postindustrial society is how to allocate new built-up areas so that contacts between different areas of economic and social interest are supported, as well as to guarantee the functioning of ecological systems to support life in the city. A main claim in the theory of island biogeography, for the shaping of biologically vital areas, tells us that green areas should be connected into as large and unbroken areas as possible.

The spatial growth of metropolitan regions such as Stockholm, with its relatively strong public planning component, has been strongly determined by transport systems. The railways have promoted a spatial regime with a finger form, where the fingers consist of residential neighbourhoods and workplace districts. The road network has developed in a primarily radial fashion mimicking the rail and subway networks. The wedges of green areas which have thus arisen satisfy the claims of island biogeography well. These areas are now threatened by economic interests, as well as modern life-styles calling for more freedom for dispersed travelling and more complex city structures, with the spatial shape turning into more of a road grid with many nodes. New transport routes and new development areas are thus often suggested in the form of linking structures between the fingers. The current planning activity aims to extend the finger structure to the hinterland around Lake Mälaren which contains several medium-sized industrial, commercial, and university cities.

If expansion has to be accommodated within the borders of the existing metropolitan region, the crucial locations are to be found where the possibilities for contacts are the greatest, and, at the same time, where the ecosystems are most resilient. Metropolitan planning authorities may also use green arguments to conclude that the urban area must not become more densely built. In that case the growth must be located in pockets of green space or deteriorated urban milieus at the smallest possible distance from the downtown border, if the choice is made to fill up green space within city borders. Other interesting locations are at points of high accessibility at the urban–rural fringe, or among the other cities at commuting distance.

Although the arguments are not mainly ecological these three solutions (to build in between existing fingers, to expand the existing city into current suburban areas, and to organise a stronger connection between towns and cities in the hinterland region) are all being discussed in Stockholm today.

At the local level in a city like Stockholm, there is an ongoing process of rejuvenation and transformation. And the same interests as at the regional level are at work preparing the city for its postindustrial life. From the ecological point of view, the ambition should be to have a good mix of green and built-up areas, to promote recreation and local loops of material and water between nature and society. It may also be important to promote local contacts by mixing urban functions in the already built-up areas. Figure 2 gives an example from the southern border of the current downtown area.

The district illustrated here, with housing areas and industries originally constructed around 1940, is now being rejuvenated. Old industries are closed down and replaced by housing at the waterfront which gives the area its local characteristics. A new transport corridor will link traffic southbound to the west with traffic moving to the east of the area.

Although green arguments are involved in the planning process, we still lack strong and politically approved green strategies of the kind mentioned above. A green strategy for the city centre might, for example, involve a highest permitted density as well as maximum proportion of land zoned urban within a city district. Special ecological attention should also be paid to the hydrology of the Stockholm area with its strategic location at the mouth of a very large inland lake. There must be the option of closing down obsolete industrial or housing areas permanently if their land is of strategic interest for the green infrastructure in the region.

How the built environment will be structured in a region like Mälardalen during the next twenty years will depend to a large extent on regional politics, and how hopes for an international competitive region become realised through in-migration and the fulfilment of prosperity potentials. The required volume of building stock is very difficult to forecast at this stage. The issue of how development on this level is best adapted to the environment, however, is better answered by an analysis of linkages between land use and economic function as a whole than by classical urban design (see also Zuchetto and Jansson, 1985).

The regional level basically means the labour-market area around Stockholm. The decentralisation of workplaces from the core of the Stockholm region to suburban centres has directly increased the geographical extension of the labour-market region. A potential for new residential settlements has been created. At this level the issues are: how such areas should be grouped relative to one another and relative to the landscape; the optimal size of neighbourhoods; access to unexploited areas; and limits to the total environmental burden on the region. As working life develops and transport speed increases, the boundaries between established labour-market regions currently not connected to one another will also become more and more diffuse. Plans are traditionally made according to a growth forecast within a labour market. The extension of the region may depend more on the travel time to work than on the geographical distances involved. A further extension of the region will come from the tendency towards more flexible working hours, implying that the

Figure 2. Potential local land-use conflicts at the southern fringe of the Stockholm downtown area.

standard assumption of everybody making one work trip per day is no longer valid.

In the extended Stockholm area the issues are whether gaps in the region's central and semicentral areas should be filled in, whether new areas should be planned near existing areas at the urban fringe, or whether exploitation should leapfrog to the closest established medium-sized cities. Another issue is whether to build along new ring-road highways or to create new building capital together with radial network expansion. A further policy would be to establish satellites on the other side of a green belt, or alternatively to support growth centres within adjacent existing labour-market areas.

The local level in Sweden is the municipality, which is the administrative entity responsible for comprehensive and detailed land-use planning. The Building and Planning Act gives full responsibility for land-use planning to the municipalities. On this level the issues are urban density, the interaction between land use and transport, the balance between green and exploited areas, and the promotion of public participation in planning.

At the local level, the space for future activities is the central issue. The quantity of new dwellings, for example, is decided in negotiations with other muncipalities in the labour-market area. Structurally it is a matter of building along the lines of existing housing areas, replacing them completely, or building in between the current districts. At the level of the district, questions of the following type are to be answered. Which mix of denseness and sparseness, separation and integration, high-rise and low-rise, grouped and detached buildings should be selected? How high can the exploitation rate of the land become? What is economic in transportation and district heating? What is efficient for solar heating? What are the costs of adapting the built environment to recycling? A prerequisite is that there is a pressure for development, creating an as yet unformed building context to work with. Also, we suppose that the conditions for building will allow a sustained development with long-term societal and economic considerations at work.

Local and regional levels are both of interest in this study. The regional structure will influence the extent, type, and length of work travel, but also the need for goods transportation, including the handling of products that can be manufactured within the region instead of being imported. How should cities be built that are self-sufficient at least in employment, daily contact patterns, and basic needs fulfillment, but that still may have an intensive exchange of information with other societies at the national or international level? Densities that prove sustainable at the local level will indirectly influence the extension of the region and thereby affect travel to work. Density and structure at the local level will also influence the need to carry supplies to the local community and the disposal of waste products.

4 The environmental aspects systematised

Urban structure planning, including the choice of density of urban development, from an environmental perspective may be determined by the following concerns (see also Orrskog 1989): the carrying capacity of the land, the potential arising from the landscape of the site, the recycling adaptivity and resilience in urban supply systems. These concerns are technical. To make man-made systems sustainable we must also consider a host of democratic and humanistic demands on understanding, cooperation, and participation. Although important, these issues are not at the centre of interest in this study.

The carrying capacity of the land determines the ultimate degree of development. The creative potential that emanates from the landscape and natural conditions determines the specific location and direction of the development. Natural and landscape determinants are water and its motion (hydrology), rock and soil composition (geology), topography and climatic conditions (meteorology), and vegetation and biotope structure (ecology), including the borders between different biotopes.

The water flow through the landscape, and the character and composition of the ground and the soil should have a major influence on the choice of areas for development and on the structure of the environment to be built. Inflow and outflow areas in the landscape could guide us to permitted development. Water-system borders could also serve as district borders, and activities along a water system could be reciprocally arranged depending on the direction of the stream.

The borderline between forest and agricultural land, or between land and water, is often biologically vital and valuable. The desire to build and dwell on shores and coastlines should therefore be restricted if sustainability is to be promoted. Also, waterway transportation systems, which are good from an energy standpoint, should be carefully planned, so as not to disturb breeding places for fish, and other vital water-based activities. The city should be organised so that fresh air, fresh water, and active biotopes may pass through the city to regenerate it. Green areas in the city or its surroundings must be large enough that life can regenerate itself and nature can repair damage.

Demands on efficiency, recycling adaptivity, and resilience in the supply systems of urban areas have an impact on the supply of district heat and fresh water, sewage collection, waste disposal, transportation, and communication. It is all about metabolism. The claim of green planning is that the metabolism of the city should be adapted to that of nature's own systems.

Energy sources should as far as possible be renewable and local. Other energy sources must be treated as scarce resources. The stream of nutrition to and from urban areas should fit into recycling processes. Other material should as far as possible be recycled. Water supply and sewage should follow the pattern of watersheds in the landscape.

Demand for energy conservation also implies claims on how the city and region are arranged for efficiency in transportation, and how houses are adapted to the landscape and climatic conditions in order to reduce heating needs and facilitate district heating. District heating systems are also preferable to minimise the air pollution from energy transformation. Relying on such local renewable energy sources as sun, wind, and water will imply demands on minimum density and maximum distances to the source of energy. An energy-conservation strategy should also include the mingling of types of activities, especially work and housing districts.

The demand to recycle flows of nutrients determines the structure of the city and will have an influence on its density. Sludge and compost material from houses and gardens can be taken care of centrally in the city or at a local level, and can be used in agriculture and gardens or even for energy production. Demands on material management will include attempts to economise on and sort garbage, especially to sort out toxic substances for possible recycling.

Demands on resilience and flexibility imply that different technical systems should be connected, which requires proximity and density. Centrally arranged systems should be able to function locally as closed loops. This places demands on the grouping of buildings. There should be space for alternative future technologies as well, implying a certain dispersal in housing, and segments of unexploited areas in the city.

Planning both at regional and local level will be influenced by recycling, with an emphasis on local level solutions, and on regional level solutions when it comes to energy and basic needs. Energy-saving policies will influence both regional and local structures.

5 Principles for building sustainable urban structures

At a regional level the planning concern is with quantities of people and their activities, over the different types of landscape and milieus that they make use of, and the balance between exploited and unexploited areas.

Locally, land-use planning may be conceived as basically a matter of density and structure. Two notions of density are of interest. The first is in essence the number of inhabitants and activities per square metre. The second boils down to the proportion of an area that is exploited. The first notion provides information on how loaded the landscape is with human activities, to be compared with the carrying capacity of nature. The second notion provides information on how much green area there is for nature's functions, for leisure, or for cultivation. With a high degree of exploitation within a given area it is important that free space is not reduced too much. It is preferable to have some high-rise buildings rather than a uniform carpet of detached houses.

The structure variable is more difficult to define. The highest number of buildings in a city are dwellings; therefore the design of dwelling areas is especially important. Travel within a region demands consideration of how different kinds of activities should be located relative to each other. Extensive travel means that large amounts of land need to be placed under hard cover. We live in a more and more specialised goods-transporting and people-transporting society, and this has a direct impact on urban and regional structures. Cities are supplied with basic commodities through huge centralised trade and transport systems.

With increasing living standards, cheaper energy, and developments in transport technology, housing has decentralised successively in European urban areas. Europe exurbanised from the 1970s onwards. Following rapid increases in energy prices from the mid 1980s, however, it seems that development has again turned towards an increased number of more densely populated areas being added at the urban fringe. In Sweden this tendency has often been associated with the establishment of remote-heat systems.

The urban area has during the 20th century grown faster than the number of urban inhabitants, that is, cities have become more sprawling. On the other hand, there are statistics indicating that housing areas are built with increased density. Density in the city is influenced only partly by the conditions in housing areas. Some 37% of the urban area is land for houses, 14% is taken up by other types of buildings, 12% is traffic and transportation areas, and 37% is undeveloped land such as sports grounds, agricultural plots, forests, etc. Local transport areas which are included in residential districts generally take up 40%–50% of that total.

At the district level, the necessary density to have customers living within walking distance from a shop, will decrease quickly when the distance is increased only slightly. Walking distances to shops and public transport facilities, which have been common parameters in local land-use planning, will thus not necessarily result in a need to specify density exactly.

Rådberg (1988) distinguished between three doctrines in town planning during the 20th century: regularism in dense and high-rise houses; garden cities in low-rise and green city areas; and functionalism in open and dense city areas. The first and the third doctrines emanate from the same idea of building high to keep some local land unexploited. Functionalism was basically launched for economic reasons. The task was to solve problems of hygiene and traffic. The solution was high-rise apartment buildings in parks.

Because of energy and environmental crises during the last decade, a number of studies have been published containing energy-motivated guidelines on city density. Owens (1989) gives an account of modelling efforts concerning energy conservation and urban structure. She distinguishes between three levels—regional, urban, and local—and sketches physical structures with different energy-density structures. Rickaby and de la Barra (1989) model an urban system at regional to local levels on the basis of a set of background conditions. Energy efficiency in urban structures should be met within given transport technology, aiming at maximum accessibility to work and service. Modelling starts from an archetypal configuration of towns and villages based on spatial patterns in eastern England. Through plausible investments in infrastructure and service provision the archetype is modified, implying that the settlement pattern is influenced. Among the prerequisites are upgrading of existing housing, as well as migration patterns where the migrants come mainly from the suburbs.

After some numerical calculations Rickaby and de la Barra (1989) conclude that the most energy-effective structure is a massive concentration in the city core. Second comes building in existing villages near to the city. If good and cheap housing is given higher priority and traffic congestion can be avoided, this second-best energy solution becomes the best one overall. City growth in a linear mode is not very efficient unless public transport clearly surpasses motorism. They conclude that Ebenezer Howard came to the same ideal distribution of people in the city in 1898.

Some of the rules for energy conservation, especially regarding travel, undoubtedly point towards high density in urban areas. Other energy rules on how to utilize renewable fuels, for example with biomass products for heating, will generally lead to more spacious housing districts. This spaciousness applies mainly at the regional level. A tentative conclusion is that the relatively dense city should be completed in the periphery until it reaches a maximum size. Further expansion should be located in places in the surrounding hinterland.

When it comes to conservation of energy for transport it is important to transfer as much as possible from individual to collective travelling. Because working life and daily life are presently becoming more diversified in space and time, tram traffic will not function very well. Nevertheless, the assumption here is that transportation is to a high degree collective and by rail or by water.

Rules for recycling flows of material and energy between nature and society mean that the urban city should be made less complex and intertwined. Green spaces are needed to let in fresh air and connect nature to the urban core. This also makes us all aware that there is a nature on which we depend. Yet another reason to leave some green areas is to have space to utilize composted material locally. Areas should be set aside in the immediate outskirts of the city for handling waste products and for production of food nearby. These spaces can be coordinated with the green belt that is needed for the regeneration of biotopes. Water flows also demand space.

Thus the picture of the energy-conserving city is one of dispersed concentration. It is provided with green inputs locally. It is completed by transport networks to the next city. Local communities should be built along public traffic routes and be sufficiently large for district heating to be competitive. The settlements should be placed sufficiently far from each other to keep up the productivity of the land in between but not further away from each other than daily commuting by public transport would allow. Demands for participation, and shared responsibility, require that the city be composed of local neighbourhoods. Demands for self-reliance by supplying commodities to fulfil basic survival needs within the region completes the regional level. This leads to further arguments for a modestly dense region.

Cities are often located on lakes and seas because water maintained life and facilitated transport prior to the petroleum-based society. In an environmentally healthy society, it is desirable that growth in such regions is located so that transportation on water can be reestablished. A sparsely populated region means massive interregional transportation, but less intraregional transport work. For a densely populated region the opposite is true.

The fact that we keep radial tracks as the main transport system may be the explanation for the similarity between the well-known city of today and our picture of the sustainable city. The expansion in the 1940s to 1960s was arranged in neighbourhood units with green areas in between, moti-vated by social and hygienic reasons. This may well be only another way to express the same kind of demands that are presented in this paper on free space for nature and people in the city. The uncertain element is whether development in the information society towards increased mobil-ity, new residential preferences, and social patterns of interaction will give rise to totally different considerations. Is there convincing cause to reconsider our reasoning?

6 Prospects of planning for sustainability
Conflicts exist between different parts of the regulatory framework for planning under the heading of sustainability. The rules for energy conser-vation have built-in conflicts, as was shown above. Other conflicts may arise: for example, between demands on efficient centralised supply systems, and small more intelligible and resilient decentralised systems. The general rules can be followed only to a certain degree. The existing city with its building stock and topography is a major influence. There is a work of adaptive design to be done, whereby potential conflicts can be resolved. This applies to the local as well as the regional level. Such work puts high demands both on knowledge of environmental issues, on creativ-ity, and on empathy for local cultural conditions.

The scope of possible solutions to the design of a sustainable city and urban region will be determined by a range of factors. What is it possible to achieve? What point on the reality – utopia line should be chosen? Different demands within the concept of sustainability may be given different weights by scientists and planners. It may be that sustainability in a society cannot be judged from a distant position. It is not the physical shape of the city and its built-up areas which is important. It is how the urban society is organised and managed that counts most.

In a project carried out in the municipality of Lerum in western Sweden, consultant architects had already introduced methods for ecological consideration in comprehensive planning at the end of the 1970s. But their work did not find much response in the municipality of Lerum. Why? In their final report they pointed to a number of reasons for the decisionmakers not adopting the ecological approach. One was that modern society develops through its sectors rather than as a local whole. Another was that planners prefer to go deep into norms and quantities rather than into problem analysis. The state of the art of planning was neither focused nor inventive enough. A third reason was that attention paid to nature is mostly in the form of preservation instead of adaptation between society and nature. What, then, are the prospects?

The fact that housing is not adapted to nature in situ depends to a great extent on sheer lack of knowledge. Better knowledge about, for example, hydrological circumstances and their implications will probably in itself lead to better adaptation. Conflicts may, however, arise between demands on the adaptivity to nature and the built environment in existence. What is the overriding factor?

An economy of the network type and its spatial consequences, that among other things will mean that new satellite cities may be formed, could provide better adaptivity to nature's claims. As an example, new thinking in the handling of garbage may be a milestone. The incentive originated from the conflict between those who manage waste products, who saw their stations filled to the brim, and those people who did not allow new refuse stations near their residential districts. Better resource efficiency and recycling techniques will also come up within other areas, if only the right market and political signals come. And the signals will come. A market for new sanitation techniques will be developed, with stimuli coming, inter alia, from developments in Eastern Europe. Higher energy prices are predicted, which together with international conventions for the reduction of greenhouse gases, will lead to the development of new vehicles and heating systems.

Prospects are less bright, though, for nearby production of food supplies and for other basic needs. Also, the substitution away from cars and airplanes to trams, trains, and boats will take place only after crises and commotion, because high economic interests are at stake for the individual, for firms, and for society as a whole.

Finally, there is uncertainty as to what extent the present sectoral handling of the supply of technical infrastructure will be replaced by more resilient and pluralistic systems. Vulnerability of specialised, large-scale systems has so far been judged less significant than their reliability and efficiency.

The neighbourhood unit, the postwar model for organising housing districts, is a subsystem that functions well. It is to some extent possible to influence it locally. A modest progress in social ambitions to maintain this form of housing, in the face of an increasing market orientation in housing, probably means that the neighbourhood idea will not survive. This fact, together with a tendency towards dissolving territorial integration in general, bring us to the most serious conflict between current urban development tendencies and ecological norms.

References
Alonso W, 1964 *Location and Land Use* (Harvard University Press, Cambridge, MA)
Hettne B, 1983, "Main stream and counterpoint in western development debate", background report to The Commission on Natural Resources and Environment, Departmentens reprocentral, Stockholm
Metropolitan Investigation, 1990a, "Urban challenges", report to the Commission on Metropolitan Problems, SOU 1990:33, Allmänna Förlaget, Stockholm
Metropolitan Investigation, 1990b, "Metropolitan life: rich possibilities—hard conditions", SOU 1990:36, Allmänna Förlaget, Stockholm (in Swedish)
Orrskog L, 1989, "The municipality and natural resources: about knowledge creation and planning in a new policy area", RR TRITA RP-89/1003, Department of Regional Planning, Royal Institute of Technology, Stockholm (in Swedish)
Owens S, 1989, "Models and urban energy policy: a review and critique", in *Spatial Energy Analysis* Eds L Lundqvist, L G Mattsson, E A Eriksson (Avebury, Aldershot, Hants) pp 227 – 244
Rådberg J, 1988, "Doctrine and density in Swedish town planning 1875 – 1975", RR R11:1988, Swedish Council for Building Research, Stockholm (in Swedish)
Rickaby P, de la Barra T, 1989, "A theoretical comparison of strategic spatial options for city and regional development, using the TRANUS model", in *Spatial Energy Analysis* Eds L Lundqvist, L G Mattsson, E A Eriksson (Avebury, Aldershot, Hants) pp 315 – 334
Wiman B, 1988, "Maintaining natural resources", Institute for Future Studies, Stockholm (in Swedish)
Zucchetto J, Jansson A M, 1985 *Resources and Society: A Systems Ecology Study of the Island of Gotland, Sweden* (Springer, New York)

Growth Regions and the Future of Dutch Planning Doctrine

A van der Valk, A Faludi
University of Amsterdam

1 Introduction

In Europe much attention has been given recently to the idea of the 'compact city' (Breheny, this volume; CEC, 1990). The Netherlands is at the forefront of the movement and amongst the initiators of this idea. What is striking in the various pleas for the compact-city idea is the, mostly implicit, assumption that concentrating urban development in itself contributes to improving the state of the environment. It is only recently that this assumption has been questioned in the Netherlands. Elsewhere, particularly in the English-speaking countries, where the garden-city idea is more deeply rooted, this criticism could be heard earlier.

In this paper we argue for keeping open the option of a more suburban form of development. We do so with a view to growing uncertainty as to the feasibility of future development in historic towns conforming to minimum standards with respect to air and water quality, subsoil conditions, energy savings, and the use of local resources. For the more suburban form of development we have introduced the term 'growth region'. The notion fits well with the Dutch postwar planning tradition. For planning it offers the opportunity of forging an alliance with the strong environmental lobby existing both within and outside the government apparatus. Now that, after more than one hundred years, the marriage of convenience between planning and housing policy seems to be coming to an end, through the transfer of central government housing funds and powers of control to the provinces, municipalities, and semiprivate and even private institutions, there is a crying need for such a new alliance.

2 Dutch planning doctrine and the 'Fourth Report'

With the Fourth National Physical Planning Report under discussion, planning is a controversial issue in the Netherlands. Accompanied as it is by surveys and advisory documents, this report is a new milestone in the development of national planning.

Dutch national planning is distinguished by having a clear doctrine. By planning doctrine we mean a set of principles guiding planners and politicians 'in the field' (Alexander and Faludi, 1990; Faludi, 1989a; 1991a). Doctrine comprises notions relating to: (a) spatial arrangements within an area of jurisdiction; (b) the development of that area; and (c) the way both are to be handled. For a doctrine to be fully developed, views about spatial arrangements and development need to be integrated into an overall principle of spatial organisation for the plan area. This principle relates to the overall arrangement of land uses. It incorporates planning concepts such as 'overspill' or 'balanced growth' as building blocks. The principle of spatial organisation and the planning concepts must be compatible with the planning principles governing the way spatial arrangements and development are to be handled.

Underlying Dutch planning doctrine is a philosophy of 'rule and order' (Faludi, 1991b). The new perspective for national planning which we suggest in this paper is nothing but an extension of this philosophy. Like 'growth control' in the USA (Chinitz, 1990), Dutch doctrine takes shape through influencing the location, intensity, and timing of development. Authorities in the Netherlands are more involved in growth control than is the case in the United States. Ever since the 1950s, all three levels of government have shared responsibility for such control. The development of growth control has gone through three stages:

(1) Until the middle of the 20th century, the aim had been concentric growth in and around towns and cities so as to preserve open space and to minimise the costs of serviced land.

(2) The decades which followed saw 'rule and order' crystallise in the oxymoronic concept of concentrated deconcentration. This denotes controlled dispersal; allowing for suburban development, but only in designated growth centres.

(3) Since the mid-1980s, controlled dispersal has been abandoned in favour of a policy of concentrating development yet again in major urban centres. This is the current compact-city policy.

The Dutch planning community is small, and Dutch political culture conducive to consensus building (van der Heiden et al, 1991). An agreed doctrine is a strategic planning asset. However, consensus courts the danger of changes in the knowledge base of the doctrine and/or values going unnoticed. The argument of this paper is that the prevailing emphasis on the 'compact city': (a) fails to take account of uncertainty as regards population growth and dispersal and (b) is out of step with the emergent form of urban civilisation which Fishman (1991) signals. He refers to 'growth corridors', stretching from 80 to 160 km, which characterise present urbanisation in the United States and may be relevant for the future of Europe.

Nevertheless, the Fourth Report endorses the 'compact city'. The policy is the joint product of central government and the large cities. In the 1980s, the cities suffered the effects of the previous policy (which they themselves had pursued vigorously) of 'concentrated deconcentration'. They suffered a decline in population, public services and employment, and their income (primarily dependent on central government funding, based mainly on the number of inhabitants) was being eroded.

The idea was to abate income erosion by allocating more housing to the cities, if necessary at the expense of open space. So initially the compact-city policy was concerned mainly with housing. However, it soon got caught up in another, more fundamental change which entailed much more emphasis on the economy (van der Knaap and van der Laan, 1991, pages 9–12). This is not surprising. Unemployment rates in centres like Amsterdam and Rotterdam are more than 20%, and the Dutch economy faces the challenge of having to compete in an integrated Europe. Even though densely populated, the Western Netherlands are still the engine of the Dutch economy. This 'Randstad', or rim city, comprises numerous towns and cities, including Amsterdam, Rotterdam, the Hague and Utrecht, arrayed around an open area called the 'Green Heart' (van der Valk, 1991; van der Wusten and Faludi, 1992). Emphasis on the Randstad complements the compact-city policy, which now focuses not only on housing, but on office development, infrastructure, and the like. The emphasis in housing policy has shifted from subsidised to more expensive forms of housing, catering for the new urbanites whom planners want to attract back to the cities.

So the compact-city policy constantly evolves. So does the Fourth Report (MVROM, 1988). The 1988 draft bears the stamp of the centre-right government then in power. It gives priority to economic recovery. Public–private partnerships played a pivotal role in housing, infrastructure, and the restructuring of inner cities. The present centre-left government has brought out a revised Fourth Report 'Extra' (MVROM, 1991). The theme is 'sustainable development'. Economic goals must be squared with environmental concerns. A capital programme specifies major investment in housing in and around the big cities. So there is renewed commitment to planning goals. In the same spirit, the government seeks to counteract provincial and municipal plans that encroach upon the Green Heart and/or increase mobility.

Laudable though it is, this policy (and here we return to the theme of consensus around established doctrine) has its risks. Attention focuses exclusively on the compact cities. Rural communities and the previous growth centres alike are left in limbo. Open space in the cities is being taken up and environmental quality suffers. Rising real estate prices deepen social segregation. To make things worse, it is questionable whether population decline in the cities can be halted. Priemus (1991) shows that, as a proportion of existing stock, home construction in these cities has reached the national average only once, in 1984, and has fallen behind ever since. The most telling indicator of uncertainty is the erratic fashion in which forecasts of housing need in the Randstad fluctuate.

In 1988, housing need between 1990 and 2015 was estimated to amount to one million new houses, a figure much higher than everybody had thought. A million new houses in the Randstad caught everybody's imagination. Planners were particularly pleased. This appeared to signal the demise of the 'end of growth' philosophy. The tasks ahead of managing more urban growth seemed massive.

However, the Fourth Report Extra is based on a different assumption: 485000 new homes needed between 1995 and 2015. Note that the two figures are not compatible. Within a matter of only a few years, expectations have been lowered considerably. Recent provincial figures seem to indicate that this latest national forecast is too low. Some analysts think that the government estimates reflect wishful thinking. Environmental considerations may have played their part in bringing them about. What matters here is the indifference which planners show to uncertainty. The report contains not a shred of evidence of scepticism as regards goals, concepts, and the proposed instruments of policy. The compact city is the one and only growth-management strategy.

However, there are several factors that cast doubt on the compact-city policy. To judge from recent experiences it will be difficult to find land for half a million homes in the existing cities, and virtually impossible for a full million. Proposed sites sometimes turn out to require massive clean-ups. There are conflicts over open space, allotments, and playing fields, and there is growing resistance against proposed infrastructure. The authorities in the four big cities themselves seem convinced that it is impossible to find enough land for housing within the city limits. So present national urbanisation policy carries within it an incalculable risk.

Our educated guess is that the future will reveal yet more problems besetting the compact city. Inevitably, research flows from policy, instead of the other way round. This draws attention to another weak spot which we have already hinted at. Much energy has gone into generating consensus about the compact city. Substantial commitments have been entered into as regards, for example, subsidies for housing, infrastructure, and cleanup operations. This makes it harder to conceive of alternatives. In an effort to engender necessary discussion, we propose an alternative concept of 'growth regions'.

The logic behind the growth region is a simple extension of that under-lying 'concentrated deconcentration'. Thus, growth regions should deflect pressure away both from the cities and from major open space in need of preservation. It is a concept with both spatial-environmental and admin-istrative implications. Before going into more detail, we discuss our main source of inspiration; the growth-centre policy (Faludi and van der Valk, 1991). Lessons from the past can help us face similar challenges in the future. That future will see the postwar Dutch societal project of remedy-ing the postwar housing shortage replaced by a new one of revitalising the economy whilst at the same time upholding the ideal of sustainable devel-opment. Our contention is that growth control in the sense in which we use the term here has a direct bearing on this.

3 Lessons from the past

The growth-centre policy is a rare case of successful large-scale planning. More than half a million people found new homes in the Dutch growth centres between 1970 and 1990 (see figure 1). These homes now account for over 5% of the Dutch housing stock. As an achievement this more than equals the British new-towns policy. It can also serve as an example for the societal project of the future, the more so as some of the factors responsible for suburban sprawl are gaining new prominence.

Traditionally, the Western Netherlands is perceived by planning professionals as congested and overcrowded (Postuma, 1991; van der Valk, 1991; Zonneveld, 1989). In 1958 the Working Commission for the Western Netherlands (comparable in importance to the Barlow Commission in Britain) recommended that congestion should be remedied by designating overspill centres. These could be new towns or existing towns ten to twenty miles away from the donor cities. The First Physical Planning Report (Ministerie van Volkshuisvesting en Wederopbouw, 1960) endorsed this policy. However, the mere designation of localities as overspill centres was to no avail. To make things worse, in the decade that followed, estimates of need were revised upward. In this situation, national planners put too much faith in instruments of control. These instruments failed to stem the tide of suburban sprawl in the Green Heart and on the outskirts of the Randstad.

Glasbergen and Simonis (1979) have analysed the failure to stem suburban sprawl. During postwar reconstruction, the housing shortage was public enemy number one. Channeling growth away from suburban communities to designated overspill centres was one thing, implementing this policy without endangering housing production was quite another. In the 1960s planning was simply subordinate to housing. The overspill centres were not yet ready for an annual production of hundreds, and in some cases thousands, of homes. Some had problems with neighbouring municipalities. In most, political support for growth was weak. The authorities also lacked planning expertise. In the meantime car-owning

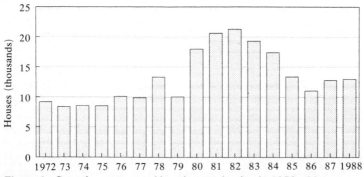

Figure 1. Growth centres, total housing production in 1972–88.

families showed a profound predilection for suburban homes with gardens. Many rural communities went out to attract them. The reason was twofold. First, it helped them to bring their facilities in line with contemporary requirements. Second, they could thereby combine subsidised housing for people on their housing list with more expensive development for suburbanites. Such mixing of various forms of development is standard in the Netherlands.

Mixing makes it possible to cross-subsidise public housing and thereby meet government cost-ceilings. By the time the growth centres were ready to meet the challenge, around 1970, developers were strongly committed within the smaller communities. Given these circumstances, the accomplishments of the growth centres are very impressive.

The foundations for this success were laid in the early 1970s by a number of working parties involving representatives of various departments and levels of government. They devised ways and means to cut through the red tape. Arrangements were made for a package of financial instruments. This package contained: a 100% subsidy on main infrastructure which otherwise would have to be paid for out of the proceeds of the sale of land to developers; additional grants over and above the usual amount allowed for housing and other facilities; and an extra increment added to the allocation to growth centres from the Municipal Fund, the main source of local finance.

There were flanking strategies by the provinces exercising planning control. Not the least important was the appointment of growth-minded burgomasters in the growth centres. However, the crucial factor was the flow of funds. After 1972, housing and planning thus contracted a marriage of convenience.

However, this marriage shows signs of breaking up. Planners might look for other partners, especially in the environmental sector. The argument is over money. In the early 1980s some 90% of all new housing was subsidised in the Netherlands, so an alliance with housing made sense. However, soon the proportion of subsidised housing will fall below 50%. Even more important, remaining government funds are increasingly handled by the provinces and the municipalities. The decline of funds for housing is equalled by a rise of funds for the environment. This is no coincidence. Housing and environmental policy are part of one and the same department (which also happens to be responsible for planning). Planning itself has virtually no funds. By carefully choosing its allies, it can profit from the change of priorities.

Now, the breakup of the marriage between housing and planning would cast a shadow on the compact-city policy. Already, cuts in housing have forced the four big cities to reduce their urban renewal programmes. The distributional effects of housing shortages in the Western Netherlands, with concomitant increases in property values making housing prohibitively expensive for starters, may give rise to political problems. On the other

hand, it seems just a matter of time before rural municipalities in the
Green Heart and on the outskirts of the Randstad start once again attracting suburbanites. (Figures indicate that this may already have started.) To
stem the tide, a concerted effort similar to the growth-centre policy may
be needed. Suburban sprawl would be contrary to the present policy of
achieving sustainable development. Growth regions should pave the way
for a new era of systematic urbanisation in the pursuit of this goal.

4 Growth regions

With notable exceptions, in 1990 most of the growth centres were
deprived of extra assistance. For some of them this spells nothing less
than impoverishment. In the Netherlands local authority deficits lead to
strict financial control by the Ministry for the Interior, enforced savings,
cuts in services combined with tax increases to the maximum allowed
under the law. Responding to the untimely demise of the growth-centre
policy, we have introduced the concept of growth regions (Faludi and
van der Valk, 1990). A growth region comprises a relatively large area,
usually (but not necessarily) spanning several municipalities. It is designated by central government and/or the respective province for intensive
urban growth. Like the growth centres before, because of its special
status, a growth region can count on extra financial resources.

Drawing inspiration from the British new town development corporations (but also from the special agencies set up for developing the polders
and implementing the Delta Plan in the Netherlands) we propose for such
a growth region a new type of authority endowed with special powers in
the fields of planning, environmental protection, transport, economic
development, land acquisition and landscaping. Although the size of
growth regions may vary, the production of 50 000 dwellings over a period
of twenty-five years seems a realistic target. This number may be much
higher (ranging up to 100 000 or even 200 000) if established growth
centres are included in future growth regions. So-called key cities, designated as economic growth poles in the Fourth Report are, however,
excluded. The thirteen key cities are the spearheads of the compact-city
policy. Thus the growth regions are a supplement to, and not a replacement for, existing policies.

A growth region must be large enough to comprise both existing and
new settlements. The *villes nouvelles* of Cergy-Pontoise, Melun-Sénart, and
St Quentin-en-Yvelines in the Paris region offer models. The *syndicats
d'agglomération nouvelle* (council) and the *établissements publics d'aména-
gement* (planning service) are also worth studying.

If planning, transport, and housing are not sufficient justification for
new administrative bodies, then the need for comprehensive environmental
planning will have to do the trick. Growth regions can and must play an
important role in the implementation of the ambitious strategies of the
National Environmental Policy Plan, the Second Structure Scheme for

Traffic and Transport, and the Nature Policy Plan. In the next section we elaborate upon this. Suffice it to say that growth regions should be as self-contained as possible, including sewage works and other waste disposal, recycling plants, and the like. This should be a top priority in planning. A related area for concern is the 'ecological infrastructure'. Growth regions provide a chance of delivering the ideal of urban life close to nature, but in a way that does justice to wider ecological concerns.

The area called Het Gooi near Amsterdam may serve to illustrate what a growth region may look like twenty-five years from now. This area of about one hundred square miles comprises three medium-sized and a few smaller towns. All of these are compact, although not unduly so. They are separated by forests, heath land, and extensively used agricultural land, all carefully landscaped. Needless to say this is an attractive area for the well-to-do and high-tech enterprises alike.

Another example is the new town of Almere in the Flevo-polder. It was designed in the 1970s and developed in the 1980s and 1990s. The original master plan enunciated an open spatial organisation principle. It foresaw seven settlements and various commercial areas interspersed with open space, lakes, and canals. The alignment of the railway and the location of the settlements have made it possible to slow down or increase, as the case may be, the pace of development over a period of twenty-five years. Within limits the layout can also be changed without violating the overall concept. Such flexibility is a guarantee of continuity in planning; political, financial, and demographic uncertainties notwithstanding.

The example which has inspired us most to think along these lines has never gone beyond the provincial drawing board. As a proposal it has evoked considerable discussion, both in the region concerned, as well as within the planning community. What we refer to is a plan by the province of South Holland. Recently, this province has published a comprehensive proposal for a polynuclear 'Park City' in the more or less undeveloped area between The Hague, Zoetermeer, and Rotterdam (see figure 2, over). The proposal is to build at least 50 000 new dwellings and to create 20 000 new jobs there. This embodies many of the characteristics of our notion of a growth region such as: a regional perspective, open spatial organisation, a finely tuned multifunctional layout, optimal use of natural amenities, an ecological infrastructure, space for purification and recycling plants, employment close to housing areas, and priority for public transport.

The striking thing about this is that the 'Park City' does not include the existing buoyant growth centre of Zoetermeer. Situated to the north of the plan area, Zoetermeer would seem a natural coalition partner for the municipalities designed to participate in this scheme. However, this is only one of many administrative and financial questions still awaiting an adequate answer. Precisely these questions form a bottleneck in the negotiations between central government, the province, and the munici-palities. So the 1991 version of the Fourth Report does not endorse the

'Park City'. At best, it leaves the option open. Unfortunately, recent decisions about new housing locations north of Rotterdam seem more in line with the compact city than with the proposed growth-regions policy.

Other areas to be considered for growth regions are: Haarlemmermeer – Lisse – Hillegom in the provinces of North Holland and South Holland; Barendrecht – Rijsoord – Heerjansdam in South Holland; Vleuten – IJssel-stein – Nieuwegein in Utrecht; Heerhugowaard – Alkmaar in North Holland; Almere – Lelystad in the province of Flevoland.

Figure 2. A proposal for a growth region: a 'Park City' between the capital and the port.

Lack of space prevents us from presenting the detailed arguments for each of these possibilities. Suffice to say, these pose a challenge for urban and regional research in the Netherlands. Note that the above examples merely concern spatial – visual aspects. The administrative dimension seems more problematic. Almere is of course an exception. It has been developed by the Ministry of Transport and Waterworks as the department responsible for the reclamation scheme of which it forms part. Similar cases are hard to find in the Netherlands.

The growth-centre policy bears some resemblance to what we propose, but one important element is missing. This is an overall body, including a democratically elected council supported by technical expertise. Proposals along these lines have always foundered on the rocks of fear of a fourth layer of government. Central government, the provinces, and the municipalities are the three traditional layers of Dutch government and administration. Naturally, the balance of power between them is delicate, and in the past it has always proved impossible to change this.

On the other hand, after twenty-five years of constitutional discussion and experiments, there is a strong impetus now for reform. Government is willing to hand over powers and (diminishing) resources to regional bodies. There are also many ad hoc arrangements for cooperation between municipalities in environmental control, transport, employment, policing, economic development, housing, recreation, and nature conservation. Needless to say that this is not an ideal situation from a democratic point of view. To tackle this problem the government has proposed legislation to establish city-regional authorities. (At the same time the provinces taking part in the Randstad are discussing setting up a metropolitan authority.) Growth regions seem a logical complement to the proposed city-regional authorities.

City-regional authorities are the administrative answer to the economically inspired concept of key cities in the Fourth Report. Authorities for growth regions would be a logical complement. An added dimension is the possibility of involving private actors in the development of growth regions. Traditionally, housing and planning have been areas in which Dutch authorities have taken the lead. However, there is much talk now about spreading the burden through public – private partnerships. Such joint ventures are now considered for major projects, including infrastructure. Even one of the most spectacular projects currently under discussion for reclaiming land off the coast near the Hague and Hook of Holland, is now envisaged to be implemented by a public – private partnership. A consortium by the name of 'New Holland' is considering developing the reclaimed land for the top segment of the housing market, for nature and recreation. The city of The Hague is supportive, hoping that the government will participate (*Binnenlands Bestuur* 1991). There is no reason why similar arrangements should not be possible in growth regions. In the next section we elaborate on the concept of the growth region.

5 Opportunities for environmental planning

Dutch environmental policy has drawn inspiration from the Brundtland Report (WCED, 1987). In trying to understand the complexities of environmental planning, it is helpful to differentiate between two meanings of what Dutch environmental planning entails. The limited interpretation of environmental planning refers to the set of sanitary laws concerning industrial pollution, waste management, nuclear energy, soil pollution, zoning of areas around noisy, dangerous, and pollutant activities, and so forth (see figure 3). Until recently, environmental management concerned the sum of such regulations. However, success in one sector could be detrimental to others. In addition there is now a second, more ambitious interpretation of what environmental planning entails. The Dutch Ministry for Housing, Physical Planning and the Environment, in cooperation with other relevant departments, produced a proposal in 1984 for new comprehensive legislation. Over a period of six years many chapters have been added to the General Regulations for Environmental Management which resulted from this effort (SDU, 1989). In 1991 a chapter on environmental planning was included. At the same time central government has published the first National Environmental Policy Plan (MVROM, 1989; 1990a).

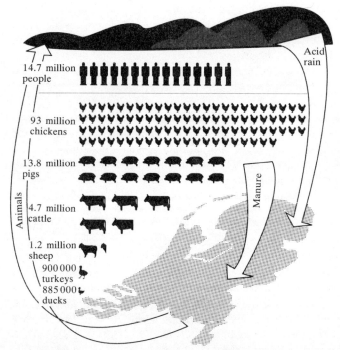

Figure 3. Pressure on the environment (source: *NRC Handelsblad* 5 November 1988; reprinted with the permission of the publisher).

This bears fruit in other national planning documents (like the Fourth Report, the Second Structure Scheme on Traffic and Transport, the Third Report on Water Management) and also in investment programmes. So, like physical planning before, environmental planning is now considered a form of overall coordination for which the Dutch have invented the term 'facet planning'. However, unlike physical planners, environmental planners control a sizable and growing budget, a precondition, if any, of success.

The National Environmental Policy Plan defines categories of measures directed to specific areas. Often what they come down to is zoning. Obviously, close cooperation between environmental and physical planning is essential for success. The National Physical Planning Agency and the Directorate General for the Environment have responded to this situation by introducing the concept of 'ROM' areas; ROM being the Dutch acronym for physical planning and environment.

The objectives of the ROM-area policy are:
1. To develop a strategic vision, a comprehensive plan, and a commitment package with a view to achieving spatial and environmental quality.
2. To accelerate the implementation of environmental policy and to focus the efforts of various authorities and of private organisations for the sake of a better environment.
3. To find solutions to problems which are specific to the regions.
4. To promote active involvement of environmental planners with implementation outside the domain of statutory environmental policy.
5. To create broad consensus by promoting active involvement of all relevant groups in plan-making (MVROM, 1990b; 1990c).

Eleven regions have been designated ROM areas. Some are rural and others urban–industrial in character. The urban areas are Schiphol Airport near Amsterdam, the Rijnmond area around the port of Rotterdam, and the Sas-van-Gent Canal Region in Zeeuws-Vlaanderen near the Belgian border. Designated ROM areas are entitled to administrative and moderate financial support. The results so far have been the formation of networks, the making of comprehensive strategic plans, and, in one or two instances, the formulation of commitment packages. The ROM areas serve as testing grounds for a new form of comprehensive planning and for the application of new technologies.

The above environmental plans propose ambitious standards to reduce air pollution, abate soil pollution, prevent noise, achieve energy efficiency, and the like. As a corollary, radical measures have to be taken in the domains of private transport, the location of housing and employment areas, parking provision, the location of waste-disposal plants, and the introduction of environmental technology. In existing urban areas these aims are difficult to achieve. Large well-planned new developments seem to afford better opportunities. The fewer the impediments from existing structures and routines, the better. It is in this respect that growth regions can play an important role.

Dutch physical planners usually show a good instinct for international planning fashions. As regards the 'nature-city', so far they have missed the boat. Only a small 'in-crowd' of biologists and landscape-architects are familiar with British and US literature on this subject. The garden-city tradition and the parkways are only a weak echo from a distant past. A special edition of the periodical *Stedebouw en Volkshuisvesting* (1991), an article in the yearbook of the National Physical Planning Agency (van Selm, 1990) and the 1991 planning competition organised by the prestigious E O Weijers Foundation (Weijersstichting, 1991), all dedicated to the 'ecological city', are signs of change.

The wording of the brief for the competition states the issues. The nature-city will be the product of radical change in the patterns of consumption, production, and communication in our highly urbanised country. As agricultural production becomes more and more efficient, producing large surpluses on the way, the traditional division between the urban and rural domain is becoming less meaningful. On the other hand, demand for urban land will continue to increase, if for no other reason then because of the decline in household size. The effects of immigration also need to be considered. Surprisingly, the Dutch migration balance overall still showed a net surplus of 2.6 per 1000 in 1989.

The nature-city can bring an end to the traditional conflict between city and nature and lead the way to a sustainable urban environment. According to the E O Weijers Foundation, key notions in this process are: efficiency in land use, small-scale living in combination with massive disposal of refuse, improved exchanges of information, nature and technology combined, and sustainable methods of industrial and agricultural production.

The 1990 National Nature Policy Plan mentions the same concept of the nature-city, relating it to that of a national 'ecological infrastructure'. On the regional and local scale this concept can be translated into park systems and green corridors. These elements offer a safe habitat and migration routes for indigenous plants and animals otherwise threatened with extinction.

The National Physical Planning Agency, too, has published interesting proposals for the application of environmental technologies in a book published in 1990 describing various pilot studies (Rijksplanologische Dienst, 1990). The thirty plans coming under the heading 'recycling and urban form' are good, valuable building blocks for the nature-city. The following examples are noteworthy:

(a) Application of hylofyte-filters for the purification of water which is being suggested for rural as well as urban areas. These draw upon bacteria in swamps with reed vegetation. This method seems to fit many low-lying peat areas in the Western Netherlands.

(b) The use of indigenous building materials. Some municipalities are seriously exploring the possibility of grass roofs in subsidised housing projects.

(c) The design of self-contained neighbourhoods with green fields for the purification of water, small-scale facilities for waste disposal, and recycling.

These ideas are no longer the domain of long-haired activists. They are proposals submitted by municipalities willing to implement them. (For example, the fourth-largest Dutch city, Utrecht, is now considering building 800 houses with grass roofs in an ecologically sound and carefully landscaped environment.) The point is that growth regions offer the best opportunities for large-scale applications of such ideas. They would become more effective because growth regions would also afford the opportunity to go beyond the application of environmentally sensitive technologies. The very layout of growth regions would reflect the same aim of sustainable development. The responsible authorities would constantly have this goal in mind. After all, achieving sustainable development would be one of the rationales for their existence.

Growth regions could also become building blocks for a new national principle of spatial organisation. This is what a daring scheme by the prominent Dutch architect-planner Tummers (1990) proposes. Inspired by the US park movement and park systems in British, French and German metropolises, he has made proposals for a reconstruction of the existing Randstad – Green Heart Metropolis into a Park Metropolis. This seems a more realistic perspective than the forced attempt, such as in the Fourth Report Extra, to keep the Green Heart open by drawing a firm line around it on a map. We must not forget that, when it was first proposed in 1958, the Green Heart was seen as a hedge against future urban growth. Now that more growth may be upon us, growth regions in selected parts of the Green Heart may point the way.

6 Conclusions

Gloomy financial prospects and a growing understanding of the limitations of state intervention notwithstanding, the Fourth Report reflects the contours of a new societal project, the restructuring of the economic engine of the Netherlands, the Randstad. This needs to be done within constraints imposed by the goal of sustainable urban development. Systematic urbanisation through growth management should be part of the overall strategy, fitting the proposed urban nodes and city-regional authorities into one scheme alongside growth regions. Such a policy could achieve prosperity coupled with sustainability in the future Green Heart – Metropolis.

Growth regions are the building blocks for this strategy. Growth regions may serve as a safety valve in an open principle of spatial organisation. Recent planning reports and other writings suggest that the underlying design principles might attract support. The concept of a nature-city

can be a source of inspiration. The bottleneck lies in the administrative
dimension. The planning principles practised in the growth-centre policy
between 1970 and 1985 is a source of inspiration.

References
Alexander E R, Faludi A, 1990, "Planning doctrine: its uses and applications",
Werkstukken van het Planologisch en Demografisch Instituut 120, University of
Amsterdam, Amsterdam
Binnenlands Bestuur 1991, "Den Haag wil buitengaats 'Goudkust'wijk bouwen",
27 September, page 2
Breheny M J, 1992, "The contradictions of the compact city: a review", in *European
Research in Regional Science, Volume 2: Sustainable Development and Urban Form*
Ed. M J Breheny (Pion, London) pp 138–159
CEC, 1990, Green Paper on the Urban Environment (Commission of the European
Communities, Brussels)
Chinitz B, 1990, "Growth management: good for the town, bad for the nation"
Journal of the American Planning Association **56** 3–8
Faludi A, 1989a, "Keeping the Netherlands in shape: introduction" *Built Environ-
ment* **15** 5-10
Faludi A, 1989b, "Perspectives on planning doctrine" *Built Environment* **15** 57-64
Faludi A, 1991a, "Fifty years of Dutch national physical planning: introduction"
Built Environment **17** 5–13
Faludi A, 1991b, "'Rule and order' as the Leitmotiv: its past, present and future
meaning" *Built Environment* **17** 69–77
Faludi A, van der Valk A J, 1990 *De groeikernen als hoekstenen van de Nederlandse
ruimtelijke planningdoctrine* (Van Gorcum, Assen)
Faludi A, van der Valk A J, 1991, "Half a million witnesses: the success (and
failure?) of Dutch urbanization strategy" *Built Environment* **17** 43–52
Fishman R, 1991, "The new American city" *Dialogue* number 3, pp 49–54
Glasbergen P, Simonis J B D, 1979 *Ruimtelijk beleid in de verzorgingsstaat* (Uitgeverij
Cobra, Amsterdam)
Ministerie van Landbouw, Natuurbeheer en Visserij, 1990, "Natuurbeleidsplan;
regeringsbeslissing" *Handelingen van de Tweede Kamer 1990–1991* **21** 149 (SDU,
The Hague)
Ministerie van Volkshuisvesting en Wederopbouw, 1960 *Nota inzake de ruimtelijke
ordening in Nederland* (Staatsuitgeverij, The Hague)
MVROM, 1988 *On the Road to 2015: Comprehensive Summary of the Fourth Report
on Physical Planning in the Netherlands* Ministerie van Volkshuisvesting,
Ruimtelijke Ordening en Milieubeheer (Ministry of Housing, Physical Planning
and Environment) (SDU, The Hague)
MVROM, 1989 *National Environmental Policyplan (NEPP)* Ministerie van Volkshuis-
vesting, Ruimtelijke Ordening en Milieubeheer (Ministry of Housing, Physical
Planning and Environment), The Hague (comprehensive English translation now
sold out)
MVROM, 1990a *National Environmental Policyplan Plus (NEPP-plus)* Ministerie van
Volkshuisvesting, Ruimtelijke Ordening en Milieubeheer (Ministry of Housing,
Physical Planning and Environment), The Hague; a comprehensive English
translation can be obtained from the Department for Information and Inter-
national Relations of the Ministry, PO Box 20951, 2500 EZ The Hague
MVROM, 1990b *Voorbeeldplannen Ideenboek* Ministerie van Volkshuisvesting,
Ruimtelijke Ordening en Milieubeheer (Ministry of Housing, Physical Planning
and Environment) (SDU, The Hague)

MVROM, 1990c, "Actieplan gebiedsgericht milieubeleid" *Handelingen van de Tweede Kamer 1990 – 1991* **21** 896 Ministerie van Volkshuisvesting, Ruimtelijke Ordening en Milieubeheer (Ministry of Housing, Physical Planning and Environment) (SDU, The Hague)

MVROM, 1991 *Summary of the Fourth Report Extra on Physica Planning; Part 1: Key Planning Decisions* Ministerie van Volkshuisvesting, Ruimtelijke Ordening en Milieubeheer (Ministry of Housing, Physical Planning and Environment) (SDU, The Hague)

Postuma R, 1991, "The National Plan: the taming of runaway ideas" *Built Environment* **17** 14 – 22

Priemus H, 1991, "De Randstad: winnend of verliezend woonmilieu?", in *De Randstad: Balans van Winst en Verlies, Volume 1* (Stedelijke Netwerken/NETHUR, Rotterdam) pp 11 – 16

Rijksplanologische Dienst, 1990 *Ruimtelijke Verkenningen 1990* Ministerie van Volkshuisvesting, Ruimtelijke Ordening en Milieubeheer, The Hague

SDU, 1989, "Wetsvoorstelplannen en milieukwaliteitseisen", *Sec. Ch. Parl. 1988/89* 21163 (SDU, The Hague)

Stedebouw en Volkshuisvesting 1991 **72** May supplement on "Stadsecologie"

Tummers L, 1990, "De uitgroei van de Randstad tot een groene metropool", ir. L J M Tummers, Bureau Tummers, Nieuwe Plantage 25, 2611, XJ, Delft

van der Heiden N, Kok J, Postuma R, Wallagh G J, 1991, "Consensus-building as an essential element of the Dutch planning system", paper given at the joint ACSP/AESOP conference "Planning Transatlantic" Oxford, 8 – 12 July; copy available from Department for Urban and Regional Planning, University of Amsterdam, Amsterdam

van der Knaap G, van der Laan L, 1991 *Stedelijke vernieuwing: Onderwerpen voor onderzoek*, *PRO-Voorstudies 31: Analyse van de onderzoeksbehoefte ter voorbereiding van de Meerjarenvisie Ruimtelijk Onderzoek 1991 – 1996 van het PRO* Programmeringsonverleg Ruimtelijk Onderzoek, The Hague

van der Valk A J, 1989, "Amsterdam in aanleg: planvorming en dagelijks handelen 1850 – 1900", Planologische Studies 8, Institute of Planning and Demography, University of Amsterdam, Amsterdam

van der Valk A J, 1991, "Randstad – Greenheart Metropolis: invention, reception, impact of a national principle of spatial organization" *Built Environment* **17** 23 – 33

van der Wusten H, Faludi A, 1992, "The Randstad as the playground of physical planners", in *The Randstad: A Research and Policy Laboratory* Eds F M Dieleman, S Musterd (Kluwer, Dordrecht) pp 17 – 38

van Selm A J, 1990, "Het beest in de stad", in *Jaarboek Rijksplanologische Dienst* Rijks Planologische Dienst, Ruimtelijke verkenningen, Ministerie van Volkshuisvesting, Ruimtelijke Ordening en Milieubeheer, The Hague, pp 97 – 110

WCED, 1987 *Our Common Future* (The Brundtland Report) World Commission on Environment and Development (Oxford University Press, Oxford)

Weijersstichting E O, 1991, "Het stromende stadsgewest; vormgeven aan de ecoregio Breda", E O Weijersstichting, PO Box 30833, 2500 GV The Hague

Zonneveld W, 1989, "Conceptual complexes and shifts in post-war urban planning in the Netherlands" *Built Environment* **15** 40 – 48

The Contradictions of the Compact City: A Review

M J Breheny
University of Reading

1 Introduction: a new integrity?

One of the unexpected benefits of the recent revival of interest in environmental issues is that it has served to promote and to link previously disparate areas of academic work. It has also brought together academic and practical interests that previously made little or no contact. The result is a richness of work and an integrity of effort in the urban field that has not been witnessed for a very long time.

The common denominator to these new endeavours is the loose notion of 'sustainable development'. There is a considerable amount of debate about what this term means (Pearce et al, 1989), and of how it might be interpreted in an urban context (Breheny, 1990). For present purposes, and indeed for most local applications, sustainable development implies the adoption of policies that minimise both local resource consumption and pollutants. Around this common denominator of sustainable development we can identify a number of areas of work—some basically academic, others more practical—that suddenly appear to be linked: urban form and energy consumption, the merits of the 'compact city', transport and energy efficiency, urban and rural qualities of life, development pressures, environmental protection, new settlements, urban intensification, and strategic planning.

This newly integrated—or more correctly integrating—debate has produced a number of 'sustainable' policy stances, most notably the promotion of the 'compact city'. However, such policies also give rise to a number of contradictions. It is these contradictions that are the focus of this paper. However, before we consider these, a brief review of the elements of the debate that are coming together may be useful.

For urbanists, the recent environmental debate has given a major spur to the question of the contribution that certain *urban forms* might make to lower energy consumption and lower pollution levels. Surprisingly, the UK government's White Paper on the Environment *This Common Inheritance* (DoE, 1990) takes the lead in this and refers directly to the role that urban form and planning can play in achieving sustainability. Arising out of the White Paper was a major research project—currently underway—on "Reducing Transport Emissions Through Planning". Separately, the Department of the Environment has commissioned research on "Land Use Planning Policy and Climate Change" (Owens and Cope, 1991). The brief for its "New Settlements" research project also stressed the need to consider the effect of such new developments on sustainability. Until these research projects are completed the UK government will reserve judgment on the question of the most appropriate forms of development. The European Commission has not been so circumspect. Its *Green Paper on the Urban Environment* (CEC, 1990) advocates very strongly a '*compact city*' solution to the problem. This approach is consistent with the line taken by a number of environmentalist groups, such as Friends of the Earth (Elkin et al, 1991), whose views are also expounded by Sherlock (1990).

Some academics, such as Newman and Kenworthy (1989) have found in favour of the European Commission solution, following detailed analysis of urban form and energy consumption levels. Much of the energy consumption debate rests, of course, on *transport* issues. Contributions here range from the very practical, such as Banister's (this volume) review of information on transport usage in different urban forms, to the theoretical, such as Rickaby's (1991 and Rickaby et al, this volume) modelling of hypothetical urban forms.

The EC Green Paper has broadened the debate because its advocacy of the compact city rests not just on strictly environmental criteria of energy consumption and emissions, but also on *quality of life* grounds. It is argued that the compact city, at its best, provides a superior cultural, social, and economic base for society. The Green Paper has produced a wealth of counterresponses, which challenge its views both on environmental and on quality-of-life issues. Owens (1986) had earlier questioned the energy efficiency of high-density compact cities. Gordon and Richardson (1990) have challenged the Newman and Kenworthy findings. Green and Holliday (1991) advocate a decentralised exurban life-style, as being desirable on the very same quality-of-life considerations addressed by the European Commission. Robertson (1990) likewise promotes a decentralised life-style, but one which takes advantage of modern telecommunications. This debate about concentrated or dispersed forms of settlement takes place against the background of continuing decentralisation from Britain's cities, a process viewed by some as so profound as to be labelled *counterurbanisation* (Cross, 1990; Fielding, 1991).

In the United Kingdom, this whole debate about urban form, transport, and quality of life coincides with a longer standing debate about the *accommodation of development*. In the South of England in particular, this is a major political issue. With a million houses to be built over the next twenty years, there is widespread resistance to development, most obviously in the outer parts of the region that have witnessed the fastest rates of growth in recent years. This resistance—often posed pejoratively as the NIMBY (not in my backyard) syndrome—is well organised and well argued. The reasoning by pressure groups is largely on altruistic *environmental protection* grounds, but carries a suspicion of selfish protectionism. The resistance is not restricted to private pressure groups. One county council—Hampshire—has recently refused to accept the housing allocation to the county made by the Secretary of State for the Environment.

The general view is that other counties would also like to refuse their allocation, but dare not confront the Minister. In the United States, the home of free market decentralisation, the disbenefits of urban 'sprawl' seem to have been recognised late in the day. A major debate is now underway about the need for, and form of, 'growth management' (for example, see Chinitz, 1990; Gordon and Richardson, 1991).

An important element in this development debate in the United Kingdom concerns 'new settlements'. Since the mid-1980s there have been nearly 200 proposals in Britain to build privately funded new settlements (Breheny et al, 1992). These proposals range in size from 300 to 5500 houses. Initially these were speculative developments and were largely resisted. Now they are being promoted by developers through the planning system, and an increasing number of local authorities are proposing such schemes themselves. Such developments are extremely controversial and have been vigorously opposed by environmental groups. An increasingly important element in the debate concerns the sustainability of new settlements, relative to other means of accommodating development.

In response to the rural protectionist lobby, there are signs now of a counterargument in favour of protecting urban areas. This is as yet poorly articulated, but may gather force. The concern is manifest in complaints about 'town cramming'. Given the long-standing policy of urban containment in Britain, it is felt that urban intensification has produced congestion, loss of amenity, and a general lowering of urban quality of life, particularly in suburbs. The Open Spaces Society (personal communication, 1991) is one of the few bodies to have documented their concerns over this problem, but there is a lobby in favour of 'greening the city' (for example, Lusser, 1991). It is possible that, as urban residents become increasingly concerned about urban intensification, the debate will focus more sharply on a clash between urban and rural protectionists' interests.

Also closely related to this whole debate is the 'renaissance of strategic planning' in the United Kingdom (Breheny, 1991). Arguably, the British government, which had been steadily dismantling the strategic planning system as part of its programme of deregulation, has reversed its policy because of the coincidence of all of the issues discussed here. The environmental debate, transport issues, the highly charged arguments over development, and the complaints of its own supporters about the effects of a free-for-all policy on land, have all contributed to this fundamental change of policy. It was significant that the decisions to reprieve structure plans and develop a nationwide system of regional guidance were announced in the 1990 White Paper on the Environment (DoE, 1990).

2 The European Commission's 'compact city'
There is, then, a new rich web of work—focused on the sustainability issue—that has given a boost to old academic ideas, has generated new ideas, and has brought these together with directly practical concerns.

Within this new web of work, the idea that has generated most response is the European Commission's (CEC, 1990) *Green Paper on the Urban Environment*. Its simple, yet extremely profound, conclusion—that the existing high-density compact city should be the focus of future development—has implications for all of the areas of work discussed above. For this reason, in this paper I review the arguments around that simple conclusion. In particular, I suggest that the compact city proposal is in important respects contradictory. The word 'contradiction' is used loosely here. It both covers instances where there are elements of the EC's policy statement that are internally contradictory, and covers cases where the proposals seem to be in potential conflict with other legitimate policy objectives.

The Green Paper is not the only source of the compact city proposal. There are earlier proposals such as those by Goodman and Goodman (1947) and Dantzig and Saaty (1973). During the current debate there have been arguments in favour of the compact city, such as those by Friends of the Earth (Elkin et al, 1991) and Sherlock (1990), that are in many ways more thoroughly articulated than those of the Commission. The critique offered here will focus on the Green Paper because it is an important document, produced by an important organisation, but one that has been accepted a little too readily. We have a solution being proposed by the Commission before the problem has even been debated properly, and certainly before optional solutions have been assessed.

The European Commission's (CEC, 1990) Green Paper is particularly interesting because it combines concerns with the effects of urban growth on the environment and the future quality of life in urban areas. For the Commission, the one solution—the compact city—achieves the two aims of making urban areas more environmentally sustainable and improving quality of life. The report provides both an analysis of the causes of urban environmental problems and proposals towards a Community strategy to overcome these problems. The analysis suggests that the twin problems of environmental degradation and poor quality of life in urban areas result largely from the same cause. Two factors in particular are identified:

"The first of these is the uncontrolled pressure placed on the environment by many of the activities which are concentrated in the cities. The second—and not unrelated—factor is the spatial arrangement of our urban areas." (page 48)

Much of the report focuses on this second issue; the spatial arrangement of European cities. Two problems are identified: urban 'sprawl' and the spatial separation of functions. These together, by undermining the intensive milieux provided by the compact city, in turn undermine creativity:

"The enemies of this source of creativity are, on the one hand, undifferentiated urban sprawl in quasi-rural settings which isolate the individual; and highly specialised land-use policies within cities which create functional enclaves and social ghettos where like speaks to like; university campuses at the city's edge, banking districts at the centre, industrial zones deprived of simple services and far from habitations. Both suburban sprawl and specialisation are linked to the urban environment: they exist because they provide escape or protection from urban blight, poverty and pollution." (page 21)

The report suggests there has been a recent rediscovery of the value of urban living, and that this:

"reflects the failure of the periphery: the absence of public life, the paucity of culture, the visual monotony, the time wasted in commuting. By contrast, the city offers density and variety; the efficient, time and energy-saving combination of social and economic functions; the chance to restore the rich architecture inherited from the past." (page 19).

Thus, the one solution—the compact, functionally mixed compact city—appears to solve neatly the two major urban problems: the desire to protect the natural environment and to preserve the quality of life that the healthy city provides. It must be appreciated, in considering the merits of this solution, that the Commission's vision of the compact city is a very radical one. One of the policy 'orientations' in the proposal is to "avoid escaping the problems of the city by extending its periphery; solve its problems within existing boundaries" (page 45). The question of the feasibility of doing this will be addressed later.

The Friends of the Earth, in a recent major review (Elkin et al, 1991) of the sustainability of the city, come to the same basic conclusions about high density and mixed land uses as the European Commission:

"We have outlined alternative transport, but the built form of the city dictates the overall demand for transport, which can be reduced. The maintenance of high 'urban' densities of population alongside integrated land use can achieve this while providing the social interaction that makes cities desirable." (page 8).

The European Commission, then, has proposed an elegant, if rather poorly substantiated, vision of the future of European cities. It is a seductive argument, because it catches the prevailing mood in favour of environmental protection and resource conservation, and it also promises cleaner, healthier, and more prosperous cities. However, the compact city proposal immediately raises doubts about its feasibility and desirability. Before the compact city notion gathers yet more momentum—and we must bear in mind that the Commission rarely sets ideas into motion that do not ultimately bear on Community policy—it has to be subjected to a much more thorough examination than it has received to date. The rest of this paper contributes to that examination.

3 The contradictions of the compact city
Although the European Commission's Green Paper is to be welcomed in raising the debate about the future form of our cities, there are many possible contradictions that arise from the advocacy of the compact city that it fails even to consider. Listed below are some of these possible

contradictions:
compact city versus energy efficiency,
compact city versus suburban quality of life,
compact city versus the green city,
compact city versus telecommunication-rich dispersal,
compact city versus renewable energy sources,
compact city versus rural economic development.
These have been derived on a rather idiosyncratic basis. Other researchers may conceive of others or give different priorities to these. The coverage given here to the six contradictions reduces with each one. This is based on a personal assumption about their relative priority, but also reflects the quantities of available literature and the degree of controversy in that literature.

It could be argued that there is one basic contradiction that is not considered in this list; that is, the advocacy of centralisation in the face of deep-seated counterurbanisation trends in virtually all Western countries. In the United Kingdom, for example, the preliminary 1991 results show that during the decade 1981–91 there was a clear inverse correlation between the rate of population growth of an area and the existing population of that area. Thus, the more remote areas have seen the highest rates of growth and the largest cities the highest rates of decline. This trend is consistent with that in previous postwar decades, and undermines the suggestion of a number of commentators that the decentralisation trend has slowed down. Perhaps these trends are so powerful that a realistic solution to the sustainability issue might be one that goes with the tide and tries to reshape rather than one that tries to swim against it.

Another important issue not addressed directly here concerns the economic implications of centralisation. It is to be expected that congestion and property costs will rise in the compact city. As Gordon and Richardson (1991, page 15) state: "Nostalgia for the compact city carries its penalties". But the potential penalties of the compact city may extend well beyond just monetary costs.

3.1 Compact city versus energy efficiency
From a sustainability perspective, the most important characteristic of the compact city is that in principle it should reduce the need for travel, and hence reduce fuel consumption and emissions. It seems to have the merits of short private journey lengths and the greatest prospects for increasing the patronage of public transport. It also seems to offer the best prospects for the introduction of communal heat and power systems. In the European Commission's *Green Paper on the Urban Environment* (CEC, 1990) it is argued that one of the major merits of the compact city is its contribution to environmental sustainability. This interesting and provocative conclusion is, however, simply an assertion. It is based on a number of contentions which ought to be substantiated. It is imperative that such an

important policy conclusion—the advocacy of the compact city across Europe—be based on rigorous analysis. To date it has not been.

The question of the energy efficiency of different types of urban form has been addressed by many researchers. However, although considerable evidence is available, it does not lead to a consensus [(for example, see the series of articles on the debate in the United States by Chinitz (1990), Fischel (1991), and Neuman (1991)]. According to Owens (1990), this should not be a surprise. She provides a thorough review of research on the energy efficiency of urban forms, and warns that it is to be expected that clear relationships will be difficult to determine either theoretically or empirically. The relationship between energy systems and urban form is complex, and it is difficult to predict how changes in one will affect the other. She argues that spatial structure is only one of the factors influencing energy consumption. Life-styles, for example, have a major effect, but are notoriously difficult to predict. Owens (1990) also questions those researchers—largely modellers—who assume that travel is sufficiently price elastic for fuel price rises to be reflected directly in shorter journey lengths. None of these doubts is evident in the Green Paper.

One of the major disputes in this energy–urban form debate, and one that relates directly to the compact city issue, concerns the energy-consumption consequences of urban decentralisation. The disagreements tend to focus on the question of whether changing urban forms, including the suburbanisation both of homes and of jobs, tend to hold down journey lengths and frequencies, and hence energy consumption, despite the apparently energy-intensive effects of urban decentralisation.

The nature of this dispute can best be illustrated by reference to a recent debate on petroleum consumption and urban form that has taken place recently in the pages of the *Journal of the American Planning Association*. Newman and Kenworthy (1989) provide an analysis of the relationship between levels of petroleum consumption and various features of a number of large US and other world cities. Their aim is to seek some ideas on how changes to urban form and transport modes might reduce fuel consumption. Gordon and Richardson (1990) have produced a savage reply, which criticises the validity of Newman and Kenworthy's analysis and questions the whole logic of the arguments in favour of constraining the private car and promoting public transport.

Newman and Kenworthy (1989) have collected a range of data for thirty-two cities around the world, including ten in the USA. These ten US cities have petrol consumption rates that vary by some 40%. In an attempt to explain this variation, they have correlated petrol consumption per capita with, for example, incomes, petrol prices, car ownership, city size, and population density. Most of these variables are dismissed as having insignificant correlations with fuel consumption. The analysis then focuses on the correlation with urban density. The conclusion is that "The relative intensity of land use in the ten US cities is clearly correlated with gasoline use overall and in the inner and outer areas. The strongest relationship is with the population density in the inner area .... These patterns suggest that urban structure within a city is fundamental to its gasoline consumption." (page 25). The least densely populated cities in the sample, Houston and Phoenix, with 8 people and 10 jobs per acre in inner areas, have gasoline consumption rates of 567 and 532 gallons per capita, respectively. The most densely populated, New York and Chicago, with approximately 40 people and 20 jobs per acre, have consumption rates of 335 and 367 gallons per capita.

Table 1 shows Newman and Kenworthy's consumption and urban density figures for different parts of New York, demonstrating very clearly the decline in consumption with density. They contrast the 90 gallons per capita in central New York with the most extravagant consumers, in exurban Denver, who accounted for 1043 gallons each in 1980.

Newman and Kenworthy's (1989) conclusions from their study of US cities is that there is a potential fuel saving of 20 to 30% in low-density cities such as Houston or Phoenix if they were to develop urban structures more like Boston or Washington. This would involve the creation of higher density inner areas and the provision of basic public transport systems.

The analysis is extended from US cities to the full thirty-two worldwide sample. Here, much lower per capita petroleum consumption rates are found in the non-US cities. Asian cities have very low rates. European cities also show modest rates compared with the US cities, and Canadian and Australian cities fall between the US and European examples. Again, the analysis shows that generally high inner area densities and high levels of public transport provision correlate closely with low per capita petrol consumption. Newman and Kenworthy (1989) account for this form of relationship by explaining how at each extreme the situation is compounded. Thus very low densities require almost total reliance on the car and prohibit any public transport system. Very high-density urban areas have extreme, but opposite, effects.

Newman and Kenworthy (1989) dismiss previous studies which show that little can be done to reduce petroleum consumption other than by taxation. They conclude that other policies can save significant amounts of

Table 1. Gasoline use and urban density in New York by region (source: Newman and Kenworthy, 1989).

Area	Gasoline use (gallons per capita)	Urban density (persons per acre)
Outer area	454	5.3
Whole urban area	335	8.1
Inner area	153	48.3
Central city	90	101.6

fuel:
  "—increasing urban density;
    —Strengthening the city center;
    —Extending the proportion of a city that has inner-area land use;
    —Providing a good transit option; and
    —Restraining the provision of automobile infrastructure" (page 33).
They conclude that processes of reurbanisation, evident in some parts of the world, should be boosted by land-use and transportation policies, not only to reduce fuel consumption, but also to make our cities more 'livable'.

Gordon and Richardson's (1990) reply to Newman and Kenworthy suggests that the latter's "analysis is faulty, that the problems are wrongly diagnosed, and that their policy and planning prescriptions are inappropriate and infeasible" (page 342). They are accused of adopting "Maoist planning methods" and of wanting the "Beijingisation of US cities" (page 344). Gordon and Richardson (1990) argue for economic—that is, pricing policies—to determine the consumption patterns of scarce resources, including petrol. They also argue that petrol consumption should not be singled out; it should be considered as one of a number of potentially scarce resources that should be allocated such as to maximise social welfare. The answer, if petrol is to be conserved—the need for which they doubt—is a fuel tax.

Gordon and Richardson also point out that much of the variation in petrol consumption between cities that Newman and Kenworthy attribute to urban form may be caused simply by variations in life-style and travel behaviour; that the analysis merely asserts, does not prove. Even if it were the case, they argue, the worldwide experience with the building of new major public transport systems is not encouraging: "Declining transit use and high costs per passenger mile are common phenomena" (page 343). They also argue that rail transit is likely to accelerate decentralisation, rather than achieving Newman and Kenworthy's goal of further centralisation.

One major omission from the Newman and Kenworthy (1989) analysis is highlighted by Gordon and Richardson (1990). The latter point out that journey trips to urban cores are now a small proportion of total work trips in most cities. Most commuting now takes place from suburb to suburb; hence, the lack of relationship between fuel consumption and average journey-to-work length in US cities. Newman and Kenworthy's own analysis shows that average journey lengths are shorter in the 'gas guzzling' cities than in the apparently efficient New York and Chicago. Indeed, in an earlier paper, Gordon et al (1988) argue that urban decentralisation, particularly of jobs, has actually reduced average work-trip lengths. However, Gordon and Richardson (1990) do ignore the evidence put forward by Newman and Kenworthy on average work-trip lengths in non-US cities, which shows a positive relationship with petrol consumption.

Gordon et al (1988) and Gordon and Richardson (1990) argue that the importance of nonwork trips has been ignored. The growth of these trips—many of them short—has been facilitated by decentralised life-styles. During the period 1969–83 Gordon et al (1988) observe that nonwork trips in the USA grew at a substantially higher rate than work trips, and that the highest rates of growth were in suburban areas, and at peak times. Their conclusion from this is that conventional policy measures aimed at reducing peak-time car-borne work trips to central areas, are misguided. With decentralisation reducing average work-trip length, efforts should be directed at reducing peak-time suburban nonwork trips.

One of the major policy initiatives proposed by Newman and Kenworthy is the introduction of new mass rail transit systems into the 'inefficient' cities. Gordon and Richardson point out both the enormous cost of doing this in cities such as Los Angeles, and the likelihood of low patronage because of existing low population densities. They point out that the cities chosen for treatment, such as Houston and Phoenix, have much stronger economies, faster commuting, and less congestion than the desirable models such as New York and Chicago: "the last thing they need is a basic rail transit system" (page 343).

Basically, the Gordon and Richardson paper is pro-motor car, pro-market (although they seem to regard fuel taxes as somehow outside this), pro the status quo, and antiplanning to an extent rarely witnessed in Europe. Some of their critique throws a new light on important, but neglected, issues, particularly over the nature of contemporary journey-to-work flows, the importance of nonwork trips, and the questioning of the practical merits of massive investment in rail. However, the whole paper is very complacent about the issue of energy consumption. Possibly, both sets of papers were written before the present alarm over fuel consumption and CO_2 emissions. But now, in the context of national governments having set target dates for CO_2 stabilisation, the Gordon and Richardson (1990) view seems to be remarkably antiquated. They may be correct in challenging the detail of the analysis and prescriptions put forward by Newman and Kenworthy (1989), but at least the latter seem to be concerned about what is now generally regarded as a major problem. It may be that Gordon and Richardson are in tune with thinking in the USA (Newman and Kenworthy are from Australia), but not with the rest of the world, given that the US government is the only major national government not to have set a CO_2 stabilisation date.

Banister (this volume) has contributed to this debate by trying to assess the energy efficiency of different sizes of towns in the United Kingdom. Table 2 shows the result of multiplying distance travelled per week, from the National Travel Survey of 1985/86, by energy consumption figures (MJ per passenger mile), for each type of area. The table shows the results of summing all modes. It can be seen that energy consumption is highest in the smaller, and usually remotest, settlements. Interestingly, given our concern here with the compact city, London, the largest city in the United Kingdom, is not the most efficient. Urban areas with populations larger than 25 000 but smaller than London are the most efficient. Although this band is extremely wide, the analysis does cast doubt on the assumption that the largest, most compact cities will always be the most energy-efficient.

Another approach to the question of urban form and energy consumption is that of hypothetical modelling, as developed in a series of studies by Rickaby and associates (for example, de la Barra and Rickaby, 1982; 1987; Rickaby, 1987; 1991; Rickaby et al, this volume). They have produced a model of an 'archetypal' English town, based on actual data for twenty towns, and modelled various changes to land use and transport structure in order to measure relative energy consumption. Earlier work (Rickaby 1987), with the town set within a city region, suggested that a concentrated city form and a village dispersal form both showed significant energy savings over other options. More recent work (Rickaby et al, this volume), with a more specifically urban focus, shows no such advantages for one form of development relative to another.

However one chooses to interpret the Newman and Kenworthy, Gordon and Richardson, Banister, and Rickaby et al analyses, it is clear that the efficiency of the centralised compact city is not yet proven, as the advocates of the compact city would have us believe. Further debate and research are required before major policy decisions are made. Some researchers are willing to argue, in the absence of a clear conclusion on the merits of the compact city, that an urban form that may improve matters and is unlikely to make them worse is 'decentralised concentration'. Owens (1991) and Rickaby (1987) both come to this conclusion. Owens, in her recent plea for more 'energy-conscious planning', argues that: "Appropriate planning policies would therefore include discouragement of dispersed, low density residential areas or any significant development heavily dependent on car use; some degree of concentration, though not necessarily *centralisation*, of activities; integration of development with public transport facilities and the maintenance of moderately high densities along transport routes" (1991, page 30).

This approach would promote the development of a number of suburban centres in a large urban area, which would be the focus of improved public transport systems, and would help to avoid the congestion, and

Table 2. Energy consumption (MJ) per person per week by type of area (source: Banister, this volume).

London	Urban (>25 000)	Intermediate (3 000 – 25 000)	Rural (<3 000)	Overall
248.19	234.18	307.72	384.34	268.57

hence high fuel consumption, associated with a single core. This solution would maintain overall city densities, but would favour public transport, and would provide for the suburb-to-suburb movements that are neglected by most transport systems. The provision of good public transport systems, serving suburban centres, is crucial to this approach. Bell (1991) shows the consequences of not doing so. He presents the results of a 'before and after' study of the travel modes of workers in a major service company that has recently moved from central Melbourne, Australia, to a suburb that is poorly served by public transport. Before the move 34% of trips were undertaken by car; after the move the figure was 76%!

Interestingly, the emerging planning strategy for Paris is based on the development of new growth centres in the outer suburbs (but well inside the ring of new towns which was the basis of the previous plan), linked both by new circular metro lines and, in part, by a loop of the TGV network. This strategy appears to have emerged before the current debate over energy-efficient urban forms, but seems to be consistent with the 'decentralised concentration' proposal.

The 'decentralised concentration' solution generally assumes that the deconcentration element remains within the city. However, it is possible to consider the inclusion of new noncontiguous development within this scheme. Indeed, Rickaby (1987) found that one of the most efficient urban forms that he modelled included urban concentration plus nearby village developments. The EC Green Paper comes out very strongly against the idea of new towns or new settlements. It claims that they are unacceptable on two grounds: by detracting from the compact existing city, they are energy inefficient, and they fail to create the quality of life of the urban core. Again, however, there is little evidence presented to support this view. Breheny (1992) and Breheny et al (1992) have suggested that the postwar new towns in Britain now show no advantages in terms of journey-to-work self-containment relative to other towns. It is suggested that if new settlements are to be energy-efficient, they must be: small and remote, large and remote, or very close to existing urban areas.

The review above of the general features of the European Commission's Green Paper pointed out that, in addition to sprawl, the greatest enemy of 'urbanity' is the separation of land uses. What is required, it is argued, is "the efficient, time and energy-saving combination of social and economic functions" (page 19). Friends of the Earth (Elkin et al, 1991), Owens (1991), and Cervero (1991) concur with this advocacy of mixed uses. Such mixed uses are regarded as desirable because they both create a richer urban milieu and reduce journey lengths. The first reason is difficult to contradict, although, as we shall see below, Osborn was sceptical about this argument. The superior performance of mixed uses on energy grounds is, however, more questionable. Again, this superiority is asserted rather than demonstrated [although Cervero (1991) does address the issue more rigorously than most]. For certain basic nonspecialist goods and services, local provision may reduce journey lengths and facilitate walking and cycling. But for work trips and many other trips originating from home, the need for specialist destinations—particular jobs, specialist goods, particular recreational facilities, for example—local provision is impossible. Thus, it is doubtful that segregated or mixed land uses will necessarily produce different trip lengths or patterns. The success of changes in mixed land uses will depend in part, as with all of the changes that planners can introduce, on the prevailing propensity to travel. If this is high, as at present with low fuel costs, then mixed uses are likely to have little effect on travel patterns. If the propensity is low, because of high fuel taxes, then mixed uses would facilitate more localised travel. But, again, benefits one way or the other need to be demonstrated not simply asserted.

3.2 Compact city versus suburban quality of life

The most radical statement in the European Commission's (CEC, 1990) Green Paper is that further urban growth should be accommodated within the boundaries of existing urban areas. But is this possible, even if it were desirable, and is it desirable? In Britain, the aim is impossible. In the South East region, for example, it is estimated that more than one million houses will have to be built in the next twenty years. On the basis of past evidence, it is to be expected that a large proportion of this development will take place within existing urban areas. Table 3 shows the results of two recent research projects which have attempted to measure this proportion in the recent past. The urban infill proportion, at 50–60% for the South East is probably higher than most people would assume. Rather than this proportion rising in the future, as the compact city argument would prescribe, it is likely to fall. SERPLAN, the body responsible for regional planning in the South East, suggests that this estimated proportion of 60% will lower to 50% through the 1990s, largely because of objections to 'town cramming' (Grigson, 1988).

This implies that a large proportion of the one million new houses will have to be built outside existing urban areas: either as suburban extensions to existing cities, towns, and villages or as new settlements. Table 4, taken from Breheny et al (1992), shows the calculations required to arrive at a

Table 3. Housebuilding by type of development in the United Kingdom, 1990s.

| | Roger Tym and Partners (1987) South East (%) | Bibby and Shepherd (1991) | | |
		United Kingdom (%)	metropolitan districts (%)	shires (%)
Urban infill	55	45	60	30–50
Suburban or new settlement	34			
Villages	11			

housing requirement on greenfield–village sites in the South East, on the assumption that 50% of new housing will be built within existing urban areas. Of the 590 000 houses as yet unaccounted for in ROSE (rest of the South East, that is, the region minus London), after subtraction of those allowed for in structure plans, 50% will have to take the form of extended suburbanisation, village extensions or new settlements. This, then— 295 000 houses—may be the scale of the housing that will have to be built on greenfields. If SERPLAN's (Grigson, 1988) 50% figure for urban infill is a little high for ROSE, as the Bibby and Shepherd (1991) work implies, then the housing level to be accommodated in ROSE outside existing urban areas may be higher than this. In addition, the national household forecasts upon which this analysis is based are now out of date. More recent forecasts (DoE, 1991) suggest that housing provision in the South East for the period 1991–2001 is underestimated by 50 000 households. Thus, the greenfield requirement is likely to be higher still than that estimated here.

This, then, implies that the European Commission's goal of building all new development within existing urban boundaries is simply not possible, unless very drastic policies are introduced. Indeed, the changes of policy and implementation that would be required to push all of this growth into existing urban areas are unthinkable.

Having dealt with the question of the feasibility of accommodating all growth within existing urban boundaries, we can now turn to the question of desirability. Even if it were possible to contain all new development within existing urban boundaries, for environmental reasons, would this be socially desirable? The European Commission's (CEC, 1990) Green Paper extols the virtues of living in a compact, culturally diverse, exciting urban core, and denigrates suburban living. 'Cities'—that is, historic cores—are contrasted with the totality of 'urban areas':

"At the extreme 'urban areas' negate the concept of the city itself: they become 'post-urban phenomena', far removed from the traditional image of the pre-industrial and even 19th century city…. Urban areas are a statistical concept. Cities are projects for a new style of life and work" (page 19).

Table 4. Housing requirement on greenfield–village sites, 1991–2011, South East England (source: Breheny et al, 1992).

Total requirement	1 140 000 houses (SERPLAN)
minus	350 000 in London (790 000 in ROSE[a])
minus	200 000 allocated in structure plans in ROSE (590 000 new houses in ROSE)
minus	295 000 as 50% urban infill
gives	295 000 on greenfield–village sites

[a] ROSE rest of the South East.

This impassioned defence of urban cores would seem strange to many people who would come to the exact opposite conclusions. Although a few European cities do have cores which exhibit the desired characteristics, the large majority do not. Indeed, many cities have cores which have been declining physically, economically, and socially. There is abundant evidence that people have been fleeing these cores, in favour of suburban or exurban living, because of these problems. The large majority of Europeans live happily in the very kinds of suburbs that the Commission denigrates as 'sprawl'. There seems, then, to be a direct clash between the Commission's vision, as it would affect the suburbs, and the life-style chosen in practice by most residents.

Most commentators would support the Commission's commitment to the revival of our urban cores. It would be wonderful to see them restored to the degree of historical, architectural, innovative, and cultural richness that the Commission advocates. This is a project that few would disagree with. However, this project has become muddled with the broader question of the ways in which the mass of the population, and all of the activities that they generate, can be best accommodated.

For the majority of people, the implication of the compact city proposal is higher density suburban living. Given that most people have opted for low-density suburban living, it is to expected that rather than welcoming the intensive urban milieu that the Commission likes so much, most urban residents would object to increased densities. Even if the idea were acceptable, how could it be achieved? This is an important question that the Commission ignores. In practice, the biggest challenge in any move towards compact cities would be the redesigning of the very suburbs that are dismissed so readily.

There is, in the United Kingdom at least, a continuing antiurban movement that challenges the very bases of the European Commission's vision of the compact city. This movement is centred on those who have remained faithful to the long-standing garden city tradition in British planning. Ebenezer Howard's (1898) vision has been carried forward by generations of enthusiasts, and is still advocated passionately by the Town and Country Planning Association. Green and Holliday's recent (1991) vision of a dispersed—but not necessarily low-density—life-style is consistent with this tradition.

Frederic Osborn, the most celebrated follower of Howard, anticipated the compact city lobby, and their criticism of alternatives, some years ago when he wrote of the 'fetish of urbanity' (Osborn and Whittick, 1977):

"Attempts have been made by architectural writers to discredit the two garden cities and the new towns influenced by their design on the ground that they lack 'urbanity' .... The criticism reveals in those who make it a verbal confusion and aesthetic narrow-mindedness. If the word 'urbanity' is used in the accepted sense of 'good manners' or 'educated tastefulness', then the charge that the new towns are without it is an affront to the architects who have taken part in their design. If it is used in the simple etymological sense of 'towniness', the users unjustly accuse themselves of crass ignorance of the infinite diversity of shape and character—openness, compactness, ugliness, beauty, healthfulness, squalor, culture, vulgarity, etc, etc—that the world's towns display. And if it is used (illegitimately) as a synonym for high urban density or crowdedness ('cosiness' and 'snugness' are among the further synonyms) it stands for a quality most townspeople regard as a drawback and escape from it if they can" (page 81).

A less principled, but no less serious criticism of 'urbanity' has come recently from those concerned about the effects of so-called 'town cramming' or 'urban intensification'. This line of argument holds that containment policies have forced excessive development into existing urban areas, with a resultant loss of open space, gardens, and general amenity, and a resultant increase in congestion, pollution, and environmental degradation. The argument against 'town cramming' is as yet poorly articulated [Whitehand and Larkham (1991), do review the phenomenon, but from a microscale architectural perspective] but is being taken increasingly seriously. Interestingly, the protests about town cramming can be seen as a backlash against the rural protectionist lobby, who by arguing successfully in favour of containment policies, have exacerbated the problem. To date, these issues have not been seen as a straight fight between urban and rural interests, but this may become increasingly the case in the future.

3.3 Compact city versus the green city

There is within the Commission's Green Paper what appears to be a direct contradiction between two environmental objectives. It argues, obviously, for high-density cities but also extols the virtues of more 'greening' of cities. Other protagonists of the compact city, such as Friends of the Earth (Elkin et al, 1991), are also keen to 'green the city':

"In practice, an important issue is bringing nature ... into the life of city dwellers through a diversity of open landscapes: formal parks in the Victorian tradition, playing fields, extensive informal parks, public gardens, adventure playgrounds, shared streets (such as the Dutch woonerven), walkways and cycle ways, small greens, copses and thickets, meadows, and rough wild areas. In this way urban dwellers can experience nature without always having to visit rural areas" (page 116).

Elkin et al (1991) are aware of the possible contradiction between higher urban densities and the need for more green space, but they fail to resolve it. In principle, the answer might be more green spaces alongside considerably higher density development. However, they are not in favour of high-rise living in British cities. This leaves low-rise, high densities and the inevitable squeezing of space standards. In practice, the problem is that opportunities to increase the densities on sites that are already developed occur only infrequently. Thus, the opportunities to increase urban densities tend to involve the loss, not the gain, of green spaces. This danger is recognised by the Open Spaces Society, who "are ... concerned at the contemporary loss of open space—including derelict land which is frequently used on a de facto basis—within our cities and towns to built development. An argument frequently put forward is that use of derelict ground and other open space within cities and towns prevents the need to build on green land outside the city or town. We consider this argument is spurious" (personal communication).

For some protagonists of the compact city, this contradiction does not occur. Sherlock (1990), for example, following the arguments of Jacobs (1965), regards urban green space as undesirable because it detracts from the intensity of the built form that he regards as essential to the degree of urbanity that he favours. The European Commission does not go this far, but there is a contradiction in their proposal between high densities and urban greening that has to be resolved.

Another variant on the urban greening argument stresses not the recreational value of open space, but its ecological value in towns (Elkin et al, 1991). Lusser (1990) explains how policies in the London Borough of Sutton aim to preserve both garden land and verges and other green areas. The policies were prompted by David Bellamy's comment that the "attack on garden land ... is one of the current biggest threats to the natural environment in the UK" (page 1). Lusser (1991) goes on to explain that "areas abutting our streets and railway lines ... probably contain as much greenery (Biomass) as many of our parks put together. These types of areas are important not only as havens for wildlife, but also as pollution filters and CO_2 absorbers. Indeed they have an important impact on micro climate and the general wellbeing of people. Our policy suggests no development should be permitted that unsettles this important resource" (page 2).

Possibly, with very clever design, this apparent contradiction between higher densities and greater greening of our cities can be resolved. But it is a necessary resolution that is not addressed by the advocates of the compact city. The limited evidence that we do have on increasing densities—pejoratively labelled 'town cramming'—suggests that the contradiction does exist: increasing densities are at the expense of green spaces. Possibly, this is because the town cramming that we have witnessed is the result of piecemeal, largely unplanned activity, carried out without regard for environmental consequences. But, will a planned version be any more sensitive to such consequences?

3.4 Compact city versus telecommunications-rich dispersal
The compact city proposal challenges another view of future urban form and life-styles that is currently being promoted. This alternative proposes an antiurban life-style that is decentralised both geographically and institutionally. The proposal is in line with a long tradition of antiurbanism, but has been resurrected as a concept in recent years. In its current form,

it reiterates the previous antiurban–rural values arguments. Ash, for example, stresses the need to switch from materialist urban values to rural values, which are "to do with ways of life, with wholes and what is qualitative, and hence with where we belong" (Ash, 1987, quoted in Robertson, 1990, page 135).

The traditional arguments, however, are now supplemented by an emphasis on the potential for new communication technologies to facilitate this decentralised life-style. The need for face-to-face contact provided historically by the city is now obviated by telecommunications. Thus, it is now feasible to work in rural areas, in the proverbial 'electronic cottage', and remain in direct contact with others. Robertson (1990) argues for continued urban dispersal, the reaffirmation of rural values, and the use of new facilitating technologies.

This proposal raises many interesting questions; not least whether the idea is not undermined if many people choose to adopt this life-style. Certainly, one feature of the proposal is that it is more consistent with existing decentralising trends than is the compact city proposal. For the purposes of considering sustainability, however, the important question is whether the saving in travel, and hence energy consumption, that result from 'telecommuting' exceed the energy consumption resulting from the greater distances travelled. Views on this vary. For example, Beaumont and Keys (1982) suggest that telecommunications would give a net benefit, particularly if decentralised communities were focused in polynucleated settlements. Gillespie (this volume), on the other hand, is doubtful that a net benefit would ensue. He also points out that the range of telecommunications facilities available in rural areas will always be limited, because they inevitably focus on major nodes; that is on the cities.

The European Commission states that telecommunications can never provide the spontaneity and creativity of face-to-face contact:

"The telephone and data-link are no substitute for many kinds of communication which go beyond the exchange of information .... This is especially true ... of exchanges of information which yield the unexpected, even unsought answer from which true innovation results" (CEC, 1990, page 21).

3.5 Compact city versus renewable energy sources

Just as there appears to be a direct clash between the two environmental objectives of the compact city and the greening of cities, so there appears to be an inconsistency between the desires for the compact city and the development of renewable energy sources. Steadman (1979) and Owens (1986), for example, suggest that for any large-scale development of solar heating or wind power in cities, lower density development is required. Owens suggests that the linear grid form of development might facilitate both high-density living and opportunities for renewable energy sources. Likewise, it might also accommodate green open space.

3.6 Compact city versus rural economic development

A major set of issues ignored by the Green Paper concern the distributional effects of the compact city, and indeed of the alternatives to it. It
can be argued that the compact city proposal would put at a disadvantage
those people living in what are already economically declining or marginal
rural areas. Newby (1990), for example, has argued that the success of
existing urban containment policies in Britain has deprived rural areas of
economic activity that could have sustained them. Yet further drastic
containment of the kind implied by the compact city proposal would
exacerbate this problem enormously.

The corollary to this argument is that current levels of urban decentralisation have weakened the economies of inner urban areas. The compact
city, it could be argued, will help to regenerate inner urban areas, and thus
redistribute benefits in favour of those residents who are currently disad-
vantaged by decentralisation. These are difficult issues, but ones that must
be addressed in any full consideration of appropriate urban forms.

4 Conclusion

In this paper I have suggested that the notion of sustainable development
has served to bring together previously disparate parts of the debate about
urban problems and urban futures. A central theme in this newly integrating work is the 'compact city'. Although there are a number of advocates
of this concept, the most important is the European Commission (CEC,
1990) in its Green paper on the Urban Environment. It does not give the
most fully articulated case for the compact city, but the prospect of the
study actually influencing Commission policy gives it enormous significance.
The Green Paper tries to relate together the environmental sustainability
of the city with the question of quality of life. The task is to find solutions
that perform well on both grounds. The Commission tentatively suggests that
the solution is to promote the high-density, compact city—in the European
tradition—as both energy-efficient and socially desirable. The debate is
not just a European one. In the United States, for example, there is a
newly discovered concern with urban form, after decades of largely
unbridled decentralisation, and with the energy-consumption implications
of different urban forms.

The debate about sustainable development and urban form has excited
a large number of urban researchers and practising planners. They feel
that they now have a genuine contribution to make to an issue—the wider
sustainability debate—that appeared to be dominated by environmental
scientists. However, the potential contribution of planning must be put
in its place. The relationship between urban form and environmental
improvement may not be as direct as planners would like. Complex
political, economic, and social factors determine this relationship as well
as physical form. Disentangling the physical effects from the others is
difficult. However, there is little doubt that they do have an effect,

and that planning can contribute. Thus, research into urban forms that can help· to move towards sustainability is required. But it must be put into context.

While instantly appealing, the compact city proposal does warrant careful examination. It promises to determine a major policy agenda in Europe without any serious attempt to justify its conclusions. The Green Paper asserts rather than demonstrates. Possibly, its conclusions are valid. But before radical decisions are made about the future structure and functioning of our cities, the proposal must be subjected to the fullest scrutiny. This paper has made a small contribution to this scrutiny by suggesting that there are possible contradictions in the compact city idea: perhaps it is not energy-efficient; perhaps the life-style it would provide is undesirable; perhaps it undermines the desirable aim of further greening of cities; perhaps there are equally valid, but diametrically opposed, urban futures; perhaps it undermines the development of ambient sources of energy; perhaps it would undermine rural economies. These and other questions need to be explored. As these questions are addressed, the problem may seem to become more, not less, problematic. This is bad news for planners, who are under immediate pressure to respond practically to the sustainability problem. But with so much at stake, despite the obvious urgent need for action, we need to get our thinking straight.

References
Banister D, 1992, "Energy use, transport, and settlement patterns", in *European Research in Regional Science 2. Sustainable Development and Urban Form* Ed. M J Breheny (Pion, London) pp 160 – 181
Beaumont J, Keys P, 1982 *Future Cities: Spatial Analysis of Energy Issues* (John Wiley, Chichester, Sussex)
Bell D A, 1991, "Office location—city or suburbs? Travel impacts arising from office relocation from city to suburbs" *Transportation* **18** 239 – 260
Bibby P R, Shepherd J W, 1991 *Rates of Urbanization in England 1981 – 2001* Planning Research Programme, Department of the Environment (HMSO, London)
Breheny M, 1990, "Strategic Planning and Urban Sustainability", in *Proceedings of the Town and Country Planning Association Annual Conference on Planning for Sustainable Development* (Town and Country Planning Association, London) pp 9.1 – 9.28
Breheny M, 1991, "The Renaissance of Strategic Planning?" Environment and Planning B: Planning and Design **18** 233 – 250
Breheny M, 1992, "Towards the sustainable city", in *Environmental Issues in the 1990s* Eds A Mannion, S Bowlby (John Wiley, Chichester, Sussex) forthcoming
Breheny M, Gent T, Lock D, 1992, "Alternative development patterns: new settlements", paper prepared for the Department of the Environment; Department of Geography, University of Reading, Reading
CEC, 1990 *Green Paper on the Urban Environment* EUR 12902 (Commission of the European Communities, Brussels)
Cervero R, 1991, "Congestion relief: the land use alternative" *Journal of Planning Education and Research* **10** 119 – 129

Chinitz B, 1990, "Growth management: good for the town, bad for the nation?" *Journal of the American Planning Association* **56** 3 – 21

Cross D, 1990 *Counterurbanisation in England and Wales* (Gower, Aldershot, Hants)

Dantzig G, Saaty T, 1973 *Compact City: A Plan for a Liveable Urban Environment* (W H Freeman, San Francisco, CA)

de la Barra T, Rickaby P A, 1982, "Modelling regional energy use: a land use, transport and energy evaluation model" *Environment and Planning B: Planning and Design* **9** 429 – 443

de la Barra T, Rickaby P A, 1987, "An approach to the assessment of the energy efficiency of urban built form", in *Energy and Urban Built Form* Eds D Hawkes, J Owers, P A Rickaby, P Steadman (Butterworth, Sevenoaks, Kent) pp 5 – 28

DoE, 1990 *This Common Inheritance: Britain's Environmental Strategy* Cm 1200, Department of the Environment (HMSO, London)

DoE, 1991 *Household Projections, England, 1989 – 2011* (HMSO, London)

Elkin T, McLaren D, Hillman M, 1991 *Reviving the City: Towards Sustainable Urban Development* (Friends of the Earth, London)

Fielding A, 1991, "Migration to and from South East England", report to Department of the Environment, School of Social Sciences, University of Sussex, Brighton, Sussex

Fischel W A, 1991, "Good for the town, bad for the nation? A comment" *Journal of the American Planning Association* **57** 341 – 344

Gillespie A, 1992, "Communications technologies and the future of the city", in *European Research in Regional Science 2. Sustainable Development and Urban Form* Ed. M J Breheny (Pion, London) pp 67 – 78

Goodman P, Goodman P, 1947 *Communitas: Means of Livelihood and Ways of Life* (University of Chicago Press, Chicago, IL)

Gordon P, Richardson H W, 1990, "Gasoline consumption and cities—a reply" *Journal of the American Planning Association* **55** 342 – 345

Gordon P, Richardson H, 1991, "Anti-planning?", paper presented to the ACSP/AESOP Conference "Planning Transatlantic", Oxford Polytechnic, July; copy available from School of Urban and Regional Planning, University of Southern California, Los Angeles, CA

Gordon P, Kumar A, Richardson H W, 1988, "Beyond the journey to work" *Transportation Research* **22A** 419 – 426

Green R, Holliday J, 1991 *Country Planning—A Time for Action* (Town and Country Planning Association, London)

Grigson W S, 1988, "Housing provision in the South East", RPC 1230, SERPLAN Ltd, 50 Broadway, London SW1H 0DB

Jacobs J, 1965, The Death and Life of Great American Cities (Penguin Books, Harmondsworth, Middx)

Lusser H, 1991, "The greening of development control", paper to TCPA Development Control Seminar, 19 – 20 February, London; copy available from Town and Country Planning Association, 17 Carlton House Terrace, London SW1Y 5AS

Neuman M, 1991, "Utopia, dystopia, diaspora" *Journal of the American Planning Association* **57** 344 – 347

Newby H, 1990, "Revitalizing the countryside: the opportunities and pitfalls of counter-urban trends" *Journal of the Royal Society of Arts* **138** 630 – 636

Newman P, Kenworthy J, 1989, "Gasoline consumption and cities—a comparison of US cities with a global survey" *Journal of the American Planning Association* **55** 24 – 37

Osborn W, Whittick A, 1977 *New Towns: Their Origins, Achievements and Progress* (Leonard Hill, Bishopbriggs, Glasgow)

Owens S, 1986 *Energy Planning and Urban Form* (Pion, London)

Owens S, 1990, "Land use planning for energy efficiency", in *Energy, Land, and Public Policy* Ed. J B Cullingworth (Transaction Books, New Brunswick, NJ) pp 53 – 98

Owens S, 1991 *Energy-conscious Planning: The Case for Action* Council for the Protection of Rural England, Warwick House, 25 Buckingham Palace Road, London SW1W 0PP

Owens S, Cope D, 1991, "Land use planning and climate change", final report, 2nd draft, prepared for the Department of the Environment; UK Centre for Economic and Environmental Development, 3e Kings Parade, Cambridge CB2 1SJ

Pearce D, Makandya A, Barbier E, 1989 *Blueprint for a Green Economy* (Earthscan, London)

Rickaby P A, 1987, "Six settlement patterns compared" *Environment and Planning B: Planning and Design* **14** 193 – 223

Rickaby P A, 1991, "Energy and urban development in an archetypal English town" *Environment and Planning B: Planning and Design* **18** 153 – 176

Rickaby P A, Steadman J P, Barrett M, 1992, "Patterns of land use in English towns: implications for energy use and carbon dioxide emissions", in *European Research in Regional Science 2. Sustainable Development and Urban Form* Ed. M J Breheny (Pion, London) pp 182 – 196

Robertson J, 1990, "Alternative futures for cities", in *The Living City: Towards a Sustainable Future* Eds D Cadman, G Payne (Routledge, Chapman and Hall, Andover, Hants) pp 127 – 135

Roger Tym and Partners, 1987, "Land used for residential development in the South East: summary report", Roger Tym and Partners, 9 Sheffield Street, London WC2A 2EZ

Sherlock H, 1990 *Cities are Good for Us* (Transport 2000, Walkden House, 10 Melton Street, London NW1 2EJ

Steadman P, 1979, "Energy and patterns of land use", in *Energy Conservation Through Building Design* Ed. D Watson (McGraw-Hill, Maidenhead, Berks) pp 245 – 260

Whitehand J, Larkham P, 1991, "The suburban-cramming problem in the United Kingdom", paper presented to the ACSP/AESOP Conference "Planning Transatlantic", Oxford Polytechnic, July; copy available from School of Geography, University of Birmingham, Birmingham

Energy Use, Transport and Settlement Patterns

D Banister
University College London

1 Introduction and context

Renewed interest has arisen in sustainable patterns of urban development and the relationship between energy consumption and land use. The focus on energy use is important, as it is primarily a nonrenewable resource and because of its contribution to environmental pollution and global warming. Transport is a major contributor to that picture. As with other developed economies, carbon emissions from fossil fuels in the United Kingdom are above the world average (1.08 tonnes per person) at 2.73 tonnes per person. Road transport makes a significant contribution to emissions of carbon monoxide, hydrocarbons, nitrogen oxides, and carbon dioxide in the United Kingdom (table 1), and in each case there has been a marked increase in the trends over the last decade. If one examines the trends in energy consumption in transport over the same period, the same conclusions can be drawn (table 2), namely that all the trends point towards increased energy depletion and more environmental pollution. Transport's share of all energy consumption is now 31.2% (in 1979 it was 22.8%) and the growth within the transport sector was over 34%, with the most notable increases being in energy use for road and air transport.

The picture is not one of an environmentally concerned transport system, but one in which all the trends are in the wrong direction. The notion of sustainability is a slippery one, particularly when one attempts to define it precisely. Catalogues of definitions have been presented (for example, Prezzy, 1989; Breheny, 1990), but as yet there is no generally applicable or acceptable form. Breheny (1990) concludes that much greater care is required in assessing the role that cities play in consuming

Table 1. Emission of pollutants from road vehicles 1978–88 (source: DoE, 1990a).

Pollutant	Increase 1978–88 (%)	Road proportion of 1988 total (%)	Effects
Carbon monoxide	20	85	Morbidity, fertility
Black smoke	57	35	Toxic trace substances
Volatile organic compounds	17	30	
Nitrogen oxides	25	45	Acid rain
Carbon dioxide	33	18	Global warming
Sulphur dioxide	0	1.5	Acid rain, bronchitis
Lead	−58%	50	Mental development

and degrading natural resources, and he promotes the idea of a city as a resource that should be subjected to the rigorous "development-sustainable development-conditions – intergenerational-equity examination" (page 2). Cities and transport are consumers of resources and producers of pollution and environmental degradation. However, the city itself is a resource and produces wealth, culture, innovation, and education, which in turn sustain much of modern economic, social, and cultural life. It is a question of balance between the environmental arguments and those things necessary to maintain and improve standards of living.

In this paper I take the important role that transport plays in the consumption of resources and attempt to assess how different urban forms may affect the amount of energy used. Four approaches have been developed to analyse the traffic implications of various settlement patterns.

Approach 1: Energy use is assumed to be based on *modal shares, journey lengths,* and *vehicle occupancy.* Aggregate analysis can be carried out from National Travel Survey data on distance travelled per person per week. These data cover all trips over one mile in length, but relate only to four location types: London, urban (population >25000), intermediate (3000 – 25000), and rural (<3000).

Approach 2: Energy use is assumed to be a function of *modal shares, trip distances,* and *settlement types.* Analysis of household data collected for six different types of settlements in South Oxfordshire has been carried out to determine the relationships between these variables.

Approach 3: Energy use is assumed to be a function of *density and intensity of land use.* The Newman and Kenworthy data (1989a; 1989b) for different world cities can be used to establish a relationship between fuel use and urban density or job density. Aggregate analysis is possible, but there are some questions over the comparability and quality of the data. A complementary approach to the empirical methodology developed by Newman

Table 2. Energy consumption in transport (source: DoT, 1990).

Mode	1979		1989		Change 1978 – 89 (%)
	million therms[a]	%	million therms[a]	%	
Rail	495	3.5	388	2.1	−21.6
Road	10925	77.8	15009	79.7	37.4
Water	543	3.9	538	2.9	−1.0
Air	2074	14.8	2901	15.4	39.9
All transport	14037		18836		34.2
All energy	61695		59078		−4.2

[a] This is the energy content of fuels delivered to consumers. For electricity it does not include energy lost in generation and distribution. The thermal efficiency of power stations is about 32% (Energy Efficiency Office, 1990). For petroleum about 7% of energy in crude oil is consumed in the refining process.

and Kenworthy is the simulation analysis of six different settlement patterns by Rickaby (1987).

Approach 4: Energy use is assumed to be a function of *containment for the journey to work.* Census information can be used to establish labour market catchment areas and the proportion of people living and working in the same location. The locations with the highest levels of containment will have the lowest levels of energy consumption. The Cresswell and Thomas (1972) research on new towns has been updated and extended (Breheny, 1990). This approach can be further developed to cover commuting inflows and outflows (Mensink, 1990), the degree of dependence on a single outside employment centre and the proportion of the total labour force working outside the local area.

2 Trends in demand

Over the next twenty years there will be no revolutionary new mode to replace the car as the principal means of transport. Even if a new mode were to appear, the cost of any innovation would be high and the diffusion of those ideas would take time. It must be remembered that mass car production was started by Henry Ford at his Highland Park works in 1913, but it took until the 1950s for mass consumption to take place in Britain. Possible developments might be the adaptation of existing technology through greater efficiency in engine design, the widespread use of unleaded petrol and catalytic converters, and the more speculative development of guidance systems for cars. Experiments have been carried out by Volkswagen in Germany, but the main deterrent to widespread acceptance is likely to be public concern over safety and individual control.

The car is likely to remain the principal means of motorised transport, and growth in car ownership and use is likely to increase over the next twenty years. The actual scale of increases is less clear. In their latest statement on roads the government observe that road traffic has increased by 35% since 1980 and that traffic will increase by between 83% and 142% from 1988 to 2025 (DoT, 1989). The European Commission estimates that car ownership per 1000 inhabitants will increase from 379 in 1990 to 515 in 2010 for the twelve EC member countries [a 36% increase (EC Directorate General for Energy, 1989)]. Society is now in transition from one based on work and industry to one in which leisure pursuits will dominate—the postindustrial society. This society will be highly mobile and depend increasingly on the car and technology. Cities will cease to be centres of manufacturing and production, and will increasingly become centres for information processing, for financial activities and service-based activities.

Both the function and the form of cities will radically change over the next twenty years. Less time will be spent on travelling to work as more people work from home, travel to different locations on different days, and go to head offices less frequently. Long distance commuting is becoming more attractive with high-speed rail links and there is a new flexibility and complexity in people's work patterns, particularly if there is more than one worker in the household. Work, business, and education trips now account for under a third of all trips made [31.8%, (DoT, 1988)], and this proportion is likely to continue to decrease as the leisure-based society makes more trips for social, shopping, and recreational purposes. Cities will have to adapt to these changing patterns of travel demand.

In the period 1965–85 there were fundamental changes, with significant increases in mobility. In Britain, people are making more journeys (11.2 per week in 1965 and 13.2 per week in 1985) and are travelling further, with average journey lengths increasing by over 43%. Total passenger km by all road transport has increased by 67% and the increase for cars and taxis is 95%. Part of this increase can be explained by increases in population (4%), but the growth is mainly the result of increases in car ownership and changes in the range of activities people participate in and the distances needed to travel to reach them. The density of the urban centres has declined and there has been a growth in suburban development and development pressures along accessible motorway corridors. The net effect is unprecedented levels of mobility with the associated increases in the consumption of petroleum (table 2) and production of pollutants (table 1).

The recent Department of Energy (1990) report on energy use and efficiency in the transport sector over the next twenty years takes three scenarios for all forms of transport and predicts energy consumption on the basis of the expected increase in transport demand. Scenarios I and III are intended to form upper and lower boundaries to the future energy demand by transport and the intermediate Scenario II is used to explore sensitivity to the effects of various market factors. Each scenario has a slow take-up and a rapid take-up option. The conclusion reached for surface transport is that between 8% and 18% of the energy consumption, which would otherwise have been projected if no change in the 1986 specific energy-consumption values were assumed, could be saved. If there were no improvements in energy efficiency the levels of energy consumption would be 57% greater in 2010 than the reference year (1986). Two different land-use and settlement patterns were tested. The first was a no-change option with the present distribution of population between urban and rural areas being maintained, and the other tested the effects of a continued shift of population from cities to small towns and rural areas.

Each option results in a different car travel demand pattern and calculations were carried out for traffic on built-up roads, non-built-up roads, and motorways. For the no-change option the present distribution of traffic is assumed to continue—45%, 41%, and 14%, respectively. For the deconcentration option the distribution becomes 35%, 50%, and 15%, respectively. The effect on vehicle-specific energy consumption is a reduction to 2.47 MJ per vehicle kilometre for the deconcentration option from a projected 2.58 MJ per vehicle kilometre for the no-change option (4.26% reduction). It should be noted that the patterns of travel are assumed to remain unchanged as are trip lengths. It is only the distribution of traffic between the different types of road and their associated average energy-consumption patterns that change.

The background is one of increasing demand for travel, greater levels of car ownership, and longer trip distances. Technological changes may make vehicles more efficient, but the net effect is likely to be greater energy consumption as the function and form of cities change over the next twenty years, and as people's travel patterns become more oriented towards leisure activities. The analysis now presents in detail the implications of the four approaches outlined in section 1 for energy consumption given the different transport and settlement patterns.

3 Approach 1: aggregate analysis from the National Travel Survey

Calculations in this approach are based on data taken from the National Travel Survey 1985/86, (DoT, 1988) the Primary Energy Consumption figures (Hughes, 1990), and figures from the Advisory Committee on Energy Conservation (ACEC, 1976). The distance travelled per person per week by type of area and the main mode of transport have been multiplied by energy-consumption figures for the appropriate mode. Any conclusions reached should be treated with caution, as the data are all aggregated and do not take account of any local factors. The public transport figures would be increased if empty running was included, and the figures only cover the direct costs associated with each mode, not the indirect costs such as the construction of buildings and vehicles, track construction and maintenance, and other equipment costs. ACEC (1976) suggest that 30% should be added for car and that the rail figure may be as high as 50%. As with the calculations carried out for the Department of Energy (1990), and as with all other calculations in this paper, the figures are based on current patterns of passenger travel demand at one point in time (table 3; see over). No attempt has been made to assess energy consumption in the freight sector.

However, despite these limitations on the available data, certain clear messages come through

(1) The car is the dominant user of energy.

(2) Occupancy rates are crucial to overall energy-efficiency calculations for all modes.

(3) Diesel is more efficient than petrol. Empirical studies for different types of vehicle suggest that 22% is the approximate difference (Redsell et al, 1988).

(4) Journey-length distributions make the urban (population >25 000) category the most efficient urban form.

(5) To complement the transport assumptions, others need to be made on density, sufficiency and containment to combine the land-use factors with

those on travel. Unfortunately, data problems preclude such an analysis at the aggregate level, but in approach 2 these factors can be included at the local level.

As expected energy use is dominated by the car, with over 90% of all consumption attributed to this mode. Its dominance relates to its modal share of all trips (77%), its longer average journey length (8.66 miles for car drivers, 5.89 miles for non-car-drivers, and 7.5 miles overall), the assumption of 1.5 persons per car, and its higher basic energy-consumption figure. Even if some compensation is made for improved efficiency of the car operating in less congested conditions (row 2 of table 3), the overall

Table 3. Simple energy efficiency and consumption calculations.

Transport mode[a]	MJ per passenger mile	London	Urban (>25 000)	Inter-mediate (3 000–25 000)	Rural (<3 000)	Overall
Car petrol	3.21	218.28	212.50	286.01	362.73	245.89
adjusted[b]		218.28	191.25	228.81	239.40	
British Rail Electric[c]	0.89	9.35	4.98	4.45	5.87	5.52
London Transport						
tube[d]	1.08	6.26	0.11		0.22	0.86
bus[e]	0.83	4.57		0.08		0.58
Other public bus[e]	0.83	0.50	5.56	3.65	2.99	4.23
Minibus	1.15	2.76	3.91	3.91	1.96	3.57
Bicycle[f]	0.10	0.08	0.08	0.07	0.08	0.08
Motorcycle	3.13	2.82	2.50	4.38	3.44	3.13
Private bus[e]	1.40	2.10	3.22	4.20	5.60	3.50
Other private	1.15	1.04	0.69	0.46	1.15	0.69
Walk >1 mile	0.25	0.45	0.63	0.50	0.30	0.53
Total		248.19	234.18	307.72	384.34	268.57
Car proportion (%)		87.95	90.74	92.95	94.38	91.55

[a] The calculations have been based on distance travelled per person per week and the primary energy requirements (MJ per person per week).

[b] The figures give reduced values of energy consumption in non-London locations because of greater fuel efficiencies (ACEC, 1976): rural = 66%, intermediate = 80%, and urban = 90% of the London level. ACEC (1976) quote two figures for car energy consumption: rural = 3.20 MJ per passenger mile and urban = 4.96 MJ per passenger mile. The ratio of these two figures is about 66% and this is the figure used here. The other two figures are interpolations between the rural and the London figure.

[c] BR Electric suburban occupancy is 60% full: note that diesel suburban at the same occupancy level is 27% more costly and Intercity is 43% more costly at the same occupancy levels.

[d] Tube occupancy is assumed to be 33%.

[e] The bus is assumed to be 33% full.

[f] Only walk and bicycle use renewable forms of energy and all short walk trips (under 1 mile) are excluded from the aggregate analysis.

picture is only marginally modified. It is also interesting to note that outside London energy consumption in transport other than car is very similar at about 21.6 MJ per person per week; the figure for London is higher at 29.93 MJ per person per week and this may reflect a greater use of public transport and other forms of transport in the capital as well as the greater congestion experienced.

Table 4. Journey lengths by type of area (source: DoT, 1988).

	London	Urban	Intermediate	Rural	Overall
Total journeys (miles)	13.6	13.1	12.9	13.9	13.2
Total distance (miles)	98.5	88.9	109.4	133.1	99.5
Average journey length (miles)	7.24	6.79	8.48	9.58	7.54

Table 5. Travel distance by mode and energy consumption.

Distance (miles)	Walk	Bicycle	Motor-cycle	Car	Bus	Rail	All trips (%)
(a) *Travel distance by mode*							
<1	82	3		15			35
1–2	42	4		40	14		17
2–3	10	2		67	18	3	10
3–5	2	2	2	73	18	3	14
5–10		1	1	77	16	5	14
10–25				86	7	7	7
>25				85	5	10	3
(b) *Energy use by mode and distance* (MJ)[a]							Overall
<1	359	5		843			1207
1–2	268	10		3274	296		3848
2–3	63	5		5377	374	67	5886
3–5	28	11	351	13123	837	150	14500
5–10		11	329	25953	610	467	27370
10–25				33817	712	763	35292
>25				28649	436	935	30020
Total	718	42	680	111036	3265	2382	118123
(c) *Overall energy consumption per journey*							
Total energy (MJ)	718	42	680	111036	3265	2382	118123
Percentage of journeys	37.12	2.35	0.42	48.32	9.58	2.21	100.0
Energy per journey (MJ)	19.32	17.96	1617.16	2297.92	340.71	1077.51	1181.2

[a] Note that the energy-consumption figures are approximate as they relate to the midpoint of each distance range. This explains the difference in the car contribution of 91.5% in table 3 and 94% in table 5 despite short walk trips being included in the latter.

Overall, the figures for the different area types do seem to be intuitively plausible in that there is a greater use of the car in rural areas, and that urban energy consumption (settlements >25000) is less than that for London. The reason for this is that the total travel distance per person per week is lower, and the average trip length is also lower (table 4). This finding is at odds with the analysis by Newman and Kenworthy (1989), reviewed below, which finds that the very largest of (non-US) world cities tend to be the most energy efficient.

Journey length is closely correlated to mode, with the more energy-intensive modes being used for the longer journeys. The same assumptions have been used as in the previous calculations, and it should again be noted that the figures are approximate. Short walk trips are also included (less than one mile). If these figures are now converted into primary energy consumption (in MJ for each mode weighted by distance and importance), an overall view of the contribution that reductions in trip lengths and switches in modes can be obtained, and their relative importance in achieving energy-saving objectives assessed (table 5).

Even though these figures are approximate, a series of ratios can be worked out for energy efficiency of modes for an average journey by the mode under consideration. The bicycle is the most efficient mode. followed closely by walk. These two modes account for 39.5% of journeys but only 0.64% of the energy. The bus is the most efficient public transport mode being some three times as efficient as rail. The difference is mainly explained by the longer journey length of rail trips. Car and motorcycle are the least efficient modes, using over 100 times the energy required for a walk or bicycle journey. Car accounts for 94% of the energy consumption in making 48.3% of the journeys.

4 Approach 2: disaggregate analysis from survey data

The disaggregate analysis complements the aggregate analysis carried out in approach 1 and focuses on survey data collected from six parishes in the South Oxfordshire area of England (Banister, 1980). Data have been extracted on 689 persons in 440 households on trips, trip purpose, trip lengths, and trips by mode. These raw data have been analysed according to energy consumption and mode. The transport and energy calculations are then matched with information on settlement patterns to see whether any conclusions on settlement form and energy consumption can be made. It is at this microlevel analysis that the impact of local factors and social characteristics might have an important influence on energy consumption in transport. However, as with all analysis at this level of disaggregation one is dealing with small numbers and the data set is old (1978).

The survey area was in South Oxfordshire which is itself a relatively affluent area. Population density at 2.07 persons ha^{-1} is low, but household size is above the national average at 3.19 persons per household, and the housing stock is good (5.61 rooms per household). The population has increased by over 30% (1971–1981), with 24% of them being under 15 years and a further 18% over 60 years of age. Car ownership is high with 53% of households having one car and a further 24% having more than one car. In short the area is affluent and one which is undergoing considerable growth with intense pressure for development.

Overall, 41% of respondents in full-time employment lived and worked in the same parish. This average ranged from 65% in Henley to only 14% in Chalgrove. In total, the six parishes plus Oxford, Reading, Cookham–Maidenhead, and West London account for 76% of all workplaces. The journey-to-work patterns are commented on more fully in approach 4. As a context to the travel and energy analysis, a summary of the characteristics of the six parishes is presented in table 6. The range of parishes surveyed was selected to reflect the different types of parishes in the South Oxfordshire area. Originally, fifty-two parishes were surveyed and six parish types were obtained from cluster analysis (Banister, 1980). Each of those parishes selected for the household survey came from a different cluster and so the six parishes represent the full range of parishes in South Oxfordshire.

Overall, within the six survey parishes there were 2.59 trips per person per day, with work (27%), social (21%), and shopping (18%) accounting for two thirds of all trip purposes. The car was naturally the main mode, accounting for over 70% of all trips either as a driver or as a passenger, with walk being the other most important trip mode (17%). The mean trip length was 8 miles, but there was considerable variation between the parishes ranging from 5.8 miles in Henley to over 11 miles in Chalgrove and Ewelme. This variation is in part explained by the higher proportion of walk trips in Henley (26%). One other observation is that car-passenger trip lengths tend to be longer than car-driver trip lengths in almost all situations, suggesting that where lifts are taken in cars that do not belong to the household they tend to be to the more distant destinations (the average trip length for car drivers is 9.7 miles and that for car passengers 10.8 miles: an 11% difference). It seems that from the travel patterns there are three types of settlements which approximately coincide with ranges of population size:
(1) Henley—population over 10 000, high proportion of walk trips, and a low mean trip length;
(2) Woodcote, Chalgrove, Checkendon—population 1000–2000, high levels of car use, about 10% of trips by walk, longer trip lengths;
(3) Ewelme—population under 1000, very high levels of car use (>90%), very long trip lengths, remote from other settlements.

However, when the travel data are matched up against the energy-efficiency calculations (table 7), a slightly different picture emerges. Henley again stands out as the most energy-efficient form, with a higher consumption figure for non-car modes and a lower than average figure per person. Ewelme is the least energy efficient in terms of the average per person and has a high energy-consumption figure per trip. This is because the average trip rate is high, with over 90% of all trips by car and a high average trip length. Checkendon and Woodcote are both near the average energy-consumption levels per person and per trip. Woodcote's higher energy figure per trip is explained by the greater than average trip length (9 miles as compared with the average of 7.3 miles). In this middle group, Chalgrove seems to have a different pattern with a higher than expected consumption figure per person and per trip. Again, the explanation is in the highest average trip length for all parishes, and this is turn accounted for by its function as a dormitory village for Oxford. Interestingly, the

Table 6. Summary of the settlement patterns in the six parishes surveyed.

Adwell[a]	Population under 100, low-density rural area (0.26 person ha^{-1}), no services or facilities, no public transport (nearest point 1-mile walk), elderly population (51% >60 years), population loss (-17%), 16 miles to Reading and 13 miles to Oxford, all households have at least one car.
Henley	Population over 10 000, high-density urban area (20.4 persons ha^{-1}), all services and facilities (post office, primary and secondary school, food, clothes and other shops, doctor), rail service and good bus services, 23% population <15 years and 20% over 60 years, population gain (25%), 6 miles to Reading and 21 miles to Oxford, 65% of households have at least one car.
Checkendon	Population about 1000, with lower density than average (1.14 persons ha^{-1}), poor facilities (only a primary school), limited public transport to Reading and Henley, 15% population <15 years and 8% >60 years, population increase (39%), 7 miles from Reading and 20 miles from Oxford, 78% of households with at least one car.
Chalgrove	Population about 1000, with above-average density (2.18 persons ha^{-1}), some facilities (primary school, doctor, food and clothes shop), average public transport (to Oxford, Wallingford, and Watlington), young population (35% <15 years and 7% >60 years), huge population increase (272%), 15 miles from Reading and 11 miles from Oxford, 83% of households have at least one car.
Woodcote	Population over 1500, with lower density than average (1.77 persons ha^{-1}), good facilities (doctor, food shop, post office, primary and secondary school), good public transport (Reading, Watlington, Didcot, Henley), 23% population <15 years and 17% >60 years, population increase (39%), 7 miles from Reading and 20 miles from Oxford, 81% of households with at least one car.
Ewelme	Population under 1000, with low density (0.79 person ha^{-1}), limited facilities, poor public transport (Reading, Wallingford, Watlington), 29% population <15 years and 13% >60 years, population increase (50%), 12 miles from Reading and 15 miles from Oxford, 80% of households with at least one car.

[a] As Adwell is so small and different to the other parishes it has been omitted from the remainder of the analysis .

average consumption figures for the Oxfordshire villages (389 MJ per person per week) is very close to the 384 MJ of consumption averaged by the rural category in the National Travel Survey analysis (approach 1). What the Oxfordshire data show, however, is that there is likely to be great variability around such figures, with Ewelme's figure being 619 MJ as compared with Henley's figure of 295 MJ (table 7).

What conclusions can be drawn from the variability within the South Oxfordshire data? It seems that the most efficient settlement pattern is the larger town (Henley) with good provision of facilities, services, and public transport, with shorter trip lengths and a higher proportion of walk trips. It should be noted that Henley has the highest trip-generation rate but the lowest energy-consumption rate per person. The least energy-efficient form is the small remote settlement with limited facilities and services, and with poor public transport (Ewelme). This type of settlement is too small to be self-sufficient and travel by car is essential to reach work and facilities, and these journeys are long because of its remoteness.

Table 7. Energy-efficiency calculations for the South Oxfordshire data.

Mode[a]	Henley	Checkendon	Chalgrove	Woodcote	Ewelme	Overall
Car driver	8 741.47	1 544.36	9 656.48	5 848.52	2 312.45	28 196.51
Car passenger	2 262.09	942.54	2 602.93	1 324.70	836.55	8 024.44
Walk	46.62	1.32	4.28	8.06	0.17	60.45
Bicycle	4.19	1.20	1.07	1.55		9.01
Motorcycle	197.35	6.26	112.68			316.29
Bus	361.44	29.12	275.03	221.89	17.92	905.40
Rail	402.14			54.24		456.38
Other	47.88			256.73	16.92	321.54
Total	12 063.18	2 524.80	12 652.46	7 715.70	3 184.01	38 290.01
Average per person						
per day	42.18	45.09	83.24	52.85	88.45	55.57
per week	295.26	315.63	582.68	369.95	619.15	388.99
Percentage						
car driver	72.46	61.17	76.32	75.80	72.63	73.64
car passenger	18.75	37.33	20.57	17.17	26.27	20.96
pvte transport	91.22	98.50	96.89	92.97	98.90	94.60
other modes	8.78	1.50	3.11	7.03	1.10	5.40
Average per trip	14.46	19.13	32.53	24.73	31.84	21.49

Assumptions: Car occupancy for driver 1.5 persons and for car passenger 2.0 persons. The bus energy figure is the average of the double and single decker with an assumed occupancy of 33%. Rail is taken as the diesel suburban with an assumed occupancy of 60%. Other (diesel lorry, taxi, and coach) is taken to be in equal proportions and weighted accordingly.

[a] The units are in MJ for each mode, for each village, for all people in that sample. The average energy use for each person in each village per day and per week is then given (MJ). Finally, the modal shares are given in percentages for each village together with the average energy use per trip (MJ).

The intermediate sized settlements (Woodcote, Checkendon, and Chalgrove) produce a slightly confused picture. Population structure, distance from employment and other facilities, and levels of car ownership may all influence energy efficiency. Checkendon seems to be the most efficient with shorter trip distances, a close proximity to Reading (7 miles) and a large proportion of the population between the ages of 15 and 60 years (78%). Woodcote is very similar with a slightly longer average trip length, the same distance from Reading, but with more young and more elderly people (only 60% between the ages of 15 and 60 years). However, its energy consumption figures per person and per trip are 17% and 29%, respectively higher than those for Checkendon. If the physical characteristics are similar, it could be argued that social composition then becomes important, with the young and the elderly being more mobile or using less energy-efficient modes. Chalgrove has the longest average trip length and the highest energy consumption figures per trip. It is about 10 miles from Oxford (table 6) and has a very large proportion of young people (35%). The tentative conclusion drawn from the South Oxfordshire data is that settlement size together with the availability of local facilities, services, and employment are the key determinants of travel and energy consumption, but that this pattern is modified by the structure of the population and car ownership levels. All six parishes have high levels of car ownership (77%), and it seems that the higher proportion of young people leads to higher levels of travel and energy use. The physical characteristics of settlement patterns, modified by socioeconomic characteristics, seem to hold the key to transport energy consumption at the microlevel of analysis.

5 Approach 3: energy use as a function of density and intensity of land use

As argued by Newman and Kenworthy (1989) in their world survey of energy use in cities, it is population density, job density, and city-centre dominance that control petroleum use. There is a strong increase in petroleum consumption when population density falls below 29 persons ha^{-1}, and they argue for cities with strong centres and intensively used suburbs which are more suitable for better quality public transport and more walking and biking (figure 1). A basic dichotomy of view is apparent between those like Newman and Kenworthy who prefer a planning approach and those who suggest that the price system is the only way to determine urban structure (Gordon and Richardson, 1989). The argument is not clear cut, as large single-centre cities may not be efficient, but polynucleated centres with a hierarchical structure may minimise travel distances and times as people travel to local facilities wherever possible, and only go to the city centre for specific reasons.

The difficulty with such an international comparative analysis is the quality of the data and the opportunity for large-scale generalisation with policies being rather prescriptive. The key dependent variable in most of their analysis is annual gasoline use per capita (measured in GJ, 1980).

Although they have been meticulous in their search for consistent sources of data, it is notoriously difficult to collect any reliable information on this variable, and so any results must be interpreted cautiously. Gasoline consumption figures have been obtained from specific sources in the US (for example, Transportation Department), from the Triennial Survey of Motor Vehicle Usage (SMVU) in Australia, and from a variety of local government agencies in Europe and Asia. Average trip lengths have been taken from national travel surveys broken down for individual cities, but these are mainly irregular surveys. Vehicle-occupancy rates tend to be between 1.2 and 1.3 in the peak, but other data suggest a higher figure.

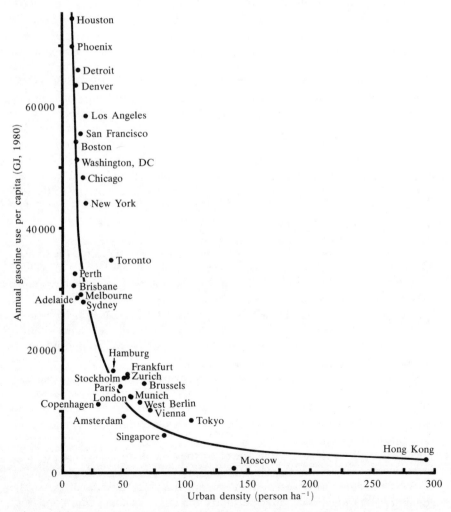

Figure 1. Petrol use per capita versus urban population density (source: Newman and Kenworthy, 1989).

The most interesting conclusion from the Newman and Kenworthy (1989) work is the lack of a relationship between gasoline use and city size, either measured by population or by extent of the urban area. The correlation was weakly significant, but negative; this means that smaller cities have higher, not lower, car travel. Most of the analysis is based on journey-to-work data, and, as Gordon and Richardson (1989) comment, the work journey is accounting for a decreasing proportion of the total trip making. They argue that colocation of firms and households can reduce journey times, and decentralisation can reduce city-centre congestion. Their evidence from the US Nationwide Personal Transportation Study supports the case that there is no relationship between city size and trip length times or speeds, and average speeds did not decline (Gordon et al, 1988).

Complementary to these empirical studies have been a series of simulation analyses of the relationships between urban form, density, and energy consumption. Sharpe (1982) suggests that Melbourne's energy savings could be 11% if density were increased three times. Small (1980) suggests that an energy-induced land-use control that results in densities of 15 units per acre compared with the US average of 5 units per acre would reduce car usage for work by only 1.4% after six years. One of the most interesting recent studies has been Rickaby's (1987; 1991) comparison of six different energy-efficient city-regional settlement patterns against three economic growth scenarios. He compares energy use and accessibility so that the spatial patterns can be compared. This means that both transport energy and fuel use in building services are included, and the energy savings are measured against the total benefit gained by the population through cost-effective interaction. A comparative evaluation of the development options for variations on an archetypal town was made by means of the TRANUS land-use, transport, and energy-evaluation model.

The six settlement patterns are
1. existing,
2. concentrated nucleated with density from 33.9 to 45.5 persons ha^{-1},
3. concentrated linear with density of 16.96 persons ha^{-1},
4. dispersed nucleated (satellite towns) with primary density of 33.9 persons ha^{-1}, and secondary density of 28.9 persons ha^{-1},
5. dispersed linear with density of 10.96 persons ha^{-1},
6. dispersed nucleated (villages) with density of 28.9 persons ha^{-1}.
It should be noted that all of these densities except in options 1 and 5 are close to the critical 29 persons ha^{-1} (12 persons per acre) identified by Newman and Kenworthy (1989). Some of the assumptions used seem optimistic. For example, bus occupancy rises from forty passengers to fifty passengers per vehicle in the high and low scenarios, and car occupancy also rises from 1.85 to 2.50. Nevertheless, the findings are important in that energy use in each of the alternatives is less than that in the existing case, but each alternative also results in a loss of benefit. This loss is mainly in the domestic sector and not in the transport sector, and

Rickaby concludes that the existing configuration is efficient in terms of accessibility and cost. Patterns 2 and 6 show both fuel savings and increased transport benefits. With respect to pattern 6, Rickaby concludes "thus it appears that modest concentration of development into local centres within the hinterland of the existing city both saves fuel in transport and improves accessibility" (1987, page 217).

The Rickaby findings are at odds with conventional thinking which suggests that the compact city (CEC, 1990) or the archipelago pattern of compact urban subunits (10000–30000) which are self-sufficient in service provision and employment (Owens, 1987) are the two most energy-efficient forms. Rickaby concludes that either the concentrated nucleated settlement or the dispersed nucleated (village) settlement patterns are the two most appropriate urban forms if energy use and accessibility are considered. This debate highlights a series of problems which are apparent when the complexity of urban problems is examined along a single dimension. If energy use is the only variable to be considered, then ideal patterns can be established, but in most cases one is dealing with an established settlement pattern and any radical change to that system has to take account both of the complex interactions between transport, land, labour, and capital, and the time required for any change. The high-density compact city proposed in the European Commission's Green Paper (CEC, 1990) may seem attractive as journey lengths would be short, public transport provision would be more effective, and land consumption would be minimised. But traffic congestion would be increased, as would journey times, and more emissions and higher fuel consumption would also result. Superimposed on all these travel-related factors is the changing role that the city has in postindustrial society and the increasing concern of people over quality-of-life factors.

6 Approach 4: energy use as a function of containment for the journey to work

Any analysis of journey-to-work data should be qualified by the declining importance of work as a proportion of all journey purposes. In Britain the journey to work accounts for 22.3% of the total distance travelled per person per week and 23.4% of all trips (1985/86), and the corresponding figures for work and school in the Netherlands (1984) are 29.8% of the total distance travelled per person per week and 23.7% of all trips.

Cresswell and Thomas (1972) devised an independence ratio for new towns in Britain and for other comparable towns in southern England over the period 1951 to 1966, and this analysis has been updated to 1981 by Breheny (1990). The independence ratio is defined as the ratio of residents working in a town divided by the sum of the residents working outside the town and the workers in the town residing outside. A high level of self-containment in the new towns was found and this level increased with distance from London. Self-containment reached its peak in the mid-1960s before the growth in mass car ownership. Breheny in his updating (1990) of the Cresswell and Thomas work concludes that both in new towns and in other towns self-containment has declined since that time, and that the decline has been greatest in the new towns (table 8). The explanation is not clear, but may be related to the concept of the new towns as centres of employment as well as population. However, it is likely that the advent of mass car ownership and increases in the numbers and lengths of all trip purposes has had a fundamental influence on the containment of all settlement types. Breheny (1990) concludes that, as settlements become more distant from London or more remote generally, the level of self-containment becomes higher. This finding is not surprising as intuitively one would expect isolation from other employment opportunities would be likely to influence the level of self-containment.

In a similar piece of work, S Potter (personal communications, 1991) examined the relationship between commuting out to work and distance from London (1981). This showed a negative relationship between proportion of working residents commuting out and distance from the capital, and Potter suggests that new towns have about average out-commuting which is in contrast with the earlier results for 1966 and 1971. The converse

Table 8. 'Independence index' values for new towns, 1951–1981 (source: Breheny, 1990).

New town	1951	1961	1966	1971	1981
Aycliffe	0.08	0.52	0.57	0.44	0.74
Basildon	0.36	0.96	0.96	0.87	0.76
Bracknell	0.90	1.13	1.02	0.87	0.82
Central Lancs				1.88	1.88
Corby	1.41	1.91	2.51	0.69	1.79
Crawley	0.98	1.59	1.58	1.69	1.15
Cwmbran	0.72	0.74	0.88	0.75	0.80
Harlow	1.42	2.04	2.05	1.92	1.44
Hatfield	0.65	0.63	0.66	0.32	0.45
Hemel Hempstead	1.31	1.82	1.72	1.43	1.00
Milton Keynes				1.36	1.44
Newtown				1.03	1.32
Northampton				2.88	2.43
Peterborough				1.84	1.99
Peterlee	0.34	0.20	0.36	0.41	0.39
Redditch				1.30	1.12
Runcorn				0.73	0.94
Skelmersdale				0.67	0.87
Stevenage	0.92	2.29	2.03	1.63	1.14
Telford				2.61	2.41
Warrington				1.74	1.32
Washington				0.56	0.67
Welwyn	1.12	1.09	1.12	0.97	0.68
All new towns	0.85	1.24	1.29	1.00	0.95

to this, namely that the amount of in-commuting to a town should be related to the scale of employment, does not seem to be supported by the evidence. Overall, it seems that new towns now have the same proportion of out-commuters as other comparable towns and probably generate slightly more in-commuting. Breheny (1990) concludes that energy efficiency can be best achieved through short journey-to-work distances, hence settlement patterns should be large and relatively isolated, or small and relatively isolated, or small and close to existing urban areas.

If a similar type of analysis is carried out on the six South Oxfordshire parishes surveyed as part of approach 2, some of the comments raised above are supported. It should be remembered that all the parishes are relatively small and close to two large employment centres (Reading and Oxford). Two measures have been used which are slightly different from the independence ratio of Cresswell and Thomas, as the number of workers in the parish residing outside was not available. The first measure is the number of residents working in the parish divided by the number of residents working outside the parish, and the second measure is the sum of the number of residents working in the parish and those residents working in the single largest employment centre outside the parish divided by the number of others working outside the parish. The first measure is a simple ratio of employment inside and outside the parish, whereas the second determines whether the parish is a dormitory centre for a single nearby town (table 9). The third measure is the proportion of the total labour force working outside the parish. The measures are not comparable with those in the previous table.

It is only in Henley that the employment within the parish is greater than that outside (Adwell has only twelve households and is not discussed), with the modified independence ratio averaging at 0.70 for all six parishes. However, if the single most important employment centre outside each parish is included, the picture changes as the measure of independence now becomes a dependence ratio. In all parishes except Woodcote the ratio has been increased to over 1.0 with an average figure of 1.44. Small numbers may partly explain this increase, but more generally it seems that

Table 9. Employment measures applied to South Oxfordshire parishes (see text for definition).

Parish	Measure 1	Measure 2	Measure 3 (%)
Adwell	1.33	2.50	43
Henley	1.88	2.90	35
Checkendon	0.83	1.06	55
Chalgrove	0.16	1.50	86
Woodcote	0.31	0.44	75
Ewelme	0.77	1.56	57
Overall	0.70	1.44	58

each parish, with the possible exception of Henley, is a dormitory for a larger town. In Chalgrove, for example, only fifteen people from the sample work in the parish but a further forty six work in Oxford which is ten miles away. The settlement is too small to maintain an employment base. The final measure simply reinforces the picture as only in Henley do more than 50% of the residents work in the parish. The overall proportion of the labour force working outside each parish is 58% (table 9).

On a much larger scale Mensink (1990) has examined the commuter outflow from seventeen Dutch cities and the changes that have taken place between 1960 and 1981. In 1960 about 75 000 people were commuting between cities, but by 1980 this figure had increased to 170 000 and the average distance travelled had increased from 3 to 15 km. The proportion of the labour force commuting out from each of these seventeen cities was considerably less than that in the six South Oxfordshire parishes in table 9. For the largest cities (Rotterdam, Amsterdam, Den Haag, and Utrecht) the figure was about 5%, for the intermediate sized cities (for example, Alkmaar, Dordrecht, Haarlem, Leiden) the range was between 12% and 29%, and for the smallest cities (for example, Maastricht, Breda, Eindhoven, Tilburg) the level was again around 5%. From this survey of the situation in the Netherlands, Mensink suggests that an ideal urban form would be a ring of small towns (20 000 – 25 000) with all essential services. These partly self-sufficient suburbs would form a ring around a central silent area and support each other making up a self-sufficient city of 160 000 – 250 000. These cities would be connected with the national motorway and rail systems and the main aim of the national strategy would have been achieved, namely to reduce the average trip length for car journeys.

It seems that the levels of independence have been reduced over the last thirty years and this has coincided with the growth in mass car ownership. It is now less likely that any individual lives and works in the same location than it was in the 1960s. Against this general trend, it can also be concluded that the larger the settlement size the greater the likelihood of self-containment as regards employment. However, in the middle range of settlement size, commuting may take place outside the local area. Again, it should be noted that the Dutch data relate only to the journey to work, not to the other 77% of trips made for reasons other than work.

7 Conclusions
In this paper I have presented a synthesis and integration of a wide range of data from international, national, and local sources on travel and energy consumption. The primary requirements for such an analysis are for details of travel by purpose, mode, distance, and frequency of trips. Certain assumptions have then been made on average energy-consumption figures for different types of vehicle, together with comment on the robustness of those assumptions (table 3), in particular the crucial importance of occupancy rates in determining energy consumption. All the data have

been collected at one point in time and so represent a static view of both travel and energy consumption. Some of the data form a repeated cross-section taken at several points in time, but even here it is difficult to interpret the changes that have taken place between the survey points.

However, despite these limitations, certain conclusions can be drawn:

1. In the domestic passenger transport sector the car is the dominant mode, accounting for 48% of journeys but over 90% of energy consumption. Conversely, walk and bicycle account for nearly 40% of journeys but under 1% of energy use.

2. The vehicle-occupancy assumptions are important in determining energy consumption. Relatively small changes in car-occupancy levels or in public transport occupancy levels significantly affect energy-consumption figures per passenger mile. Energy use per vehicle is almost independent of the number of people travelling. Perhaps a more stable measure would be to give estimates of energy consumption per vehicle mile (that is, with an assumed occupancy of one):

Car   4.82 MJ per car mile,
Bus   20.72 MJ per bus mile,
Rail (Super Sprinter Diesel) 78.32 MJ per train mile.

3. Significant increases in energy consumption have taken place since the 1960s when mass car ownership became a reality, and this is reflected in an increase of 37% in road energy consumption in the period 1979–89 (table 2). It seems likely that this growth will continue in line with the expected growth in car ownership and traffic over the next two decades, whether predictions are taken from the Department of Transport, the Department of Energy, or from the European Commission Directorate General on Energy (section 2).

4. The importance of the journey to work is declining and it now accounts for around 20% of all trips. This reduction is partly explained by the decline in work journeys as more complex work patterns evolve, but more importantly by the growth in other activities, particularly leisure, social, and shopping activities. Almost all of the growth is in car-based activities.

5. There has been some compensation through improvements in the energy efficiency of vehicles and through road construction which may reduce the amount of inefficient running of vehicles caused by congestion, at least in the short term.

6. Overall however, it seems that life-styles and trip patterns are becoming more complex and car oriented. There has been an unprecedented growth in travel over the last decade and it could be argued that the transport system has been taking the strain. Family relations are becoming more varied with the diminished importance of the nuclear family, and the growth in single-parent families and young adults with no children. The work force has expanded with part-time labour, job sharing, and increased female participation. More recently, these changes have been compounded by a stagnant housing market, high interest rates and growing unemployment.

The uncertainty in the economic situation may result in people not moving so frequently but adopting temporary patterns of travel to work and other activities, which in turn results in more and longer trips being made, principally by car (Banister and Bayliss, 1991).

7. However, as Gordon and Richardson (1989, page 342) emphasise, the pursuit of a single objective such as "minimising gasoline consumption makes no sense". They quote Lowry who points out that "efficiency does not imply rearranging our lives to minimise transport costs. Rather it implies a search for a suitable balance between transport costs of compatibly configured land uses". The complexity of the urban policy process requires the use of several policy levers (for example, pricing, regulation, and taxation) to achieve a spatial structure that reflects the land, labour, and housing markets as well as the transport market.

From the four approaches investigated and the evidence cited from other sources, some tentative conclusions can be drawn on the relationships between transport, energy, and settlement patterns. At the general level it seems that travel distances and trip rates should be reduced so that residential areas can be related to local jobs and services, and not develop as dormitory settlements (Owens, 1987). However, concentration of new development into smaller centres outside the urban area may save less fuel than concentrating that same level of development into the urban area itself. But fuel savings in developments outside the urban area are less costly because of reduced levels of traffic congestion and the greater availability of space (Rickaby, 1987).

Notions of self-containment are perhaps less valid in a highly mobile car-oriented society, as it would be impossible for any one town or city to have a complete range of activities. Even though many people may commute to another centre for employment, that settlement may still be relatively efficient if a range of other facilities and services are provided within walking or cycling distance. The large and isolated settlement would probably be more self-contained than the small and isolated settlement, but a series of small free-standing towns in close proximity to each other (and perhaps a major city) would probably be the most energy-efficient form in a society that is dependent on the car for most travel. The free-standing town (about 25, 000) would have the shortest trip lengths, lowest door-to-door trip times, and a high proportion of facilities and services within walking and cycling distance. The National Travel Survey information supports this conclusion (table 3). Henley (population 11 000) is the largest and most energy efficient of the microlevel analysis parishes, and the most urban. It has the highest trip-generation rate but the lowest energy consumption figures per trip and per person. This is because of the availability of good local services and facilities, local employment, good public transport, and a high proportion of walk trips.

This conclusion contradicts that reached by Newman and Kenworthy (1989) on density of development being the most important single determinant of energy consumption. It seems that the physical characteristics of the urban settlement are important (size, availability of facilities and services, public transport), but that this basic relationship is modified by the socioeconomic characteristics of the population as different people have different propensities to travel with different frequencies, trip lengths, and modes.

The European Commission's (CEC, 1990) notion of a compact city with greater diversity and people living close to their workplaces simplifies the complexity of life-styles. A holistic view must encompass the full range of activities that people participate in. Many would argue that the car has improved their quality of life, the opportunities available to them, and the flexibility and independence offered by personal transport. The concept of the sustainable city goes beyond one which is energy efficient or transport efficient and explores the city as a place in which people want to live.

In September 1990, the Department of the Environment published a White Paper *This Common Inheritance* (DoE, 1990b) which claimed to present the first comprehensive review of every aspect of Britain's environmental policy. Conservation of energy was identified as an issue in development plans as was the reduction in emissions of greenhouse gases. It was suggested that locations should be selected which reduce the need for car journeys and distances driven or which permit the choice of more energy-efficient public transport (paragraph 6.34). Walk and cycling should be added to that list of more energy-efficient modes. It was also suggested that the planning of transport routes should take account of the potential impact on settlement and development plans. This paper is intended to take the debate further and I have attempted to present four different approaches to the analysis of energy use in transport and the links between transport and settlement patterns. As such it is a contribution to the ongoing debate on sustainable development.

References
ACEC, 1976 *Passenger Transport: Short and Medium Term Considerations* Energy Paper 10, Advisory Committee on Energy Conservation, Department of Energy (HMSO, London)
Banister D, 1980 *Transport Mobility and Deprivation in Inter Urban Areas* (Saxon House, Farnborough, Hants)
Banister D, Bayliss D, 1991, "Structural changes in population and impacts on passenger transport demand", paper presented at the European Conference of Ministers of Transport Round Table 88, Paris, June; copy available from author
Breheny M J, 1990, "Strategic planning and urban sustainability", paper presented to the Town and Country Planning Association Conference on Planning for Sustainable Development, London, 27–28 November; copy available from the author, Department of Geography, University of Reading, Berks
CEC, 1990 *Green Paper on the Urban Environment* EUR 12902 (Commission of the European Communities, Brussels)
Cresswell P, Thomas R, 1972, "Employment and population balance", in *New Towns: The British experience* Ed. H Evans (Charles Knight, London) pp 66–79

Department of Energy, 1990 *Energy Use and Energy Efficiency in UK Transport up to the year 2010* Energy Efficiency Series 10 (HMSO, London)

DoE, 1990a *Digest of Environmental Protection and Waste Statistics* number 12, Environmental Protection Statistics Division, Department of the Environment (HMSO, London)

DoE, 1990b *This Common Inheritance: Britain's Environmental Strategy* Cm 1200, Department of the Environment (HMSO, London)

DoT, 1988 *National Travel Survey 1985/86 Report* Department of Transport (HMSO, London)

DoT, 1989 *National Road Traffic Forecasts (Great Britain)* Department of Transport (HMSO, London)

DoT, 1990 *Transport statistics Great Britain 1979–1989* Department of Transport (HMSO, London)

EC Directorate General for Energy, 1989 "Major themes in energy: energy in Europe" (European Commission, Brussels)

Gordon P, Richardson H W, 1989, "Gasoline consumption and cities: A reply" *Journal of the American Planning Association* **55** 342–346

Gordon P, Kumar A, Richardson H W, 1988, "Beyond the journey to work" *Transportation Research* **22A** 419–426

Hughes P, 1990, "Transport emissions and the greenhouse effect", paper presented to the Universities Transport Studies Group Conference, January; copy available from the author, Energy and Environment Research Unit, The Open University, Milton Keynes

Mensink G M, 1990, "Creating self sufficient cities", paper presented to the PTRC Conference, September; copy available from the author, ARJUNA Consulting Group, Amersfoort, The Netherlands

Newman P W G, Kenworthy J R, 1989a, "Gasoline consumption and cities: a comparison of US cities with a global survey" *Journal of the American Planning Association* **55** 24–37

Newman P W G, Kenworthy J R, 1989b *Cities and Automobile Dependence* (Gower, Aldershot, Hants)

Owens S, 1987, "The urban futures: does energy really matter?", in *Energy and Urban Built Form* Eds D Hawkes, J Owers, P Rickaby, P Steadman (Butterworth, Sevenoaks, Kent) pp 169–189

Prezzy J, 1989, "Definitions of sustainability", DP9, Centre for Economic and Environmental Development, 3E Kings Parade, Cambridge CB2 1SJ

Redsell M, Lucas G, Ashford N, 1988, "Comparison of on road fuel consumption for diesel and petrol cars", Transport and Road Research Laboratory, Crowthorne, Berks RG11 6AU

Rickaby P, 1987, "Six settlement patterns compared" *Environment and Planning B: Planning and Design* **14** 193–223

Rickaby P, 1991, "Energy and urban development in an archetypal English town" *Environment and Planning B: Planning and Design* **18** 153–175

Sharpe R, 1982, "Energy efficiency and equity of various urban land use patterns" *Urban Ecology* **7** 1–18

Small K, 1980, "Energy scarcity and urban development patterns" *International Regional Science Review* **5** 97–119

Patterns of Land Use in English Towns: Implications for Energy Use and Carbon Dioxide Emissions

P A Rickaby
Rickaby Thompson Associates, Milton Keynes
J P Steadman
Open University, Milton Keynes
M Barrett
Earth Resources Research, London

1 Introduction

Research has been going on into the relationship between patterns of land use and the use of energy since the early 1970s. Recently the subject has acquired a new urgency in the context of global warming and the control of emissions of carbon dioxide. In this paper we describe a series of studies made of the use of energy in English towns of around 100 000 population. We consider alternative patterns of land use both within the urban boundary and at the city-regional scale. Our principal concern is with fuel used in passenger transport. First, however, we put this work into context by presenting some figures for current national patterns of energy use and resulting emissions of carbon dioxide.

2 The current pattern of energy use and carbon dioxide emissions in the United Kingdom

Table 1 shows energy used (in PJ) in the fuel conversion industries and by final user in the United Kingdom, for 1988, disaggregated by type of fuel. Some of these figures are worthy of special comment. Very large quantities of coal and oil are used for the production of electricity, resulting in a major loss of potentially useful energy as reject heat. Some of this waste heat could in principle be put to good use in combined heat and power (CHP) and district heating schemes, which would have significant implications for patterns of land use and for development densities.

Among the final uses there is a major use of oil in transport, as would be expected, and substantial use of gas, electricity, and other fuels in the domestic sector, principally for space heating and water heating. A large part of the energy used in the 'other industry', 'public administration', and 'miscellaneous' categories is also devoted to the heating, lighting, and servicing of buildings.

If the fuel used in the conversion industries is allocated to the relevant end-use sectors, and appropriate carbon coefficients are applied to the different fuels, it is possible to arrive at estimates of carbon dioxide emissions (in Mt) for each end use. Table 2 presents the picture for 1988: transport accounts for 24% of all carbon dioxide emissions, the domestic sector for 30%, and the service sector for 16%. If the emissions are broken down by purpose, it emerges that approximately 45% of all emissions are associated with space heating, water heating, and lighting, all of which may be affected by building design. The remaining categories are made up largely by the generation of process heat for industry, and the use of electricity and other fuels to power fixed machinery of all kinds.

The energy-use sector which is most directly and significantly affected by the distribution of land uses is of course transport. Table 3 shows fuel use in, and carbon dioxide emissions from, the transport sector in 1988, broken down in more detail. Emissions of carbon dioxide direct from transport amount to some 130 Mt, or 22% of emissions from all sources.

Table 1. Energy use (PJ) in the United Kingdom by sector, 1988.

	Coal	Coke	Solid fuel	Gas	Elec- tricity	Oil	Total
Conversion industries							
Refineries	0	0	0	0	0	230	230
Electricity	2036	0	0	9	0	229	2274
Coke ovens	64	0	0	0	0	0	64
Manufacturing fuel	18	0	0	0	0	0	18
Total	2118	0	0	9	0	460	2586
Final users							
Iron and steel	1	229	0	47	29	35	341
Other industries	218	15	1	524	288	392	1436
Transport	0	0	0	0	12	1888	1899
Domestic	199	13	38	1082	333	102	1766
Public administration	28	6	0	131	68	113	347
Agriculture	0	0	0	3	15	38	57
Miscellaneous	6	5	2	182	176	59	429
Total	452	268	40	1969	920	2626	6275
Gross	2570	268	40	1978	920	3086	8862

Table 2. Carbon dioxide emissions (Mt) in the United Kingdom by end use, 1988.

	Space heating	Water heating	Light	Heat	Other	Trans- port	Total	%
Domestic	97	32	6	0	41	0	176	30
Iron and steel	0	0	0	0	36	0	36	6
Other industries	12	12	4	79	43	0	152	26
Services	44	8	27	0	16	0	95	16
Transport	0	0	0	0	0	134	134	24
Agriculture	0	0	0	0	7	0	7	1
Total	153	52	37	79	136	134	593	100
%	28	10	7	14	25	24		

The addition of the bulk of refinery emissions takes this to the gross figure of 140 Mt (24%) which we saw earlier. Notice that road transport accounts for around 80% of transport emissions. Aircraft produce 16% of transport emissions, the greater part of which is from international flights. This is the fastest growing transport sector in the United Kingdom.

In order to examine how this national pattern of fuel use and emissions might change as a result of changes in the passenger transport system, we use an accounting framework model called PASS (Steadman and Barrett, 1991). PASS uses National Travel Survey data on total distances travelled and numbers of trips. These are disaggregated by fifteen travel purposes, fourteen stage-distance bands, and twenty-five modes. In the PASS model the numbers of trips are normalised to the whole of the United Kingdom. A chain of calculations is then made which relates the following variables: journey frequency by distance (% of all journeys), total distance (passenger kilometres), modal split (% distance by mode), modal distance (passenger kilometres), vehicle load factor, vehicle distance (vehicle kilometres), vehicle-specific fuel consumption ($MJ\,km^{-1}$), vehicle fuel consumption (PJ), and carbon dioxide emission. Values for such parameters as load factors and specific fuel consumptions of vehicles are introduced as necessary. Specific fuel consumption is assumed to be constant for each vehicle type, and load factors are assumed to vary by trip purpose.

Table 3. Fuel use in, and carbon dioxide emissions from, UK transport in 1988.

	Fuel		CO_2	
	Mt	PJ	Mt	%
Rail				
Burning oil	0.01	0	0.0	0
Gas or diesel	0.69	31	2.1	2
Fuel oil	0.01	0	0.0	0
Electricity	–	12	2.5	1
Total	0.71	43	4.5	2
Road				
Motor spirit	23.25	1090	73.1	57
Derv	9.37	425	28.5	23
Total	32.62	1516	101.5	80
Water				
Gas or diesel	0.98	44	3.0	2
Fuel oil	0.1	4	0.3	0
Total	1.08	49	3.3	3
Air				
Aviation spirit	0.03	1	0.1	0
Aviation turbine	6.2	292	19.6	15
Total	6.23	293	19.7	16
All sectors	40.64	1912	129.1	100

Thus, private cars are assumed to have lower load factors for trips to and from work than for social trips.

Using the PASS model it is possible to make hypothetical changes in such variables as journey lengths and modal split, in order to study their overall impact on fuel use and emissions. At this stage these experiments are not supported by any kind of evidence, either empirical or theoretical, as to whether the changes are realistic or could actually be achieved by means of planning or economic policy. We will offer some such evidence later.

The first experiment involves the assumption that trip lengths become generally shorter. In the PASS model this is simulated by shifting different percentages of trips to the next shortest distance band. Table 4(a) shows how both the average stage length and the total distance travelled are progressively reduced as the percentage of trips shifted in this way increases. As trips are shifted to the very shortest distance bands there is some effect on modal split, as car trips are transferred to other modes such as cycling and walking. However, this effect is small, and, in general, fuel use and carbon dioxide emissions are nearly linearly related to the total distance travelled. Thus a 40% reduction in total passenger-kilometres results in a 40% reduction in emissions.

The second experiment relates directly to modal split. In the PASS model different percentages of trips are shifted from cars to walking, cycling, or trains, up to certain assumed maximum shifts for each distance band. (In energy use per passenger-kilometre, public transport is typically twice as efficient as car travel, and cycling is about thirty-five times as efficient.) The results of the experiment are shown in Table 4(b).

Table 4. (a) The stage-shift and (b) the modal shift experiments.

Shift (%)	Average stage length (km)	Billion pass-km [a]	Pass-km [a] by car (%)	Vehicle distance (billion veh-km [b]	Energy (PJ)	CO_2 (Mt)
(a) *Stage-shift*						
0	6.4	644	77	333	1123	76
20	6.0	595	71	308	1039	71
40	5.5	547	70	283	954	65
60	5.0	499	70	259	870	59
80	4.5	450	69	234	785	53
100	4.0	402	68	209	701	48
(b) *Modal shift*						
0	6.4	644	77	333	1123	76
20	6.4	644	65	293	1032	70
40	6.4	644	52	252	941	64
60	6.4	644	40	212	850	58
80	6.4	644	28	171	758	52
100	6.4	644	15	131	667	45

[a] Passenger-km.   [b] Vehicle-km.

Average stage length and total distance travelled now remain the same, but the distance travelled by car drops as increasing proportions of the maximum assumed modal shift are put into effect. At the extreme, only 15% of passenger-kilometres are by car, and carbon dioxide emissions are reduced by about 40%.

If the two experiments, on stage length and modal shift, are put together, then the combined effects of the maximum changes considered in each case result in a reduction of 50% in carbon dioxide emissions.

3 Simulation of the effects of urban planning policies on energy use

Studies with the PASS model provide some broad indications of the scale of reduction in energy use and carbon dioxide emissions which might in theory be brought about by changes in transport patterns. But what order of change might in fact be practically feasible, and by what means? There are several possible ways of investigating such questions. The approach which we have taken in two projects over the last ten years is to make experiments with land-use and transport simulation models.

Our most recent study (Rickaby, 1991) began with an empirical analysis of land-use and transport patterns in a representative sample of twenty English towns with populations between 50000 and 150000 (figure 1, table 5). For each town, data were collected describing the pattern of land use and the extent and form of development. Sources of data included local planning authorities, land-use maps, large-scale maps, and a brief survey visit to each town.

Figure 1. The distribution of the twenty study towns.

For each town, land-use maps were updated from information provided by the local planning authority, and land-use data were digitised from the maps. Measures were also made of the pattern of roads and streets in each town. The land-use data were then processed using the ARC/INFO geographical information system (ESRI Inc., Redlands, CA), in order to obtain a breakdown of land uses according to a standard pattern of zones which was applied to each town. This permitted the construction of a representation of an idealised 'archetypal town', consisting of a pattern of land uses and a road network which embody average or typical values for various characteristics of the pattern of development in the sample towns, and from which site-specific characteristics resulting from accidents of local history and topography had been removed (figure 2, see over). The population assumed for the archetypal town is the average population of the twenty study towns, distributed between zones in proportion to the average area of residential development in each zone in the twenty study towns. Distributions of households, and of basic employment, were derived from the distributions of population and land uses using national average figures for towns of this size.

The next stage of the research was to study the local authorities' planning documents for each of the sample towns, and to make a survey of the planning literature, in order to establish the likely ways in which the sample towns might develop, or be under pressure to develop, during

Table 5. The twenty sample towns.

Town	Location	Population, 1971
Cambridge	Cambridgeshire	98 840
Carlisle	Cumbria	71 582
Colchester	Essex	76 531
Crawley	West Sussex	73 000
Crewe	Cheshire	51 421
Darlington	Durham	85 938
Exeter	Devon	95 729
Gloucester	Gloucestershire	90 232
Halifax	West Yorkshire	91 272
Hastings	East Sussex	72 410
Hemel Hempstead	Hertfordshire	76 000
Lincoln	Lincolnshire	74 269
Maidstone	Kent	70 987
Poole	Dorset	107 161
Reading	Berkshire	132 939
Rotherham	South Yorkshire	84 801
Southport	Merseyside	84 574
Swindon	Wiltshire	91 033
Worcester	Hereford and Worcester	73 452
York	North Yorkshire	104 782

the next twenty years. The most evident trend was the pressure being experienced by all the towns, and particularly those in the south of England, to accommodate new private housing and large peripheral retail developments.

Although fuel conservation does not appear to have a high priority in contemporary British planning, the need to absorb new private housing in many towns does raise the question of how to do so in a way which improves the overall energy-efficiency of those towns. In order to examine

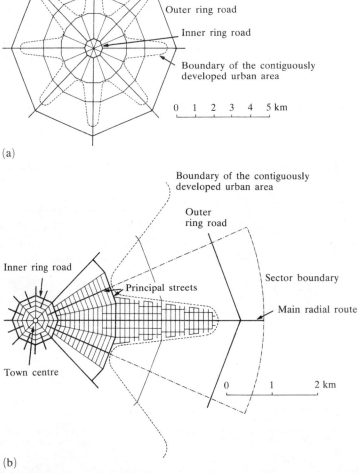

(a)

(b)

Figure 2. (a) The pattern of main roads, and (b) the pattern of streets in a one-eighth sector, of the archetypal town.

the energy efficiency of various strategies with which new development might be accommodated in the sample towns, a number of modified versions of the archetypal town were constructed. The modified versions all had the same overall population as the original, but in each case households, employment, and services were assumed to have relocated over a period of twenty years in response to development-control policies. It was also assumed that average household size decreased (from 2.5 persons to 2.1 persons per household), and that employment was maintained at an average of one job per household, resulting in increases of approximately 20% in the number of households, the number of jobs, and the amount of floorspace.

Five modified versions of the archetypal town were devised (figure 3, see over). These included three versions in which new development was contained within the original urban area, and two versions in which it was directed into areas of peripheral expansion. In the containment options, development was directed either into existing subcentres, or into new development corridors along existing main routes, or both into subcentres and into corridors. In the peripheral expansion options, development was directed either into large low-density areas between the original contiguously developed urban area and the outer ring road, or into smaller areas where densities were chosen to be suitable for the provision of CHP or district heating systems.

Option (a) is a containment option in which new development is concentrated into four of the eight existing suburban subcentres. Development densities in and around the subcentres are increased, together with the capacities of both the roads and the public transport services connecting the subcentres to each other and to the town centre.

Option (b) is a containment option in which new development is concentrated along four of the main radial roads leading out of the town centre. Development densities are increased along these routes, creating 'corridors' of relatively high density along which the capacities of roads and public transport services are increased.

Option (c) is a combination of options (a) and (b), in which new development is concentrated into four of the eight existing subcentres and along the radial routes which connect them to the town centre. The capacities of the appropriate roads and public transport services are also increased.

Option (d) is a peripheral expansion option in which it is assumed that all the land between the boundary of the contiguously developed urban area and the outer ring road is made available for new development. This results in extensive low-density peripheral development, including new local subcentres connected to the existing town centre by new radial roads and public transport services.

Option (e) is a peripheral expansion option in which new development is concentrated into eight limited areas between the radial 'arms' of the

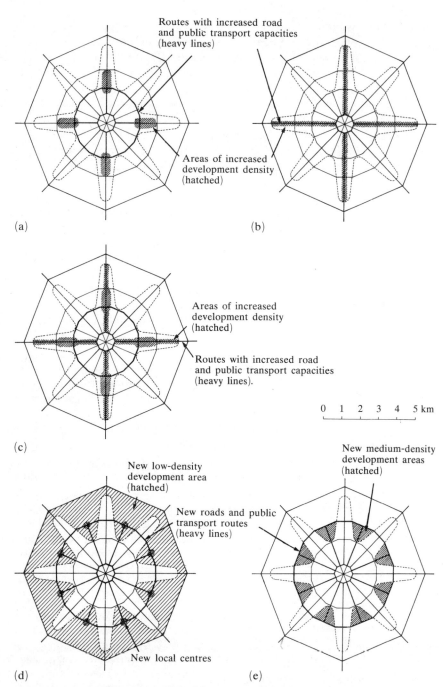

Figure 3. Development options (a)–(e) for the archetypal town.

existing town, at relatively high densities to suit the economics of district heating or CHP systems.

The TRANUS integrated land-use and transport model was then used to simulate the pattern of land use and transport within the archetypal town, and to compare the five options for its future development. This model was originally developed by de la Barra at the Central University of Venezuela, and has been extended to include urban-scale energy analysis by de la Barra and Rickaby (de la Barra and Rickaby, 1982; 1987; de la Barra et al, 1984). For a given urban area with known distributions of households and floorspace, and a given system of roads and public transport, the model provides an analysis of land values and rents, a projection of the distribution of new households and floorspace, an analysis of the resulting trips made to work and to services by public and private transport, and an estimate of the use of fuel in domestic space heating and in transport.

Some of the land-use and road network data for the archetypal town were used as input data for the TRANUS model, and the remainder were used in calibration, in order to ensure an accurate simulation. For each of the modified versions of the archetypal town it was assumed that they would be developed from the original version over a twenty-year period, each option being the result of a different set of planning, transport, building control, and investment policies. The development of each modified version was therefore simulated in four stages, occurring at notional five-year intervals, the town simulated at each stage having a configuration intermediate between those analysed in the previous and subsequent stages. For options (a)–(c), the path to the required pattern followed the same first two stages, the options only beginning to be differentiated at the third stage, after fifteen years of development. By contrast, options (d) and (e) were differentiated from the beginning of the development process, following completely separate paths to the required patterns. At each stage the output data from the simulation model became the input data for the next stage. Figure 4 (see over) illustrates the seventeen complete simulations of the land-use and transport system which were required in order to obtain a comparative evaluation of the five modified versions of the archetypal town on the twenty-year horizon.

The results obtained from the TRANUS simulations were essentially negative ones (table 6). No significant variations in fuel use, either in transport or in domestic heating, were found between the modified versions of the archetypal town. [The possible independent savings from CHP or district heating schemes in option (e) were not taken into account.] Examination of the division of trips between private cars and buses (that is, the modal split produced by the transport submodel of TRANUS, table 7) reveals almost no variation between the five options.

This somewhat disappointing outcome contrasts sharply with that of an earlier study following a very similar methodology, at the city–regional

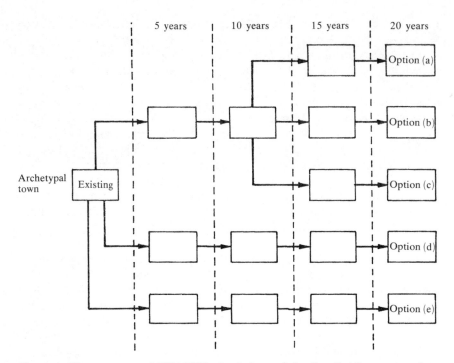

Figure 4. The sequence of TRANUS simulations of the five development options for the archetypal town over the notional twenty-year period.

Table 6. Fuel use (GJ per year) for urban options (a)–(b) the twenty-year horizon.

Option	Transport			Domestic space heating	Total
	private	public	total		
(a)	4303	151	4454	308	4762
(b)	4262	153	4415	308	4723
(c)	4261	153	4414	308	4722
(d)	4337	148	4485	317	4802
(e)	4329	147	4476	310	4786

Table 7. The split between private and public transport, as a proportion of all trips, for urban options (a)–(e) at the twenty-year horizon.

Option	Private	Public	Total
(a)	0.746	0.254	1.000
(b)	0.749	0.251	1.000
(c)	0.744	0.256	1.000
(d)	0.757	0.243	1.000
(e)	0.757	0.243	1.000

scale (Rickaby, 1987). That work made use of the same 'archetypal town' but set in the framework of an 'archetypal city region' divided into the central urban area, a surrounding 'rural hinterland', and a 'rural background' beyond that. The changes to this pattern which were studied for their predicted effects on fuel use all involved relocating 25 000 people from the rural hinterland, along with their associated places of employment and services, over a twenty-five year period, into five alternative new configurations of land uses (figure 5, see over). The road network was kept the same throughout.

The five options studied at this regional scale consisted of various permutations of concentration or dispersal of new development, into either nucleated or linear patterns. Specifically, option (a) concentrated all new development into the central city; option (b) created narrow high-density linear corridors along the eight main radial routes; option (c) created eight new satellite towns, four medium-sized and four smaller, on the edges of the region; option (d) concentrated development into high-density linear corridors along the network of secondary roads; and option (e) dispersed all development to twenty-four new or expanded villages. All five patterns were evaluated using the TRANUS model, along similar lines to the experiments at the urban scale.

The results were that two patterns—option (a), the concentrated central city, and option (e), the village dispersal scheme—showed significant savings in transport fuel use ranging between 9% and 14% for option (a) depending on different background economic scenario assumptions, and rather smaller savings in option (e). In both cases it appears that, by concentrating the previously scattered population of the rural hinterland, average journey lengths both to work and to services were shortened. Option (c), the pattern of satellite towns, was not on the other hand successful in reducing average journey lengths. This was because the rural population was moved outwards to the periphery of the region. Although some jobs and services were relocated to the small towns, there was still extensive commuting from these towns to the central city.

In no case was any significant modal shift from car to bus achieved, and so no transport fuel savings were attributable to this cause. In particular the advantages which it was thought that the two patterns of high-density linear development, options (b) and (d), might have for encouraging public transport were not borne out by the analysis. This can be partly explained by the fact that the public transport in question was assumed to be buses, without special bus lanes. The concentration of car journeys along the linear corridors, especially those on the main roads in option (b), resulted in traffic congestion, which in turn slowed the buses. The buses did not offer time savings, and were unattractive.

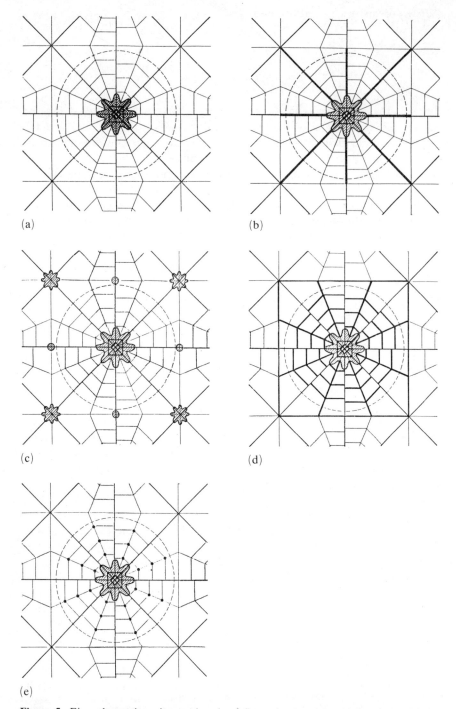

Figure 5. Five alternative city–regional configurations compared by means of the TRANUS model. Heavy lines show main roads, thin lines show secondary roads, shading shows urban areas: options (a) concentrated development in the central city, (b) high-density linear development along main roads, (c) new satellite towns, (d) high-density linear development along secondary roads, (e) development dispersed to villages.

4 Conclusions

The results of the urban-scale study suggest that within towns of this size quite radical variations in policy towards the location of new development may have only slight implications for the use of fuel in passenger transport. The apparent reason for this is that the towns are compact, and the predominant use of fuel is in short journeys to work by private cars. Large variations in fuel use are therefore only likely when patterns of development promote a substantial shift away from private cars and towards public transport or non-fuel-consuming modes such as walking and cycling. The TRANUS simulation of the original (that is, 'existing') archetypal town, and of options (a)–(e), suggests that there is insufficient congestion to discourage the use of cars and encourage the use of public transport. Public transport by bus, which is the only available mode, is particularly unattractive because it involves longer journey times, including waiting. In the urban options (a)–(e) the differences in the location of new development do not significantly affect congestion, and improved bus services to areas of new development fail to make public transport more attractive than the private car.

At the regional scale, on the other hand, the TRANUS experiments indicate that perhaps 10% to 15% savings in fuel use for passenger transport might be achieved through land-use changes alone over a twenty-five year period. These would translate as indicated earlier into a 10–15% cut in carbon dioxide emissions, by the year 2015. The effect is the result entirely of shorter journey lengths, resulting from higher densities of development. This finding is in general agreement with the conclusions of other studies, both empirical and theoretical, of the relationship of fuel use in transport to the density of settlements. It should be emphasised that the assumptions behind the experiments are generally quite conservative, and do not posit large changes in travel behaviour. (They do on the other hand apply only to cities in the chosen size range and their hinterlands, and it would not be safe to extrapolate to larger provincial cities, let alone to London.)

In neither case, at the urban or the regional scale, did the options studied result in any significant modal shift from private to public transport. It is perhaps reasonable to conclude that in the absence of other policy measures, the planned location of new development in itself is unlikely to encourage increased use of the bus network within provincial towns of this size. If combined, however, with measures to discourage car use such as higher taxation of private vehicles or fuel, or central area traffic restriction, then the effects could well be different. It would also seem possible that high-capacity high-speed public transport such as light rail rapid transit might be more effect in encouraging modal shift than the bus services running on the public roads considered here—especially at the city–regional scale. New experiments to look at such options would be a logical next step in this programme of research.

The TRANUS model can now simulate walking trips, trips by bicycle, and freight transport; and so in principle all these could be taken account of in new studies of transport energy use, alongside cars and public passenger transport. A further extension would be to attempt to estimate energy use at the urban scale in nondomestic buildings as well as in houses. To do this, however, will require much more detailed knowledge than currently exists, both of the composition of the nondomestic stock itself, and of the complex range of factors which affect uses of fuel in these very heterogeneous building types.

References
de la Barra T, Rickaby P A, 1982, "Modelling regional energy use: a land use, transport and energy evaluation model" *Environment and Planning B: Planning and Design* **9** 429–443
de la Barra T, Rickaby P A, 1987, "A hierarchical land-use and transport model for energy evaluation", in *Energy and Urban Built Form* Eds D U Hawkes, J Owers, P A Rickaby, J P Steadman (Butterworth, Sevenoaks, Kent) pp 5–28
de la Barra T, Perez B, Vera N, 1984, "TRANUS-J: putting large models into small computers" *Environment and Planning B: Planning and Design* **11** 87–101
Rickaby P A, 1987, "Six settlement patterns compared" *Environment and Planning B: Planning and Design* **14** 193–223
Rickaby P A, 1991, "Energy and urban development in an archetypal English town" *Environment and Planning B: Planning and Design* **18** 153–176
Steadman J P, Barrett M, 1991, "The potential role of town and country planning in reducing carbon dioxide emission", report to the Department of the Environment; Centre for Configurational Studies, The Open University, Milton Keynes

City Transport: Strategies for Sustainability

H Barton
University of the West of England at Bristol

1 Introduction

The promoters of light rail transit (LRT) in Bristol, England, claim that investment in LRT will lead to less car use and reduced congestion—with environmental benefits locally and globally (ATA, 1990). In this paper I evaluate that claim in the light of the experience of LRT schemes worldwide. I set the LRT issue in the broad context of transport energy use and aim to establish which urban transport–land-use strategy would have a chance of being environmentally 'sustainable'. In so doing I raise questions about prevalent theories of energy-efficient urban form.

For the purpose of this paper the potentially all-embracing concept of 'sustainability' is narrowed to a concern for global warming, with the level of CO_2 emissions the key indicator.

The first main section of the paper sets the Bristol transport scene, highlighting important trends and the changing policy context. The second part is a look at transport energy use and pollution, contrasting trend-based CO_2 emission forecasts with possible CO_2 targets for the Bristol area. The third section is an examination of the role that LRT could play in an integrated transport strategy. The fourth and longest part relates LRT to questions of urban form. Drawing on lessons from Dutch experience, I focus on three critical issues: urban density levels, job or facility location, and housing patterns.

The conclusions are intended primarily for the Bristol case study, but do no doubt have some relevance for other British cities faced with similar intractable problems; that is, with increasing car dependence leading to unacceptable environmental costs.

2 Transport in Bristol

Bristol provides an unpromising setting for an energy-efficient transport strategy. A successful city in the M4 corridor, with an expanding journey-to-work hinterland, it has the highest car ownership of any comparable city in Britain. Even in 1981 the Country of Avon had 63% of households with one or two cars. Most suburban districts around Bristol have more than one car per household, and car ownership per thousand population is now (1991) estimated at 400; compared with a British average of around 350 (figure 1).

Traffic growth has been generally above the recent British average of 4 – 5% a year. The outer cordon figure probably gives a reasonable guide to the general level in Avon (table 1). Congestion has, in popular opinion, become progressively worse, with some parts of town now experiencing

severe peak hour conditions (5.5 mph on the Bath Road radial). Buses,
having no general road-space priority, have been suffering consequential
delays and steady decline (except for a three-year demand fillip following
deregulation in 1985).

Pollution levels reflect the high reliance on cars, with, for example, NO
levels exceeding EC recommended limits at 56% of monitoring sites
(Bristol City Council, 1990), and annual transport CO_2 emissions estimated as 575000 tonnes a year. The journey-to-work figures for the
central area give some scale to the car dependence—64%, with public
transport accounting for 21% and walking or cycling 14%. With the
exclusion of nonmotorised trips, 75% of work trips are by car and 25% by
public transport, which is a considerably higher degree of car dependence
than in most British and European cities (table 2).

The overall modal split for Bristol city region gives even less ground for
satisfaction: car 64%, bus 6%, train 1%, walking 27%, and cycling 2%.
Without non-motorised transport, that gives a 90% to 10% split of car to
public transport. It is obvious that public transport ridership will need to
double or triple before it makes a significant impact on the growing use of
cars. The figures also demonstrate the importance of walking as a vital,
but often rather forgotten, mode.

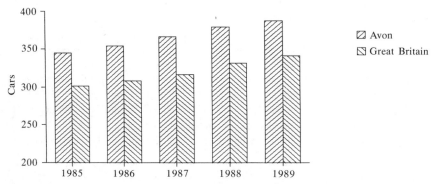

Figure 1. Car ownership per thousand population: 1985 to 1989 (sources: Driver
and Vehicle Licensing Authority, 1991, personal communication; Office for Population Censuses and Surveys, 1991, personal communication; Stead, 1991).

Table 1. Traffic flows in Bristol (12 hours 7 AM – 7 PM) 1979 – 90 (source: Avon
County Council, 1990).

Thousands of vehicles	1979	1987	1990	Change 1979 – 90 (%)
Outer cordon (new)	226.1[a]	299.4	330.5	46.2[a]
Central cordon	337.3	376.5	400.0	18.6
Inner cordon	236.1	254.1	273.6	15.9
[a] Estimated.				

Population and employment distribution patterns in Bristol mirror trends in other major cities, with a marked process of decentralisation occurring, modified by recent (1980s) inner-city revival and gentrification and the continuing growth of Bristol CBD (central business district) as a major office centre. The result has been an increasingly dispersed pattern of trips and longer average trip lengths, reflecting and reinforcing growing car dependence.

Transport and land-use policy in Avon and Bristol are currently undergoing a comprehensive review. Councillors are setting new environmental priorities, including the goal of greater energy-efficiency. Over the next year a district-wide Local Plan for Bristol and a new version of the Structure Plan will, it is hoped, convert priorities into policy. The proposal for an LRT system, once treated with suspicion, is now being evaluated as a potential key element in future strategy. The LRT proposal originated in 1985 as a private-sector initiative, under the auspices of Advanced Transport for Avon (ATA)—to be funded in large part by capturing enhanced values along the route (see figure 2).

ATA have gained parliamentary approval so far for one radial line, out to Portishead, but other routes are proving difficult to agree, and funding problems have occurred. The delay has meant that ATA's ability to carry out its intentions is uncertain. The dominant bus company, Badgerline, the most likely operator of any LRT system once built, is now investigating a bus-based alternative offering similar capacity. Nevertheless, there remains a widespread belief in Bristol that sooner rather than later investment in a local rail network will be essential.

Table 2. Motorised modal split and car ownership in selected cities (source: Avon CC, 1991; Dickens, 1988).

City	Year	Trips to CBD (%)		Cars per 1000 population
		public transport	car	
Bremen	1976	54	46	358
Munich	1980	70	30	366
Brussels	1982	57*	43*	–
Hamburg	–	50*	50*	–
Madrid	–	75*	24*	–
Newcastle	1982	42*	58*	194
Sheffield	1971	41*	58*	230
West Midlands	1979–82	55	45	290
Manchester	1971	50	50	240
Bristol	1989	25	75	385

* All trips in city.

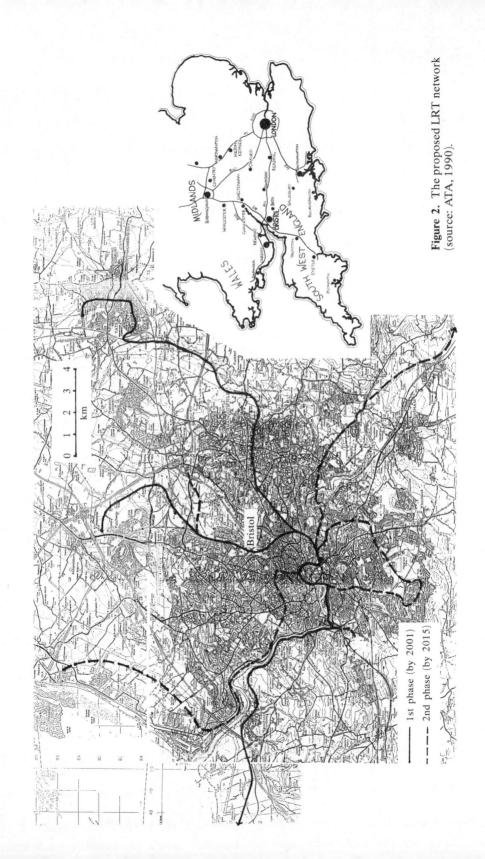

Figure 2. The proposed LRT network (source: ATA, 1990).

3 The energy and environmental context

The issue of the 'sustainability' of Bristol's pattern of movement is first addressed by looking at *general* changes in transport energy use.

The significance of transport in the pattern of British energy demand is growing. Whereas most other sectors of energy use have experienced only marginal increases or even decreases, the transport sector share of the total has risen from 22% in 1976 to 32% in 1989 (figure 3). Land passenger movement accounts for a major part of the growth, and in 1989 amounted to 20% of *total* energy use. Within the land passenger total the motor car dominates—with roughly 95% of fuel used.

The increase in passenger transport energy use reflects long-running social and economic trends. It is not only that more people now own and use a car, but also they make more trips, and each trip is on average longer. In the last few years low petroleum costs have been fuelling profligate energy use. By comparison with major competitors, some with higher car ownership, the United Kingdom has become significantly more dependent on car use.

The Department of Transport (DTp) expects these trends to continue and is planning to accommodate them. It expects a doubling of the motor vehicle population from the current 23 million vehicles by 2025 AD, with an increase in vehicle kilometres of between 86% and 142% over the period (DTp, 1989). It has been calculated that the extra parking space required in 2025 to cope with this demand would be equivalent in area to a 257-lane motorway between London and Edinburgh (Adams, 1990); even if present road building programmes were implemented in full, the expanded network could not keep pace with predicted traffic growth.

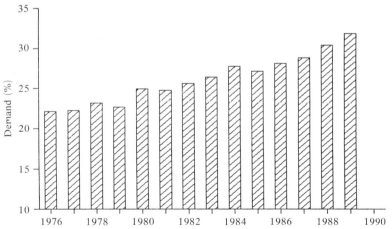

Figure 3. Contribution of transport sector to total energy demand in Britain 1976–90 (sources: Department of Energy, 1987; 1991; Stead, 1991).

Our evident infatuation with the car comes at a cost. One cost is security of resources. Despite the oil crises of 1973/74 and 1979/80, transport systems remain almost entirely oil based except for electrified railways. As yet there is no readily available substitute fuel. Continued growth in car use is heavily reliant on access to future oil resources and on price stability. The UK North Sea oil fields have only eight years proven reserves at current levels of production and, although further finds are likely, output is forecast to follow a slow downward curve (Department of Energy, 1988). World oil reserves are perhaps sufficient for another fifty years, but surplus supplies are heavily concentrated in the politically volatile Middle East. Without labouring the long-term vulnerability of oil supply, it is clear that continuation of current transport trends must be seen as a high-risk strategy. It can also be argued that rapid short-term exploitation of nonrenewable resource amounts to intergenerational robbery.

The unfortunate side effect of burning fossil fuels—in vehicles as in power stations—is pollution, treated by the transport system as a largely uncosted externality. Transport accounts for about 20% of the CO_2 that is causing global warming, and CO_2 accounts for half the total effect (figure 4).

Transport energy use also adds to the nitrogen oxides and low-level ozone which are other greenhouse gases, and is heavily implicated in acid rain (see table 3). Scientists, international agencies, and national governments (for example, DoE, 1990a) recognise the need for urgent action to stabilise global ecology. The most authoritative statement so far by the scientific community came last year in the form of the final report from the Intergovernmental Panel on Climate Change. They recommend a cut in CO_2 emisstions of 60% if we wish to halt global warming (IPCC, 1990).

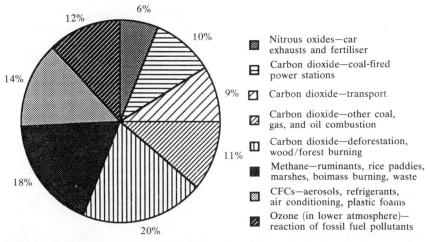

Figure 4. Greenhouse gases—relative contribution to the greenhouse effect (sources: Boyle and Ardhill, 1989; *Greenpeace News* 1989).

In this context, government plans for continued traffic growth take on a somewhat apocalyptic look. No comfort can be sought in hoping them exaggerated. Indeed, rates of traffic growth in the United Kingdom in general and Avon in particular sometimes exceed the higher DTp forecast. And at present there must be some doubt about government's intention to confront the problem: a confidential memo circulated to government departments after the publication of the environment white paper suggested "reductions in CO_2 emissions from transport could place an intolerable restriction on society" (BBC TV, October 1990—*Newsnight*). We may have a choice, it seems, between an "intolerable restriction" on society, and the destabilisation of the habitat society depends on.

The "Bristol Energy and Environment Plan" (BEEP) is an attempt to put a scale to the problem. It forecasts likely CO_2 emission levels in Avon for 2025 and contrasts these with a target level that recognises the need to tackle global warming. The forecast is based on Hugnes and Potter's work (1989). Using DTp traffic predictions and presuming continuing modest improvements in vehicle efficiency, they expect CO_2 transport emissions to rise between 65% and 118%. If we assume that Avon follows a similar pattern, this implies a 2025 range of 950 000 – 1 250 000 tonnes of CO_2— around a tonne per person per year. This is a 'business as usual' forecast (figure 5).

The target levels adopt the government's own target for 2005—to bring back CO_2 emissions to levels obtaining in 1990—and follows Fergusson and Holman (1990) in suggesting a further 20% by 2025. The 2025 target at 480 000 tonnes a year, works out at almost exactly half the lower of the two DTp-based forecasts. This divergence represents a formidable challenge, but the target is still a long way short of the 60% emission reduction called for by the IPCC (1990), recognising the inevitability of differential targets for different sectors of energy use.

In the transport field, measures to reduce energy use include technological innovation, fiscal policy, transport, and land-use strategies. All these measures are likely to be essential if the target is to be achieved. There is

Table 3. Emission of pollutants from road vehicles 1978 – 88 (source: DoE, 1990b).

Pollutants from road vehicles	Percentage increase 1978 – 88	Road percentage of 1988 total	Effects
Carbon monoxide	+20	85	Morbidity, fertility
Black smoke	+57	35	Toxic trace substances
Volatile organic compounds	+17	30	Ground-level ozone
Nitrogen oxides	+25	45	Acid rain
Carbon dioxide	+33	18	Global warming
Sulphur dioxide	0	1.5	Acid rain, bronchitis
Lead	−58	50	Mental development

general recognition that encouraging a transfer of trips from private to public transport is a vital ingredient of any 'sustainable' transport strategy (DoE, 1990a). One recent calculation shows that, if one third of passenger km by car could be shifted to public transport, then transport CO_2 emissions could be cut by a sixth [Rickaby et al, 1992, table 4(b)].

The question is, what role could LRT perform in achieving such goals?

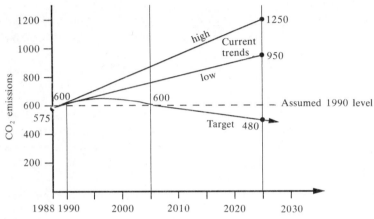

Figure 5. Forecasts and targets for CO_2 emissions (thousands of tonnes a year) by transport in Avon.

4 LRT and transport strategy

The distinctive advantage of an LRT system over equivalent bus services are capacity, speed, reliability, and image. The insertion of LRT can thus transform the pattern and quality of public transport accessibility (TRRL, 1986) and extend the catchment area significantly—Dutch operators suggest up to 30 km from the main node. One result is that public transport ridership tends to rise very significantly following the introduction of light rail (table 4). In Bristol, Kennedy Henderson (1989), using approved

Table 4. Patronage changes after LRT opening or improvement (sources: Dickens, 1988; Taplin, 1987).

City	Period	Increase in trips over the period (%)
Hanover	1975–82	24
Essen	1977–82	10
Munich	1972–82	100
Marseilles	first year of LRT	53
Lyons	first year of LRT	38
Nantes	1985	20
The Hague	first year of LRT	22

DTp forecasting techniques, estimate an 18% increase in public transport ridership once the whole LRT system is in place. The first-phase services would attract 44% of trips from previous bus users, and 56% from former car users. The trips transferred from bus represent 30% of total bus trips along the corridor served and those transferred from car represent 5% of total car trips in the Bristol area.

If we presume these estimates are reliable, such increases in public transport usage do not necessarily mean less energy used. One question concerns the actual energy use—and consequent emissions—of different transport modes. Depending on assumptions about vehicles occupancy and use patterns, public transport is around three or four times as energy efficient as petrol-driven cars. It also appears that the direct primary energy use of LRT compares favourably per passenger mile with bus and heavy rail modes (figure 6). Given the current mix of fuels in electricity production, the required primary energy gives a first rough comparison of greenhouse emissions as well, so a switch from bus to light rail should represent a net gain to the global environment (Hughes, 1991). Techno-logical innovation could change these relationships—already there are signs of new, more sustainable technologies appearing; for example, BMW's hydrogen and solar system. But no panacea is yet in sight which could obviate the need for a switch to public transport.

More significant, though, and more equivocal, is the effect on car use. Often LRT is seen as a means of combatting congestion, but evidence suggests that any slack in road use created by a new system is rapidly taken up by formerly congestion-suppressed traffic demand (Dickens, 1988;

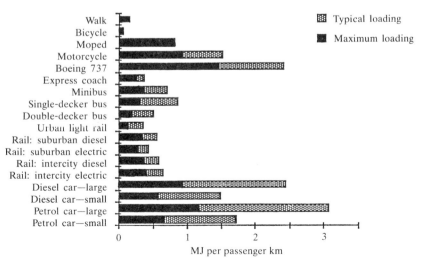

Figure 6. Primary energy consumption of different modes. (This assumes the current mix of fuels in the electricity production process, and gives a very rough approxi-mation to comparative CO_2 emissions at the moment.) (Source: Hughes, 1991.)

Simpson, 1988; TRRL, 1986). A trip transfer also may not mean a net gain for public transport and saving of a car trip because the LRT user may thereby release their vehicles for use by other household members. LRT, in other words, does not prevent congestion, but it does allow more travellers to avoid congestion, and may cause a blip on the traffic growth curve.

Some European cities have achieved more than that, and slowed or even reversed the growth of traffic. This has occurred where major investments in public transport infrastructure are seen as part of a coherent 'green' transport strategy, incorporating integrated public transport provision, strong restraint on car use, and extended pedestrian facilities, normally paralleled by determined efforts to reduce pollution and enhance the quality of the urban environment (TEST, 1988). This picture accords with long-espoused principles of energy-efficient transport (Banister, 1981; Barton, 1987; Elkin et al, 1991; OECD, 1978).

At the very broad empirical level there is also confirmation that the quality of public transport provision affects overall car use. Studies of US cities (Sullivan, 1984) and a range of world cities (Newman and Kenworthy, 1989) suggests public transport provision is a key variable explaining variations in car use. This provides some evidence that perhaps, after all, latent traffic demand in cities is not infinite, and investment in LRT will, in the long run, reduce traffic growth.

Four specific questions remain in the Bristol context. One concerns the problem of implementation. Transport initiatives in the Bristol area are in the hands of a number of semi-independent agencies. Most influential is the DTp itself, actively pushing a policy of catering for predicted traffic growth, with plans for a second Severn crossing and M4 widening which would reinforce local as well as intercity reliance on cars and lorries. At the same time the main national public transport provider, British Rail, guards its main lines against local use. On the more positive side most of the bus services are in the hands of one operator, and Avon County Council is progressively shifting its transport emphasis from one of maximising traffic capacity to one of traffic calming and the promotion of energy-efficient modes. Avon's room for manoeuvre though is limited by long-standing commitments to major road schemes (the ring road), its control over only 25% of bus services, and its funding dependence on the annual Transport Policies and Programme bid to central government. In addition, central parking provision is largely in the hands of the private sector. Achieving a coordinated transport strategy probably relies, therefore, on changed government policy and altered agency remits.

A second question concerns the routing of the LRT. Of the three radial alignments fixed so far, one is largely along the undeveloped side of the Avon Gorge, one is on an existing rail alignment at the *margin* of a major catchment zone, and the third, although well positioned in the urban fabric, takes an old rail route currently much used as a linear park, cycleway and walkway. It appears, then, that the practical problems of LRT routing through Bristol are considerable and may impair the effectiveness of the system.

A third issue concerns the effect of park and ride. Park and ride forms a natural ally of LRT in the outer parts of the city, attracting car users into the system. But it has an impact on bus services by drawing potential customers away from direct use of local bus services, thus reducing their viability. Park and ride also enables commuters to live at greater distances, spreading the tentacles of the city yet further.

Finally, there is the problem, in Bristol, that any possible expansion of public transport starts from a very low level. Although relatively well used in inner Bristol and along key radials, elsewhere—in many outer suburbs and most outlying settlements—its role has been progressively marginalised as car ownership has risen. One Northavon district planner, interviewed recently, was frank in admitting he saw no future for public transport. The major growth zone of Bristol north fringe is being developed with activity distribution-patterns, densities, and layouts that create a very hostile environment for public transport operation—and for nonmotorised modes. The development scheme for Emmersons Green—the latest growth area— treats the planning of public transport as an afterthought, even though one LRT route runs along its boundary. In these expanding outer zones, critical to LRT success according to ATA, an unholy alliance of the market and district planning authorities is undermining public transport operation.

A green 'transport strategy' could perhaps be effective in the inner, more constrained, areas of the city, but in the outlying parts car use seems set to continue its dominance. The reliance on park and ride rather than on comprehensive public transport services is an admission of that— unless, that is, the basic land-use pattern is changed.

5 LRT and urban form

Current land-use trends are progressively undermining the function of public transport. In the postwar era falling energy prices and rising car ownership have transformed cities, allowing the increased physical separation of activities and the progressive spread of urban hinterland at lower densities. The dispersal of employment, retailing, and service facilities creates an equivalently dispersed pattern of trips that is anathema to public transport operation. Lower average densities mean a decline in pedestrian accessibility, longer trip lengths, and reduced catchment populations for public transport routes. The result is increased car dependence, profligate energy use, and global pollution.

These trends have afflicted the Netherlands as much as Britain and policy in the past has strongly fuelled them. In the last two years, however, the Dutch government, aiming for 'sustainability' has committed itself to radically different policies aimed at levelling of transport CO_2 emissions. The new strategy is expressly aimed at promoting public transport and appears, at least in principle, widely supported. The three key land-use elements of the strategy are (1) higher urban densities, (2) concentration of jobs and facilities at public transport nodes, (3) compact urban development, with new areas closely linked into existing public transport, walking, and cycling networks, often in broadly linear pattern.

Public transport planners in the United Kingdom suggested roughly similar principles (CPT, 1981; White, 1976) and they are in general accord with some theories of efficient urban form (Barton, 1987; Steadman, 1980). The uncertainty, though, is whether ideas of concentration are valid for larger cities such as Bristol. Owens has argued consistently for a pattern of "*dispersed* concentration" (1986; 1990). She has also suggested that interspersion of land uses is better than a centralised pattern.

These various tensions are examined below, with three Dutch land-use principles as starting points. The search is for a feasible land-use strategy that could reinforce, not undermine, integrated LRT-oriented transport strategies.

5.1 Density
The residential density in the new parts of the Hague is much higher (perhaps double) than in equivalent areas in Bristol; development is planned from the outset to ensure public transport accessibility, with all households no more than 500 m from a good service.

In Britain consumer expectations and market conditions are different, and there is a long-standing caution about 'town cramming'. What is more, any theory of sustainability has to recognise that, although the benefits of higher densities are very clear (including shorter trips, more reliance on walking, cycling, and public transport, and reduced heat loss from buildings) there are also benefits in urban 'greening', not only for wildlife and recreation, but also to help modify climate (for example, shelter belts) and increase pollution-absorbtion rates.

Two points can be made to try to overcome this apparent dichotomy. First, support for public transport is enhanced not merely by higher *average* densities, but by the *disposition* of higher density zones within this average. It is this *form* of development, increasing the number of people close to public transport stops, which is critical (CPT, 1981). The introduction of LRT can aid this process, encouraging higher land values close to stations (Cervero, 1984; Hall and Hass-Klau, 1985).

Second, it is useful to distinguish between *net* and *gross* densities. Higher housing density need not mean the exploitation of 'soft' open spaces for housing if planning policies, backed by government, are clear. Essentially, one can envisage linear concentration of relatively intensive urban development, including local facilities, focused on upgraded public transport routes. Between those high-density zones would be green corridors, providing for outdoor recreation, allotments, wildlife habitat, and urban forests, plus other low-intensity urban activities. A historic city illustrating such principles is Oxford. Bristol still retains density variations reflecting linear development along the original tramlines and subsequent backland development. Elsewhere (Barton, 1988), I have suggested how these variations could be re-emphasised again to create a more sustainable environment.

The *practicality* of higher densities, given prevailing market conditions, is also in doubt. However, it is interesting to note the range of density in Avon. Whereas major new greenfield sites in Avon average around 30 dwellings per hectare (dph) net, and in outlying settlements the average is substantially lower (reflecting cheaper land and planning constraints) in Bristol itself the average is 50% higher at 45 dph. Indeed, many urban renewal developments in inner Bristol are above 100 dph, and charge premium rates for the privilege of living there.

It is clear there is no immutable density pattern in the market: to maximise profits developers indeed tend to favour higher densities where this does not contradict the market niche they are aiming for, and planning authorities often act to *reduce* proposed densities in order to safeguard 'amenity' and prevent 'over-development'. Government, in one rare statement on this issue, favoured "more intensive development" (DoE, 1984), and the changing pattern of household formation, with 85% of new households predicted to be single people in the year 2001, also points to higher dwelling amenities.

It would seem, then, there is some room for manoeuvre. Local plans and structure plan policies for inner Bristol already reflect a more flexible attitude. Bristol City Council and Avon County Council are concerned to make good use of available land and maintain or increase population levels despite falling household size. It is in the outer area—with district councils such as Kingswood and Northavon—that attitudes and policies would need to change if higher average densities are to be achieved. It would mean a switch from an undiluted diet of family houses, to a mixed development including a much higher proportion of flats and small terraced units to reflect overall housing demand. Many smaller households in turn, would not be attracted to outlying developments unless a good level of services, including public transport, were available there.

In conclusion, then, it would appear from these initial studies of Bristol that there are already some market and local authority pressures for higher net densities, but key changes of policy would need to occur in outlying districts. Public transport operation would be aided not so much by higher average gross densities, as by patterns of linear concentration that would allow 'green' corridors to be developed in parallel.

5.2 The location of jobs and facilities
One theme in the theoretical literature on energy-efficient urban form is the need to move away from a segregated 'apartheid' system of land uses to one where activities are interspersed throughout the urban area to allow

local access, perhaps with some clustering to permit multipurpose trips and facilitate public transport. (Newbery, 1977; Orski, 1974; Owens, 1986; Van Til, 1979).

The value of interspersion is realisable, of course, only if people choose to use facilities that are close to them. In the urban form models they may choose to do so because energy costs and the friction of distance are assumed to be high. The current reality, however, and any we can foresee for the next decade or so, is one of cheap energy. In this situation dwellers will continue to travel to find the particular job, service, or social milieu they desire, and the interspersion of employment and other facilities becomes not so much an opportunity for shorter trips as the generator of a very dispersed pattern of intersuburb trips that inevitably depends on high car use. This indeed is evident now in Bristol, where, for example, the location of new retail outlets on old industrial sites and in neighbourhood centres (that is, their 'interspersion') has generated extra traffic.

So there are dangers in promoting the concept of interspersion. The key factors are *what* is being interspersed and the *pattern* of interspersal. Facilities—normally of an unspecialised nature—that serve a local clientele are different from those which depend on a wider hinterland for employees or clients. Clearly the decline of local facilities, and the increasing unit size of most retail, educational, health, and other facilities, are trends running counter to energy efficiency. Local authorities could do much, *if* backed by government departments, to reverse this and foster localisation (that is, interspersion). But the locational criteria for activities serving a whole sector of the city or the region as a whole have to be different.

From the viewpoint of fostering use of public transport and LRT, such city-wide activities need to be located at public transport nodes. The new Dutch strategy of 'the right business in the right place' gives one model for this. Businesses are accorded a 'mobility profile' reflecting the needs of their employees, customers, or freight. This is then matched with a location having an equivalent 'accessibility profile': 'A', 'B', or 'C'. 'A' locations are major public transport nodes with good intercity rail services. 'B' locations are public transport nodes with good road access as well and 'C' locations are places with excellent motorway access. Offices, for example, are now obliged (subject to the normal political process) to go to 'A' locations, major retailers to 'A' or 'B' locations.

Such a scheme could not currently be applied in this country because of the way the Use Classes Order works to curtail planning authority powers. If it *were* to be applied in Avon, then only Bath and Bristol city centres currently fulfil 'A' location criteria. The vast growth of business in the Bristol north fringe—ill served by public transport even with the ATA scheme—would be outlawed. None of the development proposals in the latest version of the Avon Structure Plan would create any new 'A' or 'B' locations.

One further point came from discussions with public transport operators in Bristol: although centralisation of facilities is essential in order to concentrate trip demand, *excessive* centralisation results in very unequal demand patterns and inefficient use of resources. The ideal public transport route has major trip generators at both ends, and sufficient range of activities within these centres to even out demand throughout the day. The picture emerges, then, of city-wide facilities strongly clustered in the city centre plus a few major subcentres capable of supporting a full range of services, acting as nodes for public transport operation. Over time this might evolve into a multifocal urban structure.

It has been noted that LRT has the capacity to foster central area growth (Cervero, 1984). In Bristol the LRT proposals, therefore, could perhaps be designed to help create new or reinforce existing public transport nodes. As yet they have not been seen in this light.

The location of new growth points also has to recognise commercial realities. The outlying locations of Yate (16 km to Bristol centre) and Weston-super-Mare (30 km) have been promoted for some time, with quite limited success. Empirical evidence from Bristol suggests that successful commercial centres, capable in some degree of acting as a countermagnet to the CBD, have to be tied into the motorway network and closely related to the market – employee pool of the main urban area.

5.3 The shape of the city

The locational constraints on businesses discussed above have implications for general disposition of urban growth. In the urban form literature it is held that cities beyond a certain size—maybe 250 000 population—experience diseconomies of scale such as long trip lengths and increased congestion, and therefore should look to evolve towards a pattern of 'decentralised concentrations' rather than continue as a single conglomeration (Owens, 1986).

Bristol *is* such a large city. If we presume the theory is correct, the problem remains of how to effect the transition. One obvious constraint is that of the inertia represented by the existing structure—but in a boom city like Bristol, with a 53% increase in dwellings forecast over forty-five years, that problem can be exaggerated (Barton, 1987, page 78). A more fundamental problem is spatial: where could decentralised concentrations grow and succeed? An obvious suggestion would be to expand major satellites while curtailing further growth of the main city. One long-term strategy for Avon currently being evaluated involves just this—the expansion of Yate (15 km northeast of Bristol), and Nailsea (12 km to the west). Both towns lie just outside the statutory green belt. Any closer, and the growth areas would merge with Bristol. Any further off, and they cease to be in a position to cream off Bristol's surplus. This plan builds quite organically on current Structure Plan thinking. It is evaluated below from the perspectives of commercial viability and transport energy-efficiency.

The growth towns would have little problem in attracting the house-builder. New housing can be squeezed effectively by planning constraints anywhere within the city region. But, as noted earlier, they would not attract commerce, industry, and services on a commensurate scale unless, perhaps, major new infrastructure provision improved their level of regional accessibility—by road and (in the context of this paper) by rail. Even were such provision to be made, it is inevitable, according to Avon planners, that the main function of such settlements would remain, as now, dormitory, commuter suburbs for Bristol and its north fringe. Although an LRT system serving those movements would prosper, the general impact on energy use given current prices would be determined by longer trip lengths and heavy reliance on cars because of the greater overall spread of activities and interchange between them.

The Dutch have also experimented with new towns some distance from the principal city. The failure of such towns to achieve self sufficiency and the increased commuting which results have led to the abandonment of the programme. Now the emphasis, even for larger cities such as Amsterdam and the Hague, is on compact development. Often this takes the form of broad linear bands out from the city, served by LRT, trams, and buses. Pedestrian, cycle, and public transport priority routes integrate the new development into the existing city, reinforcing public transport viability and ensuring maximum public transport accessibility for the new residents.

In Britain several new or expanded towns—Runcorn, Redditch, Peter-borough—have adopted such linear principles. Varied degrees of linearity have been explored, from the 'single strand' (say 1 km wide) to the wider 'triple strand' variant which perhaps gives the most economical urban form for car use (Jamieson et al, 1967). Problems could arise in practice because of the increased congestion on the radial routes selected for growth corridors, so the attractiveness of the strategy depends on creating segregated, fast routes for public transport, and convivial conditions for walkers and cyclists, while car users are deterred. A recent study comparing Peterborough's linear townships with suburbs of roughly equivalent density in Milton Keynes found the former far superior in terms of local accessibility (Potter, 1990).

The key factor, clearly, is the integration of land-use planning for housing and commerce with transport planning for low-energy modes. In planning, new development location and form should be defined by the least flexible elements. Commercial development (for reasons of marketing and government attitude) cannot be pushed around to the same degree as housing. Railways also are relatively fixed elements, so the pattern of growth could take these factors as starting points; identifying locations that: (1) are now or potentially attractive to business to provide growth poles for city-wide jobs and services; (2) are now or potentially served by BR and/or LRT stations; (3) have the space for compact linear residential and mixed use growth; (4) are closely linked to the existing city so as to minimise distances; and (5) can provide reinforcement for existing public transport services and a high level of public transport accessibility for residents.

6 Conclusions

In this paper I have attempted to show what kind of land-use–transport strategy is appropriate in Bristol if the introduction of an LRT system is to be a successful catalyst for a sustainable city. The broad conclusion is that LRT will only enable emission reduction if planned as part of an integrated 'green' transport system, with traffic restrained and calmed, and walking and cycling promoted; furthermore, such a strategy could not survive unless current car-oriented development trends are reversed, to create a more compact city.

More detailed conclusions are given below. Their application to other cities, especially those much larger or smaller, may be limited. Some of the points have yet to be fully tested, but the BEEP study has arrived at the following interim findings:

1. The goal of ecological sustainability, if applied to transport in a city such as Bristol, implies a fundamental shift in travel behaviour. With CO_2 emissions as the key indicator, Bristol would need to cut its emissions expected in 2025 by at least 50%. Technological innovation and government fiscal policy have parts to play in achieving this. A shift of trips to nonmotorised and public transport modes is also vital. An initial target for public transport recommended in this report is the doubling of ridership by 2005.

2. LRT would, if developed, perform a valuable role in the transport system of the Bristol region. It would improve the level and quality of public transport accessibility for some sectors of the city region and ease access into the city centre, enabling further expansion. It would not, however, of itself, solve the problems of congestion or traffic growth. Nor would it necessarily lead to less greenhouse emissions.

3. If the reduction of greenhouse emission is the objective, then LRT needs to be part of an integrated transport strategy incorporating car restraint, traffic calming, pedestrian and cycling networks, as well as coordinated public transport provision. Such a strategy could not at present, though, achieve success comparable with that in some European cities, because of limited powers and conflicting priorities of the various transport agencies.

4. Park and ride could play a vital role in attracting car users from outer areas onto the LRT system. But at the same time it would tend to undermine further the viability of bus services in marginal areas. It would also tend to increase the distance commuters were willing to travel, and thus encourage further population dispersal from Bristol. In the long run, land-use and transport policy should aim to create a situation where all

suburban settlements are served directly by bus or rail, without the necessity of intervening car use.

5. Higher net residential densities, already being achieved in the inner city, would require a substantial shift in priorities in the outer city where car use currently dominates. Higher average densities, though, need not prevent a range of housing styles being available, and need not result in sacrificing urban green areas. On the contrary, the careful planning of higher and lower intensity zones, related to public transport corridors, could assist both sustainable transport and a more sustainable ecology for the city.

6. Some well-established concepts in the literature on energy-efficient urban form, although logical in a hypothetical energy-constrained future, could lead to increased energy use in Bristol if applied now. The principle of 'land use interspersion' should be refined, therefore, with twin principles of 'localisation' (for local neighbourhood facilities) and concentration on public transport nodes (for city-wide facilities). And the idea of 'decentralised concentrations'—which would be difficult to achieve in practice—could be replaced for Bristol at least with principles of compact linear bands, based around public transport routes and nodes, closely linked into the city.

7. Finally, there are manifold problems of moving towards the kind of sustainable land-use – transport strategy outlined. The limited power of the planning – transport authorities and the lack of a clear lead from government are key factors. Nevertheless, actions can be taken which stand to alter the climate of decisionmaking. One such action, an act of faith if you like, would be investment by Avon County Council and Bristol City Council in an LRT system. By virtue of the interdependence with all other strategic decisions in the city, it could act as a catalyst for more fundamental, and coordinated, changes.

Acknowledgements. The matter of this paper is taken from a 1991 – 92 study by the author of "sustainable transport for Bristol"—part of an EC-funded project entitled "Bristol Energy and Environment Plan" (BEEP), which was coordinated by Bristol Energy Centre (101 Philip Street, Bedminster, Bristol 3). Thanks are due to Dominic Stead, research assistant with the Severnside Research and Consultancy Unit at the University of the West of England, for help with data collection and editing; and to colleagues at the University for stimulus and support.

References
Adams J G U, 1990, "Car ownership forecasting: pull the ladder up or climb back down?" *Traffic Engineering and Control* **31** (3) 136 – 141, 176
ATA, 1990, "Light rail transit in Avon", Advanced Transport for Avon, Hotwells Road, Bristol BS8 4UD
Avon CC, 1990, "Transport policies and programme 1990/91", Department of Highways, Transport and Engineering, Avon County Council, PO Box 87, Avon House North, Bristol BS99 7SG
Avon CC, 1991, "Structure plan third alteration", Department of Planning, Avon County Council, PO Box 46, Whitefriars, Bristol, BS99 7EU
Banister D, 1981, "Transport policy and energy", WP 36, Town Planning Division, University College London, London

Barton H, 1987, "The potential for increasing the energy efficiency of existing urban areas through local planning policy", MPhil thesis, Town and Country Planning Department, Bristol Polytechnic, Bristol

Barton H, 1988, "Is energy integrated land use planning possible in Britain?", WP 10, Town and Country Planning Department, Bristol Polytechnic, Bristol

Boyle S, Ardill J, 1989 *The Greenhouse Effect* (Hodder and Stoughton, London)

Bristol City Council, 1990, "Air quality in Bristol", Environmental Health Services, Brunel House, Bristol BS1 5UY

Cervero R, 1984, "Rail transit and urban development", *Journal of American Planning Association* **50** 133 – 147

CPT, 1981, "Urban planning and design for road passenger transport", Confederation of British Road Passenger Transport, Sardinia House, 52 Lincoln's Inn Fields, London WC2A 3LZ

Department of Energy, 1988 *The Brown Book: Oil and Gas Reserves in the North Sea* (HMSO, London)

Dickens I, 1988, "An introduction to light rail transit in Europe", WP 32, Department of Planning, Birmingham Polytechnic, Birmingham

Department of Energy, 1987 *Digest of UK Energy Statistics 1986* (HMSO, London)

Department of Energy, 1991 *Digest of UK Energy Statistics 1991* (HMSO, London)

DoE, 1984, "Circular 15/84. Land for housing", Department of Environment, (HMSO, London)

DoE, 1990a *This Common Inheritance: Britain's Environmental Strategy* Department of Environment, Cm 1200, (HMSO, London)

DoE, 1990b *Digest of Environmental Protection and Water Statistics* number 12, Department of the Environment, 2 Marsham Street, London SW1P 3EB

DTp, 1989 *Roads for Prosperity* Department of Transport (HMSO, London)

Elkin T, McLaren D, Hillman M, 1991 *Reviving the City: Towards Sustainable Urban Development* (Friends of the Earth, London)

Fergusson M, Holman C, 1990 *Conference Proceedings: The Route Ahead* Worldwide Fund for Nature, Panda House, Weyside Park, Godalming, Surrey

Greenpeace News 1989, number 7, Canonbury Villas, London N1 2PN

Hall P, Hass-Klau C, 1985 *Can Rail Save the City?* (Gower, Aldershot, Hants) Henderson Ltd, Westbrook Mills, Godalming, Surrey GU7 2AZ

Hughes P, 1991, "The role of passenger transport in CO_2 reduction strategies" *Energy Policy* **19** (2) pp 149 – 160

Hugnes P, Potter S, 1989, "Routes to stable prosperity—a response to the white paper "Roads for Prosperity", The Energy and Environment Research Unit, The Open University, Milton Keynes

IPCC, 1990 *Climate Change: The IPCC Scientific Assessment* Intergovernmental Panel on Climate Change (World Medical Organisation and United Nations Environment Programme, Geneva)

Jamieson G, Mackay W, Latchford J, 1967, "Transportation and land use structures" *Urban Studies* **4** 201 – 217

Kennedy Henderson, 1989, "Initial revised ridership forecast", Kennedy Henderson Ltd, Westbrook Mills, Godalming, Surrey GU7 2AZ

Newbery G M, 1977, "Bus operation in alternative urban structures", in *Passenger Transport and the Environment* (Leonard Hill, London) pp 35 – 66

Newman P, Kenworthy J, 1989 *Cities and Automobile Dependence* (Gower, Aldershot, Hants)

OECD, 1978, "Energy problems and urban and suburban transport", Road Research Group, Organisation for Economic Co-operation and Development, Paris

Orski C K, 1974, "The potential for fuel conservation: the case of the automobile" *Transportation Research* **8** 247 – 257

Owens S, 1986 *Energy, Planning and Urban Form* (Pion, London)

Owens S, 1990, "Land use planning for energy efficiency", in *Energy, Land and Public Policy* Ed. J B Cullingworth, (Transaction Books, New Brunswick, NJ) pp 53 – 98

Potter S, 1990, "Land use and transport", paper prepared for the Milton Keynes Forum, available from the author, The Energy and Environment Research Unit, The Open University, Milton Keynes

Rickaby P, Steadman P, Barrett M, 1992, "Patterns of land use in English towns: implications for energy use and carbon dioxide emissions", in *European Research in Regional Science 2. Sustainable Development and Urban Form* Ed. M J Breheny (Pion, London) pp 182 – 196

Simpson B J, 1988 *City Centre Planning and Public Transport Case Studies from Britain, West Germany and France* (Van Nostrand Reinhold, New York)

Stead D, 1991, "Energy and transport in the UK", unpublished research report, Severnside Research and Consultancy Unit, Bristol Polytechnic, Bristol

Steadman P, 1980, "Configuration of land uses, transport networks, and their relation to energy use", Centre for Configurational Studies, The Open University, Milton Keynes

Sullivan B, 1984, "The changing nature of Western economies and associated implications for LRT", International Union of Public Transport, 19 ave de l'Uruguay, 1050 Brussels

Taplin M R, 1987, "Light rail transit today", Light Rail Transit Association, Albany House, Petty France, London SW1H 9EA

TEST, 1988, "Quality streets: how traditional urban centres benefit from traffic calming", TEST, Kingsland House, City Road, London EC1

TRRL, 1986, "The Metro report: the impact of the Metro and public transport integration in Tyne and Wear", Transport and Road Research Laboratory, Crowthorne, Berks RG11 6AU

Van Til J, 1979, "Spatial form and structure in a possible future: some implications of energy shortfall for urban planning" *Journal of the Americal Planning Association* **45** 318 – 329

White P, 1976 *Planning for Public Transport* (Hutchinson, London)

Environmental Impacts and the Property Market

Y Rydin
London School of Economics

1 Introduction

In developed countries the solution to environmental problems is inextricably linked to the issue of sustainable urban development. It is the impact of the built environment, as it changes and grows, on the systems of the 'natural' environment that generates the pollution, resource depletion, and waste which are of concern to environmentalists. There is a growing literature on the forms that the 'sustainable city' might take and a lengthening list of policy prescriptions (for example, see Elkin et al, 1991), but there has been remarkably little attention to the *socioeconomic* processes by which urban sustainability is to be achieved. Increasing reliance is being placed on the use of market-based instruments to achieve changed behaviour patterns [see annex A to the DoE (1990) White Paper *This Common Inheritance*]. However, there has been relatively little analysis in the urban context of existing behaviour patterns within markets, the potential existing for change, the ways in which market-based decisions frustrate environmental policy, and the most effective points at which to direct instruments for change. In particular, the property market, the mechanism by which land is allocated and change in the built environment occurs, has not been linked to problems of urban sustainability in any substantial analysis (but see Cadman, 1990). The constraints that property-market processes place on other planning goals are now well understood (for example, see the contributions to Healey and Nabarro, 1990); environmental policy will need a similar understanding if it is to achieve its goals.

In this paper I consider these issues in the following stages. First, the general nature of the relationship between property-market processes and environmental impacts is addressed. Second, environmental impacts are distinguished in terms of their spatial and temporal scale and their riskiness, and the significance of these distinctions for property-market processes is discussed. This requires a fuller understanding of the property market, covered in a third section. The resulting framework is then used to present the results of preliminary research into 'sustainable residential development' as a case study of the interrelation of environmental issues and a specific property market, in this case for housing.

2 The environment – property market relation

The most obvious dimension of the interrelation of environmental and property-market processes is the impacts of the property market *on* the environment. These are the impacts arising from the operation of the property market in creating, altering, and allocating the built environment.

The land and buildings which constitute our built environment have an impact on the 'natural' environment in a number of ways: as they are consumed, as they are produced, and by virtue of their continued existence (for example, see DoE, 1991).

Pollution, waste, and resource use will arise from the occupation of land and buildings. Property may play a largely passive role in this environmental impact, as the shell within which the main cause of impact is housed. But it can also be a more active ingredient. Physical aspects of the property, such as layout, level of insulation, or the incorporation of air conditioning, may encourage energy consumption. Design can promote or hinder sustainable occupation patterns, such as the provision of space for recycling or for bicycle storage or the enhancement of stairs over lifts. The legal nature of property rights over the building or site may prevent the optimal use of the physical site from the point of view of the environment, for example, preventing activities such as composting on a residential estate.

The act of creating buildings, improving sites, and generating urban development is itself a production process which entails pollution, generates waste, and has implications for resource use (CIRIA, 1990). The raw materials used in that process are often from nonsustainable sources: many hardwoods and aggregates, for example. The production of building materials, their transport to sites, and their assembly in the construction process all consume energy. The localised environmental impact of even minor development projects can adversely affect local residents in terms of air and noise pollution and disrupt habitats for flora and fauna. With major projects, such as the Channel Tunnel or the redevelopment of King's Cross Station in London, the disruption can, of course, be more widespread.

But many aspects of the very existence of the built environment, irrespective of their use or creation, can be a cause of concern. The leakage of CFCs from insulation foam and air conditioning plants, the threat from asbestos even in an unused building, and the pollutants from treated wood are all examples of the 'store' of environmental damage that a building can represent.

So the built environment can be environmentally assessed from the point of view of the consumption, production, and existence of property resulting from property-market operations; and from market-generated decisions concerning building design, management of the construction process, and site layout of individual elements of property. However, the spatial distribution of these elements within the built environment, and hence decisions about site location of individual properties with respect to each other are a further source of environmental impact. The pattern of land uses and the density of development have clear implications for transport use, both quantity of travel and mode of transport, with implications, in turn, for the use of energy resources. More generally, the nature of urban form will influence patterns of living and working, with consequences for urban sustainability that are, as yet, only beginning to be understood (Owens, 1986; 1991).

Analysing these aspects of the property market – environment relation provides both a model for sustainable forms of urban development and an assessment of how far current patterns of property development and use deviate from that model (for such an analysis in the case of residential development see Rydin, forthcoming,). But devising policy initiatives to mitigate environmental impacts and render the built environment more sustainable requires analysis of another dimension of the property market – environment relation. That is, environmental policy needs a discussion of the way in which property-market processes both underpin and react *to* environmental impacts. This involves looking at the decisionmaking of interests in the property-market and assessing the ways in which environmental impacts are integrated into that decisionmaking; for environmental change will affect property-market decisions. Environmental degradation, both existing and related to a development project, will be a factor in decisions concerning occupation, purchase, and construction. Furthermore, anticipated future environmental change will be relevant as many property-market decisions involve assessing costs and benefits over a future timescale (see below). It is this second dimension that I seek to address by looking at the characteristics of property-market decisions in the light of the key characteristics of environmental impacts.

This discussion, with its emphasis on the market, does not preclude consideration of the role of the state; on the contrary. Clearly, many of the issues already mentioned are the outcomes of state policy or regulation as much as the intentions and desires of property-market actors, such as landowners and developers. With reference to market decisions and operations, markets are seen as institutions which are created, maintained, regulated, and structured by state actions. The state and markets, in advanced capitalist societies, are intimately interconnected (McMahon, 1985). Markets depend on the state for their smooth operation, and public policy, including environmental policy, relies on market outcomes for achieving its goals.

Devising and assessing environmental policy initiatives, therefore, require a detailed analysis of the workings of markets, as already structured by current policy frameworks. This does not mean 'market-based instruments' which assume markets operating according to the abstract model of supply and demand forces. Rather it means that policy should be based on an understanding of markets as institutions, which operate through the decisions of constituent actors. Knowledge of how property-markets actually work, within a current pattern of state action, is achieved through understanding who takes important decisions concerning the built environment, what the assumptions and goals of those decisionmakers are, what the perceived constraints on decisionmaking are, and how these mesh with an environmental policy agenda. In this way policymakers can assess the extent to which market processes are frustrating environmental policy or potentially can contribute to its goals. More importantly, it enables new policy to be designed for effective implementation and with realistic knowledge of the constraints on that policy. With this in mind, in the next section I define more precisely the nature of environmental impacts and change, before going on to examine decisionmaking in the property market more fully.

3 The nature of environmental impacts

There are three characteristics of environmental change which need to be distinguished, in order to set an environmental agenda against which the decisionmaking processes of property-market actors can be judged. These are: timescale and the temporal distribution of impacts; the spatial scale of impacts; and their riskiness or unpredictability. The ways in which property-market decisionmaking meshes with environmental concerns can, of course, be investigated through data on individual topics, such as the use of CFCs, adoption of solar design principles, current site-management practices, etc. Indeed, the research presented at the end of the paper collected such data. But to explain the aggregate patterns in the data requires an explanatory framework, which the emphasis on these three key characteristics provides.

3.1 Timescales and environmental impacts

The issue of time is central to the concept of 'sustainability' which is increasingly being used to define environmental concerns (see WCED, 1987). This concept recognises that the environmental consequences of activities undertaken by the current generation only become fully apparent to future generations. The key to sustainability is to ensure an equitable *temporal* distribution of environmental impacts as well as the benefits of economic development, and the policy goal is stated in terms of passing on to future generations an undiminished stock of environmental assets along with the stock of capital assets (Pearce et al, 1989). This stock of environmental assets includes the varieties of natural resources, the availability of energy sources, and the range of biodiversity, as well as the capacity of the atmosphere to act as a pollution sink.

Property-market decisions can also be judged in terms of the temporal aspects of sustainability. This involves assessing the overall timescale within which such decisions are taken, the number of years hence within which costs and benefits are considered. If a cutoff point of a few years is used to judge the costs and benefits of property purchase, occupation, or development, then an environmental impact occurring further off will not be taken into account. It is also necessary to assess the weights that are placed on future as opposed to imminent impacts, and the ways in which appraisal techniques informing decisionmaking may have weighting implicit within them. The role of discounting procedures is relevant here (see Pearce and Turner, 1990).

The shorter as well as the longer timescale should not be forgotten in considering the role of environmental concerns in decisionmaking. Many environmental impacts of concern to the public and policymakers are more immediate than future-oriented: for example, the impact of poor air quality, aspects of visual amenity, current constraints on the availability of environmental goods. But the cumulative impact of short-range environmental impacts suggests that they may well result in even more significant long-range impacts.

3.2 Spatial scales and environmental impact

To this temporal dimension of environmental impacts must be added the spatial dimension. The term 'the environment' is used to cover a range of spatial scales. Policymakers in local, national, and international arenas claim to be involved in environmental protection and public perception of environmental problems that range from litter in the streets to ozone depletion. Indeed the UK government's own Environmental Protection Act 1990 ranged from litter to integrated pollution control, to species protection, to administrative arrangements for local waste management. Table 1 presents one way of classifying environmental impacts using an explicit spatial hierarchy.

The classification used is local, regional, and global. Clearly, the precise definition of these spatial scales can be problematic and the purpose of the hierarchy is to identify impacts of significantly different type rather than to debate the meaning of 'local' or 'regional' in the abstract. Local and regional economies are defined by the extent of external trading in labour, materials, and finished products; local and regional communities by the degree of identification of residents with the area. Similarly, local and regional scale here refer to the extent to which environmental impacts are contained within a smaller or larger area.

'Local' refers to an area in the immediate vicinity of the activity giving rise to the impact, where the environmental impact is largely felt within that area. Thus, in the case of atmospheric pollution, for example, a photochemical smog arising from heavy car and other vehicle use within an area is a local impact. Where the pollution is exported so that the impact is felt beyond the local area, then a regional impact can be identified, with acid rain arising from the 'export' of sulphur dioxide and other pollutants being a good example. Beyond both the local and regional scales, certain impacts can be considered global in scale. Again in atmospheric terms, global warming and the depletion of the ozone layer are relevant examples. Table 1 outlines the application of these spatial scales to cases of environmental impact affecting the hydrosphere (water supplies and systems), the lithosphere (soil and ground conditions), and the biosphere (flora and fauna).

Two points arise from this spatial typology. The first relates to the tendency for environmental impacts to be spatial externalities in the sense that an activity occurring in one location will impact on others, either in close proximity to the location or often further afield. Many environmental impacts are, therefore, spatially exported. Where an impact is locally contained, it is more likely to be included within an actor's decisionmaking. This is not guaranteed. Even in the case of impacts internal to a building (the sick building syndrome) these may not concern the property developer or even occupier if the main effects are felt by workers and not translated into loss of productivity or rent. Even localised air pollution from an activity may be externalised onto local residents and property owners without affecting the profitability and property values of the polluter. However, many property-market actors will be affected by localised environmental degradation. Property values and the benefits of property occupation are dependant on the quality of the local environment in many cases. As the scale of the impact and the potential for export increase, the possibility of the impact being internalised into actors' decisionmaking certainly declines.

The second point is that, as higher spatial scales are involved in the identification of the impact, so the cause is more likely to be related to the aggregate effect of many individual activities. The externality involved here is the effect of many marginal increments in the overall level of an activity or activities over a broad spatial area. In this case it becomes very difficult for individuals making decisions within the property market to appreciate the full effect of their decision and hence internalise the impacts.

The spatial dimension of environmental impacts also has relevance to the type of response on the part of the state to the environmental damage. Local impacts are the primary concern of local authorities. The cause and effect are internal to a defined local governmental area and can be dealt

Table 1. Typology of environmental impacts with examples.

Focus of impact	Scale of impact		
	local	regional	global
Atmosphere	Photochemical smog	Acid rain	Ozone depletion Global warming
Hydrosphere	'Dead' pond or lake	Pollution of water source Depletion of aquifer	Use outstripping recycling capacity
Lithosphere	Site contamination	Soil erosion	Depletion of stock of fertile soil
Biosphere	Specific habitat loss	Impact on migration patterns	Loss of biodiversity

with by regulation and other policy instruments at that scale. Much local planning is of this sort. As regional impacts are considered, then issues of negotiation between local authorities arise. These may be dealt with in the context of a regional authority with responsibility over a series of local authorities or directly over the regional area. Alternatively, negotiation between local level authorities may be more appropriate. Where the regional scale under consideration is spatially extensive, as in the case of supranational impacts, then the terms 'regional' and 'local' may describe entities such as the European Community and nation-states. As the scale of the impact increases, and particularly for global impacts, it will become more difficult to identify appropriate organisations and the tendency will be to rely more on negotiation of agreements to initiate behavioural change. This can be a complex process given the importance of aggregation of many separate activities in creating environmental damage at higher level spatial scales and the problem that the payoff for changed behaviour, in terms of environmental improvement, is often both spatially and temporally remote from the activity causing the damage.

3.3 The predictability of environmental impacts

In addition to considerations of timescales and spatial scales, there is the problem of predicting or forecasting the environmental impact. Because impacts arise in the more or less distant future, consequent upon property development or continuing activities within a property, some degree of prediction is unavoidable. This prediction process will not result in firm figures for a number of reasons: the unknowns in the data input into any forecasting method, dispute over the forecasting method to be used, and lack of knowledge about the ways in which environmental impacts are generated. Ranges for scale and timing of the predicted impacts are more likely than single figures and for some types of impact it may not even be possible to give any figures. Even where the scale and timing of impact can be identified, problems remain as to assessing the environmental significance of the impact and its incidence in the future.

This discussion of the problems of impact assessment raises the question of how property-markets deal with problems of lack of information or variable information. This is couched in terms of *risk assessment* by property-market analysts and the nature of a property-market actor's risk-assessment procedures, including their approach to complete uncertainty, is highly pertinent to the linkages between an environmental agenda and property-market decisionmaking. Some examples may help elaborate this definition of environmental impacts in terms of property-relevant risky events.

The occurrence of global warming is couched in terms of probabilities and ranges of likely increases in temperatures by given dates in the future. As more research and applied analysis of research findings are undertaken, these figures will be translated into probabilities of sea-level rise and consequent inundation of coastal and riverside locations. Property in such locations is, therefore, at risk and decisions about that property will need to take into account the nature of that risk, its timing and likelihood, and the potential costs involved. Again, location at outfalls of air pollution will carry consequential risks for agricultural production, for human health, for certain types of production activity. The impact of the environmental damage in terms of reduced usefulness of that location for occupation by households and firms has to be assessed by occupiers along with the attendant probabilities and the potential for changing location. Or, one final example, location near to certain sites such as waste disposal landfill sites, hazardous industrial installations, or mining activities, carries with it the risks of sudden ground failure or catastrophic explosion. The impact on adjoining property is obvious and the existence of such risks is a factor that property users and owners in the vicinity will have to take on board.

A final aspect of risk is policy risk, the prospects of increasing knowledge about environmental risks and associated political pressure generating state action which places restrictions on property use and development. The potential imposition of new regulatory requirements may cause market actors to revise their decisionmaking to internalise impacts previously beyond their adopted temporal and spatial scales. An assessment of the policy context, including the changing agenda at national and increasingly at European levels, will, therefore, form part of the overall environmental risk assessment process (CIRIA, 1990).

This discussion of the key characteristics of environmental impacts suggests that the timescales adopted by actors, their relation to spatial scales, and their attitudes to risk are important in understanding the relation between these impacts and the property market, and the scope for changed behaviour by market actors. This will be developed further in the next section.

4 The nature of property-market processes in the context of environmental impacts

The term 'property' has been used loosely so far, mainly to denote the physical land and buildings which make up the built environment. However, more strictly, the property market is a mechanism by which legal rights to use and benefit from land and buildings are exchanged and allocated (Reeve, 1986). The rights can vary from a tightly circumscribed right of way to a freehold ownership, subject in the British case only to the Crown. These rights are essentially enforceable claims to the physical property by one party against another party and several such rights can, and commonly do, coexist over one item of land or building. Thus the property market describes a complex network of relations between parties, social as well as economic in character, which overlays the simpler spatial map of land and buildings. The reasons for holding a property right can be separated into occupation, development, and investment, each describing a distinct sector of interests within the property market. These sectors will be used to explore further the relation of the property market to environmental impacts.

4.1 Occupation interests in property

Occupation interests hold property in order to use it as a site for a consumption or production activity, whether a household living in a dwelling, an industrialist renting a factory, or a farmer working an owner-occupied farm. The significance of the physical, legal, and spatial characteristics of the property lie in the extent to which they permit and enhance the particular production or consumption activity. The relation of the property to the environment can be an important part of its suitability for a particular occupying activity.

The environment may provide raw materials for the activity: fertile land for the farmer, timber for the forestry company, minerals for the mining corporation, 'white water' for the canoeing club. In some cases the ecological systems of the environment will be an integral part of a production process: the growing cycles of plants, animals, and trees; the capacity of the atmosphere and hydrosphere to act as a pollution sink and 'recycle' air and water. In all cases the environment will act as the location for the production or consumption activity and the spatial arrangement of positive and negative features will affect the value of that location for the activity. It is in the nature of the property market that the relative balance of advantages and disadvantages provided by the environment for a location will influence its price and hence the cost to the occupier. Where it is possible for an activity in a particular location to externalise its adverse environmental impacts beyond the timescale and spatial area of concern to an occupying interest, then the value of that location will be enhanced.

To take the temporal aspect first: the timescale of an occupier will depend on the length of the production or consumption cycle. In some production activities, this cycle is relatively short and the commitment of a producer to particular processes, products, and locations is relatively limited. Unless the consumer of the product imposes a longer timescale, through demanding 'green' products, and market conditions allow consumer pressure to carry weight, then short-termism will dominate corporate planning. In other production activities, the level of investment in the production process, the nature of the technology involved, and the relations with the consumers of the product mean that a much longer timescale is adopted. For consumption activities, some are short term, involving only a passing relation to the site of the activity, as with holiday leisure activities. Others, such as the occupation of a family dwelling, involve a commitment of possibly a generation's span. Thus it is factors internal to the production and consumption process, rather than factors related to the property, which determine the timescale of decisionmaking and detailed analysis will be needed in each case to determine this.

In spatial aspects the role of property is more important. The arrangement of the occupying activity within a surrounding pattern of land uses will in part determine the extent to which pollution, waste generation, and resource exploitation impact locally or whether the adverse environmental impact is exported. The density of different uses will also contribute to the extent to which the aggregate effect of many individual effects becomes apparent locally, as opposed to regionally. Where the local property market is spatially structured so that adverse environmental impacts are either minimised, exported, or dispersed, then the ability of the occupier to exploit the environment is maximised, the value of the location to the occupier is enhanced, and the price charged will be increased.

The property market is, therefore, an indicator of the net balance of positive and negative spatial externalities arising from the use of the environment by occupiers. Furthermore, if the local environmental impacts can be minimised, particularly during the timescale that the occupier adopts for personal or corporate planning, while exporting other negative impacts to other areas or deferring them beyond the occupier's timescale of decisionmaking, then there is very little incentive within normal property-market processes for the occupier to mitigate any environmental damage caused.

The attitude to risk further affects the incentives for changed decisionmaking behaviour. If the occupier places a low priority on certain types of risk, either in terms of when they occur or the nature of the impact, then the market is less likely to internalise the impact. There is a large body of literature on risk assessment [see Macgill (1987) for an innovative environmental example] but little related directly to property occupiers (Page, 1991). There are indications that many risks to health arising from environmental sources are given a relatively low priority. Similarly, it seems that public awareness of and concern over global environmental damage are not matched by changed decisionmaking incorporating revised risk-assessment for the future. This is not to suggest that people are risk-seeking but rather that they are risk-blind. Even if the risk can be translated into monetary terms, the perception of future changes in expenditure patterns arising from, say, an environmentally prompted investment in the property, do not always encourage such investment. This is part of the problem in demonstrating short payback periods for energy conservation measures. This area of property occupiers' response to the risks dimension of environmental impacts, local and global, short range and long range, monetary and nonmonetary, requires further investigation.

4.2 Development interests in property
Development interests own property rights in order to shape the built environment through the production of buildings and sites. As mentioned above, the development process has major environmental implications in

terms of its choice of development sites, its use of natural resources, the production of waste and pollution during production, the disturbance of natural habitats, etc. Development differs from occupation in terms both of its temporal and of its spatial dimensions of decisionmaking.

The timescale adopted by development interests is limited to the time from site purchase through to disposal of the completed development. Clearly, the complexity of the project will determine the length of this period. In some cases rights to sites are bought in anticipation of development, but this aspect of urban development is a form of investment and will be dealt with in the next section. It is likely, therefore, that the timescale of developers will be shorter than that of occupiers for many categories of property, and the commitment of a developer to a particular location is relatively short term. This will affect the conduct of the construction process and the extent to which environmental damage during the production of buildings is mitigated. Furthermore, the economic pressures for development mean that development occurs when the economic life of the current use of a site or building is ended. The economic life of a building is over when redevelopment is profitable, regardless of its physical condition. When occupiers change their building requirements rapidly, say because of new technology, or there is a demand for new buildings simply because they are new, as with the desire of institutional investors to own the prime property in an area, then the economic life of buildings is short. Regardless of the continued usefulness of the resources bound up in sites and buildings, redevelopment will occur. This works against the development of high-quality buildings which need less frequent replacement. In this sense also the timescale of development is not in tune with the needs of urban sustainability.

This means that the pressure to consider impacts arising from the use of building materials, particular building designs, and specific features such as air conditioning and space heating, are all inherently more likely to come from the occupier demanding a particular type of development, than from the development industry itself. Where the development industry is not buoyant and developers are competing fiercely for clients, then the concern with occupiers' 'green' demands will be more readily taken on board by the development industry. An example of this concerns the balance between capital costs of construction and ongoing maintenance costs for a building. This balance will depend on the details of building design and construction. Higher capital costs may mean less profit for the developer, unless the reduced future maintenance costs can be captured in the form of a higher price for the development. Yet, from a resource-use point of view, the creation of high-quality low-maintenance buildings may be preferable. If occupiers are willing to pay for low-maintenance buildings or if this is seen as a way of maintaining market share in a falling development-market, then developers may improve quality of construction.

The level of competition between firms and the relative environmental standards will also be relevant. Growing competiton at a European level, where some property developers have lived with more stringent environmental policy requirements may drive UK domestic developers into improved environment performance (CIRIA, 1990). This may make the assessment of developments under the Building Research Establishment Environment Assessment Method (BREEAM) (Raw and Prior, 1991) more attractive to developers as an aid to marketing and attracting consumers in a highly competitive or buyers' market.

Spatially, development interests are more likely to play a proactive role. This is because the development process can actively shape the spatial structure of an area. The local pattern of environmental externalities can be managed by the developer, if the project is of sufficient scale: for example a major residential estate, the King's Cross redevelopment, a new settlement in a rural area. In this way adverse local environmental impacts may be mitigated and positive externalities within the development sites and their surroundings actively created. However, the scale of development interests is such that regional or global impacts will not be considered, and, as with occupiers, the incentive to export adverse impacts beyond the development area and its surroundings remains.

In assessment of risk, the property developer will probably be more sophisticated and aware than an occupier. A number of dimensions of environmental risk will be considered: the impact on development programme and budget from new information on the immediate environment of the site; concern over future consumer demand in relation to the environmental performance of a building; and the prospects for new environmental legislation or the imposition of liability for environmental damage, which will affect the development process or the marketability of the finished development. Indeed, many property developers are now looking to mitigate the environmental impact of their projects because of changed risk assessments, particularly concerning policy risk.

It would seem, therefore, that it is market competition for consumers and the threat of policy change that will alter developers' actions. Cadman found (1990, page 267) that in a survey of twenty leading property companies "all but a few were conscious of the need to confront environmental issues and that three of the 20 were taking steps to incorporate such issues into their project work".

4.3 Investment interests in property
Investment interests differ both from occupation interests and from development interests in that theirs is an essentially passive relationship to property. The aim is to benefit financially from holding the property right, although individual investors may at times combine the activity of investment with development and/or occupation. The financial return comes from the rental flow from the occupier of the property (or an intermediary

property right holder) and the capital growth of the asset. The level of the rent and the increase in the price of a property, together with its risk characteristics, determine its attractiveness as an investment.

The usefulness of the property to an occupier, as discussed above, determines its value, measured as rent or price. As discussed above, this economic return is dependent, in part, on the ability to externalise adverse environmental impacts, both temporally and spatially. Internalising them to the undertaking of the activity would reduce the surplus from which the return to the investor is derived. Thus, more stringent pollution controls will reduce the rent due to the owners of industrial premises. The extent of the reduction will depend on the relative market strengths of those recovering and giving the rent (or price or charge)—the investor and occupier. This in turn is a function of the profitability of the occupying activity compared with the ease with which premises can be obtained. Thus, the ability of investors to benefit from environmental exploitation depends on: the relation of the occupying interest to the environment, including the extent to which adverse impacts are externalised; and the activities of the development industry in supplying property onto the market, including the use the development industry makes of spatial structuring of environmental externalities and their response to occupiers' environmental concerns.

Although this emphasises the interrelation of occupying, development, and investment interests in the property market, research has shown that investment interests, the providers of finance for urban development and property purchase, increasingly drive the processes of urban change (Healey and Nabarro, 1990). This is important, from an environmental perspective, because the timescale of investors is considerable longer than that of developers and many occupiers. To investment interests, the return from the property (rental income and capital growth) over the future is all important and property is classed as a long-term asset (Rydin et al, 1990). A generation span of thirty years could be an appropriate timescale for institutional decisionmaking. This would suggest that such interests are more likely to take environmental impacts into account even though they arise in future years. Thus, for example, it has been shown that owner-occupying households are more likely to invest in energy-efficiency measures than tenants (RICS, 1991). Again it is the owner-occupiers in the commercial sector, such as Sainsbury's, rather than speculative developers, who are promoting 'green' buildings. However, a number of factors act against this trend.

First, the desire to generate capital growth means that a rising property-market is preferred in which land values and property prices are increasing. Permanently rising markets are impossible and, instead, the pressures towards capitalising on upswings in the market encourage cyclical patterns in the supply of property, engendering wide swings in the rate of property development. The economic life of buildings can fall dramatically in an upswing, encouraging the redevelopment of sites well in advance of the end of their physical life. Yet in downswings, sites can lie idle in anticipation of the upturn. Such a market encourages land hoarding until the maximum profit can be made from development and sale. In the meantime environmentally acceptable urban development can be hindered.

Second, the valuation of property as an investment asset is based on discounting future returns, in the form of rent and capital growth, by the use of a discount rate (in property circles referred to as a yield). As Pearce and Turner (1990) have emphasised, the use of discounting downgrades costs to future generations at the expense of benefits to the current generation. Thus the expense of future maintenance will have a relatively smaller impact on the value of an investment compared with current capital expenditure. This form of valuation can inhibit many forms of property refurbishment which would enhance energy conservation and undervalue buildings which minimise their environmental impact.

Nevertheless, the longer term commitment of investment interests to their property should, on the face of it, create the potential for greater concern with environmental impacts. The substantial spatial spread of investment by many major institutions also means that negative spatial externalities can be less easily ignored, although there is always the scope for geographically differentiated buying and selling to shift investments out of adversely affected areas. The finely graded nature of spatial structuring of property markets encourages this. Furthermore, the risk-assessment procedures of investors are the most sophisticated in the property market and are becoming more so under the influence of other investment markets. In these procedures property is viewed as a class of asset and, therefore, they are concerned with the performance of property in general and, by implication, the environmental costs associated with that performance over the future.

Provided that property is seen as an important element within the investment portfolio and not substitutable (an important caveat), this discussion raises the prospect that institutions will increasingly be looking to the environmental impact of their property holdings. The decision-making of investment institutions still requires further research, particularly as there has been more emphasis on developing theoretical models of investment behaviour than on exploring this behaviour in practice. Such research could identify points within the investment market where environmental concerns could be successfully introduced into decisionmaking so that this sector of the property market could itself seek to mitigate adverse impacts.

5 Environmental issues in the housing market
As a preliminary stage in a longer research project, the Royal Institution of Chartered Surveyors Education Trust have funded a pilot research project into sustainable residential development. The results from this project

allow reflection on the above framework with its emphasis on use, development, and investment interests in property. The project comprised a number of elements besides the necessary literature review (see Rydin, forthcoming): a survey of national level representatives of organisations involved in the various stages of residential development, during which policy documents concerning the environment were collected; a postal survey of 300 estate agents, 400 housebuilders and 160 mortgage lenders; a scan of *The Housebuilder*, the house magazine of the House Builders' Federation, for 1987–90 inclusive; analysis of the company reports of eighteen major construction companies with housing interests for references to environmental concerns.

The emphasis was, therefore, on data collection in the form of a series of postal questionnaires. In many respects this was not ideal. The characteristics of property-market decisionmaking discussed above are best explored through in-depth interviews and focus groups. In particular, the survey research did not lend itself to an understanding of the detail of risk-assessment procedures. However, the questionnaires produced a set of data on a variety of individual issues concerning the environment. These are useful descriptive data in themselves, which can also act as a backdrop to future research on the dynamics of property-market decisionmaking with regard to the environment. The results are reported here under the headings of occupation, development, and investment interests in housing, and reference is made to the characteristics of temporal and spatial distribution.

5.1 The occupiers

The purpose of this part of the research was to guage, by proxy, the attitude of occupiers of dwellings towards various environmental aspects of their buildings and their locations. Estate agents were asked to guage whether certain features were valued very highly, moderately, or not at all by prospective purchasers. The features listed ranged from wildlife areas, to environmentally friendly building materials with particular emphasis on energy consumption, transport and access to nonresidential uses, and use of open spaces. Of the 300 questionnaires sent out, 136 responses were received, a response rate of 34%. The total population sampled was approximately 31 500 estate agents, not all residential.

A number of caveats must be made concerning the results from this survey besides the obviously small sample size. The original survey was of a random sample taken from the *Estate Gazette* directory, spread across the counties in England, Wales, and Scotland. This simple sampling method would not, of course, take account of the different levels of activity in the housing market across the country. In the final batch of responses 17% came from Greater London and 32% from the rest of the South East, with the remaining fairly evenly spread. In all, 79% of the responding agents described their local property market as depressed or very depressed.

Estate agents were used as a proxy for two reasons. First, the pilot nature of the research did not allow for the resources involved in sampling the homebuying public. Second, estate agents are important gatekeeper professionals, linking purchasers and sellers in the housing market, sifting the properties offered to buyers, and, most important, determining the information about the property which is given to the buyer in the early stages. It may well be that the underlying environmental concerns of housing occupiers and estate agents diverge. Certainly a variety of opinion polls and economists' valuation exercises indicate that the public place a fairly high priority on environmental quality. However, the filtering role of estate agents is important in potentially amplifying or suppressing the occupier's concerns and, therefore, merits investigation in its own right.

The overall results were that, of the features listed, the items most frequently cited as very highly valued were:

Space for one car	83%,
Garden for recreation	65%,
Garden for visual pleasure	60%

The items at the bottom of the list (valued not at all) were:

Space for recycling	93%,
Cycleways	93%,
Environmentally friendly building materials	80% ,
Energy efficient lighting	79%,
Water metering	76%,
Space for bicycles	75%,
High standard of floor insulation	70%.

Thus, in the views of estate agents, some of the key features needed to render housing more capable of supporting sustainable living patterns are not valued at all by house purchasers. Meanwhile at the top of the list of priorities is the private car, increasingly seen as *the* major environmental problem. Three issues stood out in terms of the results: attitudes to energy conservation, to open space, and to transport.

If we take energy-conservation items together (see figure 1), high standards of insulation were only moderately valued with double glazing considered the most popular feature (31% valued this highly, 64% moderately). There is some doubt whether this is valued as a cost-effective means of reducing energy bills or rather as a highly visible form of dwelling enhancement and hence an aid to marketing and a source of added housing value (see the section below on investors). Energy-efficient space heating was highly valued by 26%, and moderately by 48%, but energy-efficient lighting was considered of no importance by 79%.

There is, therefore, in the estate agents' view a long way to go in raising the house-buying public's awareness of the energy efficiency of the building they are purchasing. Perhaps an overall ranking of dwellings in terms of energy efficiency, as under the Energy Foundation's National Homes Energy Rating scheme would expand users' appreciation of this aspect of their dwellings, particularly on complex issues such as design (38% did not value design for lower energy consumption at all). The current level of concern by users of housing with energy efficiency does not seem to be particularly high and is uneven in focus. In terms of where insulation is applied, only 18% did not value a high standard in roofs, but 42% did not value this in walls and 70% did not value it in floors. The fact that 39% were indifferent to a high standard of draughtproofing, although it is a very cost-effective means of insulation, may be because prospective purchasers would undertake such works themselves, but this is unlikely to apply in the case of more major works.

Open space near dwellings was generally regarded as important for recreation and visual pleasure (see above) rather than for growing vegetables (40% valued this not at all, 49% moderately) and wildlife areas were considered of no importance by 58% (see figure 2). Substantial tree planting in the local area was also of only moderate importance. In general low densities were favoured: 33% valued them highly, 48% moderately, suggesting a preference for an 'open texture' to residential areas, though not for the open space to be used to enhance wildlife or sustainable food production. This preference for low densities has important ramifications for the demand for transport discussed next.

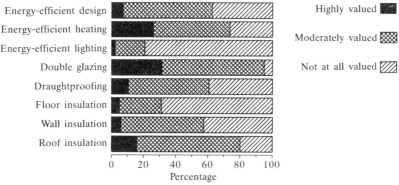

Figure 1. Estate agents' survey: energy efficiency.

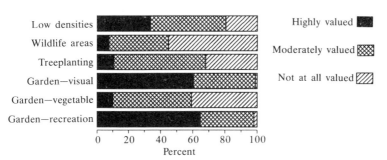

Figure 2. Estate agents' survey: open space.

The strongest finding was the perceived need to provide for a household car or even additional cars: 42% valued space for two cars highly, 56% moderately. However, space for bicycles was considered unimportant by 75% of the sample and cycleways were among the least valued features. Public transport was highly valued by only 26% and moderately by 68%. The perceived desire to provide for vehicles meant that local car-free areas were considered unimportant by 60%, although 52% moderately valued local traffic-calming. The picture put foward by estate agents is one where provision for car-borne transport within residential areas predominates. The arguments for shifting towards an urban form based on public transport clearly have a long way to go. However, it is clear that estate agents perceive a desire for facilities to be placed so that pedestrian access is possible. 49% valued being able to walk to school very highly, compared with 47% for shops and 21% for workplace. Beyond this, such pedestrian access particularly for schools and shops was moderately valued rather than not at all. Enhancing such pedestrian access implies a mix of land uses, the spread of smaller scale facilities, and a denser urban form. These implications and the clash with a low-density car-based form of development may not be fully appreciated.

These findings suggest only limited concern with environmental impacts by dwelling occupiers, as least as perceived by estate agents, focusing largely on energy conservation (and then only in limited, highly visible forms) and the planning of local land uses to maximise pedestrian access. In terms of the key dimensions identified above, the following observations can be made.

The local environment is clearly of considerable significance to housing users, but there is limited appreciation of environmental impacts which are exported beyond this area. Environmentally friendly building materials, with their global impact, were considered of very little importance. Where energy-conservation features were valued, this is likely to be because there is a financial payback within the time period that the household is likely to stay in the dwelling. The General Household Survey found that 10% of households move in under one year, 24% in under three years, and 36% in under five years. Although the payback on solar energy may be ten to twenty-five years, many energy conservation measures have a payback within lesser times. Loft insulation, condensing boilers, draughtproofing, and cavity wall insulation all have paybacks potentially within four years (BRE, 1990). To the extent that such features are still undervalued, this suggests either that households stay longer than they originally intended in their dwellings and/or that the payback periods are overestimated. Generally and not surprisingly, the factors indicate an incentive to minimise the local environmental impacts, but no more general stimulus towards valuing features which contribute towards sustainability in the choice of dwelling.

5.2 The housebuilders

The reaction of residential developers to a changing environmental agenda was investigated through a postal survey, a scan of *The Housebuilder*, and an analysis of company accounts for the major firms.

The scan of *The Housebuilder* (see figure 3) reveals the growth in concern with environmental issues. There were twenty-eight separate references in

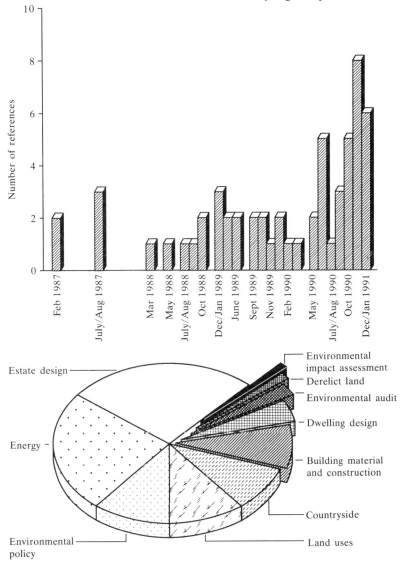

Figure 3. Scan of *The Housebuilder* (combined issues are published in December and January, and July and August; copies for February, March, and April 1989 are missing).

1990 compared with just five in 1987: this represented a six-fold increase in environmental column inches from 82 column inches to 521 column inches. Analysing the content of these articles highlights two issues in particular: energy consumption and principles of estate design accounted for the greatest share of environmental column inches at 25% and 26% each. Yet neither issue featured in 1987. Two other issues which have become important in the last two years are: the spatial pattern of land uses, particularly the home–work relation; and the environmental impact of the construction process itself, with regard to building materials and local disturbance. These accounted for 10% and 9% of total column inches, yet did not appear in 1987 or 1988. In contrast, countryside articles, which accounted for 9% of space overall, only feature in 1987 and 1988. As suggested in the framework above, it appears that the housebuilding industry is matching the user market in identifying energy consumption and the management of spatial externalities in the immediate vicinity of the development as the key environmental concerns.

A similar analysis was undertaken of a number of company accounts to determine which issues feature most prominently when individual companies are considered. Of the eighteen company reports looked at, fourteen had some mention of environmental issues, with thirty-eight specific references overall; 42% of the references concerned the nature of the sites being developed or sought for development, in particular the need to select sites carefully with regard to the locality, with an acceptance of the importance of using derelict land and redeveloping existing building stock. Besides this, there were eight references (21%) to problems of resource use and the general issue of environmentally acceptable sources and seven (18%) to planning issues, such as the role of transport, the relation of land uses, and development densities. Waste management, waste production, energy use, and nature conservation only raised five references in total. Housebuilders are clearly concerned with current problems of finding sites and developing them in the short term within the constraints of resource availability and planning policies. The scale, spatially and temporally, is an immediate one.

Differing pictures arise from the different audiences. *The Housebuilder* represents, in part, the public face of the industry, with the House Builders' Federation attempting to guide housebuilders in their thoughts and actions. Company reports are addressed to shareholders and seek to assure them that they have their immediate financial interests at heart. Neither picture suggests a substantial concern with environmental impacts, beyond the spatial scale of the housing estate or the temporal scale of payback on energy consumption measures. Indeed, the House Builders' Federation's 1990 environmental audit of the industry complacently suggested that housebuilding in general had a positive environmental effect.

The postal survey did not achieve a high response rate; only 92 questionnaires out of 400 were returned (23%—total population approximately

26 500 builders). The sample was randomly selected from the National House-Building Council handbook, with a spread across the different counties in England, Wales, and Scotland. The sample, therefore, reflected the number of firms in the industry rather than their contribution to output. Only four volume builders were included in the survey and only one of these responded (with results that were broadly in line with the overall pattern). Any future research would need to take greater account of the different types of firm within the housebuilding industry and their varying responses to the spatial and temporal characteristics of environmental change, as well as their differing risk-assessment procedures. The detail of the responses would also be affected by the type of site and development that the housebuilder specialised in: no data were collected on these aspects.

The survey results identified a number of areas where housebuilders were changing practice and a number where they were not. One of the main areas of changed activity was in increasing insulation standards: 89% said they were doing this, mainly in response to the 1990 revised Building Regulations. There was also a tendency to minimise waste produced during the construction process: 76% responded thus, emphasising the use of new information technology to reduce the quantity of materials held on site. There was also general support for environmental labelling of building materials: 76% were in favour; and 64% of firms claimed to 'always' or 'normally' take measures to protect wildlife on construction sites, although it is difficult to assess the level of protection afforded. Similarly 56% said they always included treeplanting on sites.

However, there was also considerable evidence of lack of response to environmental concerns: 53% said they were taking no measures to reduce energy consumption during the construction process, 60% said they were taking no measures to reduce water consumption (and those that did emphasised the role of dry-lining with plaster, a material which is very energy intensive), and 64% were not recycling building materials; 64% said they were not revising dwelling designs to reduce energy consumption by occupiers and 97% said they never included solar energy equipment in their developments. In planning their developments a majority in each case said they did not positively seek to reduce distances to shops (53% said they did not), schools (60%), workplace (67%), or other facilities. With regard to open spaces, 88% never included allotments and 54% never included 'wild areas' in their developments. With regard to transport provision, 54% never included public transport provision, 46% never included traffic-calming measures and 72% never included cycleways.

Internally, 62% never provided space for domestic recycling (although this is a feature that receives a credit in the BREEAM for dwellings), but almost equal numbers always or sometimes provided space for bicycles as never did (35% compared with 38%), though this does raise the question of what type of space is provided. Providing space for a second car still took priority over bicycle space. Energy efficiency of space heating was a relatively low explicit priority: 29% mentioned this as one of the two factors influencing choice of space heating. The two most commonly cited factors were: perceived consumer demand (53%) and reducing running costs (50%), which should of course relate closely to energy efficiency. In terms of kitchen and utility equipment, the most important factors were perceived consumer demand (76%) and reducing installation costs (33%) compared with 10% for energy efficiency.

From an environmental policy perspective, these findings are not particularly encouraging. It is clear that housebuilders are responding very little or only slowly to the environmental agenda. In those areas where there is change it is occurring in response to minimisation of costs (construction waste), government policy (insulation standards), or perceived consumer demand (space heating). There is an emphasis on landscape conservation and enhancement during construction and site layout, and the House Builders' Federation have been promoting the positive role that naturalistic layouts can play in marketing (Baines, 1990). Generally the concern is with enhancing the environment of the site to promote saleability and this limited spatial dimension is matched by a tight timescale for planning developments: 49% of respondents said that they assumed households bought the dwelling on the basis of current needs alone, without considering a longer timescale.

Housebuilders have moved quickly to suggest that restrictions on planning permission for residential development are hindering the ability of builders to be environmentally conscious. For, according to builders, planning constrains site choice; it limits the funds available for environmental improvements given the pressure from planning-generated high land prices; and it constrains the space given to environmental measures such as wildlife habitats. Furthermore, limited land availability means that consumers also face a constrained choice of dwellings and environmental aspects of those dwellings then get downgraded within the housebuyer's priorities. These arguments on the links between availability of new housing, the costing of environmental measures, the impact of land prices, consumer choice between dwellings and the prioritising of environmental features, all need further exploration and critical judgment in the light of empirical work. However, as in the case of the more general debate about land availability (Duncan, 1989; Rydin, 1985), it seems reasonable to expect the level of technical innovation in the industry, including the standard of energy efficiency, the pressures on site density, and other areas of environmental performance to be linked to the structure of the industry and its search for profit from different sources rather than positing a simple link between a restrictive planning system and low environmental standards.

5.3 The investors
Identifying the investors in residential property raises an interesting issue. There is a substantial body of literature (for example, Hamnett et al, 1991) in

which it is argued that owner-occupiers of dwellings have a dual interest in their property - as occupiers and investors. The large-scale capital gains that can be made from owning equity in housing over the last two decades (and losing it in specific locations and generally over the last few years) means that many house purchasers treat housing as an investment asset. Therefore, the responses to the estate agents' survey can be interpreted as much in terms of an investor's attitude to certain features as a 'pure' occupier's attitude. Features will be assessed in terms of their contribution to future resale as much as to intermediate occupation. The fact that households tend to move fairly frequently means that housing is regarded as a short-term rather than a long-term asset and, therefore, relatively short paybacks are required on any further investment in the dwelling. However, many of the features which represent an occupier's concerns with the use of the immediate local environment are also relevant to an investor, particularly a short-term investor, as they enhance the short-range marketability of the asset. These points, therefore, reinforce the discussion of the estate agents' survey.

Of course, owner-occupiers are not the only investors in the housing market. Such purchases are backed by finance supplied from building societies, banks, and other financial institutions, in the form of mortgages. Mortgages are relatively long-term commitments of finance, typically for twenty-five years, and this might suggest a longer term viewpoint on the part of the institution which would encompass a variety of environmental concerns. However, it is clear from the survey of mortgage lenders that the short-term view of the owner-occupier leads to short-termism in the mortgage lender also. This is reinforced by recent restructuring in the mortgage finance sector and the deregulation of the building societies which encouraged them to compete with other financial institutions on a range of commission-earning activities.

The response rate from the 136 mortgage lenders, listed in the Council of Mortgage Lenders handbook, was quite good at 94 responses (59% from a 100% sample of the population) and the results showed a high degree of consistency. Managers were not advised to take certain key items of environmental concern into account in the mortgage lending decision: 88% did not consider the level of insulation, 90% the overall energy consumption of the dwelling, and 77% the use of environmentally damaging building materials. There was an assumption that the valuer would take account of these items if relevant. In this light the proposals being considered by the Royal Institution of Chartered Surveyors for including a section on energy conservation in the standard House Buyers Report could be important.

The response to the introduction of the BREEAM for dwellings is likely to be muted: 74% were not currently aware of BREEAM and 66% were not sure whether they would take green labelling of a dwelling by BREEAM into account when deciding to grant a loan; 32% were sure they would not. Conflicts of interest within the mortgage lender market will also underpin the slow acceptance of BREEAM. This method was developed by BRE with Municipal Mutual and BREEAM credits carry a discount from Municipal Mutual's warranty scheme for new houses. However the National House Building Council currently underwrites 95% of new private-sector housing and they are excluded from using BREEAM for its first year of operation. Overall, the attitude of mortgage lenders to environmental issues is summed up by the letter from the Head of External Relations of the Building Societies Association which, in response to an enquiry regarding this research, said: "As a representative body for building societies rather than for house builders, this Association has relatively little interest in the matters which are the subject of your research" (personal communication). There does not, therefore, seem to be any immediate prospect of the building societies underwriting, say, energy-efficiency measures by offering funds for works at an interest rate which allows costs to be more than covered by savings in running costs, as suggested by the Environment and Energy Committee of the Royal Institute of British Architects (Smith, 1991).

The timescale involved in mortgage lenders' commitment to their property investment seems to be dominated by the cyclical swings in the housing market, with saleability of the asset depending on the next upswing, and the general business cycle. The financial standing of the mortgagor depends on the security of employment and income and the assumption that a dwelling will be sold within the short term. This is confirmed by the response to a question on the timescale taken by managers in making loan decisions in which 39% said they looked to the period within five years and 49% to the period within ten years, although another 48% did claim to look to the period beyond twenty-one years which should indicate a rather different approach to decisionmaking.

6 Conclusions
In this paper I have argued that an analysis of the property market in the various sectors is necessary to understand the environmental impact of the built environment and, in particular, the ways in which market actors will respond to growing knowledge about these impacts and to environmental policy. The research findings from the residential sector provide an indication of how this approach may assist our understanding of environment – property-market relations and, it is hoped, suggest further avenues for more in-depth work.

Acknowledgements. The author wishes to acknowledge: the funding of the Royal Institution of Chartered Surveyors Education Trust in supporting this research; the research assistance of Joanna Locks, Kevin Taylor, and Karen Ziegler; and helpful discussions with Ian Davies, Nick Dean, Mark Goodwin, and Duncan McLaren.

References

Baines C, 1990, "Landscapes for new housing", New Homes Marketing Board, 82 New Cavendish Street, London W1M 8AO

BRE, 1990 *Energy Efficiency in Dwellings: Digest 355* Building Research Establishment, Garston, Watford WD2 7JR

Cadman D, 1990, "The environment and the urban property market" *Town and Country Planning* **59** (10) 267 – 270

CIRIA, 1990, "The construction industry and the environment: the way forward" CIRIA Special Publication 77, Construction Industry Research and Information Association, 6 Storey's Gate, London SW1P 3AU

DoE, 1990, *This Common Inheritance: Britain's Environmental Strategies* Cm 1200, Department of the Environment (HMSO, London)

DoE, 1991, *Environmental Action Guide: for Building and Purchasing Managers* Department of the Environment (HMSO, London)

Duncan S, 1989, "Development gains and housing provision in Britain and Sweden" *Transactions of the Institute of British Geographers* **14** 157 – 172

Elkin T, McLaren D, Hillman M, 1991 *Reviving the City: Towards Sustainable Development* (Friends of the Earth/Policy Studies Institute, London)

Environmental Protection Act, 1990 *Public General Acts—Elizabeth II* chapter 43 (HMSO, London)

Hamnett C, Harmer M, Williams P, 1991 *Safe as Houses* (Paul Chapman, London)

Healey P, Nabarro R, 1990 *Land and Property Development in a Changing Context* (Gower, Aldershot, Hants)

Macgill S, 1987 *The Politics of Anxiety* (Pion, London)

McMahon M, 1985, "The law of the land: property rights and town planning in modern Britain", in *Land Rent, Housing and Urban Planning: A European Perspective* Eds M Ball, V Bentivegna, M Edwards, M Folin (Croom Helm, Andover, Hants) pp 87 – 106

Owens S, 1986 *Energy, Planning and Urban Form* (Pion, London)

Owens S, 1991 *Planning Settlements Naturally* (Packard, Chichester, Sussex)

Page G W, 1991, "Groundwater contamination effects of property values" paper to AESOP/ACSP Congress, Oxford Polytechnic, 8 – 12 July; available from College of Urban and Public Affairs, Atlantic University, Fort Lauderdale, FL

Pearce D, Turner K, 1990 *Economics of Natural Resources and the Environment* (Harvester Wheatsheaf, Hemel Hempstead, Herts)

Pearce D, Markandya A, Barbier E, 1989 *Blueprint for a Green Economy* (Earthscan, Aldershot, Hants)

Raw G, Prior J, 1991, "BREEAM/new homes: the BRE environmental assessment method for new homes", paper to conference on "Unhealthy Housing: The Public Health Response", Univeristy of Warwick, December; copy available from Building Research Establishment, Garston, Watford WD2 7JR

Reeve A, 1986 *Property* (Macmillan, London)

RICS, 1991 *General Practice Members Information Service* October, page 3, Royal Institute of Chartered Surveyors, 12 Great George Street, London SW1P 3AE

Rydin Y, 1985 *Housing Land Policy* (Gower, Aldershot, Hants)

Rydin Y, forthcoming, "What is sustainable residential development?" *Journal of Environmental Planning and Management*

Rydin Y, Rodney W, Orr C, 1990, "Why do institutions invest in property?" *Journal of Property Finance* **1** 250 – 258

Smith P, 1991, "Power points in the battle to build a safer future for all" *The Guardian* 7 June

WCED, 1987 *Our Common Future* (The Brundtland Report) World Commission on Environment and Development, (Oxford University Press, Oxford)

Spatial Depiction of Local Sustainable Development

V Despotakis, M Giaoutzi
National Technical University, Athens
P Nijkamp
Free University, Amsterdam

1 Introduction

There is an increasing need for enhancing existing geograpical information systems (GIS), to provide integrated policy-oriented systems to assist planners (Fischer and Nijkamp, 1992). A policy-oriented GIS should provide analysts with several relevant and feasible development scenarios (options). On the basis of a compound evaluation, the optimum scenario(s) which meets specific sustainability criteria (Opschoor and Reijnders, 1991; van den Bergh, 1991; van den Bergh and Nijkamp, 1990) may then be selected by the user.

There are several barriers to developing such a system (Nijkamp and Scholten, 1991). The main difficulty is that we have to link traditionally complex and data-driven GIS procedures (Burrough, 1983; Openshaw, 1990; Scholten and Stillwell, 1990) with procedures that monitor economic–ecological interactions (WCED, 1987; Opschoor, 1990). From this linkage we may arrive at a simple user-friendly system for assisting sustainable development (SD) within the region to which the system is applied. Simplicity and clarity are necessary characteristics if any strategic or policy decision has to be supported by this system.

We present some preliminary results for such a hybrid GIS–SD system developed in the GIS Laboratory of the Free University, Amsterdam. The system was numerically tested in a 90 km (north–south) by 100 km (east–west) area of the Greek Sporades islands in the Aegean Sea (Giaoutzi and Nijkamp, 1989) with a particular focus on the island of Alonnisos. To evaluate the scenario results, we linked the GIS–SD system to a decision support system (DSS), originally derived to operate on nonspatial data (Janssen, 1991; van Herwijnen and Janssen, 1989). Consequently, in section 2 we briefly provide the necessary theoretical background on which our system was based. In section 3 we present the most important components (modules) of our system. In section 4 we deal with numerical results in the test area of the Sporades islands. Finally, in section 5 we summarise the findings and suggest further studies that may be conducted in the near future.

2 Designing spatial models for sustainable development

First we will give some concise definitions of sustainable development. We start from the general observation that important changes in environmental and economic systems, which directly or indirectly affect their survival and/or well-being, have to be-controlled on the basis of rigorous scientific analysis. Some indicative and well-known examples of global and local human and environmental changes and their effects are described in the World Commission on Environment and Development report *Our Common Future* (WCED, 1987; see also Archibugi and Nijkamp, 1989; James et al, 1989; Opschoor and Reijnders, 1991) and include:

Global examples: sea level rise of the oceans caused mainly by global warming and climatic changes, depletion of the ozone layer, deforestation and urban decay, population growth and migration due to resource scarcities, desertification, and extinction of species.

Local examples: pollution in areas that face strong urban development, unbalanced with respect to the capacity of the environment to accept such pressures, hazards from chemical, nuclear, and radioactive toxic industries, extinction of specific species through uncontrolled hunting, road construction, etc, and local catastrophes (wars, floods, etc).

A common attribute of these examples is that they threaten human and environmental survival and hence are 'negative' or 'undesirable' changes that we should try to avoid or cope with. 'Positive' changes (regeneration of natural environmental stocks, advances in environmental technology regarding optimal resource allocation and exploitation, etc) are by definition 'welcome'. Scientific action is needed to support and enhance such 'positive' changes.

To begin our brief presentation of SD definitions and concepts, we quote the (anthropocentric) definition of the WCED (1987, page 7): "Sustainable development is a pattern of development that meets the needs of present generations without jeopardizing the ability of future generations to meet their own needs". However, SD has not only an intergenerational dimension, but also contains other concepts and definitions. Being dynamic in terms both of space and of time, SD is continuously being redefined. In analysing SD it is clear that for describing complex and dynamic economic and ecological processes we have to define at least one dimension: time. Economic and ecological development clearly take place over time.

Restricting ourselves to economic and ecological coevolutionary development (Nijkamp, 1990), we first define development as: nonnegative changes of *social welfare* over time, with social welfare being made up of two correlated components (see also Nijkamp and Soeteman, 1990; van Pelt et al, 1990a; 1990b), namely the consumption of man-made products and services (the socioeconomic system) and the consumption of environmental amenities (the ecological system).

In figure 1 a schematic simplified representation is given of the above definition. Both systems (economic and ecological) produce corresponding functions that include quantitative and qualitative components.

Within each system i ($i = 1, 2$) there are several difficulties in expressing each of the W_i as a function of the terms shown in figure 1, because a specific and common quantification (uniform measurement units in any of the existing metric systems) is very difficult within each system. Even if this can be accomplished there remains the problem that W_1 has to be compatible with W_2, so that they have to add up through the use of relative weights (a, b). Thus the addition in figure 1 is conventional and refers to some function or algorithm which should comprise welfare sources from the interacting systems of economy and ecology. In addition, there is no market and hence no price for environmental amenities (Bojö, 1991; Folke, 1991; Opschoor, 1990; van Pelt et al, 1990a; 1990b). Also, in reality, strong conflicts may exist between development in both subsystems. This complicates the effort towards clearer and stricter expressions of the interactions that take place between the two subsystems. The expression of both terms in present values is an even more complex problem.

Once we have defined the concept of development as a nonnegative change of a socioeconomic and ecological welfare function over time (that is, $dW/dt \geq 0$), the next step is to define how (under which constraints) this change should be maintained as positive. We now introduce the SD constraint, by requiring that this change take place so that certain pre-specified goals are achieved and/or constraints are met. We may claim that an important characteristic of sustainability is that it represents a dynamic state of balance between economic activities and ecology, rather than a fixed state of harmony.

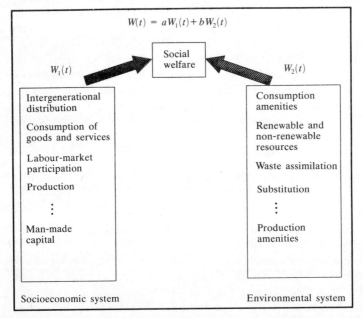

Figure 1. The main components of the social welfare function.

The next question is which goals one should try to achieve in SD. To examine this question we first define the necessary dimensions of sustainability: time and space. The *time* intervals for sustaining the economy and the environment are multigenerational. Problems arise in the way intergenerational values can be regarded and estimated uniformly in future time spans as well as in how these values can be linked among different generations (that is, eliminating unknown incompatibilities).

One can use the *spatial* dimensions (for example, fully three-dimensional coordinate intervals: geographic latitude and longitude intervals, depth or height intervals) to characterise sustainability analyses according to two broad categories: *global sustainable development* (GSD) and *regional sustainable development* (RSD). The latter is easier to apply[1] and to monitor in terms of data availability, computational efforts, management, and control; the former is much more difficult to control and can be indirectly achieved through RSD: if all regions of a global system experience RSD, then we have GSD (Nijkamp, 1990). It is thus essential that RSD functions are well understood and applied to at least one unitary cell of a test area. A formal definition of RSD (Nijkamp, 1990, page 4) is: "From a welfare viewpoint on RSD, it makes sense to define RSD as a development which ensures that the regional population can attain an acceptable level of welfare—both at present and in the future—and that this regional development is compatible with ecological circumstances in the long run while at the same time it tries to accomplish a globally sustainable development."

As we move towards concrete SD concepts, we observe that the condition that social welfare function changes should be positive $(\mathrm{d}W/\mathrm{d}t \geqslant 0)$ may hold in two different ways: (1) either $\mathrm{d}W_1 \geqslant 0$, or $\mathrm{d}W_2 \geqslant 0$, or (2) both $\mathrm{d}W_1 \geqslant 0$ and $\mathrm{d}W_2 \geqslant 0$. In the first case we have '*weak sustainability*', whereas in the second case we have '*strong sustainability*' (Daly, 1991; Opschoor and Reijnders, 1991). Although these distinctions are conceptually sound, the absence of a numéraire again makes the actual numerical illustration or application very difficult.

The definition of SD implies that economic stocks and equivalence in stocks of ecological amenities are defined first. In the development process, it is obvious that we should not allow a stock to become negative, because otherwise it does not have any meaning. However, when a stock falls below a prespecified desirable (or allowable) level, then one should explore the possibilities of substituting this stock for another stock or system of stocks. In doing so, we need a deep understanding of the mechanisms of the economic and ecological system, so that substitution is feasible; that is, the net welfare sum of substituting stocks is exactly equivalent to the scarce stock. Sometimes this cannot happen and substitution is impossible. We may then say that the scarce stock experiences a type of *irreversible change* and that SD management should avoid such

[1] However, GSD is easier (or at least less ambiguous) to define than RSD.

types of changes. If the substitution possibilities are not warranted then one has to assess (again in terms of a uniform metric) the *risk* of proceeding (or not proceeding) with substitution.

In addition, initial stock values as well as confidence intervals for upper and lower stock limits have to be known for both the economic and the ecological system. This knowledge is essential for setting the systems in an operational mode (for example, computations, decisions, etc). In defining these values, knowledge about the *carrying capacity* (CC) of a region is required. CC can be vaguely expressed (for example, in terms of population) as the upper (feasible) asymptotic rate of population growth. Various definitions of CC exist, but in general a specific context is needed for an operational definition. An example is a definition of CC in a recreational context: "CC is the maximum level of recreation use in terms of numbers and activities, that can be accommodated before a decline in ecological value occurs" (Coccossis and Parpairis, 1990, page 3). From the above definition it is clear that CC incorporates a relationship between 'amount of use' and 'user satisfaction' within the context of SD.

A link between the nonspatial and spatial models is crucial for developing a GIS–SD hybrid system. We begin to investigate this link by examining the conceptual equivalence of economic stocks to geographical layers. In Murthy et al (1990) stocks are also referred to as 'reservoirs' or 'levels' interconnected by flow paths. For a spatial layer $A(x, y)$ (referring to a specific coordinate system x, y) and a stock S_i (which is a function of time), we may write the following relationships:

$$A_1(x, y) \leftrightarrow S_1(t), \ A_2(x, y) \leftrightarrow S_2(t), \ \dots A_l(x, y) \leftrightarrow S_l(t). \tag{1}$$

We relate the idea of stocks with the idea of layers by realising that the spatial contents of a specific classified layer A can be regarded as stocks which dynamically change in time. In this way we can generalise the concept of dynamic modelling of a specific phenomenon to include all necessary stocks S_i which are needed to describe the available spatial layers of information for a region.

Let us assume that we have derived the land-use map of a specific region, for a specific time, with ten land-use classes. Our land-use map is an information layer $A(x, y)$ with ten classes ($l = 10$). We may relate each land-use class $A_i(x, y)$, $i = 1, 2, \dots, l$, to a specific stock sequence $S_i(t)$, $i = 1, 2, \dots, l$ as follows: (1) calculate the areal averages for each land-use class, (2) transform the areal totals to the properly scaled areal units, and (3) store these areas to the sequence of stocks S_i. The ten land-use classes may be entered into a differential equation system for further (numerical) integration over time. By using the above stock–layer equivalence concept, (with each layer containing n classes) we insert in a differential equation system n additional differential equations.

We can further conclude that, if there are t spatial layers available for a region, each with $l, m, \dots, q$ classes, then we need $r = l + m + \dots + q$

definitions of stocks (and flows) of the form of equation (1). Thus our generalised spatial modelling of dynamic phenomena takes the form

$$\frac{dS_i}{dt} = f_i(t, x, y, z; S_i; F_i; C_i), \qquad i = 1, 2, ..., r, \tag{2}$$

with the initial conditions

$$S_i(t_0, x_0, y_0, z_0) = S_0, \qquad i = 1, 2, ..., r, \tag{3}$$

where F_i are the corresponding flows of the stock S_i, and C_i are the values of the converters.

The sustainable development considerations can be embedded in equation (2) and in each integration step dt by: (1) imposing the necessary conditions that stock S_i should fulfil; (2) defining and examining the values of the indicators (but also the stocks, flows, and converters themselves) as functions of the stocks, flows, and converters; and (3) defining and examining alternative scenarios which, in our system, can be of any kind: no-policy (external events) scenarios (natural progress of the ecosystem), external policies (influencing totally or partially one or more functions of the ecosystem), and behavioural scenarios (creating and monitoring spatial dynamic behavioural patterns such as migration, urban growth, etc).

The important stage for the above link is to decide on the rules of three types of stock motion: (1) expansion, (2) shrinkage, and (3) outflow and inflow. These rules have to govern the propagation of the stock changes that will result from the dynamic simulation of the spatial system. Such rules can be built in a raster (or quadtree format) and will reflect the spatial reality of the region. For example, if the dynamic solution gives an increase in 'urban stock' of the land-use layer of $10\,000$ m^2, the spatial model can equally increase the x and y dimension of this class by the square root of $10\,000$, that is 100 m. The 'candidate' squares in the geographic layer that can accommodate this expansion will be determined by overlaying the land-use layer with other layers that can influence this expansion: the layer of slopes, aspects, elevation, transportation, etc (see also Méaille and Wald, 1990). In this way we can create 'suitability layers' to govern the stock motion. In the following section, where a numerical application of these concepts is provided, these suitability layers are generated by simulating specific 'force fields' in a spatial context. Of course the interaction of each class within the same layer will also play an important role in the determination of stock motion.

After all 'motion' assignments have been inserted in the geographic system in a hybrid user–computer manner, the results (maps, reports, etc) for each time period will be written on disk, and the numerical integration will proceed to the next step.

The proposed system is shown in figure 2: sustainable development constraints can be entered at the 'expansion rules formation' stage, after each integration circle has been completed. These constraints can be of the form (4) (equality constraints) or of the form (5) (inequality constraints):

$$G_{SD}(S_1, S_2, ..., S_r) = 0 \, , \tag{4}$$

$$G_{SD}(S_1, S_2, ..., S_r) \geq 0 \, , \quad G_{SD}(S_1, S_2, ..., S_r) \leq 0 \, . \tag{5}$$

The user can enter the modelling procedure for scenario generation at three points: in the differential equation forming and editing process, in the geographical analysis stage, and at the 'expansion rules formation' after each integration step (figure 2). The incorporation of the nonspatial system [in our case the STELLA[2] system (Richmond et al, 1987)] with the

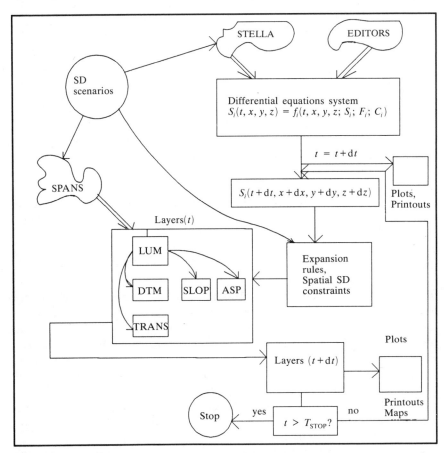

Figure 2. The link between nonspatial and spatial dynamic modelling.

[2] STELLA is a dynamic modelling software tool operating in a MACINTOSH environment. The user determines the constants of the model, the 'stocks' (any quantity that may change on time and for which initial values are known), the 'flows' (the time derivatives of the stocks), the 'converters' (any functions of time entering the model), and the 'connectors' (possible relationships between stocks, flows, or converters depicted by arrows).

spatial system [we chose the SPANS[3] GIS system (Tydac Technologies, 1988)] is achieved through the generalised stocks that form the function of layers. These layers are the land uses of the area, the digital terrain model (DTM), the terrain slopes and aspects (SLOP and ASP), the transportation model (TRANS), etc. The transition to the space domain is achieved by defining the rules of stock motion. Intermediate layers may be used to act as 'attraction' layers, simulating the force field applied to the stocks.

The GIS–SD system described above is the 'heart' of our proposed system. To complete and fully operationalise our GIS–SD system, we followed the six steps shown in figure 3: (1) Extend the GIS functions to accept the SD linking concepts. (2) Operationalize the SD concepts to fit into the GIS. (3) Link the concepts of steps 1 and 2 (GIS–SD system). (4) Create the spatial and nonspatial data for the study area. (5) Link the data to the GIS–SD system. (6) Evaluate the results by a DSS linked to the GIS–SD system.

In our case study on SD these main steps are derived in the design phase and are needed to give the theoretical background for the implementation of our GIS–SD system. The actual hybrid GIS–SD system finally contained (in its core form) eight submodules which are discussed in the next section.

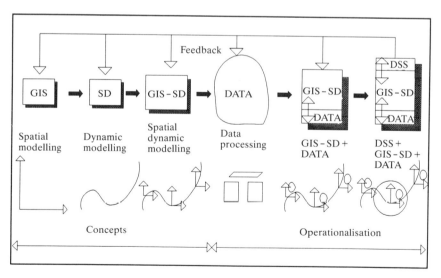

Figure 3. Design and context of the GIS–SD system.

[3] SPANS is a GIS operating on an IBM environment. The geographical objects are represented as 'entities' by the form of vectors, rasters, and quadtrees. A variety of spatial functions between these entities is available (matrix overlay, spatial queries, etc); the results are presented using most of the features offered by a computer-assisted cartographic system (labelling of points, map titles, map animation, etc).

3 Components of the general dynamic GIS–SD model

The general dynamic GIS–SD model links the GIS spatial analysis concepts to the concepts of SD. To achieve this, the following eight submodules were necessary (figure 3): (1) spatial modelling, (2) nonspatial

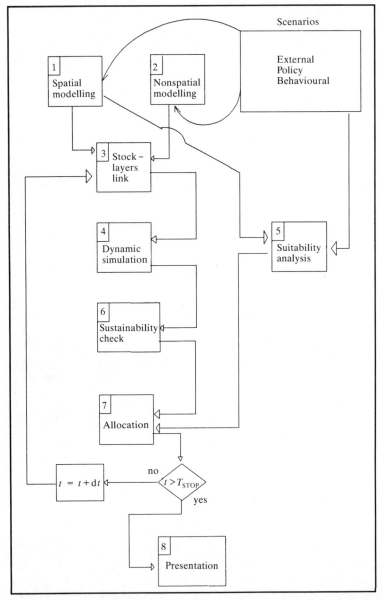

Figure 4. The eight main modules integrated into the general GIS–SD hybrid model.

modelling, (3) stock–layer linking, (4) dynamic simulation, (5) suitability analysis, (6) sustainability check, (7) allocation, (8) presentation. Figure 4 shows the various functions each submodule performs within the system.

3.1 Module 1: spatial modelling

This module creates the original spatial data layers of the digital terrain model (DTM) and the land-use model (LUM) from raw map data and air photographs [figure 5(a)]. After the original data layers have been created we compute the derived databases by using existing GIS packages, such as SPANS (Tydac Technologies, 1988) and IDRISI (Idrisi Project, 1990), or by using specially written software (that is, source programs written in C or FORTRAN). This module operates at a detailed pixel level, that is, at the originally selected spatial resolution of 100 m × 100 m.

3.2 Module 2: Nonspatial modelling

This module creates questionnaire, tabular, and cadastral (nonspatial) data taken from the processing of the relevant raw data initially collected in the field [figure 5(b)].

These data are further processed to create the necessary initial stock, stock flows, and converter values to be used as inputs to the terrestrial model (described in module 4). Other nonspatial but dynamic submodels such as rain models and rain forest models are also derived at this stage. This module operates at a nonspatial level. The spatial aggregation level may thus be defined to be at the level of the Sporades islands.

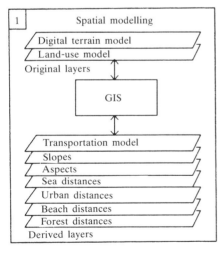
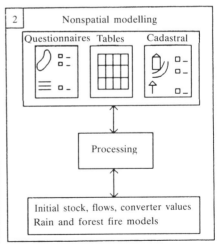

(a)   (b)

Figure 5. (a) Module 1 (spatial modelling), (b) module 2 (nonspatial modelling) of the GIS–SD hybrid model.

3.3 Module 3: Stock-layer link

This module performs the link between the spatial layers $A_K(t)$ derived from module 1 at a pixel level and the spatial stocks $S_i^{SP}(t)$ necessary for the dynamic simulation [figure 6(a)]. The *total areas* of the relevant spatial layers (at pixel level) are directly inserted as initial stocks into the dynamic model (module 4) for every time t. This procedure is necessary to obtain the next stock value for these total areas in time $t+dt$, where dt is the time step of 1 year.

At this stage we link the stock derived from module 2 (nonspatial modelling) to the stocks of the dynamic stock-flow model, by equating the areal totals derived from module 2. This procedure does not involve changes in the aggregation levels, as opposed to the spatial procedures of module 1.

3.4 Module 4: Dynamic simulation

This module is, metaphorically, the 'engine' for our GIS-SD model. Figure 6(b) describes the structure of this module. Its main operation is to solve numerically the differential equations [see equations (2) and (3)].

The dynamic simulation modelling language of STELLA software (operating on a MACINTOSH environment) was transformed to its FORTRAN language equivalent (operating on an IBM environment). During the above transformation, more emphasis was placed on the numerical integration mathematical procedures than on the graphical interfaces.

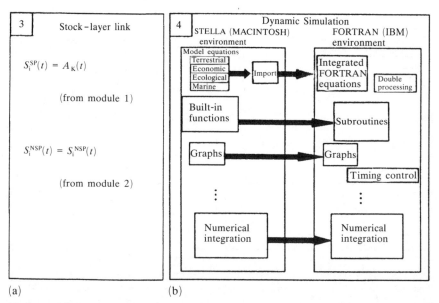

(a)   (b)

Figure 6. (a) Module 3 (stock-layer link), module 4 (dynamic simulation) of the GIS-SD hybrid model.

At this point we may provide the necessary description for the four nonspatial submodels, namely the terrestrial (see also Gilbert, 1992), economic (van den Bergh, 1991), ecological, and marine (Gilbert, forthcoming) submodels.

The locations of these four submodels within the dynamic simulation module are shown in the top of module 4 (see figure 8). All four refer to the Sporades study region. However, to simplify the GIS–SD numerical example, the four corresponding models were reduced to the Alonnisos island. The other areas can easily be integrated into the GIS–SD system in a similar manner.

The four submodels were originally provided separately in the form of STELLA equations. These equations were integrated (1) into the FORTRAN environment as figure 8 indicates, and (2) into a STELLA environment to construct an integrated marine–ecological–economic–terrestrial model base. The relationships of the four integrated submodels with GIS and the corresponding linking variables are illustrated in figure 7.

The main linking model between GIS and the four-model model base is the Alonnisos terrestrial model. The structure of the terrestrial model within the GIS is almost identical to the structure of this model within the integrated model base: only the input–output data differ.

The principles and interactions of the GIS-model base operation are as follows. The land uses (areal totals) and the island areas are fed into the economic model by the GIS for the initial year T_0; the economic model in turn feeds the terrestrial model (GIS part) with the numbers of tourists and local people in Alonnisos for every simulation year. These population values are derived from simulation runs of the integrated model base.

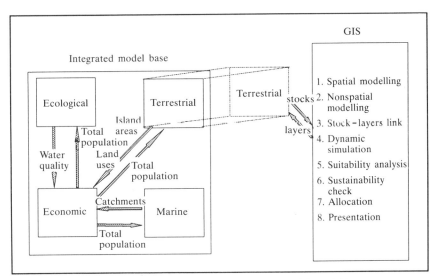

Figure 7. The linking nodes between GIS and the four-model model base.

During these runs, interactions between all four submodules are taken into account: (1) the economic–ecological model interactions through the total population and water quality and (2) the economic–marine model inter-actions through the total population and catchments (mainly fisheries).

The GIS-model-base variables interchange is performed once, at the beginning of the GIS dynamic simulation. The GIS then regards the total population for every simulation year as fixed, that is, as it is provided (exogeneously) by the model base.

Under these specific model-base functions, the GIS (using its eight submodules, as shown in figure 7) operates both in spatial and in non-spatial dynamic modes to perform urban allocation tasks, spatial simulations, alternative spatial scenarios, etc. We will now describe the terrestrial model because this model was the main linking node between GIS and the four submodels.

3.5 Terrestrial model

The terrestrial (nonspatial) model contains three interrelated submodels: (1) land-use, (2) forest wildlife, and (3) groundwater submodels. In figure 8 we can see the basic terrestrial model variables and their interrelations. In this figure the arcs joining two variables denote influence which may be positive $(+)$ or negative $(-)$. The mechanics may be briefly explained as follows: the island population growth (including tourists) increases the demand for urban land; the resulting urban growth causes the agricultural and the bare land to increase, and the maquis, low maquis, and forest areas to decrease; the forest areas are also decreased by fires; population growth also negatively influences forest wildlife and increases disturbance;

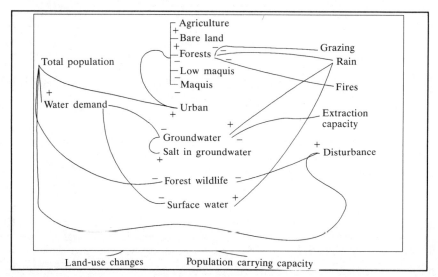

Figure 8. The main interrelations of the terrestrial submodel variables.

and, as water demand increases (mainly through population growth), surface water and groundwater are pumped out to satisfy the population's needs for water. As overall 'energy' check variables (indicators) for monitoring the operation of the system, we used (1) the population-carrying capacity of the island and (2) the land-use changes from one land-use type to another. The population-carrying capacity is computed by the GIS–SD system using the suitability layers of module 5; the land-use changes are computed specifically for each land use which is regarded as a dynamic stock.

The *state* variables of the models are defined by the ten stocks themselves: the six land-use types (agriculture, bare land, forests, maquis, low maquis, and urban land) and the forest wildlife, groundwater, groundwater salt, and surface water stocks; the *policy* variables belong to the category of converters and the user may produce alternative scenarios by changing these variables; examples of these variables are: tourism population rate, water demand, and wildlife population rate; the *instrument* variables belong to both categories of flows and converters; examples of these are: rain, fires, extraction capacity, and disturbance.

3.6 Ecological model

The ecological model constructed for our test area consists of four stocks: biochemical oxygen demand (BOD), chlorophyll, nitrogen, and phosphorus. The main sources of BOD, nitrogen, and phosphorus emissions are the inhabitants and the tourists. Olive presses add to the BOD levels. A scenario of biological treatment affects the quality of the seawater (stocks: BOD, nitrogen, phosphorus). Flushing removes a percentage of chlorophyll in each harbour.

Spatial distributions of these four stocks were not available at the time of the simulation runs. However, we may assume that the *total* stock values obtained by the ecological model simulation run refer to the harbours of the villages of the five main islands. It is then possible to rescale the results when actual data become available. The integrated GIS–SD link may then be achieved by assigning spatial zones to the ecological data. These zones will surround each of the harbours, with a specified distance from the harbours to the sea. The spatial layers in this case will consist of the BOD, chlorophyll, nitrogen, and phosphorus spatial models. The linking variables between the nonspatial ecological model and our GIS–SD hybrid model are the variables related to total population and water quality (see figure 7).

3.7 Marine model

The marine model is aimed at simulating the marine ecosystem with a special emphasis on seals, lobsters, and fishery. Tourists are the main cause of disturbance for newborn seals. Heavy storms occur once every five years and lead to the death of all newborn. The total fish catch (a very important input for the economic model) is determined by adding the fish and lobster catches. The marine model contains a total of six stocks: adult seals, young seals, three fish categories, and lobsters.

It is extremely difficult to link the marine model spatially to our GIS – SD model. This would require spatial data on fishery, seals, and lobster caught mainly by the local people. A possible benefit from such a spatial integration could be the location of areas of high threat for the survival of the seals, lobster, or fishery population.

To establish a minimum link between our model and the marine model, the following variables were used: total population and catchment (see figure 7); it was then assumed that the disturbance to young seals is caused not only by tourists, but also by local people.

3.8 Economic model
The economic model is aimed at simulating the relevant aspects of the socioeconomic reality of our study region as accurately as possible. Hotel capacity, pensions, tourism development, housing and secondary housing, gross net product, fishery, natural attractions, amenities, etc are some of the model variables of the economic model. The objective was also to include the concepts of sustainable development in the model. The structure of the model is described in detail in van den Bergh (1991) and van den Bergh and Gilbert (forthcoming). Here we will only give its working relationships with our GIS – SD model.

The economic model includes a number of variables which can be used as linking nodes to our GIS – SD model. These variables are (see figure 7) (1) population (local people and tourists), (2) land-use totals, and (3) land-areal totals. The population variables (1) were modified to correspond to the integrated model-base population outcomes for Alonnisos (input exogenous variable to GIS from the economic model). The land-use totals (2) embedded in the economic model were those referring to grazing areas, natural areas, urban land, and beaches. There is thus a straight link with our GIS – SD model (in particular the LUM) when it comes to these areal totals: the grazing areas were estimated as valley + bare rocks and the natural areas as forest + maquis + low maquis + trees. Variables (2) and (3) are inputs to the economic model from GIS.

3.9 Module 5: Suitability analysis
This module is used to simulate the spatial 'force field', necessary to generate the spatial motion of the stocks. The basic parts of the suitability analysis module are shown in figure 9(a). The purpose of generating a spatial force field is to simulate the attracting forces acting on the various stocks of the spatial layers. These attracting forces may then be used to determine the stock motion for each simulation period.

The spatial force field is generated by user scenarios. These scenarios can be: (1) *external* scenarios (nonpolicy development), (2) *policy* scenarios (policy-measure constraints), and (3) *behavioural* scenarios ('forces' generated by social, economic, or psychological reactions). These types of scenarios operate on a pixel-detailed spatial level.

3.10 Module 6: Sustainability check

This module contains the operational application of the concepts of sustainability. The location of this module with respect to the general model (see figure 4) dictates its function: it is positioned between module 4 (dynamic simulation) and model 7 (allocation) as an SD-checking module. On the assumption that SD has been typified in the form of model constraints for several stocks, this module checks whether these SD constraints are satisfied. The SD constraints may be equality or inequality constraints between stocks, converters, flows, and functions of them, obtained from module 4, every time step. The values of the indicators selected are also checked at this stage, whether they are within the threshold intervals the user has assigned for them (figure 9(b)]. If the SD conditions are met, the model proceeds to the next module (allocation). If the SD criteria are not met, then the model stops and prompts the user for instructions. At this stage the user may provide several alternatives for the system: (1) change the SD conditions, (2) revise one or more of the dynamic simulation submodels, or (3) change the scenarios. It is important that the correct decisions for the proper continuation of the GIS–SD system are taken here. For example, one may first reexamine the mathematical models before deciding to increase the SD indicator thresholds.

For our case study, the following sustainability constraints are checked:
1. All stocks should be positive.
2. No stocks should exceed the carrying capacity limits.

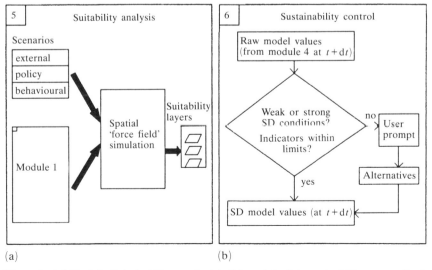

(a)   (b)

Figure 9. (a) Module 5 (suitability analysis), (b) module 6 (sustainability control) of the GIS – SD hybrid model.

3. Detection of strong sustainability constraints.
4. Detection of weak sustainability constraints.
5. Check whether indicators are within limits.

Sensitivity analysis runs, produced by modifying the above SD constraints, could be used for a more accurate determination of the Alonnisos 'environmental utilisation space' as defined in Opschoor and Reijnders (1991). In these types of runs all the other modules (spatial–nonspatial databases, allocation, numerical integration) should be regarded as fixed; then the corresponding changes of the ecoscope, produced separately by each of the modules, could be determined for the sensitivity analysis. Module 6 operates in a nonspatial level.

3.11 Module 7: Allocation

This module is used to allocate back to the spatial layers the new values for the areal totals computed by the GIS–SD model. The basic parts of this module are shown in figure 10(a).

The module again operates on a pixel level. It is used to compute the spatial distribution of the new stock values which come from module 6 (sustainability check) to the spatial model which is regarded as changing over time. In our case this is the land-use model, LUM(t). The new areal totals are allocated to LUM(t), taking into account the suitability layer which has been created from module 5. This is done through an allocation algorithm which uses the different classes of the suitability layer to assign an allocation priority to the new stock values. The allocation priority is directly proportional to the class values. These suitability classes can thus be interpreted as different degrees of attraction to the stock that is to be allocated.

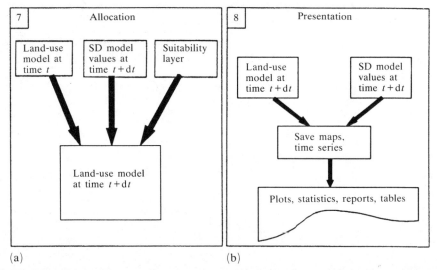

(a)   (b)

Figure 10. (a) Module 7 (allocation), module 8 (presentation) of the GIS–SD hybrid model.

3.12 Module 8: Presentation

This module plays the role of the interface between the user and the results obtained by the computer simulation. It is responsible for recording all the spatial and nonspatial information that has been derived by the GIS–SD model in the form of time series. Figure (10b) shows the basic parts of this module.

As the model can operate in a batch mode to save time, the user may interrupt the model at any time if a special result (map, stock value, etc) is to be recorded. The resulting maps of a user-defined period t are saved on disk for offline plotting at a later stage; the stocks, flows, converters, and indicators are also saved on disk as time series for further processing (for example, frequency analysis). The maps and the nonspatial results may both be used at a later stage for processing and evaluation by a DSS (see next section). The module operates at both a pixel and a nonpixel level.

4 Numerical application of the GIS–SD system in the Sporades test area

The GIS–SD system developed as described above was numerically applied to the Greek Sporades islands located in the central and western part of the Aegean sea (figure 11).

Two main conflicting objectives appear in the test area and are dealt with in this study: (1) regional economic development and (2) environmental protection. The main economic activities of the approximately 20 000 inhabitants of the region (1990) are tourism and fishery. The dramatic increase in tourism in the past thirty years in Greece has also influenced in descending order the islands: Skiathos, Skopelos, Alonnisos, and Gioura. Pilion is expected to receive spillover effects from tourism and agriculture. During the summer there is a large increase in the population of the islands because of tourism (domestic and foreign). This increase often exceeds the population-carrying capacity of the islands, and may result in abrupt high resource demands, which may cause irreversible processes in resource stocks. Similar effects have been studied by Despotakis (1989). It is apparent that the SD conflicts in the study area are dynamic phenomena. Some of these conflicts can be also expressed directly in spatial dimensions (for example, the expansion of urban land at the expense of forest areas). But it is only through the use of a spatio-temporal hybrid GIS–SD dynamic model that we can satisfactorily approach and simulate the mechanics of our ecosystem SD conflicts.

4.1 Data requirements

The data requirements for such a GIS–SD hybrid model are determined by (1) the spatiotemporal resolutions selected, and (2) the data needs for a successful GIS–SD model calibration. The data supply may not necessarily be in one-to-one correspondence with the data demand. This means that (1) digital data may have been collected and processed which are not used as an input to the GIS–SD model, but rather form an integrated digital database and (2) necessary digital data for the GIS–SD model may not have been available for the period for which the model was developed and tested. The data-collection process focused mainly on obtaining as much information as possible about the socioeconomic and natural environment of the study area.

In general, the necessary data input to both our GIS–SD model and the digital database, were determined to be:

Nonspatial data: data on the socioeconomic reality of the region (productivity and income per economic sector, tourism, fishery, houses, energy used per household, etc); demographic data (population, pyramid of ages, etc); ecological data (groundwater, sea water quality, forest fires, wildlife data, etc).

Spatial data: terrain elevation and sea depth data; land-use data; distance data from important land uses such as urban land, forests, etc; road transportation network data, etc.

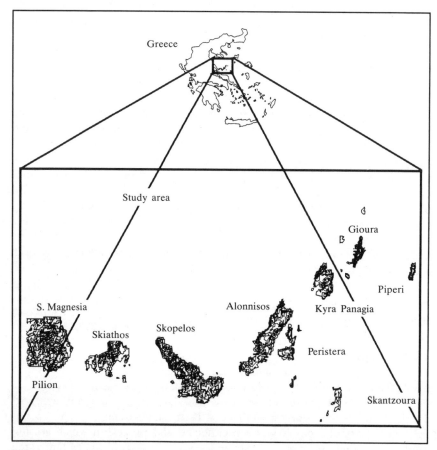

Figure 11. The location of the Northern Sporades test area.

After the necessary spatial and nonspatial data requirements had been set, the relevant data were collected from the various (mainly Greek) sources: National Statistical Service, Greek Military Geographic Service, Ministry of Environment, Planning and Technical Works, etc.

On the basis of the selected data, we ran our GIS–SD model in two ways. First, we selected—by way of illustration—transportation to be a (linear) attraction feature for urban development. This facilitated the use of a specific geographical entity in a GIS–SD model. Transportation could be replaced by any other user-specified attraction entity. The scenarios generated by including and excluding road transportation on Alonnisos island were first carried out to demonstrate the efficient use of our GIS–SD system to monitor urban development under different urban attraction conditions. The results are shown in figure 12 for the cases of 'absence' and 'presence' of transportation, plotted every five years.

The effects on urban expansion which result from the consideration of road transportation as a spatial attraction network are clearly depicted in the figure. For the 'no transportation' scenario the urban expansion takes place mainly across the seashore and the existing urban areas of the island; for the 'transportation' scenario the urban expansion presents clusters spread along the roads of the island, thus eliminating the amount of urban area to be spread along the seashore. Our GIS–SD system provides these results in form of raster images which may also be used for animation applications, so that more intuitive information may be extracted from the simulation results. These two-scenario results were not inserted into a DSS.

Second, our GIS–SD model can be used to evaluate the effects of various spatial policies on urban development. Five spatial scenarios, generated by assuming certain policies on urban expansion over Alonnisos, were considered:

Scenario 1: urban growth is encouraged within 200 m of the sea. The beaches themselves may be changed to urban areas.

Scenario 2: urban growth is encouraged in the middle of the island. The beaches and a zone of 500 m from sea may not be changed to urban areas.

Scenario 3: the urban area is allowed to expand and beach areas are allowed to change to urban in the southern half of the island only. The north half of the island remains 'untouched'.

Scenario 4: urban growth is allowed to expand and beach areas are allowed to change to urban only in the eastern half of the island. The western part of the island remains 'untouched'.

Scenario 5: the urban area is allowed to expand only in the existing urban areas of the islands. Any type of urban growth is strictly prohibited in the horizontal direction, and is only allowed in the vertical direction.

All these scenarios can be included in a GIS environment for all relevant years in beautiful colour maps. For practical reasons these maps are not included here (for full details see Despotakis, 1991).

(a)

Figure 12. Dynamic land-use changes for (a) the 'no transportation' scenario, and (b) the 'transportation' scenario. This was originally a colour figure, but for technical reasons it had to be printed in black and white.

(b)

Sea	Low maquis	Trees	Beach
Forest	Valleys	Agriculture	
Maquis	Bare rocks	Urban	

Figure 12 (continued)

For these runs we evaluated the results using a DSS (Janssen, 1991), on the basis of four criteria: tourism, nature, landscape, and transportation. The evaluation year was selected to be the final year of the simulation, T_{STOP} = 2005.

Table 1 is the effects table. The scoring units are nondimensional relative units. High scores mean 'good' results, whereas low scores indicate 'bad' results. We may observe that:

(1) Scenario 2 has a very low relative score for the 'tourism' criterion, whereas scenario 5 has the highest score for the same criterion, because urban distances to the sea—which determine the 'happy tourist' in this scenario—are maximal for scenario 2 and minimal for scenario 5.

(2) The 'best' sustainable scenario for the natural environment, as determined by land-use changes, is scenario 5, because the natural area for 2005 is almost the same as it was in 1985. The 'worst' scenario in terms of natural sustainability is scenario 2, because the scarce natural areas of the middle of the island are destroyed and urbanised. Scenario 3 results in a lesser load on the natural environment than scenario 4 because the urban area existing in 1985 is already in the southern half of the island. Scenario 4, which allows additional urban expansion in the eastern half of the island, will load the natural areas more than the southern (already loaded) areas.

(3) Scenario 2 is the 'best' in terms of preserving the original landscape of the island: urban expansion takes place in the middle of the island, so urban areas are not visible from either the sea or other parts of the island. This nonvisibility results in high scores on the landscape criterion.

(4) Scenario 5 is the 'best' in terms of road transportation, because it results in the minimum load of road transportation required for the local people or tourists to move within the island. The 'worst' scenario is scenario 4, because distances from the harbour, at the southern part of the island, are taken into account for the computation of road transportation load.

The effects table is imported to DEFINITE (van Herwijnen and Janssen, 1989), a DSS for ranking of alternatives. This DSS is based on a multicriteria method (Regime) to rank the alternatives. The selection of weights was

Table 1. The effects table used for the numerical application of the GIS – SD – DSS system in the test area.

Criterion	Scenario				
	1	2	3	4	5
Tourism	6.219	3.761	6.242	6.543	6.817
Nature	4.128	3.841	3.906	3.879	5.516
Landscape	4.663	5.742	4.575	4.427	4.353
Transportation	6.299	5.635	6.945	5.168	8.691
Rank	3	5	2	4	1

such that all the criteria were considered equally important. The ranking results for the four selected criteria are also given in the bottom row of table 1.

We thus conclude that, based on the above assumptions and ranking methods, scenario 5 is to be selected as a 'sustainable' scenario, in preference to the others. The term 'sustainable' here refers to a development (until the year 2005) which 'best' combines the four sustainability criteria selected: (1) tourist sector activities are favoured and enhanced, (2) natural areas are least destroyed and/or changed to urban areas, (3) landscape values are preserved, and (4) the road transportation load is minimised. However, such a conclusion is expected from development scenarios of type 5: if urban areas are to be restricted to their original locations, then this is the 'best' sustainable scenario, at least in an ecocentric sense. As such 'no expansion' policies tend to be unrealistic (and much more difficult to apply and control), we could, alternatively, select scenario 3, that is, the scenario which was ranked as the second 'best'.

5 Conclusions—future developments

We aimed at providing a necessary tool for linking GIS with SD in the form of a GIS–SD hybrid system. The complexity in determining the model base of our system reflects more or less the inevitable complexity when economic–ecological interactions are modelled. The database, on the other hand, is analytical and easy to access, provided that the necessary spatial and nonspatial data have been collected. Scenarios concerning external events, policy, and social behaviour are equally easy to apply. The force fields (for example, transportation attraction, forest restrictions) may be changed to reflect the spatial effects scenarios have on the 'mobile' stocks. Finally, the proper input to a DSS connection is provided for an evaluation of the alternatives. This DSS link involves transformations of the spatial results to single nonspatial outputs to be inserted in a DSS.

The GIS–SD system described in this study operates mainly on raster data; at the present time, where economic–ecological procedures are spatially simulated by a GIS, the reduced spatial accuracy of rasters does not seem to create any problems. Because the topology is easily preserved and the spatial objects are well defined with rasters, these factors make up for their limited spatial accuracy. In the future, other data structures, such as quadtree structures, may be tested.

Problems with limited or inadequate data were overcome by manually digitising the topographic maps and aerial pictures of the study area. Satellite remotely sensed data have played an important role in reducing the data-production cost for our system. Finally, spatial data in digital form related to economic and ecological quantities (for example, spatial distribution of BOD, seals, important species, and their dynamic migration patterns) are needed so that the full potential of the proposed GIS–SD model can be realised.

References

Archibugi F, Nijkamp P (Eds), 1989 *Economy and Ecology: Towards Sustainable Development* (Kluwer, Dordrecht)

Bojö J, 1991, "Economic analysis of environmental impacts", in *Linking the Natural Environment and the Economy: Essays from the Eco–Eco Group* Eds C Folke, T Kåberger (Kluwer, Dordrecht) pp 43–59

Burrough P A, 1983 *Principles of Geographical Information Systems for Land Resources Assessment* (Clarendon Press, Oxford)

Coccossis H, Parpairis A, 1990, "Tourism and the environment: some observations on the concept of carrying capacity (CC)", paper presented at the fourth Greek Regional Science Association meeting, Istanbul 1990; copy available from the authors, University of the Aegean, Mytiline

Daly H E, 1991 *Steady State Economics* (Island Press, Washington, DC)

Despotakis V, 1989, "Geoid undulation computations at laser tracking stations" *Bulletin Géodésique* **63** 342–358

Despotakis V, 1991 *Sustainable Development Planning Using Geographic Information Systems* PhD dissertation, Department of Regional Economics, Free University, Amsterdam

Fischer M M, Nijkamp P, 1992, "Geographic information systems and spatial analysis", Special issue of the *Annals of Regional Science* **26**(1)

Folke C, 1991, "Socio-economic dependence on the life-supporting environment", in *Linking the Natural Environment and the Economy: Essays from the Eco–Eco Group* Eds C Folke, T Kåberger (Kluwer, Dordrecht) pp 77–94

Giaoutzi M, Nijkamp P, 1989, "A strategic information system and planning model for marine park management", EC report, DG11, European Commission, Brussels

Gilbert A, 1992 *Natural Resource Accounting and Sustainable Development* PhD dissertation, Department of Regional Economics, Free University, Amsterdam (forthcoming)

Idrisi Project, 1990, "IDRISI users' manual", Idrisi project, Graduate School of Geography, Clark University, Winchester, MA

James D E, Nijkamp P, Opschoor J B, 1989, "Ecological sustainability and economic development", in *Economy and Ecology: Towards Sustainable Development* Eds F Archibugi, P Nijkamp (Kluwer, Dordrecht) pp 27–48

Janssen R, 1991 *Multiobjective decision support for environmental problems* PhD dissertation, Institute for Environmental Studies, Free University, Amsterdam

Méaille R, Wald L, 1990, "Using geographical information system and satellite imagery with a numerical simulation of regional urban growth" *International Journal of Geographic Information Systems* **4** 445–456

Murthy D N P, Page N W, Rodin E Y, 1990, "Mathematical modelling: a tool for problem solving", in *Engineering, Physical, Biological and Social Sciences* Ed. E Y Rodin (Pergamon Press, Oxford) pp 88–101

Nijkamp P, 1990, "Measurement in conservation planning", Series Research Memoranda, Faculty of Economics and Econometrics, Free University, Amsterdam

Nijkamp P, Scholten H J, 1991, "Information systems: caveats in design and use", in *EGIS '91, Second European Conference on GIS* Eds J Harts, H F L Ottens, H J Scholten (EGIS Foundation, Utrecht) pp 735–746

Nijkamp P, Soeteman F, 1990, "Ecologically sustainable economic development: key issues for strategic environmental management", Series Research Memoranda, Faculty of Economics and Econometrics, Free University, Amsterdam

Openshaw S, 1990, "Spatial analysis and geographical information systems: a review of progress and possibilities" in *Geographical Information Systems for Urban and Regional Planning* Eds H J Scholten, J Stillwell (Kluwer, Dordrecht) pp 153–163

Opschoor J B, 1990, "Economic instruments for sustainable development", in *Proceedings: Sustainable Development, Science and Policy, Conference Report, Bergen, 8–12 May 1990* (Norwegian Research Council for Science and the Humanities, Oslo) pp 249–269

Opschoor J B, Reijnders L, 1991, "Towards sustainable development indicators", in *In Search of Sustainable Development Indicators* Eds O Kuih, M Verbruggen (Kluwer, Dordrecht) pp 7–29

Richmond M, Peterson S, Vescuso P, 1987 *An Academic Users Guide to STELLA* High Performance Systems Inc., Lyme, NH

Scholten H J, Stillwell J C H, 1990, "Geographical information systems: the emerging requirements", in *Geographical Information Systems for Urban and Regional Planning* Eds H J Scholten, J C H Stillwell (Kluwer, Dordrecht) pp 3–14

Tydac Technologies, 1988 *Spatial Analysis System (SPANS) User's Manual* Tydac Technologies Inc., Canada

van den Bergh J C J M, 1991 *Dynamic Models for Sustainable Development* PhD dissertation, Faculty of Economics and Econometrics, Free University, Amsterdam

van den Bergh J C J M, Gilbert A, forthcoming, "SPIDER report book for Alonnisos project", Faculty of Economics and Econometrics, Free University, Amsterdam

van den Bergh J C J M, Nijkamp P, 1990, "Ecologically sustainable economic development: concepts and implications", Serie Research Memoranda, Faculty of Economics and Econometrics, Free University, Amsterdam

van Herwijnen M, Janssen R, 1989, "DEFINITE: a system to support decision on a finite set of alternatives", Institute for Environmental Studies, Free University, Amsterdam

van Pelt M, Kuyvenhoven A, Nijkamp P, 1990a, "Project appraisal and sustainability: concepts and main issues" Department of Economics, Wageningen Agricultural University, Wageningen

van Pelt M, Kuyvenhoven A, Nijkamp P, 1990b, "Project appraisal and sustainability: the applicability of cost–benefit and multi-criteria analysis", Department of Economics, Wageningen Agricultural University, Wageningen

WCED, 1987 *Our Common Future* (The Brundtland Report) World Commission on Environment and Development (Oxford University Press, Oxford)

Towards Sustainability: The Combined Production of Heat and Power

D Hutchinson
London Research Centre

1 Introduction

Concern about the environment is not new, but the nature of that concern has changed radically. In the first half of this century the concern was with protecting individual wildlife species, areas of beautiful landscape, or with particular historic buildings. Rachel Carson, with her book *Silent Spring* (1962), was one of the first writers to draw attention to the wider impacts of people on their environment.

That the environment was an international issue, rather than simply local or national, was recognised by the United Nations when it held its first conference on the environment in Stockholm in 1972, and by the subsequent creation of the United Nations Environment Programme. In 1983 the UN General Assembly also recognised the links between economic and environmental issues by establishing the World Commission on Environment and Development. The Commission's report, the so-called Bruntland Report *Our Common Future* (WCED, 1987) introduced the concept of 'sustainable development', defining it as: "Development that meets the needs of the present without compromising the ability of future generations to meet their own needs."

One of the major concerns today is global warming, resulting from an enhanced greenhouse effect. The greenhouse effect, first noted by 19th-century scientists, is now well understood (Houghton et al, 1990). It makes life on our planet possible, but the way this effect is enhanced by man's activities is of growing concern. Although emissions of one of the principal greenhouse gases, carbon dioxide (CO_2), have fallen from their peak in many industrialised countries such as the United Kingdom, economic growth exerts a constant upward pressure. 45% of the world's population now lives in cities, and that proportion is growing at the rate of 3% a year (Sadik, 1991). Traffic in cities is one of the fastest growing sources of CO_2 emissions and may well require the most radical measures to reduce it. In other areas combining heat and power production offers major opportunities for reducing CO_2 emissions, and moving closer to the goal of sustainable development.

2 Combining heat and power production

The production of heat from fossil fuels is a relatively efficient process. Conventional modern boiler plant can achieve efficiencies of over 80%, and condensing boilers are better still. The generation of electricity is far less efficient, averaging 37% efficiency, with even the best plants rejecting about 60% of the energy input as waste heat and in flue gases. By producing usable heat as well as electricity, combined heat and power (CHP) plants can convert between 70% and 90% of the potential energy into a usable form. Figure 1 shows the differences in the efficiency of separate and combined heat and power production.

The inherently greater fuel efficiency achieved by avoiding the need to burn fossil fuels in separate electricity generation and heating plant makes CHP an environmentally attractive technology. This advantage applies to small-scale CHP plant serving individual buildings or groups as well as large-scale schemes serving industry or providing heat for whole towns. There are already over 300 small-scale schemes in the United Kingdom, but the realistic potential is at least ten times this.

There are four possible systems which can be used to supply the heat and electric power.

Steam turbines. The system most commonly used to generate electricity in Britain and elsewhere is the steam turbine. Coal, gas, oil, or other fuel is burnt in a boiler in order to produce steam at high pressure. This is then used to drive a turbine which, in turn, drives an alternator in order to generate electricity. Where electricity alone is produced, the residual steam is then cooled in cooling towers or a dry cooling system before being returned to the boiler and recirculated. In a CHP system the steam

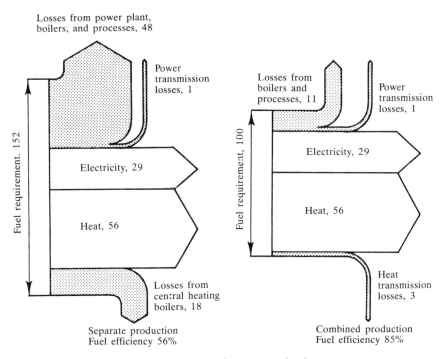

Figure 1. Separate and combined heat and power production.

can either be used directly by industry or to heat water in a district heating system before being recycled.

This is the type of system used in Scandinavia to supply heat to their large district heating schemes discussed below. Figure 2 shows the general arrangement of a CHP plant of this type.

Internal combustion engines. Adapted vehicle and marine engines running on oil or natural gas are used to drive an alternator. The heat generated in a vehicle engine is dispersed by its cooling system through the radiator. In a CHP system the heat from the cooling and exhaust systems is retained and fed to industry, or into a district heating or building heating system depending on the scale of the plant. The size of these units range from 10 kW to 10 MW in electrical output.

Gas turbines. Industrial gas turbines have been developed from aircraft jet engines. Natural gas or oil is burnt in the engine and the resultant hot gas used to drive the turbine. The turbine drives an alternator in order to generate electricity and the hot exhaust gas is passed into a boiler to produce steam or hot water. In many cases fuel can also be fed directly into the boiler so that the amount of heat produced can be increased, or the boiler can produce heat when the gas turbine is not operating. The electrical output ranges from 1 MW to 100 MW.

Combined cycle gas turbine (CCGT). This is similar to the gas turbine described above except that the exhaust gas is also used to raise steam which is then passed into a steam turbine in order to generate additional electricity.

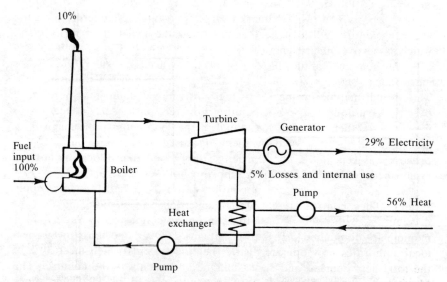

Figure 2. A typical steam turbine combined heat and power plant.

3 Combined heat and power in Scandanavia

Urban CHP schemes linked to district heating (CHP/DH) are particularly well established in Scandinavia. The Finnish energy-supply system is noted for the high proportion of district heating, and particularly schemes which make use of heat from power stations. In less than thirty years district heating has developed to the extent where 25% of all the building space in the country is heated by district heating schemes and 27% of all electricity is produced in CHP plants. The growth has been particularly rapid since the 'oil crisis' of 1973–74 because of Finland's dependence on imported fuels.

In Helsinki, in contrast to London, district heating meets over 80% of the annual heat demand of the city, with 81% of the heat and 72% of the electricity used in the city supplied from CHP plant. The Helsinki Energy Board is responsible for the supply of electricity, gas, and heat throughout the city as well as the maintenance of streetlighting. It is, in effect, a department of the Helsinki City Council, and the eighty-five members of the City Council elect nine members of the Energy Board to serve for four years. The Board's trading surplus is returned to the City and allows the local rate of tax to be set lower than would otherwise be the case.

Finnish experience has been seen as particularly relevant to the United Kingdom because of the high proportion of CHP-based district heating. The Finnish engineering consultancy Ekono has played a major part in developing the schemes in Leicester and Sheffield discussed below.

The Odense municipal district heating scheme in Denmark has just celebrated its sixtieth anniversary. It is one of the largest in Europe, supplying 75000 or 95% of homes in the city with heat. It also supplies schools, sports centres, Denmark's largest hospital, commerce, industry, and horticulture. 93% of heat comes from the Fynsværket CHP plant, which has an overall efficiency of 73%.

Swedish municipalities have also been involved in energy supply for more than 100 years. In the 1860s the first municipal gas-supply utilities were established and in the 1870s many private gas companies were taken over by local authorities. Local authorities were particularly concerned to improve streetlighting, and by the end of the 19th century the majority of gas companies were owned by them. From the late 1880s onwards this process was repeated with electricity supply, and many local authorities established a profitable subsidiary supplying both services.

Local authorities have a major influence on the Swedish energy-supply system. They control about 20% of electricity production and 60% of distribution, with over 70% of the consumers connected to municipal or municipally dominated distribution networks. Over one third of Swedish local authorities now operate district heating systems which meet 30% of the total heat demand and serve half the apartments in the country. The Municipal Energy Planning Act, originally passed in 1977 but since amended, states that "Every municipality shall have an up-to-date plan for energy supply, distribution and use within the municipality. The plan shall be approved by the municipal council."

Figure 3 shows the balance of energy use in Helsinki in 1990. The overall efficiency of the system is 71%, to a very large extent as a direct result of the high proportion of electricity and heat for space heating

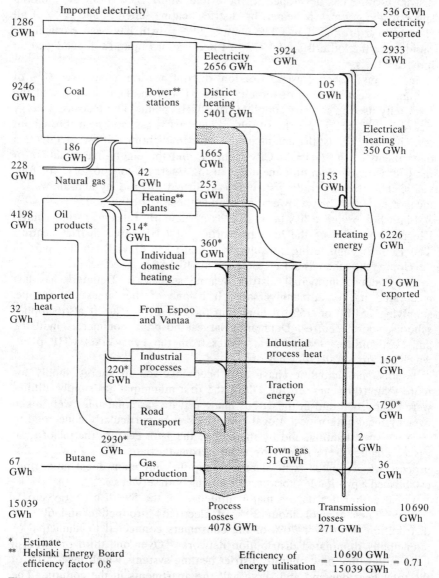

Figure 3. Energy use in Helsinki in 1990. The city is able to achieve a high overall energy efficiency of 71% because a large proportion of its demand is met from combined heat and power plants linked to a district heating network.

produced from CHP plants (Helsingin kaupungin energialaitos, 1991). Although such a system may not be 'sustainable' in the way that energy from a renewable source (wind, solar, etc) would be sustainable, it is a great deal more sustainable than the energy systems serving the vast majority of the world's cities.

Although district heating is most efficient when serving relatively high-density urban areas, because the demand for heat is high in relation to the length of the distribution network, it is feasible to connect relatively low-density housing, including detached houses. This is done in the suburban parts of Scandinavian cities.

4 A growing interest in combined heat and power worldwide

Many countries are interested in the potential of CHP schemes for improving their energy efficiency. A quarter of the world's population lives in China. It is the world's largest coal producer and the third largest oil producer. The problems caused by the inefficient and environmentally damaging use of these fuels has long been evident in Chinese cities. A failure by China to introduce effective controls over CO_2 emissions could vitiate any efforts at control by other countries.

Although these problems have frequently been commented upon by foreign observers, China's own concerns are less well documented. However, these were fully explained by Professor Qu Geping, director of the Chinese National Environmental Protection Agency at a recent energy efficiency symposium in Hong Kong (Patterson, 1991).

Professor Qu Geping said that by the year 2000 China's energy production will be 50% more than in 1989 and its GDP will have doubled. In other words, China has to raise the efficiency with which it uses energy by at least 50% in order to ensure the desired economic growth. China uses 30% of its coal production in some 400000 small inefficient industrial boilers and 20% is burnt in domestic fires. One of the ways of improving both energy efficiency and reducing pollution is to develop CHP schemes in industry and to supply heat to urban district heating systems. This will allow domestic coal burning to be phased out. Professor Qu Geping said that China will take all possible measures to reduce the emission of greenhouse gases.

In Australia the State Electricity Commission of Victoria is giving incentives to industry to encourage the development of CHP schemes. Electricity purchased from independent generators operating CHP plant attracts a 10% premium compared with that purchased from electricity-only plant. There are 41 MW of CHP plant installed with 31 MW currently under construction, and another 348 MW at the planning or discussion stage (State Electricity Commission of Victoria, 1990). Small-scale CHP schemes (see below) are also being encouraged in Australia (Sippitts, 1992). The development of CHP schemes is recognised as an important element in the state's strategy to reduce greenhouse gas emissions.

5 UK energy policy

Suggestions that local authorities in the United Kingdom should adopt a similar approach to energy planning to those in Scandinavia have, until recently, been rejected. The House of Commons Select Committee on Science and Technology (1975) recommended that the government should instruct authorities responsible for the preparation of regional plans, structure plans, and transport policies and programmes to consider the energy implications of their proposals with a view to adopting schemes of low-energy intensity. In its reply the government accepted the importance of the energy implications of plans but rejected the idea that they should be separately identified (Department of Energy, 1976).

Now, however, the attitude of government is changing. The recent environmental White Paper, *This Common Inheritance*, notes that the government has already asked local authorities to have particular regard to the conservation of energy as an issue in development plans (DoE, 1990). In respect of CHP systems, the White Paper goes a great deal further: "Because of its high fuel efficiency CO_2 emissions are reduced. CHP therefore has the potential to improve the environment and reduce energy costs to users in all sections of British industry and commerce." It goes on to set a target of a further 2000 MW of CHP capacity by the year 2000. CHP is the only energy technology or measure to improve efficiency and reduce CO_2 emissions for which a target is set.

The government's revised guidance to local authorities on their preparation of development plans (DoE, 1992) now says that one way in which development plan policies can encourage greater efficiency in the use of energy is through the location of new development. Travel patterns influence CO_2 emissions, and a way of reducing these emissions is to guide development towards locations which reduce the need to travel, or encourage the use of more energy-efficient public transport. It also says that development policies can influence the viability of CHP schemes.

6 Combined heat and power studies

CHP schemes are not a new concept in the United Kingdom. One of the first was in 1911 at Bloom Street in Manchester where the local electricity company supplied steam to local industry. CHP schemes to serve district heating (CHP/DH) were considered in the postwar years but the only one actually constructed supplied heat from Battersea Power Station to housing in Pimlico, on the other side of the River Thames, in central London (Duplock and Troop, 1986). Battersea Power Station is now closed and heat is supplied from a heat station next door. This is somewhat ironic when there is growing interest in CHP/DH.

Following the 1973–74 'oil crisis', the former Department of Energy set up a study group under the chairmanship of its then Chief Scientist Dr Walter Marshall (now Lord Marshall, the former Chairman of the Central Electricity Generating Board) to examine the potential for CHP/DH in the United Kingdom. This group, which reported in 1979 (Heat Load Density Working Party, 1979; CHP Group, 1979) suggested that about half the national space-heating load which could be served economically by CHP was in Greater London and about 90% in the five largest conurbations; Greater London, West Midlands, Greater Manchester, Merseyside, and Glasgow. If CHP serving the district heating could supply 25% to 35% of the total UK heat load the approximate savings compared with the alternatives could be as shown in table 1. In addition, a large number of other towns were identified as likely to be suitable for CHP/DH development (see figure 4).

In 1980 the Secretary of State for Energy announced that he proposed to implement a programme of further work on the feasibility of CHP/DH at specific locations. On the basis of the first stage of the work, the Government selected nine cities [Glasgow, Newcastle, London (parts of Southwark and Tower Hamlets), Sheffield, Belfast, Liverpool, Manchester, Leicester, and Edinburgh] which were then the subject of detailed study. The report on those studies, undertaken by W S Atkins and Partners, was completed in July 1982, and published later as Energy Paper 53 (Atkins and Partners, 1984).

Following the report, the government said that it was ready to encourage the formation of local consortia to draw up detailed proposals. It would help by contributing towards the cost, on condition that there was substantial private-sector participation in the consortia and on the assumption that further development of CHP/DH would be a viable private-sector investment. Proposals were submitted on behalf of all nine cities and the government agreed to support the development of schemes in Belfast, Edinburgh, and Leicester.

The work was completed on the three government supported cities and in three other areas as well; Sheffield, Newcastle, and London. In the case of Belfast (Joint Venture for Belfast CHP, 1988) and Edinburgh

Table 1. Potential energy savings resulting from the introduction of combined heat and power/district heating (CHP/DH) (source: CHP Group, 1979).

Minimum net heat load density served (megawatts per square kilometre)	15	20
Percentage of national heat load served	35	25
Alternative to CHP/DH:	Annual percentage energy savings achieved by CHP/DH in comparison to the alternatives:	
Existing mixture of fuels	6	4
Direct electrical heating	10	7
Substitute natural gas from coal	6	4
Heat only district heating from coal	3	2
Electric heat pumps	4	3
Substitute natural gas heat pumps	2	1

(Edinburgh CHP Consortium, 1988) the schemes were large scale. They involved the transfer of heat by pipeline from relatively remote power stations. To be viable they would have required financial support from the public sector and, therefore, did not meet the government's criteria. The other four studies all focused on 'core' schemes. The idea was that, if a first stage or 'core' scheme could be identified which was financially viable in its own right, but which is also compatible with the eventual development to something larger, then this could be funded from the private sector. Such a scheme could begin to generate the cash flow which would be necessary if a larger scheme were to be realistic.

Three schemes which are of particular interest are those in Leicester, in southeast London, and the Citigen scheme in the City of London.

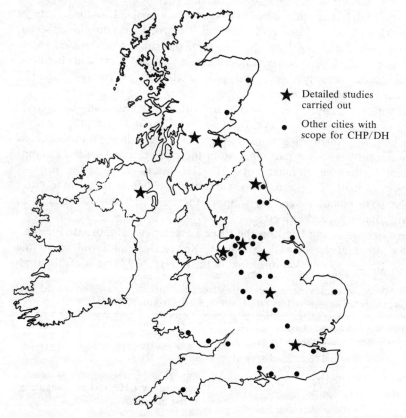

Figure 4. The scope for urban combined heat and power/district heating (CHP/DH) schemes.

6.1 Leicester

The most encouraging results came from Leicester. A consortium of five private and six public-sector organisations formed themselves into the

Leicester Combined Heat and Power Consortium. The consortium appointed the Finnish engineering consultancy Ekono to advise it because of its wide and international experience of designing and constructing CHP and district heating schemes. A customer survey undertaken by the consortium identified a substantial requirement for the supply of heat in the form of steam as well as hot water. Initial studies indicated that it would be economic to have separate networks for steam and hot water and it was subsequently decided to do this.

The requirement for steam was spread throughout the city but mainly concentrated along the line of the River Soar and the Grand Union Canal. Demand for heat in the form of hot water focused on the centre of the city where, together with steam, it amounted to some 25% of the total city demand. A significant proportion of the total heat usage would be by a small number of industrial, commercial, and institutional consumers in the central part of the city.

Various options were considered for heat supply including the laying of a pipeline from the power station at Ratcliffe-on-Soar, the construction of new coal-fired or waste-incineration plant, and gas-fired combined-cycle plant. The original Raw Dyke coal-fired power station near the city centre had been demolished by the former CEGB but it still operated two gas turbines to provide a 'peak lopping' capacity of 116 MW. These were to be converted to be dual-fired with natural gas or oil and to combined-cycle operation. Two new gas turbines each with a waste heat boiler would feed a further steam turbine. The electrical output of the combined cycle station would be between 250 and 300 MW, depending on the amount of heat being extracted.

The consortium recommended that a company be set up to implement the scheme. In July 1987 Leicester Energy Limited was established. Financial studies undertaken before the government's announcement of its electricity-privatisation proposals (Department of Energy, 1988) indicated that the best mode of operation was to maximise income by the sale of electricity rather than to follow Scandinavian practice and match heat demand. The scheme seemed therefore to be in a strong position to sell electricity to the new distribution company, particularly as the then East Midlands Electricity Board was a member of the company. If all had gone according to plan, the Leicester CHP scheme would have been 'on stream' in 1992 (Leicester Combined Heat and Power Consortium, 1986; Walton, 1987). This has simply not happened. The scheme stalled because of a failure to agree the terms for the sale of electricity, use of the former CEGB site, and contracts for the supply of gas in the context of an industry undergoing privatisation. However, some of the companies involved in the original study believe that a scheme could still proceed, although some modifications would be necessary.

6.2 The southeast London CHP project

In 1986 the London Boroughs which comprise the South East London Waste Disposal Group (SELWDG), Greenwich, Lewisham, and Southwark, commissioned a study of the options for waste disposal from the London Waste Regulation Authority (LWRA). This recommended incineration with energy recovery as an alternative to landfill or the production of waste-derived fuel. In making this recommendation LWRA took into account the earlier work discussed above, as well as a study completed in 1985 of the feasibility of converting Belvedere Power Station to refuse incineration with electricity generation.

In 1988 SELWDG set up the South East London Combined Heat and Power Consortium (SELCHP). This consisted of Asea Brown Boveri, Associated Heat Services, John Laing, the London Borough of Southwark Housing Department, London Electricity, Mainmet Holdings, Martin Engineering Systems, Lloyds Bank Capital Markets Group, as well as SELWDG. Foster Wheeler Energy and the CEGB were originally members of the consortium but later left it (Siggars, 1992).

The initial task of the consortium was to complete a detailed evaluation of an energy from waste scheme for southeast London, and to demonstrate its viability, which it did. Construction of the plant began in February 1992 and it is due to begin accepting waste in January 1994. The plant will dispose of 420000 tonnes per year of municipal refuse from the London Boroughs of Greenwich, Lewisham, and Southwark; generate 29 MW of electrical power for sale to London Electricity as part of the 'Non-Fossil Fuel Obligation'; have the potential to supply heat to six local authority housing estates in Southwark with existing district heating systems. This would include 7500 homes as well as schools and other buildings.

The regional electricity companies are required to obtain a specified amount of the power which they supply from generation plant which does not use fossil fuels. This is known as the 'Non-Fossil Fuel Obligation'. The power may come from renewable sources, such as wind generators, as well as refuse incineration plants, and, by far the dominant source, the nuclear power stations. Any additional costs incurred are recovered from customers through a 'fossil fuel levy' (sometimes called the 'nuclear levy') (Hutchinson, 1991). The SELCHP is classed as a 'non-fossil fuel' power plant and will benefit from a higher price being paid for the electricity generated than would otherwise be the case. The plant will meet all the current environmental standards.

6.3 CHP for the City of London

The City Corporation, British Gas, and Utilicom Holdings Limited announced the setting up of a CHP scheme in the Barbican area of the City of London in 1990. British Gas and Utilicom, which is part of the French Idex et Cia group, have formed a joint company Citigen Limited to build and operate the scheme which will be based on a medium-speed reciprocating engine burning natural gas, with low-sulphur fuel oil as a backup. The plant will be located at 51–53 Charterhouse Street. Many years ago this site was used for electricity generation but more recently as a cold store.

The CHP scheme will initially serve the Barbican Centre, the Guildhall, Bastion House, the Museum of London, and some other suitable City Corporation owned buildings in their vicinity. The plant will generate 32 MW of electricity and an equivalent amount of heat, but it could eventually grow to between 60 and 90 MW. The electricity-to-heat ratio has not yet been determined for later stages. At least some of the electricity generated is likely to be supplied direct to buildings in the area.

Citigen will be constructing the hot water distribution system during 1992, and expect to begin operating in the summer of 1993. Chilled water will also be supplied to air conditioning systems. In return for the use of existing boiler plant and equipment, whilst the new CHP plant is being built, Citigen expects to be able to supply electricity and heat 5% and 15% cheaper, respectively than any demonstrable lower cost alternatives.

The proposed operating standards are designed to achieve the following percentage reductions in emissions of pollutants to the atmosphere when compared with the present methods of energy supply:

Carbon dioxide (CO_2) 60%
Sulphur dioxide (SO_2) 65%
Nitrous oxide (NO) 95%

6.4 Small-scale CHP

The CHP systems discussed so far are all relatively large, as even the smaller industrial systems generally have electrical outputs of more than 1 MW. In the last few years, however, smaller 'micro'-CHP systems capable of heating buildings have been developed. There are now over 300 of these systems installed in the United Kingdom.

These are several reasons why such systems are now regarded as attractive:

(1) Self-contained packaged units have been developed which can be delivered to the site complete with their control systems and acoustic enclosure. These small units have electrical outputs of 10 to 200 KW and a heat output generally two to three times the electrical output. Rising energy costs have made both suppliers and potential users aware of the financial benefits that these systems can bring by reducing the energy costs of a building.

(2) The UK government encouraged the development of CHP systems by passing the 1983 Energy Act. This, amongst other things, required the twelve electricity distribution boards to publish tariffs for the purchase of surplus electricity from organisations which installed CHP systems, and also for the use of the electricity supply network to transfer power to a third party.

(3) The Act also placed a duty on the electricity boards to "adopt and support schemes" for CHP. Although the duty of adopting and supporting schemes was never clearly defined in law, it nevertheless encouraged the electricity-supply industry to take a more positive attitude to these schemes.

The relatively low cost of micro-CHP units and their heat and electrical output makes them suitable for use in a range of different building types from hotels and hospitals to universities and sports centres. In addition, they can also provide standby electricity-generation capacity. In the latter case they operate in parallel to the public electricity supply network for most of the time but can operate independently to meet essential electrical loads in the event of a mains failure.

In the early 1980s the potential advantages of this type of installation were not widely understood. The former UK Department of Energy supported a number of pilot projects through its Energy Efficiency Demonstration Scheme. The results of these, including appraisals of the financial benefits, were published in 1985 (Energy Efficiency Office, 1985). Since then the process of installation has built up its own momentum.

The micro-CHP schemes are attractive financially because they make use of a relatively low-cost fuel (usually natural gas) to generate both heat and electricity. The heat would otherwise be produced using the same fuel in a conventional boiler, but the electricity would be purchased at relatively high cost per unit of energy from the regional electricity company. Although a micro-CHP unit will be somewhat less efficient than a normal boiler as a heat producer, this disadvantage is more than offset by the direct savings in electricity purchases.

A recent International Energy Agency study of small-scale CHP concluded that the electrical efficiency of these systems is usually about 30%. The thermal efficiency is to a large extent determined by the characteristics of the application and can be as low as 37% or as high as 55%. High thermal efficiencies can be obtained when designing units which follow the heating load and by applying up-to-date technology. The overall efficiency of a CHP unit can be around 85%, based on the gross calorific value of the fuel (Jennekens, 1989).

Small-scale CHP units have now demonstrated that they can meet current environmental standards in relation to emissions of oxides of nitrogen, carbon monoxide, and unburned hydrocarbons as well as noise and vibration, without significant loss of efficiency. The sulphur content of natural gas is usually too low to present any problem. Biogas and landfill gas may have a higher sulphur content, but it should be cleaned before it is used. Engines which do not by themselves meet emission standards can be equipped with three-way catalytic converters to reduce emissions. The benefits in relation to CO_2 and global warming come through the higher efficiency of these units when compared with the separate production of heat and electricity.

7 District heating

District heating is most efficient when serving relatively high-density urban areas, because the demand for heat is high in relation to the length of the distribution network. The current schemes and recent studies in the United Kingdom have all focused on existing relatively high-density areas. It is, however, also feasible to connect relatively low-density housing including detached houses, and this is done in the suburban parts of Scandinavian cities. In a totally new community, the district heating system could be designed in relation to the residential and commercial development in order to produce the most efficient system. Minimising the length of the distribution network would be an important factor.

Factors which will influence the design of a CHP/DH system include: the temperature and pressure at which heat is to be supplied; size, location, density, and type of buildings in the area to be supplied; future development of the area; design of existing building heating systems; the type of CHP heat plant which will supply the heat; the form and complexity of the heat mains distribution system; business plans of the heat supply organisation.

A substantial number of heat-only district heating schemes were built in the United Kingdom in the 1960s and 1970s. The basic reasons for preferring district heating then were lower costs-in-use, maintenance problems associated with some other forms of heating, and the problems of condensation and mould which had resulted from intermittent use of warm air heating systems. Until the 1973–74 'oil crisis', it was possible to obtain fuel for central boiler houses much more cheaply than could individual domestic consumers. It then became virtually impossible to negotiate contracts for fuel supplies on such favourable terms. Charges for district heating had to be increased substantially and this eroded the cost-in-use advantage. People in many cases also became disenchanted with district heating either because the scheme was poorly designed in the first place or poorly maintained.

A major obstacle in the development of CHP/DH schemes in many areas was the generally poor opinion which the public had of the existing district heating schemes. People in homes connected to existing schemes frequently had to pay substantially more than for individual gas systems whereas the original idea was that they would pay less. The cost was a major problem for many households and district heating systems became a prime focus of tenant dissatisfaction in public-sector housing.

In the course of its work for the Department of Energy on CHP/DH, W S Atkins and Partners investigated consumer satisfaction with existing district heating schemes and were told by a number of local authorities that there were serious doubts about the acceptability of such systems to consumers (Rew, 1985). The head of one local authority engineering department with extensive experience of district heating said that "I have only one comment to offer about district heating; don't do it."

The 1990s are seeing major changes in attitudes to district heating in the United Kingdom. One particular problem with the older schemes was heat metering, but accurate electronic heat meters are now available in the United Kingdom. The replacement of old meters with new, or their installation where none existed before, is having a marked impact on public attitudes. The new metering systems provide as good a degree of control as can be obtained with any other heating system. They are frequently being installed as part of a general programme of refurbishment which is, in turn, improving the general efficiency of district heating schemes. The Association of Metropolitan Authorities (1988) issued a guide to good practice in district heating in 1988 which helped to improve its image still further. In November 1990 Doncaster Metropolitan Borough Council opened an extension to its district heating scheme, and published a new edition of its own guide to good practice (Christian, 1990).

7.1 Sheffield

Sheffield, the fourth largest city in the United Kingdom, is certainly demonstrating that it regards the poor image of district heating as a thing of the past. Preliminary studies by W S Atkins and Partners identified a potential scheme which could provide heat to some 100 000 people living in the inner city area. It could also heat seventy of the largest commercial and institutional buildings in the city centre.

The approach was the same as that at Leicester; the development of a 'core' scheme using the cheapest available source of energy, which in the case of Sheffield was refuse. The Barnard Road refuse incineration plant has one of the best operating records of any such plant in Europe. It currently treats 120 000 tonnes of refuse per year and produces 34 MW of heat. The plant already heated 2400 flats in Hyde Park and Park Hill, but much of the energy potentially recoverable remained unused.

The first phase of extension to the existing network added 1890 flats in fifteen high-rise buildings. The second was much more ambitious, and extended the district heating network into the very centre of the city. This was completed in February 1990 and included 6 km of pipeline, of which 4 km runs through the city centre. It serves major commercial and civic buildings, and allows for expansion. The success of this second stage has shown clearly that it is possible to lay district heating mains in the centre of British cities without causing unacceptable disruption and inconvenience.

The scheme now serves 3500 flats in nineteen locations, twenty shops, twelve public houses, and twenty of the largest commercial and civic buildings in the city centre. In the early stages it will remain a heat-only district heating system. Electricity generation will only be added (in other words the scheme will only be converted to CHP operation) once a substantial heat load has been connected. Sheffield Heat and Power, the operating company, plans eventually to build one or more CHP plants in the 20 to 150 MW range (Lawrence, 1988; 1992).

The City Council could, in theory, have implemented the scheme on its own, but in practice it would never have been able to commit the large sums of money needed, year by year, to expand the scheme. It therefore decided to develop the scheme in partnership with the private sector, but was concerned that its partner or partners should have an established track record in this field. After discussions with a number of British and Scandinavian organisations, Sheffield Heat and Power Limited was formed as a joint venture with Ekono from Finland. So far, £7 million has been invested in the project; in the laying of the heat distribution pipe network and consumer connections as well as in the installation of peaking and standby boilers.

8 Combined heat and power and global warming

CHP was identified in a report "An evaluation of energy related greenhouse gas emissions and measures to ameliorate them" as offering considerable potential for reducing CO_2 emissions (Department of Energy, 1990). This was on the assumption that CHP plant would be gas-fired and would displace conventional coal-fired electricity generation and heat from gas-fired boilers. On this basis, each TWh of electricity generated by CHP plant would save approximately one million tonnes of CO_2. For CHP plant with a load factor of around 55%–60%, this amounts to a 5 million tonnes of CO_2 saving for each 1 000 MW(e) of installed capacity. For gas-fired CHP units with a full heat load (that is, operating at similar levels of overall efficiency to boilers) and displacing coal-fired electricity generation, the reduction in the CO_2 emission per unit of electrical output could be as high as 70%.

The report concludes that CHP looks set to grow in capacity, possibly very significantly. With the continued shift towards the use of natural gas, CHP will make a significant contribution to reducing CO_2 emissions. Contributions of a 7 million tonnes reduction by 2005 and a 15 million tonnes reduction in CO_2 emissions by 2020 (based on plausible assumptions) could lead to reductions of as much as 5–10% in UK CO_2 emissions from fossil fuel combustion.

9 Conclusions

Definitions of 'sustainable development' abound. There is some truth in the criticism that the term has come to mean whatever suits the particular advocacy of the individual concerned (Pearce et al, 1989). Nevertheless, under almost any definition the introduction of combined rather than separate heat and power production is going to be more efficient and therefore more sustainable.

The 1980s saw a major shift in attitudes to CHP. At the beginning of the period CHP was regarded as a valid theoretical concept but with limited applicability in the United Kingdom. The initial concept of very large district heating schemes linked to large coal-fired power stations embodied in the Marshall study group report has been replaced by the concept of the 'core scheme'. The successful outcome of core scheme studies in London and elsewhere, work in Sheffield, the development of an affordable electronic heat meter, the improving image of district heating in the United Kingdom, and the need to reduce CO_2 emissions all favour the development of CHP schemes. National Power has said that it is discussing 100 own-generation schemes, with a combined generating capacity of over 500 MW, with industry. Some, at least, of these schemes will be CHP.

Micro-CHP schemes and CHP schemes in industry are now well established. What is less certain, even after a decade of study, is the rate at which large urban CHP schemes will develop. In the case of micro-CHP schemes and CHP schemes in industry, the operators generally use the electrical output themselves. In the case of urban CHP schemes the electricity will usually be sold to the regional electricity companies or through the National Grid Company. The tariffs which can be negotiated for the sale of this electricity are crucial to the financial viability of the schemes. The fact that the output from the SELCHP refuse incineration plant is likely to be sold to London Electricity as part of the 'Non-Fossil Fuel Obligation' is a significant factor in determining its viability. Similarly, the large existing heat load and the possibility of direct supply of electricity are important factors in relation to the City of London CHP scheme.

References

Association of Metropolitan Authorities, 1988, "Too hot to handle?", Association of Metropolitan Authorities, 35 Great Smith Street, London SW1P 3BJ

Atkins W S and Partners, 1984, "Combined heat and power district heating feasibility programme: stage 1: summary report and recommendations" *Energy Paper 53* (HMSO, London)

Carson R, 1962 *Silent Spring* (Houghton Mifflin, New York)

CHP Group, 1979, "Combined heat and electrical power generation in the United Kingdom" *Energy Paper 35* report by the Combined Heat and Power Group to the Secretary of State for Energy (HMSO, London)

Christian G S, 1990 "Doncaster—the district heating experience", Public Works Department, Doncaster Metropolitan Borough Council, Scarborough House, Chequer Road, Doncaster DN1 2DB

Department of Energy, 1976, "Energy Conservation", Cmnd 6575 (HMSO, London)

Department of Energy, 1988, "Privatising electricity: the government's proposals for the privatisation of the electricity supply industry in England and Wales", Cm 322 (HMSO, London)

Department of Energy, 1990, "An evaluation of energy related greenhouse gas emissions and measures to ameliorate them", *Energy Paper 58* (HMSO, London)

DoE, 1990 *This Common Inheritance: Britain's Environmental Strategy* Cm 1200, Department of the Environment (HMSO, London)

DoE, 1992, "PPG12: development plans and regional planning guidance" *Planning Policy Guidance Notes* Department of the Environment (HMSO, London)

Duplock S A F, Troop J, 1986, "Pimlico district heating undertaking—thirty five years of operating experience", Kennedy and Donkin Building Services Limited, Westbrook Mills, Borough Road, Godalming, Surrey GU7 2AZ

Edinburgh CHP Consortium, 1988, "CHAMP—combined heat and mains power", Edinburgh CHP Consortium, NEI Parsons Ltd, Heaton Works, Newcastle upon Tyne NE6 2YL

Energy Efficiency Office, 1985, "Guidance notes for the implementation of small scale packaged combined heat and power" *Good Practice Guide 1* Energy Efficiency Office, Department of the Environment, 1 Palace Street, London SW1E 5HE

Heat Load Density Working Party of the Combined Heat and Power Group, 1979, "Heat loads in British Cities" *Energy Paper 34* (HMSO, London)

Helsingin kaupungin energialaitos, 1991, "Toimintavuosi 1990" (Helsinki Energy Board, Annual Report 1990) Helsinki Energy Board, Helsinki, Finland

Houghton J T, Jenkins G J, Ephraums J J (Eds), 1990 *Climate Change—The IPCC Scientific Assessment* (Cambridge University Press, Cambridge)

House of Commons Select Committee on Science and Technology, 1975, "Energy Conservation" (HMSO, London)

Hutchinson D, 1991, "Site requirements for advanced coal-fired power stations", Coalfield Communities Campaign, 9 Regent Street, Barnsley S70 2EG

Jennekens M, 1989, "Learning from experience with small scale cogeneration", CADDET Analysis Series number 1, Centre for the Analysis and Demonstration of Energy Technologies, Sittard, The Netherlands, page 16

Joint Venture for Belfast CHP, 1988, "CHP: the Belfast case", Joint Venture for Belfast CHP, Airedale, Mundesley Road, Knapton, Norfolk NR28 ORY

Lawrence D J, 1988, "Affordable heat", paper presented at the UK National Symposium on "Combating Condensation", Sheffield, 23 July; copy available from the author, Sheffield Heat and Power Limited, Cooper Buildings, Arundel Street, Sheffield S1 2NS

Lawrence D J, 1992, "Building for the future", paper presented at the Combined Heat and Power Association Conference "CHP Powering the Future", Stratford-upon-Avon, 30–31 March; copy available from the author, Sheffield Heat and Power Limited, Cooper Buildings, Arundel Street, Sheffield S1 2NS

Leicester Combined Heat and Power Consortium, 1986, "Summary report", Leicester Combined Heat and Power Consortium, CHP Office, Town Hall, Leicester LE1 6BF

Patterson W, 1991, "Cold war tactics" *The Guardian* 10 May, page 30

Pearce D, Markandya A, Barbier E, 1989 *Blueprint for a Green Economy* (Earthscan, London)

Rew A, 1985, "Consumer acceptance of community heating systems", paper presented at the 6th National Conference of the Combined Heat and Power Association *CHP—Developments and Decisions, Torquay, 4–6 June*; copy available from the Combined Heat and Power Association, Grosvenor Gardens House, 35–37 Grosvenor Gardens, London SW1W 0BS

Sadik N, 1991, "Confronting the challenge of tomorrow's cities—today" *Development Forum* **19**(2) page 3

Siggars R, 1992, "London mass-burn power project" *Waste Management* **82**(1) 15–21

Sippitts D (Ed.), 1992, "Micro-cogeneration—targeting projects under 500 kW" *Gas Profile* **2**(1) 10–11

State Electricity Commission of Victoria, 1990, "Independent generation policy", State Electricity Commission of Victoria, Demand Management Unit, 818 Whitehorse Road, Box Hill, Victoria 3128, Australia

Walton D, 1987, "Will Leicester have the UK's first city CHP scheme?" *Modern Power Systems* **7**(6) 51–57

WCED, 1987 *Our Common Future* (The Brundtland Report) World Commission on Environment and Development (Oxford University Press, Oxford)

Index